Acclaim for **ALEXANDER STILLE**'s

EXCELLENT CADAVERS

"Absorbing, detailed history . . . lucidly and soberly recounted. . . . Mr. Stille's impressive volume may erase the illusion that, given all of the movies and other books that have appeared over the years, you already know most of what there is to know about the always compelling subject of Cosa Nostra. Until you read *Excellent Cadavers*, you probably don't. . . . Mr. Stille is a writer to watch."   —*The New York Times*

"Authoritative. . . . *Excellent Cadavers* is a comprehensive, engrossing lesson in how to interpret the signs—past, present and future—of the Mafia's role in Italian society. . . . A compelling drama."   —Jonathan Burnham Schwartz, *Newsday*

"Totally absorbing and distinctly chilling. . . . Stille's book gives us vivid insights into the courage and dedication shown by those who have to work, day by day, in constant fear of death. This is an altogether outstanding work of contemporary history." —Barry Unsworth, *London Evening Standard*

"In *Excellent Cadavers* Alexander Stille tells the story of the Italian anti-mafia campaign. It is a crucial passage in contemporary history. . . . It is also an heroic story, and Stille has the understanding, both of politics and of human character, to make this book an epic worthy of its heroes."
    —John Casey, author of *Spartina*

"Riveting. . . . Alexander Stille is a young and very able investigative reporter. . . . A fervently, lucidly written work of great importance."   —*Foreign Affairs*

ALEXANDER STILLE
EXCELLENT CADAVERS

Alexander Stille's first book, *Benevolence and Betrayal: Five Italian Jewish Families Under Fascism*, was cited in the London *Times Literary Supplement* as one of the best books of 1992, and received the *Los Angeles Times* Book Award for history. From 1990 until 1993, Stille reported on Italy for *U.S. News and World Report*, the *Boston Globe*, and the *Toronto Globe & Mail*, while contributing long articles to *The New Yorker* and *The Atlantic Monthly*. He lives in New York City and Atlanta, Georgia.

Books by
ALEXANDER STILLE

Benevolence and Betrayal:
Five Italian Jewish Families Under Fascism

Excellent Cadavers:
The Mafia and the Death of the First Italian Republic

EXCELLENT CADAVERS

CITY OF PALERMO

- - - Family territories
—— Main streets

③ Partanna
② Resuttana
① Uditore
⑨ Passo di Rigano
Noce
④ La Kalsa
⑧ Porta Nuova
S. Maria di Gesù
⑤ Corso dei Mille
⑦
⑥ Brancaccio

ITALY

MESSINA

Golfo di Patti
Golfo di Milazzo
Messina ⊙
Stretto di Messina

ENNA

⊙ Enna

▲ Mount Etna

Ionian Sea

CATANIA

Catania ⑱ ⊙

Golfo di Catania

Golfo di Augusta

Siracusa ⊙

SIRACUSA

RAGUSA

⊙ Ragusa

Golfo di Géla

Golfo di Noto

...SETTA

1 Salvatore Inzerillo, Rosario Spatola
2 Francesco Madonia & Sons
3 Rosario Riccobono
4 La Kalsa –Tommaso Spadaro
5 Filippo Marchese (Room of Death of Piazza Sant'Erasmo)
6 Francesco Mafara
7 Stefano Bontate
8 Pippo Calò, Tommaso Buscetta
9 Salvatore Inzerillo, DiMaggio Bros.
10 Gaetano Badalamenti
11 Bernardo Brusca & Sons
12 Stefano Bontate
13 Michele, Salvatore, & Pino Greco
14 Leonardo Greco
15 Salvo Family
16 Luciano Leggio, Salvatore Riina, Bernardo Provenzano
17 Giuseppe DiCristina
18 Giuseppe Calderone, Nitto Santapaola
19 Mariano Agate

EXCELLENT

THE MAFIA AND THE DEATH OF
THE FIRST ITALIAN REPUBLIC

CADAVERS

WITHDRAWN

ALEXANDER STILLE

VINTAGE BOOKS

A Division of Random House, Inc.   New York

For Sarah, Vittorio and Sesa
and in memory of Giovanni Falcone, Paolo Borsellino
and the many other courageous public servants
who have died working in Sicily

FIRST VINTAGE BOOKS EDITION, AUGUST 1996

Copyright © 1995 by Alexander Stille

All rights reserved under International and Pan-American
Copyright Conventions. Published in the United States by
Vintage Books, a division of Random House, Inc., New York,
and simultaneously in Canada by Random House of Canada
Limited, Toronto. Originally published in hardcover
by Pantheon Books, a division of Random House, Inc.,
New York, in 1995.

The Library of Congress has cataloged the Pantheon edition
as follows:

Stille, Alexander. Excellent cadavers / Alexander Stille.
p.   cm.
ISBN 0-679-42579-9
1. Mafia—Italy. 2. Italy—Politics and government—
20th century. 3. Violence—Italy. 4. Elite (Social sciences)—Italy.
I. Title.
HV6453.I83M3766 1995
364.1'06'0945—dc20
94-37863
Vintage ISBN: 0-679-76863-7

Random House Web address: http://www.randomhouse.com/

Map design by Bette Duke

Printed in the United States of America

10 9 8 7 6 5 4 3

CONTENTS

EXCELLENT CADAVERS

Giovanni Falcone and Paolo Borsellino
(Tony Gentile/Laura Ronchi)

PROLOGUE

In 1876, a young member of parliament from Tuscany, Leopoldo Franchetti, traveled to Sicily to report on the strange island that had quickly become the most troubled and recalcitrant part of the newly united Italian state. Franchetti was enchanted by the beauty of Palermo, the majesty of the baroque palaces, the exquisite courtesy and hospitality of the people, the languorous, sunny weather, the exotic palm trees and the intoxicating perfume of the orange and lemon blossoms of the Conca d'Oro's fertile citrus groves.

> Someone who had just arrived might well believe . . . that Sicily was the easiest and most pleasant place in the entire world. But if [the traveler] stays a while, begins to read the newspapers and listens carefully [he wrote], bit by bit everything changes around him. . . . He hears that the guard of that orchard was killed with a rifle shot coming from behind that wall because the owner hired him rather than someone else. . . . Just over there, an owner who wanted to rent his groves as he saw fit heard a bullet whistle past his head in friendly warning and afterwards gave in. Elsewhere, a young man who had dedicated himself to setting up nursery schools in the outskirts of Palermo was shot at . . . because certain people who dominate the common people in that area, feared that, by benefiting the poorer classes, he would

prestige

acquire some of the influence on the population that they wanted to reserve exclusively for themselves. The violence and the murders take the strangest forms. . . . There is a story about a former priest, who became the crime leader in a town near Palermo and administered the last rites to some of his own victims. After a certain number of these stories, the perfume of orange and lemon blossoms starts to smell of corpses.[1]

The perfume of orange and lemon blossoms began to smell of corpses during one of my first trips to Palermo. I went to visit Domenico Signorino, one of the prosecutors who worked on the "maxi-trial" of Palermo—the largest mafia trial in history. Signorino appeared more open and cordial than most prosecutors, especially in Sicily. During a long, pleasant interview, he spoke with great nostalgia and affection about the trial and of his colleagues who had been killed in the war against the mafia. A few days later, I saw Signorino's photograph on the front page of the Palermo newspaper *Giornale di Sicilia* with the headline: "Palermo judge suspected of collusion with the mafia." Two days after that, Judge Signorino took a pistol and shot himself.[2]

It is still not clear whether Judge Signorino was guilty or not. The *mafioso* who accused Signorino has proven a reliable witness and it seems hard to believe that someone with a clear conscience would commit suicide. But the prosecutors who worked with Signorino swear by his innocence, saying that he had a fragile psyche and insisting that the trauma of public humiliation for a person used to universal respect and approbation can be overwhelming. Some also found it highly suspicious that of the five judges accused of collusion only one name, Signorino, had been leaked to the press. Perhaps Signorino was the victim of a cleverly orchestrated maneuver.[3]

People in Sicily were unsure which possible scenario was worse: that a judge entrusted with the most delicate mafia cases had sold himself to the enemy or that an honest man had been destroyed by an occult hand. Some suggested a third possibility, that Signorino was not guilty of outright collusion but that he had committed some impropriety, accepted some favor, met or knew certain people of dubious reputation, which would invariably create an appearance of guilt with which he could not live. We will probably never know. The case was closed with the death of the suspect, taking its place among the infinite mysteries of Palermo.

Sicily is a place where almost nothing is what it seems. A few days after meeting Signorino, I went to interview Palermo's new police chief, who appeared to be an energetic crime fighter, having recently seized the assets of one of the city's main mafia clans. Several months later, he, too, was accused of having taken bribes when he worked in Naples. No one knows what to believe.[4]

Survivors of twenty-five hundred years of foreign invasions and of countless violent and corrupt rulers, Sicilians are a skeptical people. When I asked a Sicilian friend why he didn't trust a local politician with a reputation as an outspoken anti-mafia crusader, he replied: "He's alive, isn't he? If he'd really done anything against the mafia, he'd already be dead."

Death is the only certain truth. It lifts the disguise—if only briefly—from the Pirandellian world of Sicilian politics, where appearance and reality are easily confused and where the face of the mafia may hide behind the respectable mask of lawyer, judge, businessman, priest or politician.

A body found on the sidewalk can reveal secret alliances or conflicts, economic interests or changes in strategy. The notion that only the best investigators are killed is a brutal and often unfair equation for the living: when one Palermo police officer miraculously survived an ambush in which two others died, he was suspected of collusion, a taint that was not removed from his name until the mafia killed him a few years later. The importance of a given prosecutor or politician may not become fully apparent until he is gone.

The moment of truth came for Judge Giovanni Falcone on May 23, 1992, when he, his wife, and three bodyguards were killed by a massive explosion that ripped apart the highway leading from the airport at Punta Raisi to Palermo.

It came just two months later, on July 19, for Falcone's close friend and fellow prosecutor, Paolo Borsellino, and five bodyguards—blown up as Borsellino arrived for a Sunday visit with his mother in downtown Palermo.

In massive popular demonstrations, solemn funeral orations and candlelit processions, the two prosecutors were universally hailed as national heroes, as Cosa Nostra's most implacable and dangerous enemies—the heart and soul of the Palermo anti-mafia "pool," a small team of magistrates who had taken the war against the mafia further than anyone had ever dared.[5]

Falcone and Borsellino took their place among the city's other martyrs. People in Palermo can tick off the dates of major assassinations as easily as the feast days of Sicily's patron saints: September 25, 1979, Judge Cesare Terranova; January 6, 1980, Piersanti Mattarella, president of the Sicilian Region; August 6, 1980, Judge Gaetano Costa; April 30, 1982, Pio La Torre, head of the Communist Party in Sicily; September 3, 1982, General Alberto Dalla Chiesa, prefect of Palermo; July 29, 1983, chief prosecutor Rocco Chinnici; August 6, 1985, Antonino Cassarà, deputy chief of police.[6]

These are some of the city's "excellent cadavers," a term used in Sicily to distinguish the assassination of prominent government officials from the hundreds of common criminals and ordinary citizens killed in the course of routine mafia business.

But in the spring and summer of 1992, the mafia appeared to have taken a quantum leap forward with a new political/terrorist strategy. In March, Cosa Nostra had interrupted the election of a new parliament by killing an important political figure. Then, in May, as the country was busy trying to select a new president, they killed Falcone. Finally, in July, with a recently formed government trying to enact stiff new anti-mafia provisions and survive a growing government corruption scandal, they killed Borsellino.

The mafia appeared to be sending a message to the government in Rome by killing Italy's two most famous mafia prosecutors, the architects of the maxi-trial of Palermo—arguably the greatest mafia trial in history. Murders are carried out not only to eliminate a dangerous adversary but to make a clear, unequivocal statement when more subtle forms of communication have been ignored. "Everything is a message, everything is full of meaning in the world of Cosa Nostra, no detail is too small to be overlooked," Falcone wrote in an autobiographical memoir he published the year before his death. Because of strict prohibitions against discussing or even acknowledging the existence of Cosa

Nostra, the *mafioso* communicates indirectly through actions, gestures and silences. "The interpretation of signs," Falcone added, "is one of the principal activities of a 'man of honor' and consequently of the mafia-prosecutor."[7]

The meaning of the spectacular murders of Falcone and Borsellino was not immediately clear.

At first glance, their murders seemed an assertion of total invincibility. The mafia was showing that it was prepared to kill anyone—no matter how important or well protected—that the state might send up against it. By killing Falcone in Palermo and not in Rome, where Falcone worked during the last year of his life, Cosa Nostra declared that it and no one else was in charge in Sicily. It would have been easier to kill Falcone in Rome, where he often moved around without bodyguards: by blowing up an entire, bulletproof motorcade on one of the most heavily traveled stretches of highway in Sicily, the mafia made a spectacular demonstration of its complete control of its territory. But underneath the surface of these more obvious messages, more subtle semioticians of Cosa Nostra life saw something quite different. "The mafia is on its last legs," declared Tommaso Buscetta in an interview from his hideaway in the United States, where he is in the witness protection program. "The mafia is not used to these kinds of large-scale public killings. It is used to silence. I think it is fighting for its survival." It was Buscetta—in his capacity as witness—who had taught Falcone to decipher the behavior of the mafia. His interpretation of the Falcone-Borsellino assassinations was greeted with skepticism at the time, but proved remarkably clairvoyant.[8]

The killings stunned the Italian state into its most vigorous anti-mafia campaign in decades. The Italian parliament quickly passed many of the tough anti-mafia measures Falcone and Borsellino had been pushing for years: greater incentives and protection for mafia witnesses, tougher prison conditions for mafia defendants, streamlined procedures in mafia trials. Moreover, it took the extraordinary step of sending 7,000 army troops to Sicily to set up roadblocks, guard judges and politicians, and free up the police to concentrate on investigative work.[9] The results of the next two years were nothing short of revolutionary: several hundred *mafiosi* turned against Cosa Nostra and offered to cooperate with police. The Italian police dismantled entire organizations overnight and tracked down more than three hundred longtime mafia fugitives, including several of the most powerful bosses, and, in particular, the "capo di tutti i capi" Salvatore (Totò) Riina, who had eluded arrest for twenty-three years.[10]

One of the signs that convinced Tommaso Buscetta that the mafia was in trouble was an earlier and much more puzzling assassination. In March 1992—during a national electoral campaign—*mafiosi* in Palermo killed Salvatore Lima, arguably the most powerful Christian Democratic politician in Sicily and a close friend and ally of then prime minister Giulio Andreotti. The murder was a complete mystery since Lima was one of the politicians rumored to be one of the mafia's closest friends in government.[11]

Buscetta understood that the killings of Falcone and Borsellino were symptoms of a profound crisis within the mafia itself. Lima's killing represented the breakdown of the long-standing alliance between the mafia and certain parts of the Christian Democratic Party. Cosa Nostra was striking at the highest levels of the state because the political world in which the mafia had thrived was coming apart at the seams and was no longer able or willing to continue protecting it.

The new terrorist strategy of Cosa Nostra must be understood in a broad historical context. In 1992, the Italian political class that had "tolerated" mafia power in southern Italy was turned upside down by two parallel scandals: the investigation into massive government corruption known as Operation Clean Hands, and the revelations about political collusion with the mafia that followed the killing of Salvatore Lima. While separate, the two investigations are related. The same system of party patronage that lent itself to massive bribery in northern Italy has been highly porous to mafia infiltration in the south.

The back-to-back assassinations of Falcone and Borsellino mark a pivotal moment in the demise of the political class that ruled Italy from World War II until 1994. As the twin scandals of corruption and mafia collusion progressed, one-third of the national parliament and one-half of the Sicilian parliament came under some form of criminal investigation. The two most powerful figures of Italian political life—the Christian Democrat Andreotti and Socialist leader Bettino Craxi—were driven from the political stage. (Craxi because of the overwhelming evidence of his central role in highly systematic corruption. Andreotti because of mounting charges of mafia collusion.)

"For more than forty years there has been an unwritten law in Italy that corrupt politicians didn't go to jail, *mafiosi* didn't talk and you couldn't have a government without Giulio Andreotti," said Vittorio Foa, who was a member of Italy's first postwar parliament and retired from the senate in 1992. "Now we have a government without Andreotti, corrupt politicians are going to jail and *mafiosi* are talking."[12]

The radical change in Italy's political climate is due in good part to larger international developments. Perhaps more than any country in Western Europe, Italy has been dominated by the politics of the Cold War. With the largest Communist Party of any democratic country, its political life was polarized between the two opposing forces of the Christian Democrats and the Communists. "Because of the presence of a large Communist Party, the Christian Democratic Party remained in government for forty-seven years," said Pietro Scoppola, a professor of political science at the University of Rome and a Catholic scholar close to the Christian Democratic Party. "The normal alternation of governments in Italy was impossible. The DC [Democrazia Cristiana] was forced to use its power to consolidate its electoral position, through patronage. And the passage from patronage to corruption and from corruption to mafia is a quick one."[13]

Until very recently, Italian voters tended to consider corruption and complicity lesser evils compared to a government headed by the Communists. "Hold your nose and vote Christian Democrat," conservative editor Indro Montanelli advised his readers in the mid-1970s when the Communists were on the verge of overtaking the Christian Democrats as Italy's largest party.[14] But with the evaporation of the Communist threat, the stench of corruption suddenly became intolerable. Almost overnight, a nation that preferred to ignore corruption began pursuing it with the zeal of the recent convert. Crowds cheered as once-untouchable party chieftains were dragged off to jail. The traditional parties hemorrhaged votes and fought for their survival. "Either we change or we die," Vincenzo Scotti, a senior Christian Democrat leader, said. That the Christian Democrats' power depended on the presence of the

Communist threat was made clear when the party collapsed and was forced to change its name just two years after the Italian Communist Party did so in 1991.[15]

Until the collapse of the Berlin Wall, the U.S. government was also keenly interested in keeping the Christian Democrats in power and the Communists out. In the 1940s and 1950s, the CIA funded the Christian Democrats, just as the Russians funded the Italian Communist Party. And during the late 1970s the U.S. government openly stated its opposition to Communist participation in the government. U.S. policy has been schizophrenic. American law enforcement officials have worked closely and effectively with prosecutors like Giovanni Falcone and Paolo Borsellino, creating a model of international cooperation. At the same time, however, the United States' closest political allies continued to be many of the same politicians suspected of being in league with the mafia. It is one of the unfortunate accidents of history that many of the mafia's bravest opponents locally were in the wrong camp internationally. Pio La Torre (the head of the Communist Party in Sicily who was killed by the mafia in 1982) led both the fight for tougher anti-mafia legislation and the campaign to keep NATO cruise missiles out of Comiso, Sicily. The installation of the cruise missiles was the greatest priority of Reagan administration policy in Italy, and some consider it the turning point that convinced the Soviets to abandon the arms race and begin glasnost. For such a price, the United States was more than prepared to overlook the unsavory associations of some of its closest friends.

Despite the astonishing level of corruption, during the last forty-five years Italy has enjoyed its greatest period of peace and prosperity since the time of the Roman Empire. Never before have so many Italians experienced such a widely distributed level of well-being. Even in the south, problems like hunger, malaria and illiteracy have been virtually eliminated. But these achievements have come at a very high price: the region has come under the near-total domination of the mafia.

The extent of mafia control of daily life in Sicily is something that people outside of Italy cannot quite fathom. The American mafia is a parasitic phenomenon operating at the margins of society. In southern Italy it plays a central role in almost every phase of economic and political life. There are still many places in Sicily where people are forced to buy their water from private wells owned by the mafia—an almost feudal situation.

For many years, most people underestimated the power of the mafia, considering it a primitive, archaic organization that would gradually disappear as Italy modernized and the economic level of Sicily approached that of the rest of Italy. Instead, the mafia has proved an extremely vigorous and mutable virus that has adapted itself in almost perfect symbiosis with the modern Italian welfare state. Political parties in Italy control almost every aspect of economic life, running vast industries and divvying up hundreds of thousands of jobs from the mightiest bank president to the lowliest street sweeper. As the parties expanded their sphere of influence, government spending came to occupy 52 percent of the gross national product. In southern Italy, where the figure is an incredible 70 percent, political clout is the key to wealth and power.[16] "In Sicily the mafia controls all public contracts," a recent report of the parliament's anti-mafia commission declares starkly. "In my area, you can't move a pin without Cosa Nostra," Leonardo Messina, a former *mafioso* from the town of San Cataldo, Sicily, recently told the commission, barely able to hide his residual pride.[17] To create electoral consensus, the government funded pharaonic and often useless building projects—superhighways leading to nowhere, dams without water, seaports without ships, factories that never opened. These projects created jobs, enriched a series of unscrupulous entrepreneurs and provided a perfect vehicle for mafia infiltration.

Forty-five years of mafia-influenced government in southern Italy have transformed the countryside and cities. They almost all share a common physiognomy in the helter-skelter collection of cheap, cement-box buildings that clutter the skyline; in the filth of the streets and lack of basic services. Pork barrel politics have made Italy the world's largest per capita consumer of cement, and yet much of southern Italy still has a substandard infrastructure. Many of Sicily's most beautiful beaches have been covered over with cement, but the highway between Palermo and Messina— under discussion for thirty years—remains incomplete.

Artistic and archaeological sites that are among the most important and beautiful in all of Europe have been degraded almost beyond recognition. Some six hundred illegal buildings crowd the archaeological area around the magnificent Greek temples at Agrigento—to the benefit of highly suspect economic interests.[18] And although they are in direct violation of strict zoning laws, no one has had the courage to order their demolition. In any other European country, the sumptuous aristocratic villas and parks of Bagheria (outside Palermo) would be a mecca for tourists from around the world. Instead, the corrupt and mafia-infested town administration has reduced it to a squalid slum; illegally constructed concrete buildings surround the villas, while many of the architectural monuments have fallen into decay through looting and neglect.[19]

In many places, democracy as we know it has ceased to exist. In 1992 and 1993, the Italian Ministry of the Interior dissolved the elected governments of more than seventy towns and cities because their city councils were found to have been polluted by the mafia. For several years, the town of Platì in Calabria had no city council whatsoever because people were too afraid to run for office or to vote. In other places, politicians negotiate to buy packets of votes from organized crime bosses.[20]

The maintenance of this extraordinary degree of social and economic control requires the constant threat of violence. An estimated ten thousand people were killed by organized crime in southern Italy during the 1980s—three times as many as have died in twenty-five years of guerrilla warfare in Northern Ireland.[21]

Sicily, as the great novelist Leonardo Sciascia said, is a metaphor.[22] Because of its violence and extremity, Sicily contains in highly concentrated doses and highly dramatic form Italy's virtues and vices. Honor, friendship and family can take the form of great dignity, warmth and hospitality or become perverted by mafia culture. The mafia allegiance to the clan is an exaggerated form of a national disease that sociologists have called "amoral familism." Because of hundreds of years in separate states and principalities, most Italians identify to a greater degree with their region, town, neighborhood and family than with the national government. Italy is an extremely young nation, just over 120 years old, in which identification with the abstract concepts of state, law and the public good have been slow to take root. Personal relations are fundamental in Italian life. The length to which many Italians will go for their friends and relatives is extraordinary. The willingness of most Italians to discard bureaucratic rules and look at each situation in strictly human terms is often highly appealing. But it also lends itself to the current patronage system. A cumbersome bureaucratic process that might normally take months of paperwork is resolved in minutes by a friend in the right place. Getting a telephone installed or a hospital bed in timely fashion can often be accomplished only with the right connections. Jobs are reserved for *raccomandati* (those with the right recommendations). Public offices of all kinds—from the heads of museums and theaters to the local garbage collector—are treated like the private fiefdoms of Italy's political parties. Because so many things are decided by connections, most Italians seek the protection of some "clan," a political party or a faction within a party, a religious organization, social club or a secret society such as the Freemasonry or the mafia. The war against the mafia in Sicily is not a local problem of law and order, but, as Leopoldo Franchetti understood in 1876, the struggle for national unity and democracy in Italy.

ONE

The history of the mafia and of the modern Italian state begin together. Soon after Garibaldi and the troops from the northern region of Piedmont invaded Sicily in 1860 and united it with the rest of the new Italian nation, they encountered the problem of rampant crime. In the chaos that followed the war of unification, bandits terrorized the countryside, murdering government troops, while criminal bands tried to control the sale and renting of land, placing their own men as guards on the lush gardens and groves in and around Palermo. The northern Italians were struck by the Sicilians' refusal to cooperate with the new government, the stubborn silence of even innocent victims, their tendency to take justice into their own hands. The word "mafia" entered the Italian vocabulary at this time to describe the peculiarly tenacious kind of organized crime the northern Italians found deeply embedded in Sicilian life.[1]

Unlike bandits or common thieves who live outside respectable society, most mafiosi continued to work at regular jobs, using force or the intimidating power of the organization to extort advantage from others. Many of the early mafiosi were armed guards or administrators who ran Sicily's great rural estates for their absentee landlords in Palermo. Traditionally, the mafioso put himself in the role of intermediary, keeping the peasants in line and guaranteeing that the harvest would be brought in, while using his control of the land to extract concessions from the landlord. In a place where government has never been particularly effective or well liked, mafia groups usurped many of the functions of the state—administering justice, settling disputes and dividing up resources. Although *mafiosi* have often cultivated the image of being modern-day Robin Hoods who rob the rich and give to the poor, they have always been dedicated to the task of self-enrichment, never hesitating to use violence and murder in defense of their own interests.

Centuries of corrupt and brutal government by foreign conquerors taught most Sicilians to regard government with suspicion and hostility. Justice was frequently administered not by rule of law but by the private armies of Sicily's feudal landlords. The mafia draws on a code of behavior—the refusal to cooperate with police authorities, the preference for private rather than public justice, even the practice of extortion—that can be traced back centuries. While it has its cultural roots in feudal Sicilian life, the mafia, as a form of organized crime, appears to be a product of modernity, of the new freedom and opportunity of unified Italy. There was little room for organized crime in the highly static world of feudalism, where the landowners had a virtual monopoly of both economic resources and the use of violence. The breakup of the great feudal estates and the expansion of trade opened up possibilities for the lower classes to participate in the confused grab for wealth that followed unification. With no tradition of law or public administration to fall back on, violence or the threat of violence became the easiest way to gain a leg up on the competition. As Paolo Borsellino once observed: "The desire to prevail over the competition, combined with a lack of a credible state, cannot bring about a normal marketplace: the common practice is not to do better than your rivals but to do them in."[2]

Crime in Sicily reached such epidemic proportions that in 1874 it became the subject of an enormous national debate. The conservative government proposed emergency police measures to regain control of the island, which prompted Leopoldo Franchetti's trip to Sicily two years later. In the end, the question brought down the government and brought the Left to power for the first time in Italian history. Public order in Sicily was restored through a typically Italian compromise between mafia and government that set the pattern for the future. The mafia helped police track down and arrest the bandits who were the most obvious threat to public security, and in exchange the government allowed the mafia to continue its own more subtle form of economic crime. This ability to co-opt and corrupt public authority has characterized the mafia from its beginning and has guaranteed its impunity for more than 130 years of history. The advent of democracy and the expansion of voting rights gave organized crime new opportunities to acquire political influence. By controlling substantial blocks of votes, mafia groups helped elect politicians who, in turn, helped them.

Even in Franchetti's day, the disastrous consequences of this compromise were evident. "Italy, annexing Sicily, has assumed a grave responsibility," he wrote. "The Italian government has the obligation to give peace to that population and to teach it the meaning of the law, and to sacrifice any private or political interest toward that aim. Instead we see Italian ministers of every party setting the example by engaging in those 'interested transactions' that are the ruin of Sicily, by recognizing and negotiating with those local powers they ought to try to destroy in order to get their help at election time. The chief of police in order to obey his superiors ends up imitating them and thus forgets the purpose of his mission. . . . While the *carabinieri* [Italian military police] and army soldiers are marching up hill and down dale under the rain and snow, the chief brigand is passing the winter peacefully in Palermo—and not always hidden. . . . People scheduled to be arrested are warned even before the warrants have been signed and the troops who come to arrest them find them gone three or four days earlier."[3]

It was not until Mussolini's fascist regime that a first serious, if bloody, attempt to suppress the mafia was made. Between 1924 and 1929, Mussolini's "Iron Prefect," Cesare Mori, conducted mass arrests, surrounded and besieged entire towns, took hostages and destroyed property and livestock in order to track down suspected criminals. To some extent, the campaign was a success: according to government figures homicides in the province of Palermo dropped from 278 to only 25 in 1928. Grateful landowners wrote letters to Mori in which they reported that after being "freed" from the mafia the value of their land had skyrocketed, with rents doubling, tripling and in some instances increasing by 1,500 percent.[4] But if he appeared to reduce criminal activity, Mori did little to cut the social roots of the mafia. His campaign of terror, by using brutal and illegal tactics and indiscriminately arresting hundreds of innocent people along with the guilty, turned *mafiosi* into persecuted victims who enjoyed popular sympathy. The fact that the regime also used the operation to eliminate some of its own political opponents further undermined its credibility. Moreover, as the rent figures show, the chief beneficiaries appear to have been the landowners. By contrast, agricultural wages dropped by some 28 percent during the late 1920s and early 1930s. The Fascists appeared not so much to have eliminated the *mafiosi* as to have replaced them by acting as the new enforcers for the Sicilian landowning class. After Mussolini recalled Mori in 1929, saying his mission had been completed, the regime had to pretend that the mafia no longer existed and ignored signs that the *mafiosi* were cautiously coming back out of the woodwork.[5]

With the fall of fascism and the liberation of Sicily by Allied troops during World War II, the mafia was ready to emerge in full force. There is a widespread belief in Italy that the Allied landing was prepared with help from the mafia, which was then rewarded with important positions of power. According to this theory, the American government contacted the Sicilian-American gangster Lucky Luciano, who enlisted the cooperation of his Sicilian counterparts to pave the way for a rapid Allied victory.

While colorful (and politically useful), the story appears to have little basis in fact. But, as with many legends, there is a grain of truth. Naval Intelligence did contact Lucky Luciano for information about German saboteurs in the docks of New York. But Luciano, who had left Italy as a boy, denied any role in the Sicilian landing: "At home, I didn't have any contacts," he said.[6] After the war, either as a quid pro quo or as an expedient attempt to rid themselves of known criminals, the United States deported Luciano and some forty other American *mafiosi* back to Italy—where they used their American experience to help modernize organized crime.[7]

The Allied occupation undeniably gave new oxygen to the mafia. Anxious to exclude both Communists and Fascists from power, the occupying Anglo-American army—whether knowingly or unknowingly—installed several prominent *mafiosi* as mayors of their towns. (An Italian-American *mafioso,* Vito Genovese, managed to become interpreter for the American governor of Sicily, Colonel Charles Poletti, during the six months of military occupation.)[8] Criminal elements succeeded in infiltrating the Allied administration, often with the help of Italian-American soldiers. They managed to smuggle supplies from military warehouses and ran a flourishing black market in such scarce commodities as food, tobacco, shoes and clothing. While this black market trade may have involved the corruption of low- and middle-level officials, there is nothing to suggest that it was part of a strategy conceived in Washington. The Pentagon and the Roosevelt administration, in fact, registered their alarm about the situation in Sicily. As in the period after the Italian battle of unification, the aftermath of World War II was a time of chaotic freedom and economic expansion which the mafia exploited ably.

Determined to avoid the persecution it had suffered under fascism, the mafia made a concerted effort to assure itself political protection in the new postwar order. At first, many *mafiosi* backed the new movement of Sicilian separatism, helping to organize its small guerrilla army. But when the cause of separatism faded and other parties, such as the Christian Democratic Party, emerged, mafia bosses shifted their allegiances. With the Italian Left seemingly on the brink of power, the new parties accepted mafia support as a bulwark against communism.

Between 1945 and 1955, forty-three Socialists or Communists were murdered in Sicily, often at election time. On April 20, 1947, the united Left (Communists and Socialists) won an impressive 30 percent of the vote in Sicily against the 21 percent of the Christian Democratic Party. Ten days later, when Communist farmers of Portella della Ginestra gathered to celebrate May Day and their electoral victory, the criminal band of Salvatore Giuliano opened fire on the crowd, killing eleven people.[9]

The killings took place in the new chill of the Cold War. That year, the United States announced the Truman Doctrine, stating its commitment to fight Communist expansion throughout the world. Indeed, on the day of the massacre of Portella della Ginestra, Secretary of State George Marshall sent a telegram to the U.S. ambassador in Rome, expressing alarm over the rise of the Communists (especially in Sicily) and the need to adopt new measures to reinforce anti-Communist, pro-American elements. Until that time, the Communists (along with all other anti-fascist parties) had participated as equal partners in the government with the Christian Democrats—an arrangement of which (as Marshall's telegram makes clear) the United States strongly disapproved. As a result of this pressure, the Christian Democrats kicked the Communists out of the government. With the fate of democratic Europe at stake, and Stalin swallowing up entire nations whole, the excesses of local thugs in rural Sicily seemed a minor problem.[10]

The decision to enlist the mafia's help in Sicily was a quite conscious one, as one of the founders of the Sicilian Christian Democratic Party, Giuseppe Alessi, acknowledged openly many years later. While personally opposing this local pact with the devil, Alessi was outvoted by others who viewed it as a practical necessity. " 'The Communists use similar kinds of violence against us, preventing us from carrying out public rallies. We need the protection of strong men to stop the violence of the Communists,' " Alessi quoted one of his colleagues as saying. "I was in the minority and the 'group' entered en masse and took over the party." (Despite his dissent, Alessi shared a rather rosy view of the "honored society" prevalent at that time: "It was another kind of mafia, not the kind of violent organized crime we see today," he said.)[11]

"The DC decided to accept the mafia's support to reinforce itself in the struggle against communism," said historian Francesco Renda. "If one doesn't understand this, it's impossible to understand everything that happens afterwards. The people who made this choice were not criminals, nor were they joining with low-level criminals. They were allying themselves with a force that had historically played this role in Sicily. All this was justified in the name of the Cold War. The mafia was ennobled by being given the role of the military arm of a major political force, something it had never had in the past. Naturally, the mafia then drew on the power of the government and became not only a political and social force but an economic force and that's when the real adventure began."[12]

The perpetrators of the Portella della Ginestra massacre, Salvatore Giuliano and his criminal band, roamed freely around the Sicilian countryside for seven years, giving newspaper interviews, meeting with politicians and even the chief prosecutor of Palermo. "The only people unable to find Giuliano were the police," declared a court sentence issued several years later. In 1950, when his presence had become a national embarrassment, the mafia helped wipe out Giuliano's band, presenting the bandit's corpse to police. "Bandits, police and mafia are one and the same, like Father, Son and Holy Ghost," said Gaspare Pisciotta, Giuliano's cousin, whose betrayal was key in the outlaw's final capture and death. Shortly after his trial in 1954, Pisciotta was himself mysteriously poisoned in Palermo's Ucciardone prison when someone put strychnine in his coffee.[13]

The mafia's valuable role as intermediary in capturing Giuliano and other bandits was openly praised by Italian judges of the period. In 1955, Giuseppe Guido Lo Schiavo, a member of Italy's highest court, wrote an outright defense of the mafia: "People say the mafia does not respect the police and the judiciary: it's untrue. The mafia has always respected the judiciary and Justice, has bowed before its sentences and has not interfered with the magistrate's work. In the persecution of bandits and outlaws . . . it has actually joined together with the police."[14]

Well-known mafia bosses with lengthy criminal records were all accorded places of honor in the Christian Democratic Party. And it was not uncommon for prominent politicians to appear as honored guests at the christenings, weddings and funerals of major mafia figures. In Sicily, being known as a friend of a *mafioso* was not a sign of shame but of power.

Mafia bosses could move blocks of votes and the politicians turned to them at election time, as is clear from a letter written in 1951 by a Sicilian member of parliament, Giovanni Palazzolo, of the Liberal Party, to the mafia boss of Partinico.

Dearest Don Ciccio,

The last time we saw one another at the Hotel delle Palme (in Palermo) you told me quite correctly that we needed a bright young member of the Regional Parliament from Partinico who was a friend and would be accessible to our friends. My friend Totò Motisi has all these requisites and I have decided to help him with all my strength. If you help me in Partinico we will make him a member of parliament.[15]

The letter's recipient was Francesco Coppola, known as Frankie "Three Fingers" Coppola in the United States, where he had served a long prison sentence until he was freed and deported to Italy along with Lucky Luciano after the war.

In the 1950s, after land reform helped break up the last great feudal estates (a process that the mafia worked to its own benefit), agriculture in Sicily diminished in importance and hundreds of thousands of unemployed peasants emptied the countryside for the growing cities. Many headed for Palermo, the new capital of the Sicilian region. In order to undercut the separatist movement, the government in Rome had granted Sicily special autonomy, including the right to have its own parliament and regional government in Palermo. While failing to fulfill the promise of greater self-determination and dignity for the Sicilian population, the new arrangement provided an extra layer of bureaucracy, thousands of jobs to be distributed to political cronies, and control over millions of dollars in government funds with seemingly limitless possibilities for corruption and patronage. So much so that many Sicilians referred to their regional representatives simply as *i novanta ladroni,* "the ninety thieves," there being ninety seats in the local parliament.[16]

With the flow of both people and money toward the new regional capital, the city experienced a massive building boom known as "the Sack of Palermo." Real estate developers ran wild, pushing the center of the city out along Viale della Libertà toward the new airport at Punta Raisi. With hastily drafted zoning variances or in wanton violation of the law, builders tore down countless Art Deco palaces and asphalted many of the city's finest parks, transforming one of the most beautiful cities in Europe into a thick, unsightly forest of cement condominia.

Developers with close mafia ties were not afraid to use strong-arm tactics to intimidate owners into selling or to clear the way for their projects. One of the most important buildings of the great Sicilian architect Ernesto Basile was razed to the ground in the middle of the night, hours before it would have come under protection of the historic preservation laws. In the period from 1959 to 1964, when Salvatore Lima and Vito Ciancimino were, respectively, mayor and commissioner for public works, an incredible 2,500 of the 4,000 building licenses issued in the city of

Palermo went to three individuals whom the Italian parliament's anti-mafia commission has described as "retired persons, of modest means, none with any experience in the building trade, and who, evidently, simply lent their names to the real builders."[17]

The expansion of the new city was accompanied by the gradual abandonment and decay of the old. Already damaged by bombs during World War II, the center of Palermo was gradually reduced to a wretched slum, through a deliberate policy of neglect. There was little money to be made in the old center because of zoning restrictions: throwing up cheap high-rise apartments was much more lucrative than patiently restoring seventeenth- and eighteenth-century structures. Many areas were left for months or years without gas, electricity or hot water, forcing residents to move out into the new housing projects. Even neighborhoods that had not been bombed during the war began to look as if they had been. Palermo gained the distinction of not only having a Department of Housing, but a department of *edilizia pericolante* or "collapsing housing"—a disgrace that continues to this day.

The residents of the city center dropped from 125,481 to 38,960 between 1951 and 1981—a period in which the population of Palermo as a whole nearly doubled.[18] Many of the great monuments of Palermo—the onion-domed Arab mosques-turned-Christian churches, the Norman palaces, the Renaissance fountains and baroque churches—stand next to empty, rubble-strewn lots or abandoned buildings with broken windows. Those who remained behind were generally the city's poorest and most wretched, prepared to put up with Third World conditions not unlike those of the bidonvilles of Cairo or Rio de Janeiro.

The story of mafia power in Palermo can be told in terms of real estate—block by block and building by building—a legacy that is reflected both in the cheap construction and infernal congestion of the "new" city and the total degradation of the old. The changes it wrought were so fundamental that almost no one was immune. The Falcone and Borsellino families were no exception.

Born respectively in 1939 and 1940, Giovanni Falcone and Paolo Borsellino grew up during this period of transformation only a few blocks apart in an old, dilapidated neighborhood of

Palermo near the seaport known as La Kalsa. For centuries the area had been one of the most elegant in the city. In the eighteenth century, the poet Goethe admired the striking axial views created by Palermo's criss-crossing avenues, along which the city's aristocracy rode in carriages for the daily *passeggio* in order to see and be seen.[19] The Falcones lived on Via Castrofilippo, in a house once inhabited by a city mayor, Falcone's great-uncle. Paolo Borsellino and his family lived nearby on Via della Vetriera, next to the family pharmacy. As boys, Falcone and Borsellino played soccer together in Piazza Magione. The neighborhood had come down a bit since Goethe's time, but it had retained some of its elegance, and remained a healthy mix of professionals and day laborers, aristocrats and fishermen, businessmen and beggars.[20]

The Borsellinos' house on Via della Vetriera was declared unsafe and the family was forced to move out in 1956. The family pharmacy (run at the time by Paolo's mother and now by his sister, Rita, and her husband) remained, while the neighborhood crumbled around it. Homeless squatters occupied their old building and, forced to live without light or heat, partially destroyed it in a fire. During the sack of Palermo, the Falcones' own house was earmarked for demolition to make way for a road. Falcone and the rest of his family haunted the offices of various city officials, carrying photographs of the palace's frescoed ceilings in hopes of convincing them of the building's historic and artistic value. The building was destroyed in 1959, although the road it was supposed to make room for was never built—a testament to the blind and irrational urban planning of the period. Both families had little choice but to join the exodus to the anonymous dormitory community on what had been the outskirts of town.

It is probably not an accident that the two prosecutors who wound up together on the front line against the mafia came from Palermo's small but solid professional middle class. Falcone's father was a chemist, Borsellino's a pharmacist. The middle class—in Sicily as in the rest of Italy—was perhaps also the part of Sicilian society that had been the most receptive to the values of patriotism and nationalism promoted by the new Italian state and emphasized even more energetically during fascism. "Our family was very religious and very attentive to the idea of civic duty," said Maria Falcone. "We grew up in the cult of the Fatherland.

Mamma's brother died at age eighteen in the First World War, falsifying his birth certificate so he could volunteer for the army at age seventeen. My father's brother died at age twenty-four, as a career air force official. Hearing about these relatives as children developed in us, and in Giovanni, a love of country above all. 'They served the Nation!' my father would say with reverence."

The family went to church every Sunday and, for a time, Giovanni served as an altar boy. Giovanni's mother showed few outward signs of affection but communicated a very Sicilian idea of manhood: "She would often repeat to him that boys never cry, because she wanted him to grow up to be a strong man," Maria said. Giovanni's father was more affectionate but remained the stern patriarch typical of the fathers of that period. "He taught us to work and to do our duty," Falcone once said. "He was a man of strong moral principle, serious, honest, extremely attached to the family. . . . He slapped me only once during my childhood. It was during wartime when I broke a bottle of oil. Someone who didn't live through those times wouldn't understand. A bottle of olive oil at that time was a treasure. My family was not rich, we lived on a modest state salary." In this somewhat austere, frugal household, Falcone's father was proud of the fact that he had never treated himself to a coffee at a café.[21]

Falcone's parents were not politically active. "They had a rather uncritical view of fascism, they were loyal, law-abiding citizens," said Maria Falcone. As a boy he had been infatuated with a phrase of the Italian patriot Giuseppe Mazzini, "Life is a mission and duty is its highest law." In fact, Falcone considered a career in the military, spending one year at the Italian naval academy, before returning to the University of Palermo to study law.

At the university, Falcone drifted away from his family's Catholicism and became interested in communism. "Our studies—particularly with Giovanni and me—brought us to a decidedly critical attitude toward fascism, as with any form of absolutism," said Maria Falcone. The Italian Communist Party, while not breaking with the Soviet Union, had long distinguished itself as the most independent and democratic Communist Party in the West. Falcone never became a party member.

Paolo Borsellino grew up with the same "cult of the Fatherland." He, too, had two uncles who had served in the army. Although they had not been killed, both had been taken prisoner in Africa during the Second World War. Both had worked for years in the Italian colonies in Africa during fascism and had moved back to Palermo after the war. Because his father had died when Paolo Borsellino was only twenty-two, his uncles assumed a more important role in his life. One of them, Francesco (Zio Ciccio), lived with the Borsellinos for many years. "When these uncles talked about their experiences in Africa he fell under the spell of these stories," says his sister, Rita. In fact, to the end of his life, Paolo Borsellino's study in Palermo was full of African masks and artifacts brought back from Somalia by his uncle. "Paolo had this great thirst for learning; completely on his own initiative he went to city hall to trace the origins of our family," says his mother, Maria Pia Lepanto Borsellino. He also made a very elaborate and carefully designed family tree of Italy's royal family, the Savoy. This would not have been unusual twenty years earlier, but by the time Paolo Borsellino was growing up, Italy had abolished the monarchy and the Savoy were living in exile, compromised by the fascist regime. But he was named Paolo Emanuele Borsellino, after King Vittorio Emanuele, and was born in 1940, when the Savoy family still held the Italian throne. "He was passionately interested in history, he wanted to know about fascism, he joked about being a supporter of the Bourbons [the Spanish monarchy that ruled Sicily and southern Italy before Italian unification]," his sister, Rita, said.

When Borsellino was at the University of Palermo, he joined a neo-fascist student group. While this fact became the source of some scandal in later years, fascism in the Sicilian context had a specific meaning: for better or worse, the fascist regime was the only Italian government that had made a serious effort to wipe out the mafia. In a land where the rule of law has generally been feeble or nonexistent, Borsellino dreamed of a State with a capital "S." In fact, mafia witnesses have testified repeatedly that the two parties they were strictly forbidden to support were the Fascists and the Communists. So that while starting at opposite ends of the political spectrum, Falcone and Borsellino were attracted by the two political forces that seemed the most uncompromising toward what was worst in Sicilian life.

Growing up, both Borsellino and Falcone had direct experience of the mafia. Borsellino often recalled envying a schoolmate of his who bragged about an uncle who was a *mafioso*. Both prosecutors had classmates who ended up as *mafiosi*. Because the Kalsa is a port area, it is filled with both sailors and smugglers of contraband goods. As a boy, Falcone used to play Ping-Ping with Tommaso Spadaro, who became known as the "King of the Kalsa," a major smuggler of contraband cigarettes and, later, of heroin. "I breathed the odor of mafia from the time I was a boy, but at home my father never talked about it," Falcone said. "It was a forbidden word." (When Falcone later prosecuted Spadaro as a *mafioso*, the boss could not resist reminding Falcone of how badly he had beaten him at Ping-Pong.)[22]

Falcone and Borsellino became friends again while at the University of Palermo and both decided to join the magistrature. In the early years of their careers, both men left Palermo to take jobs in the Sicilian provinces, Borsellino in Agrigento and Monreale, Falcone in Lentini and Trapani. Borsellino returned to Palermo in the early 1970s and Falcone arrived in 1978, taking a job with the bankruptcy court. Borsellino was working as a prosecutor in one of the two principal prosecutors' offices, the Ufficio Istruzione, or investigative office. By the time they became magistrates, Falcone's and Borsellino's early political enthusiasms were greatly tempered and became the subject of joking and teasing between them. "*Camerata* Borsellino," Falcone would say, mimicking the standard form of address between members of the Fascist Party.

Like Falcone, Borsellino never joined any political party in order to avoid any appearance of partisanship in his work as a magistrate. "He refused numerous offers to become a political candidate by both the Socialists and the MSI (Movimento Sociale Italiano, the neo-Fascist Party)," said Giuseppe Tricoli, an activist in the MSI and a friend of Borsellino's from his university days. " 'No one should ever have any doubts about my motives, that I do what I do in order to gain notoriety for myself,' " he told Tricoli.[23]

Their middle-class origins—the fact that their parents worked in professions that did not especially interest the mafia—may have protected Falcone and Borsellino when they became prosecutors. Mafia witnesses have testified that the organization did not extort small shopkeepers (like pharmacists) in the 1950s and 1960s. Members of the Palermo upper class—wealthy landowners or businessmen—were much more likely to be on familiar terms with the mafia, either as victims or accomplices. Some simply paid protection to be left alone, others decided to use the power of Cosa Nostra by having a *mafioso* as a partner in a business deal, a land sale or a development project. Many noble families participated happily in the Sack of Palermo, eager to make a quick profit by selling or developing their old estates. In fact, some prosecutors from the Palermo upper crust found themselves under pressure from friends and relatives to go easy on this defendant or not to explore the interconnections between common criminals and respected, "legitimate" businessmen. Falcone and Borsellino did not belong to any of the exclusive social clubs frequented by some of their colleagues. Even if a magistrate went purely to pass an evening playing bridge, he could very well rub elbows with someone whose name might turn up in a police report or investigation. (Michele Greco—the notorious mafia boss known as "the Pope"—was a member of a fashionable gun club; when some members began to grumble about his presence, the club suffered a robbery that many interpreted as a warning.) Both Falcone and Borsellino led highly restricted social lives among a small circle of close friends and colleagues. They declined invitations to most social occasions and always inquired closely to find out who would be present at any event they were supposed to attend. The most innocuous-seeming event could provide an occasion for the mafia to contact or compromise a prosecutor by having him shake hands with or be seen with a person of dubious reputation.

When Falcone returned to Palermo in 1978, he was undergoing an intensely difficult personal crisis. His wife, Rita Bonnici, chose to remain in Trapani, announcing that she was leaving him for another man. To make matters worse, the other man was one of Falcone's superiors, the chief judge of Trapani, making the affair a hot topic of gossip in the courthouses of Trapani and Palermo. In Sicily, where the word *cornuto* (cuckold) is reserved for the lowest forms of human life, the collapse of his marriage was a scalding humiliation and a personal loss that left Falcone smarting for years. He never discussed his first marriage with his friends and told his two sisters that he would never marry again. Instead he threw himself into his new job at the bankruptcy court, mastering a new area of the law and the intricacies of the economic life of Palermo.

At the time, a general Pax Mafiosa reigned in the city. There had been virtually no major mafia killings in recent years, which led some people (in good faith as well as bad) to declare that the mafia no longer existed. There had been no major mafia prosecutions in several years. The mafia war of the early 1960s had led to the parliament's anti-mafia commission and to a series of massive mafia trials mounted by the Palermo magistrate Cesare Terranova. While Terranova had correctly identified all the major bosses of the Sicilian mafia, the cases all ended in disastrous failure. The culture of *omertà* (silence) and the intimidation of witnesses and judges were so great that the government's cases rarely held up in court.

Many preeminent scholars at the time insisted that the mafia, if it existed, was not an organization but an anthropological phenomenon, a set of values and attitudes common in Sicily.[24] The stories of initiation rites, highly structured mafia "families," with *capi* (bosses) and *consiglieri* (counselors)—were nothing more than the fantasy of Hollywood and the sensationalist press, they said. More attentive observers noted that the relative calm indicated something quite different, a harmony among the city's mafia clans that meant that they were going happily about their business with little or no opposition.

In fact, all the men whom the anti-mafia commission had denounced as the pillars of the mafia system in Palermo were still in place. Vito Ciancimino—the former barber of Corleone—continued to pull the strings at Palermo city hall. All of the important municipal contracts continued to be steered to Count Arturo Cassina, accused of subcontracting out much of the work to mafia firms. The island's taxes were collected by the private monopoly of the Salvo family, long suspected by police of being *mafiosi* themselves. Salvatore Lima, the mayor who presided over the Sack of Palermo, was now a member of parliament, and his political mentor, Giulio Andreotti, was prime minister, thus placing Lima at the center of power in Rome.

Despite the apparent calm, a small number of police officials and prosecutors knew that all was not what it seemed. Deputy police chief Boris Giuliano had begun to notice suitcases full of drugs and money moving back and forth between Palermo and New York. Rather than disappearing, mafia business was booming as never before. Moreover, a series of mysterious kidnappings, murders and disappearances taking place in the Sicilian countryside indicated indecipherable rumblings within the obscure world of Cosa Nostra.

Meanwhile, the rest of the country was preoccupied with what seemed like much more pressing and more important problems—the right to divorce and abortion, terrorism, the rise of the Italian Communist Party, Italy's place in the international struggle between East and West. From the mid-1970s forward the headlines of the daily papers were dominated by terrorist bombings, kneecappings and killings. The Italian Communist Party had gained 34.5 percent of the national vote, just a point less than the ruling Christian Democratic Party and the two had begun to share government power in an arrangement known as "the historic compromise." In March 1978, the Red Brigades kidnapped former prime minister Aldo Moro, one of the architects of the new alliance between Christian Democrats and Communists.[25]

Throughout that spring, the nation was so caught up with the Moro kidnapping that it barely noticed when the mafia peace was briefly interrupted on the morning of May 30, and a group of killers murdered Giuseppe Di Cristina, the boss of Riesi, a town in eastern Sicily. Although the crime was committed in broad daylight on a crowded Palermo street, there were no witnesses. There were, however, a few intriguing clues. In Di Cristina's pocket, police found a $6,000 check from Salvatore Inzerillo, the mafia boss in whose territory Di Cristina had been killed, and the private telephone numbers of Nino and Ignazio Salvo, the fabulously wealthy Christian Democrat businessmen who had the concession to operate Sicily's private tax collection system.[26]

Although his case was ignored, Di Cristina had left investigators a gold mine of valuable information. Only a few days before his death, Di Cristina held a secret meeting with police in a deserted farmhouse in order to tell them of his imminent assassination, identify his potential killers and alert police to the scourge that was about to afflict both the mafia and Sicily during the coming years. Di Cristina provided police with a rare view inside the closed world of Cosa Nostra at its highest levels. He described a widening split between the traditional, "moderate" mafia and the crude and violent interlopers from the town of Corleone and their allies. The Corleonese mafia—under the leadership of Luciano Leggio in the 1960s—had distinguished itself for its homicidal ferocity. Leggio—an ignorant former field guard—had grown into a charismatic mafia leader by showing his ruthless determination to eliminate anyone who stood in his way, often with his own hands and the long knife he carried with him. After Leggio's arrest in 1974, his place was taken by two of his lieutenants, who gave nothing away, in ruthlessness, to their boss. "Salvatore Riina and Bernardo Provenzano, nicknamed 'the beasts' because of their ferocity, are the most dangerous men that Luciano Leggio has at his disposal," Di Cristina told police. "They are personally responsible for at least forty murders each. . . ." Most dangerous of all, he added, was Salvatore Riina, "because [he is] more intelligent" than Provenzano. While the "traditional" mafia, represented by Palermo bosses such as Stefano Bontate, Gaetano Badalamenti, Salvatore Inzerillo and Di Cristina himself—favored a conciliatory attitude toward public officials, the Corleonesi preferred confrontation and violent intimidation. Against the wishes of the mafia's governing body, the Commission, the Corleonesi had murdered retired police colonel Giuseppe Russo, a tenacious investigator. They had carried out a series of kidnappings in Sicily—a practice the rest of the mafia frowned on.[27]

At the end of this secret confession, Di Cristina acknowledged that his life was in imminent danger: "In the next week, I'm expecting a bulletproof car some friends are sending me. It costs about 30 million lire [nearly $40,000 at the time]. You know, Captain, I have many venial sins to my credit and a few mortal ones, as well."

None of Di Cristina's warnings were heeded. Just as he had predicted, the investigation into his own murder concentrated on the better-known members of the "traditional" mafia. Police issued an arrest warrant for Di Cristina's friend and ally, Salvatore Inzerillo, on whose territory Di Cristina had been killed—falling into the trap Salvatore Riina had prepared.

The military offensive of the Corleonesi that Di Cristina predicted came, tragically, to pass. On July 21, 1979, mafia killers gunned down Boris Giuliano, the vigilant police officer who had shown too much interest in the suitcases traveling between Palermo and New York. In September, the Corleonesi made good on their threat to kill Cesare Terranova, the member of the parliament's anti-mafia commission who had returned to take over the investigative office of the Palermo Palace of Justice. And just four months later, on January 6, 1980, they murdered Piersanti Mattarella, the president of the Region of Sicily, the most important Christian Democrat politician on the island, because he had tried to clean up the lucrative market of government contracts, heavily polluted by mafia interests. The season of excellent cadavers had begun. The emerging new mafia was sending a clear message that anyone who dared stand up to Cosa Nostra—even the president of the Region—would meet with instant death.[28]

During this period, Falcone was given the opportunity to move from the bankruptcy court to join his friend Borsellino at the investigative office, the Ufficio Istruzione of Palermo. (At that time, there were two distinct prosecutors' offices within the Italian judicial system: the Procura della Repubblica initiated criminal proceedings against a defendant, then passed the case on to the Ufficio Istruzione to be investigated and prepared for trial. The Procura della Repubblica would then review the evidence and present the case in court.) The investigative office was run by a tough Communist prosecutor, Rocco Chinnici, who was determined to pursue the strong anti-mafia stand promised by his predecessor, Cesare Terranova, who had been murdered before he could even take office.

On the night of May 5, 1980, three mafia killers shot and killed police captain Emanuele Basile, who had taken up the drug investigations of Boris Giuliano. The following day, Palermo police ordered the arrest of some fifty-five members of three different mafia families in Palermo, the Inzerillo, the Spatola and the Di Maggio, accused of running a massive international heroin ring together with the Gambino crime family in New York. The arrests constituted one of the biggest anti-mafia operations in more than a decade. The case quickly became mired in controversy. The two assistant prosecutors to whom the case had been assigned in the Procura della Repubblica of Palermo refused to validate the arrest warrants against the Palermo clans. The head of the office, Gaetano Costa, while acknowledging that the evidence against some of the defendants was preliminary, insisted it was important for the office to show it was not afraid to keep important *mafiosi* in jail. The two young prosecutors, who had evidently told the defendants' lawyers that their clients would soon be out on bail, were reluctant to break their word. Costa and his assistants argued heatedly, while a crowd of journalists and defense lawyers waited expectantly in the hallway outside. In the end, Costa was forced to take the bold and unusual step of signing the arrest warrants by himself. When the meeting broke up, one of the assistant prosecutors apparently said to the mafia lawyers waiting outside, "He signed them, not us," leaving Costa in an exposed, vulnerable position.[29]

Immediately afterward, the Spatola-Inzerillo heroin case—with its already long trail of blood—was transferred to the investigative office, where it reached the desk of Giovanni Falcone—his first big mafia prosecution in Palermo.

TWO

Within a few days of being assigned the Spatola drug case, Falcone received an unannounced visit from the defendants' lawyers, who, in Palermo, are often the friendly, smiling faces with which the mafia presents its most deadly threats: "We're so glad you have been assigned this case," they said. "We have always admired your sense of balance and fairness . . ."[1]

The lawyers would have reason, initially, to be pleased with Falcone. After examining the skeletal initial evidence, he decided to release eighteen of the twenty-eight men who were under arrest. Despite his reputation as a tough prosecutor, throughout his career, Falcone was a firm civil libertarian, refusing to hold or arrest people when he felt the evidence was insufficient.[2]

But the mafia's relief was short-lived. Falcone began a quiet revolution in the prosecution of mafia cases. He took his experience in bankruptcy court and applied it to the financial world of the mafia. He went back to the check found two years earlier on the body of Giuseppe Di Cristina and set about reconstructing a whole network of economic relationships. Along with the check in Di Cristina's pocket were two currency exchange records from the Banco di Napoli for a total of 20 million lire each (about $24,000 at the time). He impounded every currency exchange record of every bank in Sicily from 1975 forward and, by himself, started sorting through literally thousands of checks and bank records. "The investigative method he introduced was so new that we didn't understand it," recalls Judge Francesco Lo Voi, who had just entered the judiciary and did his apprenticeship in Falcone's office at the time. "Falcone had this mountain of records and he set about doing what a team of Treasury officials would now do. There were no computers at the time, he wrote everything alphabetically in these little agendas of his, and set about interrogating all the people whose names kept coming up in the investigation."

Falcone discovered that the same Neapolitan gangster (using a false name) who cashed the $24,000 for Di Cristina had issued thirty-one different currency vouchers that same day for another $360,000 to numerous other Sicilian *mafiosi*. Not only did the Sicilian mafia families work in concert with each other, they worked hand-in-glove with the Neapolitan and Calabrian equivalents of the mafia (known as the Camorra and the 'Ndrangheta). The same network that had managed the traffic in contraband cigarettes in the 1950s and 1960s had simply been converted to running heroin. The Neapolitans were bringing in morphine from Lebanon and Turkey, the Sicilians exported it to the United States and then laundered the dollars back in Italy. Through his bank investigations, Falcone discovered traces of 3 billion lire ($3.6 million) moving between Palermo and Naples over the course of one year.

Falcone caught the suspects in hopeless contradictions: people who claimed not to know one another were discovered making transactions of hundreds of thousands of dollars or flying together on an airplane carrying a shipment of heroin. One by one, the defendants of the Spatola case began returning to jail.

Falcone was placed under police escort, beginning the restricted bulletproof existence that he would lead for the rest of his life.

The mafia did not sit idly by. On the evening of August 6, Gaetano Costa, the Procuratore della Repubblica who had signed the original arrest warrants in the case, was shot down and bled to death on one of Palermo's busiest commercial streets. Falcone rushed to the scene and as he stood looking at his fellow prosecutor's body crumpled on the sidewalk of Via Cavour, another colleague came up beside him and said: "Imagine, I was sure it was you."[3]

Falcone's mother and two sisters were worried now about his safety. When they asked why he had accepted such a dangerous case, he said: "You can only die once." "Giovanni had a very Sicilian attitude toward death—not that he wasn't extremely attached to life—but he regarded death as something inevitable that you must accept with resignation," his sister Maria Falcone explained.[4]

Rather than stopping, Falcone widened the investigation, moving on several fronts simultaneously. In May, police at the Rome airport had arrested Albert Gillet, a Belgian drug courier who was caught with eight kilos of heroin in his suitcase. Subsequently, two other European couriers, one Belgian, the other Swiss, were nabbed. The couriers, who felt no particular allegiance to the organization and were in prison outside of Italy, began to talk. The mafia's international expansion had led to massive new profits, but also exposed it to new risks, by forcing it to deal with unreliable outsiders. So although Falcone could not yet penetrate the mafia's inner wall of *omertà,* he was able to get important firsthand testimony describing the mafia's drug and money-laundering operation in Europe and was able to pin down the role of major crime figures in Sicily and the United States. "One of Falcone's great intuitions [in the Spatola case] was his decision to look for evidence outside the country. . . . It was in fact easier to find documents and witnesses overseas," said Giusto Sciacchitano, who did the work on the Spatola case for the Procura della Repubblica.[5] Gillet told Falcone that Cosa Nostra was not only selling drugs but had set up five major heroin refineries in Sicily. The mafia, the Belgian courier explained, had taken over much of the Marseilles drug operation known as the French Connection, and was even using the same team of French chemists to refine the heroin, headed by a man Gillet knew simply as "André."

French police tipped the Italians off to the arrival in Sicily of the notorious chemist André Bousquet, no doubt the same "André" that the courier had mentioned. Italian police located André and two other Frenchmen at the luxury resort hotel Riva Smeralda (Emerald Coast) in the town of Carini, outside Palermo. Undercover police posing as waiters served the men food and drinks and eventually tracked them to a heroin laboratory nearby. Finally, on August 25 (two weeks after Costa's murder), they decided to move in. When police entered the laboratory to arrest the three French chemists, they got an unexpected bonus: inside they found two Sicilian *mafiosi*. One of them, Gherlando Alberti, known as *u paccaré* (*il paccato*, the imperturbable one) was a major figure in the criminal trials of the 1960s. Not only had Italian police discovered the first known heroin refinery in Sicily, they had tied together the French chemists with a mafia boss of the first order. Later that day, they located a second, larger heroin lab; judging from the equipment they found, the refinery was capable of producing fifty kilos of heroin a week—worth some $12.5 million on the American market.

The euphoria created by the raid was quickly attenuated when, two days later, two young men entered the Hotel Riva Smeralda, ordered and paid for two beers, then shot and killed the hotel's owner. The courageous hotel keeper, Carmelo Jannì, was the fourth victim of the investigation in a line stretching back to police commissioner Boris Giuliano. The killing betrayed the weakness of the Italian anti-mafia effort, the work of a handful of determined individuals, with virtually no institutional structure behind them, incapable of, among other things, protecting witnesses.[6]

Again and again, Falcone compensated for the dearth of resources in Palermo by drawing on the strength of other Italian cities and other countries with more modern and better-financed law enforcement systems. At the time, cooperation among prosecutors' offices was more the exception than the rule; judges in Palermo rarely bothered to speak with prosecutors in other cities on the island let alone in the rest of Italy. What Falcone was doing—working simultaneously with police in France, Belgium, Switzerland, the United States and Turkey, as well as Milan and Rome—was virtually unheard of. In fact, many of his colleagues dismissed his exhaustive search for evidence as "judicial tourism."

In December 1980 Falcone made his first trip to the United States, beginning a relationship that over the next twelve years would lead to some of the biggest international law enforcement operations in history. His U.S. contacts yielded important payoffs. American drug agents discovered that Sicilian *mafiosi* of the highest level, including Salvatore Inzerillo himself, had traveled to the United States and met with his American cousins, John and Joe Gambino, to check on the arrival of major heroin shipments. By checking travel records in Italy, Falcone was able to confirm the Americans' observations, correlating the movements of the *mafiosi* and the drug packages.

The deeper Falcone got into the Spatola case, the more its boundaries expanded. "Buried in the papers of the Spatola case was an enormous new reality to be deciphered," Falcone explained several years later.[7] The implications of the case went far beyond conventional criminal activity to the heart of political and economic power in Palermo. The chief defendant, Rosario Spatola, was a characteristic figure. In the 1950s Spatola had been arrested for selling watered-down milk—a petty criminal of the lowest order. During the Sack of Palermo, he had metamorphosed into one of the biggest real estate developers in the city, with hundreds of employees. By 1980, he was, in fact, the largest taxpayer in Sicily and the fifth largest in Italy. Spatola's empire was built on the massive profits of the drug trade and on his ability to win important government contracts, which meant having powerful political connections. Indeed, Spatola sponsored an electoral banquet for Attilio Ruffino, a Christian Democratic member of parliament from Palermo, and minister of defense, whose uncle had been the archbishop of the city. "Now go home and tell your friends and the friends of friends that they must support this man of integrity and honor," Spatola told the banqueters. In Sicily the term "gli amici degli amici" (friends of friends) is a commonly used code word for mafia. Spatola was the first cousin and business partner of the two biggest mafia bosses in the heroin investigation, Salvatore Inzerillo in Palermo and John Gambino in New York. Through his banking investigation, Falcone could now show that Spatola's construction business was nothing but the façade behind which Gambino and Inzerillo hid their drug operation. The Spatola-Inzerillo group were also possible suspects in the assassination of Piersanti Mattarella, the Christian Democratic reformer who had tried to clean up government contracts in Sicily. One of the major contracts he had blocked was one that Spatola had been counting on.[8]

But the Spatola case led far beyond parochial Sicilian politics to the world of international banking and the pinnacle of Italian power. Falcone's path soon crossed with that of prosecutors in Milan who were tracking the criminal career of the Sicilian banker Michele Sindona. In the 1970s Sindona had become one of the world's largest international bankers. A close financial adviser of the Vatican, he had taken over one of the largest banks in the United States (the Franklin National Bank) and was a major financial backer of the Christian Democratic Party. In 1974, he gave $2.5 million to a former (and future) Christian Democratic prime minister, Amintore Fanfani. Fanfani claimed that the $2.5 million had been a campaign loan, but Sindona insisted it was a gift and Fanfani was never able to produce any documentation that the "loan" had been repaid. (Fanfani was never so much as censured by the parliament, let alone prosecuted, for the episode.) Sindona was also close to Prime Minister Giulio Andreotti, who had once hailed the Sicilian banker as "the savior of the lira."⁹ When Sindona's financial empire came crashing down amid revelations of widespread fraud, he began a series of desperate attempts to blackmail his political friends into sponsoring a government bailout of his banking group. But the rescue plan ran afoul of a few rigorous bank regulators who refused to swallow this unwarranted looting of the public treasury. Sindona's most implacable foe was Giorgio Ambrosoli, the lawyer overseeing the liquidation of Sindona's Milan bank. After countless futile attempts to intimidate Ambrosoli, in July 1979 Sindona sent a mafia hit man from New York to Milan to murder him. The killing only worsened Sindona's legal situation and the next month he disappeared from his suite at the Hotel Pierre in New York, where he was under house arrest. With the help of John Gambino, members of the Gambino crime family and a fake beard, Sindona staged his own kidnapping by an imaginary left-wing terrorist group. The bankrupt banker used the "kidnapping" to return to Italy and gather embarrassing documents in the effort to turn up the heat on his friends in government. The communiqués of his so-called captors were thinly veiled blackmail threats, indicating that Sindona was going to tell all during his trial in the people's prison unless he was liberated. During the first two months of his disappearance, police were prepared to believe that Sindona was in the hands of terrorists. They were therefore surprised to discover on October 9, 1979, that the person delivering a ransom note to Sindona's lawyer in Rome was none other than Vincenzo Spatola, nephew of Palermo real estate mogul Rosario Spatola. The people who were keeping Sindona in Sicily were the very same *mafiosi* who were already under investigation for running the massive heroin ring between Palermo and New York. In a desperate last attempt to maintain the fiction of a terrorist kidnapping, Sindona had himself shot in the leg, spirited back to the United States and "released" on a New York street corner.[10]

Investigators suspect that the mafia was helping Sindona in order to recover millions of dollars in drug profits it had been recycling through his financial empire. If Sindona's banks were allowed to go down the drain so would their money.

Following his policy of seeking help wherever he could find it, Falcone forged close ties with the prosecutors in Milan who were investigating the murder of Giorgio Ambrosoli. The Milan office had a tradition of relative political independence and, ironically, had had more success in prosecuting the Sicilian mafia than had Palermo. Prosecutors in Milan and not Palermo were the ones who had finally succeeded in capturing the boss of Corleone, Luciano Leggio, and sending him away with a life sentence.

When Falcone first arrived in Milan, he was greeted with some skepticism. "One of the judges in Milan . . . asked me what guarantees I could give that the case would not be sandbagged if it were handled from Palermo," Falcone later explained.[11] The Milan judges had had generally poor experience with their Sicilian counterparts, said Giuliano Turone, one of the Milanese judges who worked with Falcone. "They had a sociological approach to the mafia, which had led to the acquittals of all the major cases in the 1960s and 1970s," Turone explained. "I could quickly tell that Falcone was different. . . . He was pursuing a much more modern, scientific investigative method through the examination of money laundering and banking records . . . mafia prosecutions in Sicily changed with Falcone. . . . I had the impression he was animated by a kind of Sicilian patriotism, the desire to liberate the island from the scourge of mafia."[12]

When Falcone and the Milan prosecutors joined forces on the Sindona case, it was clear that the kidnapping was nothing but an elaborate hoax, but many of the exact details and larger purpose of Sindona's mysterious ninety days in Sicily needed to be explored. "Everyone suspected that Sindona had been hiding in

Sicily but had been unable to prove it," said Elio Pizzuti, a retired general of the Guardia di Finanza (the Treasury Police), who worked closely with Falcone on the financial part of the Spatola case. "The first trace we found was when one of my men discovered that Sindona had been staying at the Excelsior Hotel in Catania." They were intrigued to learn that the hotel bill for Sindona and his questionable company was paid by one of Sicily's most respected businessmen, Gaetano Graci, one of Catania's four "Knights of Labor"—the four men who were reputed to run the city. Falcone also learned that Sindona had been hiding in a villa outside of Palermo belonging to Rosario Spatola's family and that the banker and John Gambino had been dining openly in some of Palermo's finest restaurants.[13]

Moreover, the Sindona branch of the Spatola case showed a dangerous pattern of cooperation between the mafia and the Freemasonry. One of the chief organizers of the fake kidnapping—along with the Gambinos and the Spatolas—was a prominent Sicilian-American Freemason named Joseph Miceli Crimi, a medical doctor who had worked as chief physician for the Palermo police force. When Falcone questioned Miceli Crimi about his motivation in the Sindona affair, the doctor gave an astonishing reply: the Freemasons were helping Sindona in order to organize an anti-communist coup d'état that would separate Sicily from the rest of Italy. Miceli Crimi had relied on numerous Sicilian Freemasons for logistical help as he freighted Sindona (who was himself a mason) from town to town. Moreover, during Sindona's stay in Sicily, Miceli Crimi traveled to Arezzo to meet with Licio Gelli, the head of the secret Masonic Propaganda 2 known as the "P2"—a mysterious organization that attracted many of the most powerful members of the Italian armed services and secret services for purposes that have never been adequately explained.[14]

Some have seen the P2 as a reactionary, shadow government prepared to take power in case of a communist electoral victory, while others believe that it was nothing but a sleazy association of people eager to advance their own careers by making powerful connections. There is little doubt, however, that the grand wizard of the P2 lodge, Licio Gelli, exercised a pervasive occult influence in Italian life. The list of 950 known members included 52 top officials of the Italian *carabinieri,* 50 army officers, 37 high-level members of the Treasury Police, 29 navy officers, 11 police chiefs, 5 current and former ministers of the government, 38 members of parliament, 14 judges, 10 bank presidents and numerous top members of the Italian secret services. Also members were the principal owner and editor of Italy's largest newspaper, *Il Corriere della Sera,* and the nation's chief television magnate (and former prime minister), Silvio Berlusconi. Gelli's access to classified information from the secret services gave him formidable powers of intimidation. Through his virtual control of Roberto Calvi, the head of the Ambrosiano Bank, Gelli wielded considerable economic and political influence. Gelli brokered a multimillion-dollar payoff from Calvi to Socialist leader Bettino Craxi (as the current corruption scandal has confirmed). He was the man Giulio Andreotti turned to for introductions to Argentine dictator Juan Perón. While many P2 members may have had little idea of Licio Gelli's activities, the willingness of so many high-level government officials to swear allegiance to a secret group headed by an ardent former Fascist does not speak well for the institutional loyalty of many of the men charged with defending Italian democracy.[15]

The troubling implications of the Sindona affair were not lost on the prosecutors. "The Sindona case made it clear that in Italy, the boundary between the legal and illegal worlds, between the respectable and the criminal, is very thin and porous," said Giuliano Turone, the Milan prosecutor who worked closely with Falcone on the Sindona case.[16] (The fact that two of the country's most powerful bankers, Sindona and Roberto Calvi—both members of the P2—ended up under criminal investigation and would meet violent deaths shows just how porous this boundary is.) Sindona moved among the boardrooms of Wall Street, London and Milan, the Roman palaces of government ministers and cardinals and the Brooklyn restaurant of John Gambino. This mixing of worlds was not without practical consequences: Sindona succeeded in using mafia muscle to terrorize Italy's most powerful financier (Enrico Cuccia) and to murder an honest civil servant (Ambrosoli). Sindona clearly bragged about his political connections to his underworld associates, who, in turn, used them for their own ends.[17] Shortly before murdering Giorgio Ambrosoli, mafia killer William

Arico invoked the name of Giulio Andreotti in a threatening phone call, which Ambrosoli carefully taped:

> KILLER: They're pointing the finger at you. I'm in Rome and they're pointing the finger, because you're not cooperating . . .
> AMBROSOLI: But who are "they"?
> KILLER: The Big Boss.
> AMBROSOLI: Who's the Big Boss?
> KILLER: You understand me. The Big Boss and the little boss, everyone is blaming you. . . . You're a nice guy, I'd be sorry. . . . The Big One, you understand? Yes or no?
> AMBROSOLI: I imagine the big one is Sindona.
> KILLER: No, it's Andreotti!
> AMBROSOLI: Who? Andreotti!
> KILLER: Right. He called and said he had everything taken care of, but it's all your fault . . . so watch out . . .[18]

While these claims may well have been invented to frighten Ambrosoli, it is true that one of Andreotti's closest advisers met with Sindona in New York after Sindona was under indictment in Italy and officially a fugitive from justice. This and the many meetings Andreotti himself held with Sindona's lawyers in Rome created the impression that the prime minister supported the Sindona rescue plan that the nation's bank regulators firmly opposed.[19]

It is extremely significant that the most serious political scandal in Italy in the 1980s—the P2 Masonic lodge—should have grown out of an investigation into the Sicilian mafia. In fact, Falcone was in Milan with his colleagues on the day in March 1981 when the police raided Licio Gelli's villa in Arezzo and found the secret membership lists. The trail, in turn, led back to Palermo, where the chief of police and deputy chief of police were found to be members of Gelli's secret P2 lodge. The revelation of so many powerful government figures belonging to such a suspect secret organization brought down the government of Prime Minister Arnaldo Forlani.[20] But the Milan prosecutors were not allowed to pursue the full implications of the case; the Italian Supreme Court awarded jurisdiction of the case to the more malleable Rome office—where it died a long, slow death. The Consiglio Superiore della Magistratura (the governing body of Italy's independent judicial branch) decided not to take action against fourteen judges whose names appeared on the membership list of the P2 lodge.[21] During 1981, Falcone's investigation expanded to include some 120 defendants—the biggest mafia case in nearly two decades. But rather than receive praise, he became the object of nervous sarcasm in many quarters of the Palermo Palace of Justice. "He'll drown himself in paper," some of his colleagues remarked. "Who does he think he is, a Sheriff-prosecutor? the Minister of Justice?" they said.[22] Falcone's energetic approach was shaking up the sleepy atmosphere of the Palermo courthouse, showing up more senior colleagues, touching on vital economic interests and putting people at risk. "For the most part, the investigative office had limited itself to confirming the contents of the police report and the arrest warrants," says Leonardo Guarnotta, a close friend and colleague of Falcone's in the office. "We would call in the various witnesses and ask them to confirm what they had told the police."[23] It had become more or less accepted truth that it was useless to prosecute the mafia because the evidence would never stick. The big mafia cases of the 1960s prepared by Cesare Terranova had all ended in clamorous defeat. After these demoralizing losses, the Palermo office had done little of note on the mafia front. This attitude of passivity and resignation was both easy and safe.

Judge Turone could already feel the atmosphere of hostility that had begun to surround Falcone when he came from Milan to Palermo during the Spatola case. "People would tell Giovanni, 'You're not making statistics.' They criticized him for spending so much time on this one trial, rather than knocking off a large number of routine cases that could be done in five minutes. This bureaucratic measure of productivity was used to discourage judges who tried to push difficult and complex investigations." Turone, a man of the north, was always struck by the strangeness and duplicity of the Sicilian world, where little was ever as it seemed. "Another prosecutor would come into Falcone's office, they would be all smiles and pats on the back and then when the other left, Giovanni would whisper to me: 'Be very careful of that one!' "[24]

The atmosphere of suspicion was such that the chiefs of the two prosecutorial offices—Gaetano Costa of the Procura della Repubblica and Rocco Chinnici of the Ufficio Istruzione—used to meet in the elevator to discuss delicate cases so as to avoid being noticed together.[25]

"Falcone was very much alone in those years," said Elio Pizzuti of the Treasury Police, who worked night and day with Falcone from 1981 to 1983. His suspicion of others was not unjustified. "At one point during the Spatola case we planned a series of arrests to be made in the middle of the night. When my men arrived not one of the suspects was at home." Pizzuti was convinced that someone—perhaps even a clerk or secretary—must have leaked the names of the suspects after they were registered the day before in the Procura della Repubblica. "I went to the Procuratore della Repubblica, [Vincenzo] Pajno, and asked him if the next time we could wait to write the names in the register until after the arrests. And from that point on, we never had any problems."[26]

Throughout his career, Falcone was a figure who tended to polarize people. Unlike Paolo Borsellino, who had a gregarious, open manner that put people at their ease, Falcone was far more reserved and diffident. Nattily dressed with his carefully groomed beard, Falcone had a thin, ironic smile that was difficult to read. "Borsellino was much more extroverted and very approachable," said Judge Leonardo Guarnotta, who worked with both of them for several years. "Giovanni was much more reserved, much colder in a first meeting. Many confused his reserve with arrogance or distrust. He was very prudent but when he got to know you he opened up completely." Because Falcone held himself to extremely rigorous standards, he was equally hard on others. He did not suffer fools lightly and people sensed this and never forgave him.

"When I arrived in Palermo in the early 1980s, the Palace of Justice was already divided into the friends and enemies of Falcone and the friends were a decided minority," recalled Ignazio De Francisci, who later worked closely with Falcone. "I would say one third was for him, one third against and one third indifferent."

With his demanding nature, Falcone built a staff that became completely loyal to him. Falcone's driver during the early 1980s, Giovanni Paparcuri, remembered that when he was first transferred to work for him, Falcone asked him if he was happy about the assignment. "I said, No, I wasn't. Falcone got angry and told me to think it over and if I decided by next week that I was still unhappy about the job, he would have me transferred." Falcone understood that it was critically important that his driver, one of the people most responsible for his physical safety, not be frightened or ambivalent about his job. "The next week I told him I was happy with the job. Because he worked so hard, it made me not want to let him down: I always made a point of arriving early at his house, driving carefully, always being punctual." Although Falcone established powerful ties with the people who worked with him, it was accomplished, in typically Sicilian fashion, with few words. "We communicated with our eyes," says Paparcuri, something several of the people he worked with echoed.

"If you worked hard you had his respect and if you had his respect you had all the rest," said Barbara Sanzo, the longtime secretary of the investigative office. "He made you want to rise to the task. I don't think there is another person in the world who could work so hard without experiencing the normal sense of fatigue. He would be here at seven-thirty in the morning, work straight through without going home for lunch and at seven in the evening he was still perfectly fresh. Then you'd see him the next morning, ready to do it again."

"Falcone was unique, he had a capacity to work that was simply on another level from everyone else's," said Vincenzo Geraci, one of the magistrates of the Procura della Repubblica of Palermo most involved in mafia cases. (Given the conflicts that would later develop between the two prosecutors, Geraci's comments are high praise.) "He was a kind of human jackhammer. All of us have periods of intense work, but it ends and is followed by a period of letdown, instead for Falcone it went on every day, six or seven days a week for ten years in which he generated an extraordinary amount of work. At the same time, he had an investigative subtlety that made him explore avenues that others would not have thought of. Once he got going, he was unstoppable. Giovanni was a little like Alexander the Great who cut the Gordian knot: everyone else was trying futilely to unravel the knot, Alexander took his sword and cut right through it. Once when Giovanni and I went on a trip to Spain, we wanted to get the records of a Spanish bank to track the trail of a drug transaction. Rather than going through a lengthy bureaucratic procedure that could have taken months, Giovanni went right up to the director of the bank and asked him for the records. And to my amazement, the man gave them to him."[27]

Despite predictions of failure, Falcone accomplished in the Spatola case what no other Sicilian judge had managed before. He had tied together with a web of solid evidence—bank and travel records, seized heroin shipments, fingerprint and handwriting analyses, wiretapped conversations and firsthand testimony—defendants from four crime families on two continents. He had proved that Sicily had replaced France as the principal gateway for refining and exporting heroin to the United States. He showed the close cooperative relationship between the Sicilian mafia families and the Gambino family in New York and he had managed it all without any witnesses from within the organization—destroying the myth that because of the wall of *omertà* you could never successfully prosecute the mafia.

In preparing the case for trial at the end of 1981, Falcone made a shrewd tactical decision. "We have to avoid including any murders in the case," he told Elio Pizzuti, who was then a colonel in the Treasury Police and who began handling banking investigations for Falcone in 1981. "The reason was this: if there had been murder charges the case would have to be heard before the Corte d'Assise with a regular jury. In a normal trial it would be heard by a panel of three judges. Falcone knew that it would be much easier to intimidate a jury of ordinary citizens, and figured we had a better chance with the judges."[28] The prosecution won a stunning seventy-four convictions—reversing decades of defeats against the mafia in Palermo.[29]

THREE

Monreale, the beautiful Norman city that stands atop a hill just two miles from Palermo, was in a state of jubilation. For three days, the town had been celebrating the feast of the Holy Crucifix. The center of town was a kaleidoscope of brightly colored carnival lights. The entire population was living outdoors, attending open-air performances, eating sweets from sidewalk stands and attending services in the enormous Norman cathedral that dominates the area. The celebrations culminated in a huge religious procession that passed through the streets on Saturday evening, the last day of the festivities; afterward the mayor held a grand party that lasted until past one in the morning. Captain Emanuele Basile of the *carabinieri*, his wife, Silvana, and their four-year-old daughter, Barbara, attended both the procession and the party. As they walked home through the brightly lit streets, crowded with revelers, Captain Basile carried his sleepy young daughter in his arms. When they were only a few steps from the *carabinieri* station where Basile lived as well as worked, three men approached him from behind, took out pistols and fired six bullets into his back. Basile fell to the ground, at his wife's feet, his daughter—who was miraculously not hit by the gunfire—still in his arms.[1]

For Paolo Borsellino, the killing of Captain Emanuele Basile was much more than another mafia killing. Borsellino had been stationed in Monreale in his first years as a prosecutor and at the time of the shooting the two had been working closely together on a series of extremely delicate mafia investigations. With the police captain gone, Borsellino (like Falcone after the murder of Gaetano Costa) found himself in Basile's place in the front line. Immediately after the killing in Monreale, Borsellino was assigned the investigation into his friend and colleague's murder, at almost exactly the time Giovanni Falcone began work on the Spatola case.

"Paolo put all of himself into his work, it didn't just touch him superficially, it entered deep into him," said Borsellino's mother (Maria Pia Lepanto Borsellino), who was living with her son at the time. "Paolo became seriously religious—although I became aware of it only gradually—and I think it was because of the work he did. Once, when he was at the beginning of his career he confided in me, when he had to interrogate a man who had sexually abused his daughter. 'How can I find the words? I have to try to understand what could bring a man to fall so low.' He was tormented." Borsellino's work brought him into contact with the most brutal and depraved specimens of humanity, but rather than hardening himself and distancing himself from them, Borsellino could only perform his job by finding some redeeming quality in them and connecting with them. In the case of Captain Basile, his sense of identification was total. "He suffered enormously," his mother said. "It's as if they had killed my brother," he told his sister, Rita. "They were very close," she said. "[Basile's death] was a blow that brought out his sense of sacrifice and self-abnegation that lasted the rest of his career," said Agnese Borsellino, his widow.[2]

The chances of solving Captain Basile's murder seemed greater than usual. For once, there was an eyewitness, a policeman's wife who had seen three men running away from the scene of the crime. And within a few hours of the shooting, the gunmen were arrested in the nearby countryside, with mud spattered on their clothes and on their getaway car that matched the mud near Basile's body. The three under arrest—Giuseppe Madonia, Armando Bonnano and Vincenzo Puccio—were men of the purest mafia pedigree. Giuseppe Madonia was the son of the boss of one of Palermo's most important crime families, Francesco Madonia of Resuttana, and had initiated his criminal career planting dynamite as a teenager. Armando Bonnano had a long and impressive criminal record: he had once been arrested with other members of what looked like a mafia hit squad ready for action, armed to the teeth with a sawed-off shotgun and five pistols. The third man, Vincenzo Puccio, was believed to be a rising star of the mafia family of Ciaculli (a neighborhood of Palermo).[3]

It made sense that such prominent young *mafiosi* should be chosen for the job. Within Cosa Nostra, the more important the victim, the greater the prestige for the killer.

On their arrest, the three men, from different parts of Palermo, all claimed to have had romantic assignations in Monreale the night of Captain Basile's murder. When asked to back up their alibis, they insisted that as a matter of honor they could not name names, saying they were seeing married women whose reputations were at risk.[4]

Beyond identifying the trigger men, Borsellino wanted to figure out who had ordered the killing of Basile and why. To do so, he was led back inevitably to the investigations that Basile had inherited from police captain Boris Giuliano—murdered in July of 1979. The more he studied the careers of the two slain officers, the more Borsellino was struck by their remarkable bravery and terrible solitude. Giuliano had seized a suitcase with half a million dollars in cash at the Palermo airport and had been scouring the countryside around Palermo for heroin-refining laboratories. Shortly before his death, Giuliano had made an extremely important discovery: he had uncovered the Palermo hideout of Leoluca Bagarella, the brother-in-law of Salvatore Riina and one of the most important members of the Corleonese mafia. Although Bagarella had fled, Giuliano had found drugs, arms, photographs and documents. Any one of these investigations could have led to his murder.

Giuliano's family felt that the judges of Palermo were partly to blame for the inspector's death: Giuliano had bombarded the Procura della Repubblica with reports, but they had piled up without leading to criminal proceedings. Borsellino could not help agreeing with them. "Giuliano appeared in the eyes of the mafia families at that time like the only investigator capable of creating serious problems for them, both because of his incessant and multi-faceted activity on a wide range of fronts and because of his stubborn persistence in pursuing criminals despite the near-total indifference of the Palace of Justice, which clearly undervalued the results of his investigative work," Borsellino later wrote.[5]

The investigation into Giuliano's death had foundered. Although he had been killed in broad daylight in a Palermo café, the waiter who had witnessed the killing had suddenly suffered a severe loss of memory after receiving death threats. The work of the Palermo *squadra mobile* (investigative squad) had stalled after Giuliano's death and the investigative trails he was pursuing had gone cold. Then Captain Basile, although stationed in Monreale and not Palermo, took up where Giuliano had left off.

Basile became interested in the hideout used by Leoluca Bagarella, in the hopes of solving a murder he had been investigating. A *mafioso* named Melchiorre Sorrentino had vanished several months earlier, almost certainly the victim of the *lupara bianca,* or "white shotgun," the mafia term for a "white" or bloodless murder, in which the mafia disposes of the body without leaving a trace. Basile was able to establish that a pair of boots found in Bagarella's secret Palermo apartment belonged to Sorrentino and he found a piece of paper on which the victim's name was written in Bagarella's handwriting—then crossed out angrily.

In February 1980 Basile charged Bagarella with drug trafficking, while arresting several of his closest associates and searching their apartments. Putting together photographs he found in Bagarella's hideout and the other houses, Basile was able to tie Bagarella's gang to Lorenzo Nuvoletta (a major Neapolitan drug and contraband cigarette trafficker) and to a colony of the Corleonese mafia that was operating out of Bologna, headed by Giacomo Riina (uncle of Totò Riina) and Giuseppe Leggio (relative of the infamous jailed boss, Luciano Leggio). On the fifteenth of April 1980, Borsellino and Basile went to Bologna to question Riina and Leggio. The two *mafiosi* insisted they did not know Bagarella or any of the other men in the photographs. Basile and Borsellino charged them with perjury. Three weeks after their trip to Bologna, Basile was killed.

Borsellino found it highly significant that the three killers captured on the day of Basile's death—Madonia, Bonnano and Puccio—were members of families that were the object of Basile's investigation and thought to be closely allied to the mafia of Corleone.

One of Basile's last acts before being killed was to search Giacomo Riina's apartment in Bologna, where he found checks and banking records tying him to various other defendants arrested for drug trafficking. In pursuing these financial leads, Borsellino found himself moving onto the terrain that Falcone was exploring in the Spatola case. The two friends began trading information. While dealing with different defendants from different mafia families, they began to realize that there were surprising connections between the two investigations. In fact, their boss, Rocco Chinnici, urged all of the assistant prosecutors in the Ufficio Istruzione to familiarize themselves with Falcone's Spatola case because he was convinced that it would prove the key to numerous other mafia cases. Chinnici intuited the need for the kind of collaborative work that would later come to fruit with the anti-mafia pool.

Neither Borsellino nor Falcone had intended to become anti-mafia prosecutors. It had happened almost by chance, for both of them had been assigned cases that had continued to expand the deeper they probed. They became increasingly absorbed and disturbed by the world they had discovered. Both had then seen colleagues murdered in the line of duty, and it became impossible to turn back.

A s Falcone was bringing the Spatola investigation to a successful close, he could feel the ground moving beneath him. One by one, defendants in the case and other members of their mafia clans were murdered or had disappeared. The second great mafia war of Palermo had begun.

No one had seen it coming, but, in retrospect, there were a few warning signs, especially in a bizarre murder that had occurred several months earlier. On September 6, of the previous year (1980), two killers entered the Franciscan church of Santa Maria di Gesù, asked one of the monks where they could find *Fra' Giacinto,* Brother Hyacinth. They knocked on his door and when it opened, they shot him. As police investigated the case, it quickly became apparent that Brother Hyacinth was no ordinary Franciscan. His "monastic cell" was a rather grand seven-room suite, furnished with color TV and a refrigerator bar well stocked with the finest scotch. In his closet they found a long rack of elegant designer suits and shoes, along with several bull whips—whose precise use was never determined. There was a .38-caliber pistol and several thousand dollars in cash in his desk. In the days that followed the killing, the papers were full of stories and rumors about the murdered monk: Brother Hyacinth was said to be popular with the ladies, had powerful political friends in Rome and Palermo and close ties to the mafia. Some speculated that the monk had used the monastery's graveyard to bury the bodies of the mafia's victims. The church of Santa Maria di Gesù was in the territory of one of Palermo's most important mafia bosses, Stefano Bontate, and Brother Hyacinth was said to be Bontate's good friend and confessor.[6]

The killing at first seemed to be a weird piece of Palermo folklore, but it took on a different coloring when Bontate himself was murdered a few months later. Among the twenty-five or so mafia families in Palermo, Stefano Bontate enjoyed a position of preeminence. Known as "the Prince of Villagrazia" (because of his house on Via Villagrazia), Bontate was rich, handsome, intelligent and heir to one of Sicily's most powerful mafia dynasties. His father, Don Paolino "Little Paul" Bontate, who had died only a few years earlier, was legendary for his vast political influence. Don Paolino's trajectory followed that of many *mafiosi* of his generation: he had first backed the cause of Sicilian separatism and had then become a staunch supporter of the Christian Democrats. He was famous for having publicly slapped a member of the Sicilian parliament who had dared to displease him. Another relative of his, Margherita Bontade, was a Christian Democrat member of the Italian parliament. He had used his connections to have the factory of the huge American defense contractor Raytheon located in his district so that he could control its hiring practices. The Italian manager of the factory quickly discovered who his boss was when he came down from Genoa to present the project in Palermo. "At the end of '62, I was making a speech on the factory floor to which we had invited all the highest authorities of the regional and local governments to explain the company's goals. At a certain point, the door to the room opened and in walked a short, fat man. Everyone turned around and immediately deserted their seats to run and embrace the new arrival. 'Who is this person?' I asked, and was told: 'Don Paolino Bonta.' At that moment, I understood what the word 'mafia' meant." Despite his disgust, the Raytheon manager later testified to the parliament's anti-mafia commission about why he did business with the mafia boss. "Paolo Bonta is useful to me, he provides me with the water I need, he gives me the land to expand the factory and I depend on him for the workers to run the factory." Like so many foreign and northern Italian businesses, Raytheon eventually pulled out of Sicily, deciding it was impossible to do business there.[7]

Stefano Bontate, like his father, was known for his friendship with powerful local politicians and was the charismatic head of what was believed to be the largest single mafia family of Palermo. Perhaps out of a sense of symbolism or perhaps to catch him off guard, Stefano Bontate was murdered on the evening of his forty-third birthday, April 23, 1981, as he was returning home from a party in his honor. When his bright red Alfa Romeo stopped for a red light several killers opened fire, riddling him and his car with bullets. One of the weapons used was a state-of-the-art Russian-made Kalashnikov assault rifle. The city held its breath waiting for the ferocious retaliation of the Bontate forces, but none came. Instead, members of his "family" simply vanished. Wives and mothers began turning up at the Palermo police station reporting that their husbands and sons had disappeared without a trace. At first, it was not clear whether they had gone underground or had been eliminated by their enemies.[8]

Falcone had a natural interest in the killing because Stefano Bontate's brother, Giovanni, was one of the defendants in the Spatola case. He was charged with heroin trafficking and one of the heroin laboratories police had found during the summer of 1980 was situated on land controlled by the Bontate family. Curiously, some journalists came up with a theory that Stefano Bontate had been killed because he opposed the mafia's (and his brother's) entrance into the heroin trade. "Don Stefano, they say, was not happy about this state of affairs," wrote the Italian newsweekly *L'Espresso*. "He was the heir of Paolino Bonta', anchored to the healthy principles of the old mafia: dealing in drugs was okay, but heroin should never reach the shores of Sicily. A principled position that proved both naive and dangerous and may have provoked the break with the various Spatola, Di Maggio, Inzerillo and Badalamenti."⁹

This theory seemed to find confirmation when Salvatore Inzerillo (one of Falcone's chief defendants in the Spatola case) was murdered on May 11, 1981, just three weeks after Bontate. Although police had been looking for Inzerillo unsuccessfully since 1978, his killers had no trouble locating him. He was killed as he was stepping into his brand-new bulletproof car after enjoying a tryst with his mistress in an apartment complex built by the construction company he owned together with his cousin Rosario Spatola. Within days of the killing, one of Inzerillo's brothers, his son, and several of his top mafia soldiers disappeared. Several weeks later, a third major family was targeted: Antonino Badalamenti, the head of the family from Cinisi (a town whose territory includes the Palermo airport), was murdered as were a number of his relatives and close associates.¹⁰

The killings and disappearances that began occurring at a startling rhythm in the city was not a war between different Palermo clans in conflict over whether or not to traffic in heroin. Virtually all of the victims belonged to established Palermo mafia families that were believed to be closely allied to one another; in fact, Falcone's work in the Spatola case showed them to be working together in the drug trade. The fact that Inzerillo had acquired his bulletproof car only days before his own death is an indication he had not planned Bontate's murder: surely, he would have provided for his own security before starting a mafia war. Moreover, the same Kalashnikov had been used to kill both Stefano Bontate and Salvatore Inzerillo. The only interpretative key that made any sense of the killings was the one provided by Giuseppe Di Cristina in the confession he gave before his assassination in 1978. The established mafia families who had dominated Palermo for years were being systematically decapitated one after another. The large number of disappearances suggested that many of those killed had been led into a trap by people they knew well. The complete success of the assassination campaign and the fact that the Corleonesi had suffered no losses in the "war" further indicated that the aggressors were acting with the knowledge and connivance of people high up in the "losing" families.

Investigating the growing mafia war brought Falcone more deeply into the strange mental universe of the mafia. He interviewed the women of the Inzerillo clan who pretended to know nothing of the disappearance of their sons and husbands, even as they were visibly overcome by grief and anxiety. He was deeply struck by a speech one mafia boss made about death when Falcone had asked him about the killing of Salvatore Inzerillo. "Isn't it a shame to die so young, with so many experiences ahead of him?" Falcone asked. To which the *mafioso* replied: "Inzerillo died at thirty-seven, it's true. But his thirty-seven years are like eighty years to an ordinary person. Inzerillo lived well. He had lots of things in life. Others will never have a hundredth of those things. It is not a shame to die at that age, if you have done, had and seen all the things Inzerillo had done, had and seen. He didn't die tired and unsatisfied by life. He died sated by life. That's the difference."[11]

Looking for clues about the mafia war, police found three phone numbers on the body of Salvatore Inzerillo that belonged to the office and residence of a respectable Palermo businessman, Ignazio Lo Presti. The discovery was of particular interest since Lo Presti was related by marriage to the Salvo family, which stood at the pinnacle of economic and political power in Sicily.[12]

In the early 1960s the cousins Ignazio and Nino Salvo were described in police reports as *mafiosi* and the sons of *mafiosi,* but by the 1970s they had ascended to such a level of wealth, power and respectability as to be above all suspicion. The Salvos had the private concession for collecting taxes in Sicily—a primitive but incredibly lucrative institution believed to be a great source of political corruption. While in the rest of Italy the cost of collecting taxes amounted to an average of 3.3 percent of the total revenue, in Sicily the Salvos were allowed to keep an incredible 10 percent of all they collected. At the same time, the Sicilian parliament granted them prolonged delays in delivering the tax revenue to the government—amounting to multimillion-dollar interest-free loans at the expense of the Italian state. The Salvos were active in Christian Democrat politics and a portion of the Salvos' inflated profits were thought to be used to line the pockets of some of the island's most influential politicians. Not only did the Salvos run the tax system, they were among Sicily's leading wine producers, hotel operators, real estate developers and landowners. The Salvos were said to be the kingmakers of Sicilian politics, forming and dissolving regional governments at will. Even some prominent Christian Democrat reformers had complained about the Salvos' unhealthy influence on their party, saying they "bought" elections and dictated legislation. Proof of this suspicion was the fact that every attempt to reform their grossly wasteful monopoly of tax collection was beaten back energetically by the regional assembly. At the same time, the Salvos were whispered to be a principal nexus between mafia and political power. (The Salvos' private phone numbers were among the papers found on the body of Giuseppe De Cristina, but the lead had not been pursued.) They were simultaneously good friends with·Little Paul Bontate and his son Stefano as well as politicians with influence in Rome, such as Salvatore Lima, the former mayor of Palermo and lieutenant of Giulio Andreotti. "Everybody thought the Salvos were the *'mamma santissima'* [a term for the head of the mafia, meaning literally 'most holy mother'], but they were so powerful you didn't even mention their names," said Colonel Pizzuti, Falcone's chief investigator in the Treasury Police. Despite protests by the anti-mafia commission and even by Christian Democrat reformers, the Salvos had never been investigated.[13]

The evident connection between Ignazio Lo Presti and the slain boss Salvatore Inzerillo held the promise of taking the investigation into mafia power several rungs up the ladder. Following the lead, police put a wiretap on Lo Presti's phones, a move that quickly yielded interesting results. Within a few weeks of Salvatore Inzerillo's murder, Lo Presti received a series of phone calls from a man in Brazil, calling himself Roberto, but whom investigators quickly identified as Tommaso Buscetta, a legendary figure in the Sicilian mafia. Known as the "boss of two worlds," Buscetta left Palermo during the first great mafia war in 1963 and moved to the United States, where he was thought to have helped organize a major drug trafficking ring. He had spent most of the 1970s in Italian prisons, but broke his parole in 1980 and had reestablished himself in South America. The conversations revealed that rather than initiating the mafia war, the people around Salvatore Inzerillo were in a state of total confusion. They did not know whether their own men had gone into hiding or been murdered. "We're going crazy here," Lo Presti told Buscetta. The conversations make clear the power dynamic between the *mafioso* and the businessman: Lo Presti is in the subservient position of addressing Buscetta with the respectful, formal *lei* while Buscetta speaks to Lo Presti with the informal, familiar *tu*, as if he were a subordinate. More important, the wiretaps revealed that Nino Salvo, the powerful tax collector, was anxious to arrange for Buscetta's trip to Palermo to try to bring peace to the city's warring clans.[14]

Not long after recording these calls, police arrested Lo Presti and took him to Ucciardone prison for questioning. When Falcone arrived for the interrogation, the mafia made its first attempt to kill him. "A prisoner, Salvatore Sanfilippo, a young man from the Borgo neighborhood, succeeded in getting his hands on a pistol," Falcone explained many years later. "He reached the threshold of our room. Lo Presti saw him through the window and had just enough time to say he'd come for us, and then fainted. I was able to lock the door. Sanfilippo then changed direction and took another magistrate hostage, Judge Micciché, who was conducting an interrogation, and claimed that he was trying to escape. Finally he surrendered to the prison guards," he said in 1985.[15]

After being released from jail, Lo Presti disappeared—another victim of the *lupara bianca*. Apparently terrified by the events in Palermo, Lo Presti's in-law, Nino Salvo, head of the mighty Salvo empire, postponed the sumptuous wedding he had planned for his daughter and left for an unexpected, early cruise vacation in Greece. From then on Falcone stopped questioning defendants at Ucciardone and had them brought to his office.

Falcone began the first audit of the Salvos' financial empire. After decades of political protection, the Salvos were shocked when Colonel Pizzuti showed up with fifty inspectors of the Treasury Police. "It was a bomb for Palermo," said Pizzuti, who later retired with the rank of general. Used to operating quietly in the shadows, Nino Salvo, the family lawyer, took the highly unusual step of giving a magazine interview. Salvo proclaimed himself the victim of the Italian Communist Party, which was attacking him with "savage aggression" because he was a businessman and a Christian Democrat. He went on to send a clear warning to his political friends in Rome. "Unlike many other Sicilian businessmen, we have always been and remain Christian Democrats. . . . We pose this question to the DC [Democrazia Cristiana]: Can this party continue to permit the systematic persecution of those members of the business community that have always been the closest to it?"[16]

As it happened, Pizzuti was acting on the authority of the prosecutors in Palermo and did not inform the central office in Rome until after the search of the Salvos' home and offices had begun. The socialist minister of finance, Rino Formica, saw political capital in publicizing the courageous decision to investigate Christian Democrat businessmen "in odor of mafia" (as the Italians say) and flew to Palermo to give a press conference.

The Salvos had reasons to be nervous about the audit. Pizzuti found numerous examples of tax fraud where personal expenses and property were listed as business expenses. "Even the vacations of their employees were being deducted because they thought no one would ever audit the Salvos," Pizzuti said. One of the most interesting things they discovered was the nature of the financing of La Zagarella, the Salvos' fabulous hotel complex outside of Palermo, which had cost some $15 million to build in the 1970s, making it worth several times that in current dollars. "Of the $15 million spent to build it, the Salvos put up only $600,000," Pizzuti said. "The rest was paid for by the Cassa del Mezzogiorno"—the government agency set up to assist industry in southern Italy. This huge luxury hotel (heavily frequented by mafia bosses) was essentially a gift of the Italian state. As Pizzuti dug a little deeper, he began to find a few clues suggesting how the Salvos succeeded in obtaining such favorable financing. He remembered reading a year earlier about the wildly extravagant wedding reception given by a member of the Sicilian parliament, who was also head of the provincial government of parliament. "He had invited something like 1,800 guests, so I checked the accounts and he had never paid a lira."[17]

As Falcone continued to investigate the Salvos, it became progressively clearer that they were an essential nexus between the mafia and a corrupt political class. Symbolic of this role was their fabulous Zagarella Hotel, where both politicians and *mafiosi* held extravagant wedding receptions—paid for out of the coffers of the Italian state.

FOUR

I n the final months of 1981 and the first months of 1982, a mafia killing was taking place in Palermo every three days.[1] Whoever had eliminated Stefano Bontate and Salvatore Inzerillo was not content with just getting rid of the bosses and their inner circle. They were conducting a wholesale extermination campaign, killing relatives, friends of friends, trying to create scorched earth around any surviving members of a clan who might possibly pose a threat. One day, police found the abandoned automobile of Salvatore Contorno, one of the bravest "soldiers" of Stefano Bontate. The car was full of bullet holes, its windshield shattered, abandoned in the middle of a Palermo street in the midst of a furious shoot-out from which Contorno appeared to have escaped alive. Among the several guns used was the same Kalashnikov rifle used to kill Bontate and Inzerillo—apparently the signature weapon used by whoever was conducting the so-called mafia war. In the weeks that followed the failed assassination attempt, Contorno's would-be killers went on to eliminate anyone who might have been willing to help or hide him: cousins, in-laws, business associates. Because of his ability to keep a step ahead of his killers, Contorno came to be known as "the Scarlet Pimpernel of Brancaccio" or as "Corolianus of the Forest," a kind of Robin Hood figure out of popular Sicilian literature.[2] The same scorched earth policy was later applied to Tommaso Buscetta, whose two sons from a first marriage were murdered even though they had nothing to do with the mafia and Buscetta had lived in Brazil for years. It was enough that Buscetta had been one of Stefano Bontate's closest friends and that some of Salvatore Inzerillo's relatives had tried to flee to South America, before they were hunted down and murdered.

Anonymous letters showing detailed inside knowledge of Cosa Nostra began turning up at police headquarters. Having no other arms at their disposal, some survivors of the "losing" families decided to use the police to strike back at their enemies. The smart and energetic new deputy chief of the investigative squad *(squadra mobile),* Antonino (Ninni) Cassarà, began to develop some confidential informants who helped explain the power struggle convulsing the mafia. One of his sources, referred to simply as "First Light," was none other than Salvatore Contorno. In the spring and summer of 1982, Cassarà composed the most comprehensive report on the Palermo mafia produced in many years, identifying 162 suspects as the protagonists of the current war. One of his sources identified the cause of the struggle in the "resistance of Stefano Bontate and Salvatore Inzerillo to the presence of the Corleonesi in Palermo." Nonetheless, the Cassarà report did not fully grasp the centrality of the mafia from Corleone, portraying it as only one of a constellation of "emerging" families that were eliminating the traditional mafia of Palermo. The great novelty of the report was the role attributed to Michele Greco, "the Pope"—a figure who had been virtually unknown to police before then. "The *capomafia* of all of Palermo is 'don Michele Greco,' who is advised by several lawyers and enjoys the protection of a magistrate," one of Cassarà's anonymous informants wrote.[3] Greco was known as a prosperous, if highly secretive, landowner—even though his ancestors were prominent *mafiosi* in the area of Ciaculli stretching back to the nineteenth century. Such was the importance attributed to Greco, that Cassarà's July 12, 1982, report on the mafia war was known unofficially as the report on "Michele Greco + 161." The report was considered so important that Rocco Chinnici, Falcone and Borsellino's boss, insisted on overseeing the case himself. As the first attempt to sort out the confusion of the mafia war, it was the germ of what would expand into the maxi-trial of Palermo.

Already more than a year earlier, Falcone, in his banking probes, had stumbled on a major financial transaction between "the Pope" and Giovanni Bontate—brother of Stefano Bontate and one of the chief defendants in the Spatola heroin trafficking case. Falcone began to probe "the Pope's" financial holdings. Greco, along with the other mafia families around Palermo, controlled a large portion of the city's water supply. Greco was financing his wells with money from the Cassa del Mezzogiorno. Greco used government money to dig wells so that he could sell public water to the city of Palermo at enormous profit. According to law, landowners were only allowed to have wells for their own private use and all excess water belonged to the public. But the city of Palermo had issued regular contracts to buy water from Greco and numerous other *capi-mafia* for a full third of the city's water supply. In the hottest months of summer, when water was particularly scarce and badly needed for the irrigation of crops, Greco sold water in canisters at exorbitant prices. The perpetual water crisis was maintained, in part, by Greco and his friends in city hall. Water in Palermo is plentiful, but when the city water agency bothered to dig wells, they would generally drill on land near the coast where—not surprisingly—they found salty, undrinkable water, rather than drilling in the fertile farmland controlled by Greco and his friends.[4]

Although "the Pope" declared an extremely modest income of less than $20,000 a year, he received millions of dollars in subsidies from Italian government agencies—the Cassa del Mezzogiorno and the Dipartimento di Agricoltura e Foreste—and the European Community. The European Community (EC), in order to limit agricultural production, pays farmers to destroy part of their crops: Greco corrupted EC inspectors to falsify records so that the mafia boss would be paid for destroying crops he had never even grown. Investigators also found that Greco owned a business in Palermo with Count Lucio Tasca, using the Palermo aristocrat's distinguished name as cover.[5]

But dealing with the European Community and the Sicilian nobility did not keep "the Pope" from dirtying his hands with the nitty-gritty work of the great mafia war. One of the three killers of Captain Emanuele Basile, Vincenzo Puccio, was a member of Michele Greco's family. Moreover, Salvatore Contorno had recognized Greco's most lethal assassins—Mario Prestifilippo and Pino (*Scarpa*, "the Shoe") Greco—in the hit squad that had tried to ambush him. Even though Pino "the Shoe" Greco was thought to be the underboss of the Ciaculli family, he was not afraid to expose himself in the front line. Police suspected him of carrying out dozens of murders, and it was he who handled the infamous Kalashnikov rifle that had opened fire on Contorno.

Borsellino was assigned an important offshoot of the investigation, dealing with the crimes of Filippo Marchese and the "family" of Corso dei Mille, a long, squalid avenue that cuts through one of Palermo's most wretched slums. Like Pino Greco, Filippo Marchese seemed to enjoy participating firsthand in many of his group's bloodiest crimes—in fact, he and "the Shoe" often joined forces in the same hit squads, including the recent ambush of Salvatore Contorno. The two boss/assassins were co-owners of a concrete business and were suspected of making common cause in a long string of crimes.

Despite numerous arrest warrants against them, the two bosses, Filippo Marchese and Pino Greco, continued operating freely in Palermo. They were believed, for example, to have played leading roles in the Christmas Massacre in Bagheria. On December 25, 1981, a squad of several men opened fire on a car in downtown Bagheria carrying three leading figures of the local mafia. The wild hail of bullets killed an innocent bystander and the hit men ran out of ammunition before they had completed their mission. They were forced to drag the one surviving victim into their car and, after driving away, to finish the job with their own bare hands. Used to getting away with murder, the mafia was becoming sloppy, committing crimes in broad daylight in front of dozens of witnesses, accidentally killing ordinary citizens and leaving important clues. In the Christmas Massacre, the killers failed to thoroughly burn one of the getaway cars, leaving fingerprints on the steering wheel, identified as those of Giuseppe Marchese, nephew of boss Filippo Marchese.[6]

Borsellino indicted nine people for the Christmas Massacre, and although police were unable to catch Filippo Marchese and Pino "the Shoe" Greco, they were able to arrest Marchese's twenty-year-old nephew. An important part of Borsellino's case hinged on young Marchese's incriminating fingerprints on the getaway car—

something that the *mafiosi* understood all too well. On the morning of August 11, 1982, Dr. Paolo Giaccone, the professor of forensic medicine who had correctly identified the prints on the steering wheel, was gunned down by two killers as he arrived at his office at the University of Palermo.

According to one of Dr. Giaccone's colleagues: "He confided to me that he had received a request from a mutual friend of his and of Marchese that he 'fix' the scientific report for Marchese so as to allow room for the defense." Giaccone bravely refused this request. "Anyone can see . . . that these are the fingerprints of Giuseppe Marchese," he wrote, signing a report that unequivocally sealed Giuseppe Marchese's conviction and his own death. To Borsellino's great frustration, he was never able to identify the "mutual friend" who advised Dr. Giaccone to "adjust" his report. "We are left only with a bitter taste in our mouth since [Dr. Giaccone] did not reveal . . . the name of this squalid figure," Borsellino wrote.[7]

The slaughter in Palermo reached the level of a national scandal. As terrorism—which had dominated public life since the mid-1970s—began to fade, the mafia began to attract the attention of the media and the parliament. The death of Aldo Moro in 1978 had jolted the nation into action. New laws were passed giving sentence reductions to terrorists who agreed to cooperate with the government; special "pools" of magistrates were formed to work cooperatively on terrorist prosecutions. Specially trained police units were created and General Carlo Alberto Dalla Chiesa of the *carabinieri* was given a free hand in directing the war against terrorism. In a matter of only a few years, Dalla Chiesa's men had rounded up literally thousands of suspected terrorists, rooted out terrorist hideouts, dismantled whole networks and captured or killed virtually all of the most important leaders, bringing the Red Brigades and various other groups to their knees. The fight against terrorism showed that the Italian police—often portrayed as a modern version of the Keystone Kops—could be remarkably, even brutally, efficient when given the proper political support.

In the shadow of terrorism, Cosa Nostra had been able to orchestrate a genuine national drug epidemic. In 1974 only eight people in Italy died of heroin overdose and police found only 1.5 kilos of heroin being imported into the country. By 1980, there were an estimated 200,000 addicts in Italy, hundreds of whom died each year. People began to ask: "If the government can defeat terrorism, why can't it do the same to the mafia?" A Communist member of the anti-mafia commission, Pio La Torre, hammered away at parliament to pass new anti-mafia laws. La Torre, who was also head of the Communist Party in Sicily, wanted to make it a crime to belong to the mafia rather than having to force prosecutors to try *mafiosi* for specific crimes (murder, drug trafficking, extortion); and he wanted to give the government the ability to fight the mafia's economic power by seizing the assets of known *mafiosi*, if it could be shown that their property was acquired with ill-gotten gains. The political situation in Rome was also unusually receptive to a change in mafia policy. For the first time since 1946, Italy's prime minister was not a Christian Democrat—in June 1981, Giovanni Spadolini, of the small but respected Republican Party, became head of the government. And in March 1982 Spadolini asked General Dalla Chiesa to become the prefect of Palermo. Before agreeing, Dalla Chiesa had pushed for special powers to coordinate the anti-mafia efforts throughout Sicily, but had been persuaded to accept the more limited role as Palermo's chief law enforcement officer. Politicians in Rome insisted that it was only a matter of time before he was granted the wider powers he sought.[9]

The mafia greeted Dalla Chiesa in predictable fashion. On April 30, just before he was supposed to take over his new position, mafia killers murdered Pio La Torre. Dalla Chiesa spent his first day on the job at La Torre's funeral—a sinister augury for the future.[10]

Just four months later, on September 3, 1982, Dalla Chiesa was himself murdered together with his bodyguard and his young, second wife.

The evening of the killing, Giovanni Falcone was at dinner with his friend and fellow prosecutor Giuseppe Ayala, Ayala's wife and Falcone's future second wife, Francesca Morvillo. "Giovanni left the restaurant immediately to go to the scene of the killing and I waited behind with Francesca and my wife," Ayala said.[11] When Falcone reached Via Carini, he found the tragic scene of General

Dalla Chiesa slumped over his dead wife in a desperate, last-second attempt to protect her from the rain of bullets that sprayed their car. One of the guns used was the same Kalashnikov that ran like a thread throughout the mafia war.

The assassination of Dalla Chiesa startled Italy into an awareness of just how powerful the mafia had become. In just four years, Cosa Nostra had killed some of the most important public officials in Sicily: the head of the main governing party in Sicily (Michele Reina), the head of the main opposition party (Pio La Torre), the president of the Region (Piersanti Mattarella), two chief prosecutors (Cesare Terranova and Gaetano Costa) and two leading police investigators (Boris Giuliano and Emanuele Basile). Now they had killed Dalla Chiesa, the prefect of Palermo, a general of the *carabinieri* and a national hero. Apparently there was no one so important or powerful that they would not touch. At a demonstration following Dalla Chiesa's murder, someone carried a sign saying: "Here dies the hope of every honest citizen of Palermo." In a powerful funeral eulogy, the archbishop of Palermo, Cardinal Salvatore Pappalardo, issued a clear political denunciation. He compared Palermo to Sagunto, a city on the periphery of the Roman Empire that was allowed to fall to the barbarians because the capital had chosen not to send reinforcements.

In the weeks that followed the assassination, Falcone was struck by what seemed like a press campaign to diminish Dalla Chiesa's reputation. The general's former boss, General Umberto Capuzzo—a Sicilian general who later became a Christian Democrat senator—described Dalla Chiesa as an old man who had lost his head for a young woman, contributing to his own death by recklessly exposing himself to unnecessary risks. Dalla Chiesa had refused a bulletproof car with armed escort, insisting he would be a more elusive target if he traveled in an ordinary Fiat sedan without anyone knowing his movements—a practice he had used successfully during the terrorist period. (Dalla Chiesa's concerns about an escort were not entirely unreasonable: on arriving in Palermo he discovered that the domestic servants assigned to his official residence had relatives who were mafia suspects.) Novelist Leonardo Sciascia—who had produced some of the most important books on the mafia—insisted that Dalla Chiesa had made a series of misjudgments because he had an outmoded idea of the mafia formed during the time he was stationed in Sicily right after World War II and again in the late 1960s and early 1970s. Although clearly neither General Capuzzo nor Sciascia were members of the mafia, Falcone believed that the mafia encouraged the public denigration of its victims in order to justify its actions and to diminish public outrage over its killings.[12]

Falcone was convinced Dalla Chiesa was killed because he had understood too much rather than too little about the emerging new mafia. "By now the mafia is in all the major Italian cities where it has made considerable real estate and commercial investments," the general said in an interview shortly before his death with journalist Giorgio Bocca of the Rome newspaper *La Repubblica*. "The epoch in which the mafia was limited geographically to western Sicily is over. Today the mafia is strong in Catania, too. With the consent of the Palermo mafia, the four largest real estate developers from Catania are building today in Palermo. Do you think they could do that if there were not a new map of mafia power?"[13]

Rather than having a hopelessly outdated approach, Dalla Chiesa had adopted a highly effective comprehensive strategy that went from modern bank checks to old-fashioned roadblocks to try to regain control of the Sicilian territory. "The banks have known very well for years who their mafia clients are," he said in his final interview. "The war against the mafia is not fought only in the banks or only in the streets of Bagheria, but in a global manner."

Dalla Chiesa showed that he understood the strange, indirect way in which the mafia often acts. "The [mafia and I] are studying each other as in a chess game. The mafia is cautious, slow, it takes your measure, listens to you, checks you from a distance. Some people might not notice but I know this world. . . . Certain invitations, for example. A friend with whom you have worked asks you, very casually: 'Why don't we go for coffee at So-and-So's house,' giving a distinguished name. If I didn't know that rivers of heroin were flowing through that house I would be serving as cover. If I go knowingly it's a sign that by my presence I accept what's going on. . . ."

Far from holding any illusions that the mafia would never dare kill someone of his stature, Dalla Chiesa considered himself a likely target. "I think I've understood the new rule of the game," he said in his final interview. "They kill the man in power when this fatal combination has come about: he has become too danger-ous but he can be killed because he is isolated. The most obvious example is chief prosecutor [Gaetano] Costa. . . . Costa becomes too dangerous when, overruling the rest of his office, he orders the indictment of the Inzerillos and the Spatolas. But he is isolated and therefore can be killed, wiped out like a foreign body."

Falcone's analysis of the Dalla Chiesa killing (one of the thirty-volume indictment of the maxi-trial written in 1985) has all the subtlety, the political intrigue and sense of tragedy of a great mys-tery novel. Falcone moves between Rome and Palermo, weaving together the statements of politicians and the actions of Cosa Nos-tra in a stinging indictment of a death foretold. Rather than dis-missing Dalla Chiesa as a dottering old man who had lost his head over a younger woman, Falcone was convinced that the clues to his death lay in the general's own lucid reflections to be found among his private personal papers.

Upon receiving the offer to become prefect of Palermo, Dalla Chiesa wrote in his diary: "Once again I am about to become the instrument of a policy that is leaking water in every direction." Dalla Chiesa knew all too well that political backing was the key to his mission in Palermo; he spent the weeks before leaving trying to line up support while at the same time making clear that he was not going to pull any punches with the mafia's political protectors in Sicily. He wanted to be sure that he would still have the gov-ernment behind him if he attacked the Christian Democratic fief-doms there. "Don't worry," Minister of Interior Virginio Rognoni assured him, "you are not a general of the Christian Democratic Party." Of particular interest is Dalla Chiesa's account of a meet-ing with former prime minister Giulio Andreotti. "Yesterday An-dreotti asked me to come to see him; naturally, because of his numerous political supporters in Sicily . . . I was very clear and stated in no uncertain terms that I will not do any favors for that part of the electorate on which his political supporters draw." In the course of the conversation, Andreotti told Dalla Chiesa about a member of the Inzerillo clan (Pietro Inzerillo) who was killed in the United States but whose body turned up in Palermo with a ten-dollar-bill in his mouth. Dalla Chiesa interpreted the story as an indication of Andreotti's superficial and "folkloristic" under-standing of the mafia phenomenon, but in light of Dalla Chiesa's murder it takes on a somewhat more sinister cast.[14]

Shortly after the meeting with Dalla Chiesa, Andreotti pub-lished an article in which he expressed perplexity at the general's mission in Sicily, indicating that he was more urgently needed in Calabria and Campania. Then, the mayor of Palermo, Nello Martellucci—part of the Andreotti faction in Sicily—gave an in-terview objecting to Dalla Chiesa's nomination and the "criminal-ization of a region and a city that instead want the respect they deserve." He also objected to the new proposals (by La Torre) to seize the property of the mafia bosses, saying it would "risk block-ing the free-market economy."[15]

Dalla Chiesa regarded these public statements as important sig-nals, "messages . . . sent by the most polluted 'political family' in the region," as he referred to the Andreotti faction. Writing to Prime Minister Spadolini, Dalla Chiesa again insisted that the gov-ernment grant him the explicit power as coordinator of the fight against the mafia; otherwise it "would show that the 'messages' . . . have achieved their aim."[16]

Understanding that prestige is extremely important in the Sicil-ian world Dalla Chiesa insisted that his own stature was being gradually eroded by critical remarks of politicians and by the gov-ernment's foot-dragging in adopting a clear, decisive strategy against the mafia.

Once Dalla Chiesa arrived in Sicily, the special powers he had been promised never materialized. Among Dalla Chiesa's personal papers, Falcone found various newspaper clippings which docu-mented the growing resistance among local Sicilian politicians to his being given the authority to coordinate the war against the mafia. Contrasting the general's position with that of Mussolini's "Iron Prefect," Cesare Mori, the newsweekly *L'Espresso* referred to Dalla Chiesa as the "Tin Prefect"—a situation that prompted bitter reflections on the general's part.[17]

I have been catapulted . . . into a treacherous environment, rich in mystery and in the midst of a struggle that I might find exhil-arating except that I have no one near me, no "family" as I had during the years of terrorism when the entire force of the *cara-*

binieri was behind me. . . . Suddenly, I have found myself on alien ground . . . in a place that on the one hand . . . expects miracles from me and on the other curses the aim of my mission. I find myself in the middle of . . . a state that is looking for peace of mind not by showing a clear will to fight the mafia and the political mafia but through the use and exploitation of my name to silence the irritation of the political parties.[18]

Dalla Chiesa watched with increasingly helpless rage as his obvious isolation made him appear impotent before the mafia, which mocked him by continuing its extermination campaign with even greater audacity. Dalla Chiesa tried to make life difficult for the killers by setting up police roadblocks around the area known as the "triangle of death" among the towns of Bagheria, Altavilla and Casteldaccia. Cosa Nostra responded by carrying out further murders right under his nose. On August 7, 1982, the *carabinieri* of Casteldaccia received an anonymous phone call saying: "If you want to have some fun, go and look inside the car that is parked in front of your station." The police found two corpses in the trunk of the car. Three days later, after another couple of murders, another anonymous caller phoned a local newspaper with the message: "We are the killers of the triangle of death. Operation Carlo Alberto in homage to the prefect of Palermo is almost complete, I said, 'almost complete.' "

The day after the death of General Dalla Chiesa another anonymous caller telephoned the newspaper of Catania with the message: "Operation Carlo Alberto is complete."

"The killing of Carlo Alberto Dalla Chiesa," Falcone concluded in his later indictment, "was an essential moment in the strategy of the winning groups of Cosa Nostra which, still intensely involved in the physical elimination of their adversaries within the organization, regarded the presence of the Prefect of Palermo as a serious and extremely dangerous obstacle to the consolidation of the hegemony they had achieved with the elimination of Stefano Bontate, Salvatore Inzerillo and of their many friends and allies.

"And therefore, as the persistence of strong and well-publicized resistance to giving Dalla Chiesa more incisive powers weakened his credibility in everyone's eyes, the mafia undertook a complex operation meant to further diminish his prestige and then kill him."[19]

The day before he was killed, Dalla Chiesa spoke with Ralph Jones, the American consul in Palermo, expressing his frustrations and appealing to the U.S. government to pressure Rome into granting him the powers he had sought unsuccessfully for three months. He told Jones a story from his experience during the 1970s as a colonel in charge of the *carabinieri* unit in Palermo. "One day he received a call from the captain of the *carabinieri* for the town of Palma di Montechiaro who told him he had been threatened by the local mafia boss," Jones explained later. "Dalla Chiesa left immediately for Palma di Montechiaro, arriving in the late afternoon. He took the captain by the arm and began walking with him slowly up and down the main street. Everyone looked at them. In the end, this odd couple stopped in front of the house of the local mafia boss. The two stayed long enough to make clear to everyone that the captain was not alone. 'All I am asking is that someone take me by the arm and walk with me,' the general said. A few hours later he was killed."[20]

During his hundred and twenty days in Palermo, Dalla Chiesa had not contacted Falcone, Borsellino or the other magistrates of the investigative office, no doubt because he didn't trust anyone in Palermo. But, as Falcone began to investigate the general's death, he discovered that they had been pursuing some of the same leads. As his last public interview suggested, Dalla Chiesa had begun to focus on the emerging role of Catania in the new geography of Cosa Nostra. "With the consent of the Palermo mafia, the four largest real estate developers of Catania are building today in Palermo," he had said. Dalla Chiesa, like Falcone, was investigating these developers who had all been recognized as "Knights of Labor" by the Italian government but were referred to by others as "the Four Horsemen of the Apocalypse." Among Dalla Chiesa's papers Falcone had found a note written in shorthand that indicated that Dalla Chiesa had learned that the chief mafia boss of Catania, Nitto Santapaola, was on the payroll of one of the "Knights of Labor," Carmelo Costanzo. Falcone had become interested in Catania during the Spatola case when he learned that Michele Sindona and his band had been hosted at a Catania hotel through the hospitality of another of the Four Horsemen, Gaetano Graci.

Falcone had decided to probe the Catania businessmen by encouraging Pizzuti of the Treasury Police to audit their financial records. Pizzuti found ample signs of illegality, corruption and political influence peddling that tied together the worlds of local mafia, high finance and political power. They discovered extensive relations between the Knights of Labor and local *mafiosi*. Not only was Nitto Santapaola on the Costanzo company payroll, he was a guest at the wedding of Carmelo Costanzo's nephew and had been hiding out at the Costanzos' luxury hotel near Catania when he was wanted for questioning in a murder investigation. Santapaola, known as "the hunter," because of his passion for shooting game, had access to the private game reserve of Gaetano Graci. The corporation of Mario Rendo, another of the Knights of Labor, bought all its cars from Santapaola's car dealership and wiretaps revealed Rendo's executives discussing subcontracting with various *mafiosi*.

Pizzuti also discovered that these upstanding businessmen were making millions of dollars through a massive tax fraud scheme: they created phony receipts with the complicity of subcontractors (many of them mafia controlled) in order to qualify for enormous tax rebates for completely nonexistent business operations. In searching through Graci's records, Pizzuti found a list of payoffs to politicians and even magistrates.

Graci tried to use his political connections in Rome to get Pizzuti off his back. One day in the middle of the audit, the aide-de-camp of the minister of the treasury, socialist Rino Formica, called him and told him to stop the Graci investigation. Pizzuti replied that he would stop only if given a written order. None was forthcoming. The Treasury Police continued their investigation by auditing Mario Rendo, considered the most powerful of the four Knights of Labor. Here, too, they found massive evidence of the phony receipt scheme. Rendo told one of the inspectors that "the false receipts were necessary to create a slush fund to pay bribes for government contracts." Falcone and Pizzuti had stumbled onto the evidence of political bribery that would explode ten years later in the national bribery investigation known as Operation Clean Hands. But at that time, the politicians at risk still had the political situation firmly in hand. Minister Formica continued to put pressure on Pizzuti by sending a pair of "super-inspectors" to investigate Pizzuti. When they found that the audit had been conducted properly, the socialist minister sent another set of inspectors who found reasons to challenge the audit. Finally, the politicians passed an amnesty that let Catania's Knights of Labor off the hook.[21]

During the course of a police raid in another case—Mario Rendo's son Ugo was charged with defrauding creditors in a bankruptcy—investigators found a series of notes written by Mario Rendo about his discussions with politicians, among them Pizzuti's boss, Treasury Minister Formica. "Question of investigation by Catania prosecutors' office—soften," Rendo wrote, listing the topics he wanted to raise with his politician friends. "Substitute police chief Catania with police chief of Caltanissetta. . . . Col. Pizzuti in Palermo until September?" When Falcone questioned them, the politicians denied doing special favors for Rendo; and yet, miraculously, many of the items on his wish list suddenly came true, including the transfer of Pizzuti. Unable to punish him, they did the next best thing: they promoted him. Bypassing the usual rules of seniority, Pizzuti was suddenly elevated to the rank of general and sent as far from Sicily as possible, to Udine, near Italy's northern border with Austria. During Operation Clean Hands evidence emerged showing that the Rendo family paid hundreds of thousands in bribes annually to both the Socialist and Christian Democrat parties.[22]

Falcone was able to show that the new alliance between Palermo and Catania worked on a number of different levels simultaneously, from drug trafficking and murder to government contracts and high finance—often involving the same sets of people. By tapping the phone of a known Palermo *mafioso*, Gaspare Mutolo, police recorded discussions about heroin smuggling between Mutolo and *mafiosi* in Catania. The same *mafiosi* in Catania were taped discussing how to divide up government contracts with executives working for Mario Rendo. Having accepted the support of the mafia, the Catania Knights of Labor suddenly increased their presence in Palermo, winning government contracts there and doing business with, among others, the infamous Salvo cousins. There was growing evidence that Cosa Nostra had become a much more unified, organic entity, moving with a single purpose in different cities and different provinces. Dalla Chiesa had discovered this convergence of powerful interests and had been killed.[23]

Falcone was able to tie the boss of Catania, Nitto Santapaola, to the Dalla Chiesa assassination by using a logic not unlike that of the killers in the film *Strangers on a Train*. In the Hitchcock movie, two strangers begin to share their complaints about life when one of them comes up with an idea for a perfect murder: each would kill the other's nemesis since it would be impossible for police to connect victim and murderer, perfect strangers living hundreds of miles away. Criss-cross, as the movie called it. Falcone saw the same pattern in another murder that had occurred about two months before Dalla Chiesa's death: a car of *carabinieri* was attacked on the outskirts of Palermo as it was transporting a mafia defendant from one prison to another. Three *carabinieri* were killed but the principal target was the prisoner, Alfio Ferlito, boss of one of Catania's principal mafia families and arch-rival of Nitto Santapaola. During the last two years, the two had been conducting a ferocious war for control of Catania, with gun battles in the streets of the city and dozens of murders. The location of the attack, the license plates of the cars used by the killers, made it clear that the Palermo mafia had done Nitto Santapaola a favor by eliminating his most dangerous enemy. The arrangement allowed Santapaola's men—who were immediately suspected of the crime—to say, quite correctly, that they were at home in Catania at the time of the attack. It would be logistically extremely difficult—as well as highly dangerous—to pull off such a complex operation in someone else's territory without the consent and/or participation of the local mafia. Conversely, there was mounting evidence that the Catanese had repaid the favor by providing firepower in the Dalla Chiesa assassination. Because the killing took place in downtown Palermo, no one would recognize killers from Catania. Falcone began to collect information to this effect from the prison grapevine. "Several times . . . I heard common criminals, especially from Catania, brag about the perfect logistical efficiency with which the Sicilian criminal organizations had pulled off the [Dalla Chiesa] killing," a former terrorist who was in prison with many Sicilian criminals testified. "After the Dalla Chiesa assassination the prestige of the most important Catanese prisoners rose inside the prison in an incredible fashion."[24]

The ballistic analyses of the killings confirmed the Catania-Palermo axis. The same Kalashnikov rifle used in the murders of

Stefano Bontate and Salvatore Inzerillo was used again in the Ferlito and Dalla Chiesa killings—confirming Falcone's hunch that the Palermo mafia was responsible for eliminating the Catanese boss, Ferlito. But there was an interesting new twist in the analysis of the last two crimes: in the Ferlito and Dalla Chiesa murders, two Kalashnikovs, not one, were used, and, in each case, the same two. Why would Cosa Nostra, which presumably had an ample supply of weapons, continue to use the same guns in killing after killing? "The use of the same weapons in so many different crimes is clearly not the result of carelessness, it would appear instead to be . . . an implicit way of claiming the authorship on the assassinations," Falcone later wrote.[25] He found proof of this in a curious minor crime. A few nights before the killing of Salvatore Inzerillo, his killers tried out their Kalashnikov on the bulletproof window of a Palermo jewelry shop. With precise inside information, they had learned that Inzerillo had just acquired a bulletproof car and wanted to make sure their arms would penetrate a bulletproof windshield. In this case, however, they carefully picked up the cartridges that the rifle left after firing—anxious to avoid anything that might put Inzerillo on guard. But in the killings themselves, cartridges were left all over the scene, as if the assassins wanted to leave a signature—a statement of power within Cosa Nostra. The single Kalashnikov that had been active from the Bontate killing to the Dalla Chiesa assassination clearly belonged to someone in the Palermo mafia. The presence of a second Kalashnikov in the Ferlito and Dalla Chiesa murders was perhaps symbolic of the alliance between Catania and Palermo.

FIVE

The outcry over the death of General Dalla Chiesa shook the Italian parliament out of its slumber into one of its periodic fits of activity on the mafia front. In a classic case of closing the barn door after the horse has already been stolen, the legislature in September 1982 created the office of high commissioner for mafia investigations, granting, within a few days, the same powers that it had denied Dalla Chiesa during his months in Palermo. But, in typical fashion, the office was filled by a string of gray, bureaucratic figures until it was eliminated as being superfluous. Similarly, the Communist legislator Pio La Torre achieved only in death what he had fought for in life: for the first time in history, the parliament made it a crime to belong to the mafia and gave prosecutors the power to seize mafia assets accumulated through criminal activity.

Nonetheless, there were reassuring signs for Cosa Nostra that the war against the mafia was not going to change too radically. The minister of justice, Clelio Darida, told a convention of Palermo magistrates that rather than trying to eliminate the mafia, they should do their best to contain it within "natural limits"—as if it were an immutable part of the Sicilian landscape, like lemon groves and Mount Etna.[1] Consistent with this attitude of fatalistic resignation, the minister refused Rocco Chinnici's renewed requests for a computer for the Palermo investigative office, swamped by the flood of new information from its myriad mafia investigations. Falcone and Borsellino spent their days painstakingly filling out thousands of pieces of paper on hundreds of different defendants, with only their prodigious memories to help them correlate the data.

With the coming of the new year, the two prosecutors found themselves in the all-too-familiar position of attending the funeral of yet another colleague. On January 25, 1983, Judge Giangiacomo Ciaccio Montalto was murdered in Trapani, an hour from Palermo. In a city whose mayor denied the existence of the mafia, Montalto had been a fish out of water, vigorously prosecuting both local *mafiosi* and corrupt politicians. He had received more support from his colleagues in Palermo than from those down the hall. In the last weeks of his life, he found out why. While conducting wiretaps of the dominant local mafia family, he had overheard conversations between the mafia boss and one of his fellow prosecutors, Antonio Costa, discussing a bribe to fix an upcoming case. Shortly after making this discovery, Montalto was killed.[2]

The funeral service was marked by a highly unusual and extremely moving event. Although Montalto was almost completely unknown outside of the restricted world of the courthouse—a swarm of Trapani students appeared entirely on their own initiative to pay homage to this man who had died fighting the mafia in their city. This surprising, spontaneous gesture suggested that something was changing in Sicily and contrasted starkly with the relative paucity of government officials present. After the funeral, one of Montalto's friends, Rosario Minna, a prosecutor from Florence, issued a public challenge to the minister of justice. "I want to know what is the 'natural limit' of mafia killings? What is the 'natural number' of kilos of drugs to be sold each year in Italy?"[3]

In March, the Italian government granted Raffaele Cutolo, boss of the Camorra—the Neapolitan equivalent of the mafia—the unusual privilege of being married in prison. Information was leaking out that Cutolo had been instrumental in obtaining the release of a Christian Democratic politician, Ciro Cirillo, who had been kidnapped by the Red Brigades in 1981. Publicly, the Christian Democrats had refused to negotiate with terrorists; privately, leading politicians and members of the secret services had visited

don Raffaele in prison and asked him to negotiate with imprisoned members of the Red Brigades. A large ransom had been paid
to win Cirillo's freedom.[4]

In Palermo, when Cardinal Pappalardo—who had spoken out
so strongly at the funeral of General Dalla Chiesa—went to give
his annual Easter mass at the Palermo prison, Ucciardone, not a
single inmate showed up. The boycott demonstrated clearly the
mafia's iron control not only of its own members but over the
much larger army of common criminals as well.[5]

During this period, Paolo Borsellino's case against the murderers of Captain Emanuele Basile went to trial. The prosecution's
case seemed unusually strong, but before it reached the jury, Judge
Carlo Aiello suddenly declared a mistrial, calling for a new scientific analysis of the mud that tied the three killers to the murder
scene. Although the new study of the mud confirmed the original
finding, the new jury absolved Giuseppe Madonia, Vincenzo Puccio and Armando Bonnano on March 31, 1983. Borsellino was
shocked by the verdict. According to recent mafia witnesses, the
judges at both trials had been corrupted and the jurors threatened.

Embittered by the decision, Borsellino used the only means left
to him to keep Puccio, Madonia and Bonnano off the streets: he
had them sent to Sardinia. In Italy, defendants who are considered
a public danger can be sent into a kind of "internal exile," away
from their hometown and out of contact with their fellow criminals. But the Italian state did very little to enforce the measure and
almost as soon as the three killers arrived in their new homes, they
disappeared, returning, presumably, to Palermo. Puccio, Bonnano
and Madonia took their place among the hundreds of mafia fugitives in Sicily, including Borsellino's other nemeses, Filippo
Marchese and Pino "the Shoe" Greco. It is not hard to understand
why so many eluded capture: only a few months earlier, a young
police agent (Calogero Zucchetto) was shot and killed only a few
days after he identified the hideout of an important fugitive boss
(Salvatore Montalto).[6]

The notion of these three killers on the loose created terror in
the Borsellino household; they had already murdered one zealous
investigator (Basile) and might well decide to kill another. "Puccio, Madonia and Bonnano, Puccio, Madonia and Bonnano—we
heard those names again and again throughout my childhood,"

said Manfredi Borsellino, the second of the magistrate's three children. "They haunted us for years."[7]

The panic in the family was such that Paolo Borsellino's father-in-law, who had been the chief judge of Palermo, tried to talk him out of working on mafia cases. When that failed, the retired judge went over his head to Rocco Chinnici, Borsellino's boss, complaining about the dangerous cases that his son-in-law was being assigned. Borsellino was furious when he learned about this unwanted interference. But Chinnici, who was uncompromising and irascible, reacted by excluding Borsellino from all new mafia cases. As Borsellino later remarked, the mafia is so effective because it can reach you not just through your enemies but through your friends.[8]

Falcone's investigations into international drug trafficking and into the assassination of Dalla Chiesa began to merge. In April 1983, Falcone flew to France to question an important new witness, Francesco Gasparini, an Italian courier who was bringing drugs from Thailand to the mafia in Palermo. Gasparini had been arrested in the Paris airport with heroin in his suitcase, and after spending two years in prison was feeling abandoned and ready to talk. Although he was only a common criminal being used by the mafia, Gasparini was able to update Falcone on mafia drug trafficking after the Spatola case. The discovery of four heroin refineries in Sicily, he said, had disrupted the Sicilian connection so that now the mafia was importing heroin from Thailand that had already been refined in order to avoid setting up elaborate refineries that might attract the attention of police. Gasparini would fly to Bangkok and receive the goods from a Chinese supplier named "Kim" and then deliver it to Gaspare Mutolo in Palermo, a *mafioso* whose phone Falcone had already been tapping. Gasparini was able to confirm Falcone's suspicion about the new alliance between the Palermo and Catania mafias: he had participated in a meeting at Mutolo's house in Palermo, where one of the principal bosses of Palermo, Rosario Riccobono, and the top boss of Catania, Nitto Santapaola, met to discuss a massive shipment of 500 kilos of heroin. It was on Riccobono's territory that Santapaola's archenemy, the Catanese boss Alfio

Ferlito, had been killed. This fit Falcone's hunch that Ferlito's killing had been a favor granted to Santapaola by the Palermo mafia, repaid when Santapaola helped in the assassination of General Dalla Chiesa.[9]

Gasparini's testimony was followed almost immediately by an even more dramatic breakthrough: on May 24 Egyptian police seized a Greek ship in the Suez Canal carrying some 233 kilos of heroin. Guarding the shipment was a Sicilian *mafioso*—another member of Gaspare Mutolo's drug ring and of Rosario Riccobono's crime family. His passport showed that he had just come from Bangkok, Thailand.[10]

On July 9, Falcone indicted fourteen people for the Dalla Chiesa murder, which he believed had been decided collectively by the top bosses in Sicily, including the Corleonesi, Salvatore Riina and Bernardo Provenzano, Michele "the Pope" Greco, and his brother Salvatore Greco (known as "the Senator" for his political connections), as well as Nitto Santapaola of Catania.[11]

At the same time, Italian police were able to locate the mafia's heroin supplier in Thailand. By examining the handwriting on postcards that Francesco Gasparini had received from Bangkok, police identified the man Gasparini knew incorrectly as "Kim," as Ko Bak Kin, a convicted heroin trafficker from Singapore who had spent time in Italian prisons during the 1970s. On July 12, Italy issued arrest warrants for eleven members of the heroin ring, including Ko Bak Kin, whom Thai police picked up in Bangkok. The documents in Kin's possession confirmed their suspicions: police found the addresses of Gaspare Mutolo, of Francesco Gasparini and of the *mafioso* who had been arrested in the ship carrying the 233 kilos of heroin.[12]

Immediately after the arrest, Gianni De Gennaro—the Criminalpol agent in Rome who had been working closely with Falcone—flew to Thailand to talk to Kin. To De Gennaro's surprise, Kin immediately agreed to come to Italy as a witness. Apparently, serving time in an Italian prison where he risked the vendetta of the mafia seemed a mild punishment compared to whatever fate he could expect in the hands of police in his native Singapore.[13]

Hearing the news of Kin's decision from De Gennaro, Falcone prepared to join him in Thailand. Before leaving for Bangkok, Falcone went to see his boss, Rocco Chinnici, together with Colonel Elio Pizzuti of the Treasury Police. " 'Be careful,' Falcone told Chinnici, 'this is a delicate moment,' " Pizzuti recalled. Falcone was particularly bothered by the lack of security around Chinnici's house. "Why don't you have a no-parking zone in front of your house?" Falcone asked Chinnici. "The other people in this condominium would raise such a ruckus, it's not worth it."[14] Because Chinnici's personal driver was going on vacation, Falcone's driver, Giovanni Paparcuri, was assigned to Chinnici's protection while Falcone was in Thailand.

Falcone and Pizzuti flew to Bangkok together with Domenico Signorino from the Procura della Repubblica. Signorino brought his wife and Falcone his fiancée, Francesca Morvillo, and because they were forced to take the first two days off, due to a bureaucratic snag, it felt almost like a vacation. "It was the only time we traveled with our wives," Signorino said. "And we went to one of these tourist shows of alligator wrestling."[15] Then one evening came the phone call from Palermo saying that Rocco Chinnici had been killed—blown up by a car bomb parked in front of his building as the magistrate left the house to go to work. Killed along with Chinnici were two bodyguards and the concierge of Chinnici's building. Some fourteen people were injured, including Falcone's driver, Giovanni Paparcuri, who was badly injured but miraculously alive.[16]

Chinnici had been instrumental in reviving mafia investigations and stirring the Palermo Palace of Justice out of its torpor. He had had the courage to take over the investigative office after the assassination of Cesare Terranova and had encouraged Falcone to persist in his banking investigations. Chinnici had understood the need to bridge the gap between the judiciary, operating in its marble bunker, and the rest of Sicilian society. He made frequent public appearances speaking out against the mafia, in a city where judges for many years had avoided using the word. He accepted invitations to speak in schools around Palermo, trying to break down the culture of *omertà* and building a new anti-mafia counterculture. He had appreciated the importance of Ninni Cassarà's "report on the 162," and had signed the first arrest warrants against Michele Greco, "the Pope."

Soon after the bombing it was revealed that an informant had warned police that a Palermo magistrate would be blown up in response to the arrest warrants in the Dalla Chiesa case—signed by Falcone and Chinnici just two weeks before the bombing. Yet no special measures had been taken to improve the protection of the two prosecutors. The informant was a Lebanese drug trafficker named Bou Ghebel Ghassan, who was providing morphine base for members of the clan of Michele Greco. Shortly after the arrest warrants were issued against Greco for the Dalla Chiesa killing, members of the Greco clan told him of his plans for retaliation. "They told me that it had been a mistake to kill Dalla Chiesa because it stirred up a 'mess,' but having started it was necessary to continue with these actions against anyone who 'stuck their nose in the mafia's business.' . . . [Vincenzo] Rabito said that the family headed by the Grecos, to which he belonged, was responsible for carrying out these killings in order to eliminate those who worked against the mafia and to send a message to those who came afterward so that they would limit themselves or run the same risk. . . . I remember he said almost verbatim: 'We'll blow them up in Palermo like you do in your country, we'll blow them all up so that there will be no witnesses.' . . . And after the killing of Chinnici . . . they were clearly satisfied with the result and said to me: 'See how it turned out?' "[17]

Soon the scandal of the unheeded warning of Chinnici's assassination was joined by persistent rumors that the old magistrate had kept a private diary in which he denounced many fellow judges and prosecutors for their benevolent attitudes toward the mafia. In September, soon after Falcone returned from Thailand, someone leaked the diary to the newsweekly magazine *L'Espresso,* which published the most significant extracts. From beyond the grave Chinnici pointed his finger at judges, prosecutors and lawyers whom he considered the accomplices of his mafia killers.

"If something bad happens to me there are two men responsible: (1) That great coward Ciccio Scozzari. (2) The attorney Paolo Seminara," he wrote. The first, Francesco ("Ciccio") Scozzari, was a prosecutor of the Procura della Republica, while Seminara was a prominent Palermo defense lawyer who represented the powerful Salvo family, tax collectors of Sicily, suspected of being *mafiosi.* "Ciccio Scozzari is the filthiest creature in the world, a cowardly servant of the mafia," Chinnici wrote in his diary. "Either out of envy or on orders from the mafia he has fought me since I came to Palermo."

Many had long nursed suspicions of collusion, cowardice and sabotage in the Palermo Palace of Justice but Chinnici's diary articulated them with names, dates and examples. The sarcastic remarks and corridor gossip directed at Giovanni Falcone and his work was only the tip of the iceberg of a much wider resistance to his investigative work. Chinnici described a heated exchange with the president of the Palermo Court of Appeals, Giovanni Pizzillo (the highest magistrate in the city), who told him that Falcone's financial investigations were "ruining the Sicilian economy." Pizzillo "told me clearly that I should load Falcone down with routine cases so that he 'doesn't try to discover anything, because the investigating magistrates in Palermo have never discovered anything.' . . . He tries to control his anger, but is unable to. He tells me that he wants to come to inspect the office (and I invite him to do so). . . . This is a man who has never done a thing to fight the mafia, rather with his relationships with major *mafiosi* has helped to support it."[18]

Pizzillo had not hesitated in pressuring Falcone to go easy on certain defendants with whom he was on friendly terms. "Giovanni Falcone told me that the President of the Court called him into his office to talk to him in favor of the Knight of Labor Gaetano Graci, implicated in the Sindona affair," Chinnici wrote in the diary entry of July 14, 1981.[19]

Moreover, the procuratore generale of Palermo, Ugo Viola (the most senior prosecutor in the city), had discouraged a witness who had come forward in the Mattarella case from testifying. The witness, Raimondo Mignosi, was the public inspector whom Mattarella had asked to conduct the investigation into public contracts in Palermo. "In my last conversation with President Mattarella, at the end of November, I told him to be careful because I ran the risk of ending up in a cement block, at which he replied, 'That's not true, I'll end up in the cement.' To break the tension, we jokingly agreed that we would both end up in cement blocks side by side."

When Mignosi finished telling his tale to Viola, the chief prosecutor could not hide his own terror. "Put everything you wanted to tell me in a letter and send it anonymously. Use a typewriter, no signature." Mignosi expressed his disappointment at this response, reminding Viola of public appeals he had made to encourage cooperation with authorities. To which the prosecutor replied: "Yes, it's true I have spoken out about the need for citizens to come forward . . . but citizens can help in many different ways. If you want to make a deposition I can call the Procuratore della Repubblica, otherwise . . . an anonymous letter.' 'In substance,' I answered, 'you urge me to be cautious,' " Mignosi later testified. "Very cautious," Viola answered.[20]

Chinnici also revealed a possible plot to kill Falcone. "Giovanni Falcone is extremely worried," Chinnici wrote. "At one in the afternoon he came to my office to tell me he was going by helicopter tomorrow to Caltanissetta to meet with assistant prosecutor Favi of Siracusa. A prison inmate told Favi that someone is organizing Falcone's assassination and that the organizers are the businessmen of Catania and the Catania mafia. The Knight of Labor [Mario] Rendo, according to the prisoner, is regularly informed about Falcone's activities by the High Commissioner [for antimafia investigations]. Incredible."

Living in this climate of suspicion and betrayal, Chinnici appeared to slide into generalized paranoia, distrusting everyone and everything, including Falcone himself. On June 17 (just a month before his death) Chinnici wrote: "It's been six months since I've written in this diary. It was a mistake because many things have continued to happen. Many regard Giovanni Falcone. . . . Why does he take the papers from his investigations home? And why does he meet with all these people (prosecutors, police?) in strict secret?"

Four days later Chinnici wrote: "Mandalari, accountant and consultant to the mafia has been released for lack of evidence. . . . Falcone says: in a state of law you must have the proof before making an arrest. But he hasn't done this with dozens of other defendants."[21]

If Rocco Chinnici had an Achilles' heel, it was jealousy. And after encouraging Falcone's investigation, he became envious of his success and sudden notoriety. With the Spatola case suddenly in the public eye, Falcone had become *the* anti-mafia prosecutor. Through his incessant traveling on the trail of international drug trafficking, he had become the person that investigators from Washington and Paris to Ankara and Bangkok turned to. When the U.S. government organized a convention on mafia prosecutions, it was Falcone they invited to speak. Chinnici was furious. When the American consulate in Palermo became aware of Chinnici's unhappiness, it quickly procured him an invitation. But the damage was done, the poison of envy had entered his bloodstream.

"Many people at first considered me Chinnici's right hand, as if I were merely an acritical executor of his orders," Falcone said in a 1986 interview. "When they realized that I made my own autonomous judgments, they did everything they could to pit us against one another."[22]

The mafia—probably through its eyes and ears among Palermo criminal lawyers—has always been acutely aware of the alliances and conflicts within the Palace of Justice and tried to exploit Chinnici's weakness. One day, as he noted in his diary, Chinnici received an anonymous letter saying: "No one in the investigative office moves a single piece of paper without Giovanni Falcone's permission." This poison-tipped dart was clearly meant to stimulate Chinnici's jealousy and get him to turn on Falcone.[23]

Although Chinnici expressed his feelings of jealousy and suspicion in his private diary, to his credit he never allowed it to affect his behavior toward Falcone. At one point, Falcone became aware of the problem and discussed it directly with Chinnici, clearing the air. "When things came to a head, I brought it up with Chinnici myself," he said. "The problem ended there." The final months of Chinnici's life were ones of particularly fruitful collaborations, marked both by the breakthroughs in the Thailand-Palermo drug connection and the Dalla Chiesa case.[24]

And yet, because of the diary, Falcone was forced to appear before the Consiglio Superiore della Magistratura along with the other judges and prosecutors Chinnici had accused of misconduct. Thus within weeks after losing a friend and mentor to a mafia bomb which might just as well have been meant for him, Falcone found himself in the position of defendant rather than prosecutor. Although he emerged unscathed from the proceedings—earning high praise from the judges of the Consiglio Superiore—the episode gave him a taste of how quickly the tables could be turned against him.[25]

In the months after the assassination of Rocco Chinnici, the Palermo investigative office remained at a standstill. A crowd of tired judicial hacks from Sicily lined up to fill his position. Despite his preeminence in mafia prosecutions and nearly twenty years of service, Giovanni Falcone did not even bother applying for the job. In Italy, seniority rather than merit has always been the guiding principle of judicial appointments: people who have never distinguished themselves in decades of employment expect to be automatically rewarded with the prestige and authority of higher office. But this time, in a surprising move, the Consiglio Superiore della Magistratura overturned the usually rigid rules of seniority and looked beyond Palermo to pick Antonino Caponetto as Chinnici's successor. Although he was sixty-three at the time, Caponetto was not the most senior candidate for the job. Moreover he had spent most of his career working in Florence. Caponetto had no background in mafia cases, but he had a reputation for seriousness and professionalism and his readiness to trade Florence for Palermo was a clear indication that he was animated by much more than a desire to close out his career with a comfortable sinecure. For Caponetto, going to Palermo meant leaving behind his wife and children in Tuscany for a life spent as a virtual prisoner shuttling between his bulletproof office and the heavily guarded barracks of the Treasury Police. As a magistrate and a Sicilian by origin, he was profoundly affected by the assassination of Rocco Chinnici and felt a powerful urge to return home and take up the fight against the mafia. When a Florentine television station asked him whether he was afraid of taking a job in which his two immediate predecessors had been murdered, Caponetto replied: "At the age of sixty-three one should be used to living with the idea of death."[1]

One of the first to congratulate Caponetto was Giovanni Falcone, who called to ask him to come to Palermo as soon as possible. "What struck me about Giovanni's telephone call was his completely friendly and confiding tone," Caponetto said. "He spoke as if we had known one another all our lives, when in fact we had never met."[2]

Not all the greetings Caponetto received on arriving in Palermo were as friendly. Marcantonio Motisi, one of the judges who had competed to become chief of the investigative office, warned Caponetto that he was planning to take legal action to win the job. More disturbing was a sinister message from the mafia. Someone within either the telegraph office or the Palace of Justice itself had tampered with a telegram of congratulations from the High Commissioner of anti-mafia affairs, changing the word "success" (successo) into the word for "killed" (ucciso) so that instead of saying "I wish you success," the note read: "I wish you killed."[3]

In Palermo Caponetto took up residence in the austere Treasury Police barracks, in whose cafeteria he ate each evening and where he slept in a small monastic cell with a narrow single bed. When Giovanni Falcone visited him there in order to fill him in on his work, Falcone found a thin, plainly dressed man with wire-rimmed glasses and a balding head with a few thin wisps of white hair. Despite his avuncular air and advanced age, Caponetto—from his wiry body to his coal-black eyes—had a hard, ascetic look that seemed in keeping with his Spartan accommodations in the Treasury Police barracks. Like Falcone, he was a man of simple, direct manner, and few, carefully measured words. Although Caponetto was the boss, he had the humility to respect Falcone's expertise on the mafia. "In that first encounter Falcone told me that we could count on only a few friends in the Palace of

Justice. . . . I would soon see that his views were well-founded," Caponetto has written.[4]

Caponetto decided to form a "pool" of magistrates who would dedicate themselves exclusively to mafia cases and share information collectively. Used successfully in the prosecution of terrorism, the "pool" concept reduced the risk of any single magistrate becoming the exclusive repository of dangerous secrets or the target of retaliation. At the same time, bringing together the work of several prosecutors would allow the office to deal efficiently with the growing mass of evidence and mount much more sweeping, large-scale cases in keeping with the new understanding of the mafia as a vast, complex network. Falcone was Caponetto's first choice for the pool. He then asked Giuseppe Di Lello, a favorite of Rocco Chinnici with experience in mafia cases. When asked to suggest a third member of the team, Falcone strongly recommended that they "rescue" Paolo Borsellino, who had been shunted aside after the Basile case. Somewhat later, Caponetto added Leonardo Guarnotta, a conscientious magistrate who was one of the senior prosecutors in the office. From now on they would all work together developing the case with 162 defendants that Rocco Chinnici had kept for himself.[5]

The other principal prosecutor's office, the Procura della Repubblica, which worked in synchrony with the investigative office, presenting its cases at trial, followed Caponetto's example, setting up an anti-mafia pool of its own.

The choice of Paolo Borsellino, Caponetto said, was one of the best decisions he made in his years in Palermo. He had a deep knowledge of Palermo, of the mafia and was a tremendous workhorse like Falcone, but with a very different character. "He was more open to human relations, to the pleasures of life, even the simplest, like jumping on a motorbike or going sailing," Caponetto wrote in his memoir *I miei giorni a Palermo* (My Days in Palermo). "He managed to communicate a marvelous sense of inner serenity that only later I realized came from his religious faith . . . which he never spoke about."[6] If Falcone was a figure who invariably commanded great respect, Borsellino was a person who elicited both respect and universal personal affection. "He had this enormous gift of incredible humanity," said the anti-mafia pool's secretary Barbara Sanzo. "He was interested in everyone's lives—the secretaries', the bodyguards', the file clerks'. He knew about everybody's situation, that this person had a sick son, someone else an unemployed husband and so on. He always wanted to know if people needed help."[7]

Falcone was far less communicative. "It was as if an invisible barrier stood. between himself and others," according to Caponetto. "It was a part of his character, a form of self-defense, because he was fundamentally shy. . . . Nonetheless, he was a captivating personality. His experience, the prestige he enjoyed, and his own maturity as a prosecutor had succeeded in giving him a confidence and authority in dealing with others, at any level. . . . Our relationship, despite his timidity, was very affectionate. . . . My character was very similar to his."[8]

While freeing the four members of the pool to work exclusively on mafia cases, Caponetto took on his own shoulders an extra share of the great mass of routine cases flowing each day to the investigative office, involving crimes from purse snatching to the bouncing of bad checks. Despite his age, Caponetto handled the highest number of cases of any of the sixteen prosecutors in the office, while at the same time overseeing everyone else's work. "Some people like to portray Caponetto as a mere figurehead for Giovanni Falcone, but that's not the case," said Leonardo Guarnotta. "Every morning before going up to his office, Falcone stopped in Caponetto's office to keep him abreast of what he was doing and to discuss what to do next. Falcone and the rest of the pool never did a thing that Counselor Caponetto didn't know about in advance and approve of. . . . For us Caponetto was like a father, as well as being a marvelous man and a magistrate of uncommon ability."[9]

The creation of the anti-mafia pool coincided happily with a change of the guard in Rome. In August 1983, after a prolonged government crisis, Bettino Craxi became the first socialist prime minister in Italy's history. At the same time, two Christian Democratic reformers, Mino Martinazzoli and Virginio Rognoni, were named, respectively, ministers of justice and of the interior. Both were politicians from northern Italy, where the party's electoral base did not depend on mafia support.

Minister of Justice Martinazzoli sent one of his aides, Liliana Ferraro, from Rome to inspect working conditions in Palermo.

Ferraro was appalled by what she found. Not only did the judges on the front line against the mafia have almost no protection, and no computers, they lacked even the most basic office equipment, such as typewriters, desks and chairs. "I entered [Falcone's] office and I saw him sitting on a beaten-up old chair at a teetering desk, off of which paper was falling in every direction," she said. " 'Let's start with the basics,' I said, 'a comfortable chair, a table that doesn't tilt.' After the chair and table, we put together a computer system to deal with all the data. Then a place for the Treasury Police which was overwhelmed by a blizzard of paper from the banks, then a computer for the financial investigators, the microfilming of the paper because there was so much paper that no one could find anything."[10]

Ferraro was also determined to improve the almost nonexistent security at the Palace of Justice. Criminals roamed freely through the vast marble lobby of the building and there was no police block preventing people from walking through the area where the prosecutors worked. She had Falcone and Borsellino moved to a hallway on the mezzanine level behind a guarded iron door. Falcone's door was bulletproof with a little television camera that allowed him to see who wanted to enter his office. Borsellino was put next door. "Martinazzoli gave the order to put Palermo in the fast lane, and suddenly we began to receive typewriters, computers and bulletproof cars," said Caponetto.

For the first time, by 1984, Palermo had the manpower and the machinery to wage a serious battle against the mafia.

A t the same time, the scattered threads of Palermo's numerous mafia investigations were beginning to come together.

Some three hundred people had been killed in and around Palermo in the first two years of the so-called mafia war. The unheard-of brutality of the manhunt and the presence of a new group of prosecutors, who appeared to be serious about fighting the mafia, combined to create an unprecedented phenomenon: mafia witnesses.

In the United States *mafiosi* had been talking for decades. Joe Valachi had broken the bonds of *omertà* in the 1950s and infamous mob bosses, like Lucky Luciano and Joe Bonnano, had actually published books about their careers. (The American mafia had assimilated to a much greater degree into the surrounding society. Italian-American *mafiosi,* like Luciano, made common cause with Jewish gangsters like Meyer Lansky.) Living in the land of Hollywood and Madison Avenue, American mobsters enjoyed the limelight, sometimes granting newspaper interviews or, as in the case of starstruck Bugsy Siegel, giving a screen test at a movie studio.

The idea of a Sicilian *mafioso* who talked had always been considered a contradiction in terms. This had essentially been the reaction of the Palermo judiciary when Leonardo Vitale appeared voluntarily at the Palermo police station in 1973 and announced he was ready to talk about his life in the mafia. Vitale, who had committed several murders, was suffering from a personal, religious crisis and wanted to unburden himself. Not only did he confess to a long string of crimes, he implicated more than a hundred other *mafiosi,* including future boss of bosses Salvatore Riina. Vitale's story checked out down to the smallest detail: he said that a certain victim had been smoking a cigarette when he was shot and, sure enough, when police checked their records they found that a cigarette had been found next to his body. And yet judges were skeptical of Vitale because of his mystical, religious crisis—in a bizarre act of contrition, he had burnt his clothes and covered himself in his own feces—but also because of a stubborn belief that *mafiosi* don't talk. The Palermo Court of Appeals overturned the convictions of the *mafiosi* he had implicated and placed Vitale into an asylum for the criminally insane. When he was released many years later, Vitale was brutally murdered. "Unlike our justice system, the mafia understood the importance of Leonardo Vitale's revelations and at the moment it considered most opportune, executed the inexorable punishment for breaking the law of *omertà,*" Giovanni Falcone wrote.[11]

Giuseppe Di Cristina, the boss of Riesi, killed in 1978, had opened up partially to police. But he was murdered only a few days later and his confessions were largely ignored.

The Italian parliament had passed special legislation granting sentence reductions to terrorists who became cooperative government witnesses, but refused to consider similar legislation for the mafia. Opposition came not only from politicians afraid of losing their electoral strongholds in mafia-dominated areas but also from left-wing groups worried about defendants' rights.

Despite the deadly precedents set by previous mafia witnesses and the total absence of government support, the wall of *omertà* began to crack under the strain of the great mafia war. The prosecutors had first worked patiently on outsiders who did business with the mafia—drug couriers and foreign suppliers. Then they began to win the cooperation of common criminals from Sicily who often lived on close terms with the mafia. In 1983, prosecutors in Palermo made a quantum leap forward: two witnesses with detailed inside information began to cooperate. Vincenzo Sinagra was not a "made" member of the mafia, but was an "affiliate" who had participated in and witnessed numerous murders by the sanguinary boss Filippo Marchese and the "family" of Corso dei Mille, the perpetrators of the Christmas Massacre of Bagheria and the subsequent assassination of Dr. Paolo Giaccone. Another witness, Vincenzo Marsala, stepped forward after his father, the boss of the small Sicilian town of Vicari, was murdered in 1983. Although insisting that his father had wanted to keep him out of the mafia, Marsala seemed to know a great deal about mafia business. His testimony indicated that the rural mafia was much more closely tied to that of Palermo than many people supposed: Salvatore Riina himself had come to Vicari to settle a local clan dispute—the first eyewitness report of the elusive Riina in over ten years. Moreover, the repercussions of the mafia war of Palermo were felt immediately in the countryside: Vincenzo Marsala's father and another older boss from the area had been eliminated by ruthless younger *mafiosi* tied to the Corleonese mafia.[12]

While each of these witnesses provided valuable pieces to the puzzle, none of them had anything like a complete picture of the organization—something that prosecutors in Palermo badly needed. The possibility seemed to present itself in March 1982, when police in Rome finally captured Salvatore Contorno, the Scarlet Pimpernel of the mafia, who was hiding out from his would-be assassins in Palermo and plotting his revenge. But despite having lost more than a dozen close relatives and scores of close friends in the extermination campaign directed against him and his boss Stefano Bontate, Contorno refused to cooperate. Every few months, Giovanni Falcone would travel to Rome to visit him in prison with hopes of persuading him to change his mind, but each time he would find himself faced with the same wall of silence.[13]

Then, in late 1983, Brazilian police finally arrested Tommaso Buscetta.

Buscetta, the so-called boss of two worlds, was a figure of mythic proportions. The last of fourteen children of a poor Sicilian glass cutter, Buscetta was born in a wretched Palermo slum in 1927. He quit school after fifth grade, married at age sixteen and at eighteen was initiated into the mafia. A tough guy, with wavy oiled hair and a pencil mustache, Buscetta was rumored to be one of the favorite hit men of Angelo and Salvatore La Barbera, the bosses of the "family" of the Porta Nuova neighborhood. "I was a *mafioso* by nature long before being made," he later said. "Everything they told me to do was already part of me." In 1957, he used a combination of muscle and corruption to obtain a large government contract for a Palermo builder, allegedly involving a $50,000 payoff.[14] In 1959 he was caught red-handed with four tons of contraband cigarettes and was convicted *in absentia* for a double murder committed in 1963. But Buscetta had fled the jurisdiction, with assistance from a Christian Democratic member of parliament, Francesco Barbaccia, who helped him obtain a passport. Writing a letter of recommendation to the chief of police, *Onorevole* Barbaccia (all members of parliament in Italy are "honorable") referred to Buscetta as "una persona che mi interessa molto" (a person who interests me a great deal).[15]

Buscetta spent the next ten years or so moving between the United States and South America, allegedly operating a major narcotics ring, according to American police. Leaving his first wife in Palermo, Buscetta made a second, bigamous marriage in the United States. In 1970, with a fake Canadian passport, he slipped through the hands of Italian police, together with several of Sicily's biggest bosses, on his way to a major mafia summit meeting. The following year, Buscetta was expelled from the United States and moved to Brazil, where he met his third wife, glamorous young Maria Cristina Guimaraes—daughter of a prominent Brazilian lawyer, with powerful political friends and a shady reputation. In 1972, Buscetta and his wife's entire family (including his prominent father-in-law) were arrested on charges of heroin trafficking and

Buscetta was sent back to Italy to serve the sentence for murder that had been hanging over his head since 1968.[16]

Giovanni Falcone heard about Buscetta from Francesco Gasparini, the drug courier turned witness, who had encountered "the boss of two worlds" in the Palermo prison of Ucciardone in 1979. "He enjoyed a position of supremacy over the other inmates," Gasparini said. Buscetta's stature within the prison was on a par with that of Luciano Leggio, the greatly feared boss of Corleone, believed to be running the mafia from prison through his lieutenant Salvatore Riina.[17]

"Buscetta was very meticulous about his person, using only the finest products," according to another inmate. "He never finished a bottle of eau de toilette or a bar of soap; he gave the rest away as gifts. His casual clothes, his jeans, were always designer-made. . . . Only his coffee was prepared in jail; men would take turns bringing it to him, piping hot. Otherwise, his breakfast, lunch and dinner came from the best restaurants in Palermo. . . . Buscetta was a boss—in fact, The Boss. He never raised his voice, he never asked for anything; but he always knew everything. . . . I never heard him threaten anybody, but I'd hear him say: 'This guy in cell 8 is making too much noise and he would do well to cut it out. . . .' "[18]

In 1980, with three years yet to serve on his sentence, a judge in Turin allowed Buscetta to leave prison during the day to participate in a work program that was part of Italy's new liberal prison reform laws. "The prisoner's conduct has been irreproachable. He was always respectful to the personnel and sociable with his colleagues, and participated with interest in the process of personal resocialization. . . . There is absolutely no sign that the prisoner cultivated or tried to cultivate relations with elements of the mafia in prison. On the contrary, his personality shows a sincere desire to be resocialized. . . . It is beyond doubt that he is ready to be reinserted into an orderly, civil way of living."[19]

Ignoring the objections of Sicilian police, the judge accepted Buscetta's stated desire to return to his family's glass-making business. This naive assessment failed to take into account the fact that mafia bosses are always model prisoners, ruling prison life with an iron fist inside a velvet glove. Predictably enough, after gaining his "semi-liberty" in June of 1980, Buscetta broke his parole and fled Italy.

In September of 1982, his two sons from his first wife, Antonio and Benedetto, disappeared in Palermo. Journalists and police investigators imagined that Buscetta—in disguise—had returned to Palermo as a kind of avenging angel to exterminate his mafia rivals. "We know that Tommaso Buscetta has had plastic surgery and had his vocal cords modified," the newsmagazine *L'Espresso* quoted unnamed investigators as saying. "Possibly, he even has new fingerprints. . . . We know that he returned to Palermo four or five weeks ago and has already made contact with other *mafiosi* . . . waiting for the right moment to go on the attack."[20]

In late November 1982 mafia boss Rosario Riccobono and most of his closest lieutenants all vanished into thin air. A couple of days later, a group of soldiers from Riccobono's family were shot and killed in Palermo's Singapore Two nightclub. Fanciful journalists reported that Tommaso Buscetta—"the godfather with a hundred faces"—had invited Rosario Riccobono to a peacemaking banquet at which he had poisoned him and his entire entourage.[21] They failed to grasp the diabolic cleverness of Totò Riina, the boss of Corleone, who had first used Riccobono and then eliminated him. But then Riccobono—a ruthless mafia boss, himself capable of enormous treachery—had been fooled as well. Although a traditional *capo* of one of the main Palermo families, Riccobono had sided expediently with the more powerful Corleonesi with the advent of the mafia war. In order to ingratiate himself with Riina, he used his old friendships with Stefano Bontate and Salvatore Inzerillo to lure members of their families to their deaths. Riina, no doubt correctly, figured that if Riccobono would turn against Bontate and Inzerillo, he was an untrustworthy ally, to be done in at the earliest convenience. And so, after he was confident of having triumphed over the Bontate and Inzerillo clans, Riina took care of Riccobono himself.

Several days later, Buscetta's son-in-law was murdered in the Palermo pizzeria where he worked, and two days after that Buscetta's brother and nephew were gunned down in the window-making business they ran. It looked like retaliation from Riccobono's forces and perpetuated the fantasy that Buscetta, with his new face, vocal cords, and fingerprints, was a protagonist of the so-called mafia war in Palermo.

Instead, Buscetta was hiding out on his 65,000-acre farm near the mouth of the Amazon, trying to avoid the national manhunt that the Brazilian police had unleashed against him. They were convinced that Buscetta was the mastermind of a huge international drug trafficking ring involving several countries and some two hundred people. When they arrested him and eleven others in October 1983, an official from the Brazilian narcotics squad was quoting as saying: "Tommaso Buscetta was the principal coordinator of the cocaine market between Brazil, Bolivia, Peru, Colombia, Europe and the United States."[22]

In order to strengthen their case, Brazilian police allegedly resorted to torture, pulling out Buscetta's fingernails, attaching electric wires to his genitals and threatening to throw him from an airplane. But he refused to talk. Meanwhile both the United States and Italy applied for Buscetta's extradition. Buscetta's wife Maria Cristina apparently begged American Drug Enforcement Agency officials to take her husband, fearful that he would be killed if he set foot in Italy. But the United States ceded to Italy's claim, since he still had an unfinished sentence left to serve there.

Given his behavior in Brazilian custody, it looked highly unlikely that Buscetta would cooperate with Italian authorities, but Falcone felt it was worth a try. He arrived in Brazil in June 1984 with Vincenzo Geraci, his counterpart from the Procura della Repubblica. Contrary to the reports that Buscetta had become unrecognizable after elaborate operations of plastic surgery, he had the same unmistakable face as always, with the dark complexion and features that made him look like a South American Indian. The Italians had prepared some fifty questions for the defendant, which were read aloud by the Brazilian magistrate. Buscetta sat there impassively, his wife Cristina nearby. Buscetta answered the questions quickly and evasively, giving the Italians the feeling that they were wasting their time. But as Buscetta gave his pro forma answers, Falcone noticed that the mafia boss was watching him closely, studying him. At a certain point, when Buscetta failed to answer a question, the Brazilian magistrate asked him: Do you intend to answer? But instead of addressing the Brazilian, Buscetta turned to Falcone and made a cryptic remark: "It would take all night to answer." Claiming fatigue, Buscetta then asked that the session be adjourned.

"I think he's decided to spill the beans," Falcone told Geraci. "You must be kidding," Geraci answered. It seemed too good to be true that a boss of Buscetta's stature, the keeper of more than thirty-five years of mafia secrets on three continents, could become a government witness. The two magistrates returned to Palermo and the Italian police continued with the extradition procedure. Geraci's skepticism proved justified initially: when Buscetta learned that he was to be put on a plane to Italy, he tried to commit suicide, swallowing a stash of strychnine he had kept hidden. Buscetta was convinced that, unless he died, the mafia would continue killing off his relatives and that as long as he was alive he represented a mortal threat to everyone connected to him. Suicide, he decided, was the only way to save his wife and children. But having survived, a few days after arriving in Italy Buscetta asked to talk to Judge Falcone.[23]

SEVEN

As he began the interrogation of Tommaso Buscetta, Giovanni Falcone tried to calibrate his own behavior carefully for fear that Buscetta's sudden willingness to talk would harden just as quickly into silence. He wanted to keep a professional distance but convey a sense of understanding and empathy, to show respect to Buscetta without losing sight of the fact that Falcone was a prosecutor and Buscetta a criminal defendant. Some prosecutors had made the mistake with *mafiosi* of adopting an excessively confidential tone, using the familiar *tu* instead of the formal *lei*, which a *mafioso* would invariably find offensive or disrespectful. Others tried too hard to assert their authority, raising their voice or issuing orders. It was important to be well prepared, with serious, concrete questions that didn't insult the intelligence of the interlocutor. Falcone had heard the story of a Rome prosecutor who began the interrogation of the old Italian-American gangster Frankie "Three Fingers" Coppola with a brash, provocative question: What is the mafia? Coppola paused for a minute and answered with a story. Three people were in line for the job as chief prosecutor. One was extremely intelligent, the second had the backing of the political parties and the third was a fool. The fool got the job. "That's the mafia," Coppola said, putting an end to the discussion.[1]

At the beginning, Buscetta wanted to put Falcone on notice. "I trust you, Judge Falcone, and I trust deputy police chief Gianni De Gennaro. But I don't trust anyone else. I don't believe the Italian state has the real intention of fighting the mafia. . . . I want to warn you, Judge. After this interrogation you will become a celebrity. But they will try to destroy you physically and professionally. And they will do the same to me. Never forget that you are opening an account with Cosa Nostra that will only be settled when you die. Are you sure you want to go ahead with this?"[2]

That day, Buscetta, still recovering from his nearly fatal suicide attempt, limited himself to making a brief statement. "I want to make clear that I am not a stool pigeon. . . . I am not a 'penitent,' in that my revelations are not motivated by base calculations of personal interest. I have spent my life as a *mafioso* and I have made mistakes, for which I am prepared to pay the consequences, without asking for sentence reductions or special treatment. In the interest of society, of my children and other young people, I intend to reveal all that I know about the cancer of the mafia, so that future generations can live in a more human and dignified way."[3] Then, sick and exhausted, he asked to return to his cell to rest. Falcone did not press him to continue.

This was the first of an extraordinary series of sessions that would last for the rest of the summer, that would radically alter Falcone's understanding of the Sicilian mafia. Buscetta started their second session like a professor beginning an introductory course. "The word 'mafia' is a literary creation, while the real *'mafiosi'* call themselves simply 'men of honor' . . . and the organization as a whole is called 'Cosa Nostra,' as in the United States," he explained.[4] "Before Buscetta, we didn't even know the mafia's real name," said Antonino Caponetto. The term 'Cosa Nostra' was thought to refer to the American mafia, now it appeared to be a Sicilian term imported by America.[5]

The Cosa Nostra that Buscetta described was a much more highly evolved and hierarchical organization than investigators had imagined. Italian police had heard stories about the mafia's "parliament," but only in the sketchiest of terms. Buscetta, instead, was able to provide a precise organizational map of Cosa Nostra from the lowliest "man of honor" to the Commission that stood atop the pyramid of mafia power and explained its fairly elaborate rules of governance. "Every man of honor belongs to a family, which, in the city of Palermo, corresponds to a neighborhood. In the small towns, the family takes its name from the town itself," Buscetta said. "At the head of each family is a *capo* elected directly by the men of honor. He, in turn, selects a *sotto-capo* (underboss) and one or two *consiglieri* (counselors). . . . The ordinary soldiers of each family are organized in groups of ten with a 'captain' over them who oversees the actions of the individual men of honor."[6]

The approximately thirty families in the province of Palermo, in turn, are organized into ten districts *(mandamenti)*, with each district consisting of three families operating on contiguous territory. Each group of three families chooses a "district leader" or *capomandamento,* who represents them in the governing body of the organization, known as "the Commission." The purpose of the Commission, he explained, was to lay down major policy, mediate disputes between the families, and to decide the most important murders, of police officers, judges and politicians as well as major mafia figures. This point was extremely important to prosecutors because it meant that they could hold the members of the Commission responsible for all of the "excellent cadavers" that had littered Palermo in recent years. It was inconceivable, Buscetta assured Falcone, that figures of the stature of General Dalla Chiesa or Rocco Chinnici could have been assassinated without the consensus of the Commission and without the knowledge of the bosses on whose territory they were carried out.[7]

Originally conceived as a form of collective, "democratic" governance, the Commission, according to Buscetta, had become "the instrument through which the dominant group imposes its will." The dominant group, which had recently achieved hegemony within Cosa Nostra, were the Corleonesi, led by Luciano Leggio, and after Leggio's arrest in 1974, his lieutenants Salvatore Riina and Bernardo Provenzano. Buscetta's description of the dynamics of power within Cosa Nostra matched perfectly with that given six years earlier by Giuseppe Di Cristina, including the evaluation of individual men. "Salvatore Riina and Bernardo Provenzano . . . enjoy equal power, except that Riina is much more intelligent than Provenzano and therefore has greater weight," Buscetta said.[8]

Falcone was impressed by Buscetta's bearing and manner. Although polite, soft-spoken and respectful, he was a man used to commanding and being obeyed. "Buscetta was clearly a person of extraordinary intelligence who would have succeeded at anything he had done," said Richard Martin, one of the assistant U.S. attorneys in New York who worked with Falcone on a number of American mafia cases that ran parallel to those being investigated in Palermo. "Most members of the mafia are basically thugs . . . Buscetta was extremely articulate, he spoke Italian, and not just Sicilian, he spoke Spanish and Portuguese, he understood the world on all its levels. And in that respect he was a very important person for the mafia because he could talk to almost anybody."[9]

"Buscetta was always serious and thoughtful," said Antonio Manganelli, a police investigator who worked closely with Falcone and is now the head of the Servizio Centrale Operativo in Rome. "If you asked him something he might say, 'I'd like to think about that before answering.' Then two hours later, after you had forgotten the question entirely, he would return to it and give you a very careful, considered answer."[10]

Buscetta's knowledge of the Commission stretched back to its foundation in the late 1950s. According to some accounts, it was Lucky Luciano, after being deported from the United States to Italy in 1946, who first advised the Sicilians to form the Commission, which had helped to keep peace among U.S. mob families. Buscetta was present when a collection of American and Sicilian bosses held a kind of international mafia summit at the Hotel delle Palme in Palermo in 1957. According to police investigators, the American mafia—under severe police pressure at the time—approached the Sicilians to take over the lion's share of the international narcotics traffic and to formalize the Commission structure. The importance of the Palermo meeting became apparent the following month when police broke up a gathering of some one hundred American mafia bosses who had descended on the small town of Apalachin, New York, to discuss the results of the Sicilian summit.[11]

The new mafia order worked for a while, as the Palermo clans divided up the growing pie of contraband cigarettes, government contracts and real estate money during the 1950s and 1960s. But the Commission fell apart in 1963 with the outbreak of the first mafia war. The war, according to Buscetta, was orchestrated by mafia boss Michele Cavataio in a devious manner not unlike that used later by Totò Riina. Cavataio was worried by the growing power of the aggressive young bosses of Buscetta's family, Angelo and Salvatore La Barbera. Taking advantage of a dispute between the La Barbera brothers and another Palermo boss, Calcedonia Di Pisa, Cavataio's men gunned down Di Pisa knowing that suspicions would fall immediately on the La Barberas. The other families fell into the trap and declared war on the La Barbera family. As Cavataio's rivals systematically killed each other off, his own men continued throwing gasoline on the fire by secretly carrying out assassinations and planting car bombs against both sides. This clever scheme backfired in June 1963, when a car bomb meant for the boss of Ciaculli and head of the Commission, Salvatore Greco (a.k.a. Cichiteddu, "Little Bird"), blew up and killed seven Italian police officers.

With the bomb of Ciaculli the first mafia war suddenly turned into the first war *against* the mafia. Some 10,000 police officers combed Sicily and in a matter of months arrested 1,903 *mafiosi*, including Cavataio and most of the major bosses. The public outrage over the police killings forced the parliament to convene the first anti-mafia commission, which conducted an enormous, detailed inquiry into the mafia phenomenon. Moreover, the bombing tipped off the other mafia clans to Cavataio's underhanded role in the mafia war. When the episode occurred, Salvatore La Barbera was already dead and his brother Angelo had fled to Milan, where he was seriously wounded. It became clear that Cavataio—and not the La Barberas—had planted the bomb and fomented much of the trouble.[12]

Many *mafiosi* including Buscetta and the head of the Commission, Salvatore Greco, left the country, "nauseated by what was happening" and emigrated to South and North America. The Commission, Buscetta revealed, was actually dissolved and the *capi* of Cosa Nostra agreed to suspend all activity until government pressure cooled off.

Unfortunately, the anti-mafia campaign seemed to slacken as soon as the shooting and the public clamor died down. The first war against the mafia ended in a string of not-guilty verdicts in 1969; virtually all of the major bosses, from Cavataio, Stefano Bontate and Giuseppe Di Cristina to Luciano Leggio and Totò

Riina, were absolved and released from prison. With a renewed sense of its own impunity, the mafia celebrated its court victory by settling its score with Cavataio. On December 10, 1969, six *mafiosi* dressed in police uniforms burst into a real estate office on Viale Lazio in Palermo, where Cavataio was holed up with some of his men.[13] They succeeded in killing Cavataio, but he managed to return fire, killing Calogero Bagarella, one of the hit men. Bagarella was the older brother of Totò Riina's sweetheart, Antonietta Bagarella, and of another important *mafioso* of Corleone, Leoluca Bagarella. The composition of the hit squad, as Buscetta explained to Falcone, was a clear indication that the killing had been sanctioned collectively by all the major Sicilian families: not only did it include Calogero Bagarella from Corleone, and a member of Stefano Bontate's family in Palermo, but also a soldier of Giuseppe Di Cristina's family on the other end of Sicily in Riesi.[14]

The killing of Cavataio, Buscetta explained, marked the new beginning of Cosa Nostra. In its phase of reorganization, it was governed by a "triumvirate" composed of Totò Riina, Stefano Bontate and the boss of the town of Cinisi near Palermo, Gaetano Badalamenti, another friend of Buscetta. Falcone was surprised to learn that Totò Riina was already at the pinnacle of Cosa Nostra in 1969, even though he was officially standing in for his boss, Luciano Leggio, who was ill and living as a fugitive in Milan at the time.

Riina did not wait long before making his first moves toward supremacy within Cosa Nostra. When the other two members of the triumvirate, Bontate and Badalamenti, were rearrested in 1972, Riina took advantage of the situation to strengthen his position and undermine theirs. Riina organized the kidnapping of the son of Count Arturo Cassina, one of Palermo's richest businessmen. For years, Cassina had enjoyed the lucrative private monopoly over the maintenance of the city's streets, electric lighting, and sewage system—among the worst-kept and most expensive in Italy. Cassina enjoyed the backing of the Palermo mafia clans, who intimidated any local politicians who thought about reassigning city contracts, and in exchange got to place a certain number of their own men in Cassina's operation. Kidnapping Cassina's son was a typical example of Corleonese bravado: not only did it win them a multimillion-dollar ransom, it damaged the prestige of the principal Palermo clans, exposing their inability to protect one of their principal clients.

When they emerged from prison, Bontate and Badalamenti were furious and protested vehemently. Luciano Leggio intervened to defuse the crisis with characteristic skill. Appearing to sympathize with their point of view, he dissolved the triumvirate, reinstituted the old Commission and placed Gaetano Badalamenti at its head. Since the hostage had already been released and the ransom paid, Leggio declared the kidnapping a *fait accompli,* unworthy of further fuss. The Commission adopted a policy against kidnappings on Sicilian territory, arguing that extensive police searches for the victims was bad for mafia business. But the Corleonesi continued to show a complete lack of respect for the traditional mafia families: "In the meetings of the Commission (which were always held on the estate of Michele Greco, even before he became head of the Commission itself) Luciano Leggio never failed to . . . make fun of Badalamenti . . . pointing out his errors in grammar and syntax when he tried to express himself in Italian rather than in Sicilian dialect," Buscetta told Falcone. (Although Leggio was himself the son of dirt-poor farmers, and a vicious killer, he cultivated the image of mafia intellectual and liked being called "the professor.")[15]

With Leggio's arrest in 1974, Riina resumed his place on the Commission and was soon up to his old tricks again. In 1975, he organized the kidnapping of Luigi Corleo, father-in-law of Nino Salvo, the fabulously wealthy head of Sicily's private tax collection monopoly. The move was another humiliating blow to Stefano Bontate, who was extremely close to the Salvo family. Not only was Bontate unable to free the hostage, he could not even produce his body, which the family wanted, not only as a matter of honor, but for purposes of inheritance. The Corleonesi denied knowing anything about the kidnapping and no one could prove otherwise.

Falcone began to understand the Machiavellian logic of the great mafia war. The assassination of Stefano Bontate in 1981, rather than being the opening shot of the war, was the culmination of a carefully plotted campaign conducted over a period of more than ten years. Totò Riina and the Corleonesi had always been several moves ahead of their adversaries. The big city bosses in Palermo had made the fatal error of underestimating the Corleonesi, whom they referred to disparagingly as *i viddani* (the peasants). "Already back then [the mid-1970s] the Corleonesi had an extremely lucid plan to progressively isolate Stefano Bontate in order to be able to eliminate him without any negative consequences," Buscetta told Falcone. "Bontate was without doubt the only one who represented a serious obstacle to their hegemonic designs."

The Corleonesi's subterfuge was facilitated by the fact that no one even knew the identity of the "men of honor" belonging to the family of Corleone. "One of the characteristics of the 'family' of Corleone is not revealing the names of its own members, something that Gaetano Badalamenti always complained about," Buscetta said. This dovetailed with something Giuseppe Di Cristina had said six years earlier when he told police that Luciano Leggio had a secret group of fourteen killers prepared to commit murders at his bidding at any moment anywhere in Italy.

The bosses of Corleone were almost as mysterious as their legion of nameless soldiers. While the traditional bosses of Palermo and of much of Sicily enjoyed living openly in their own lavish homes as respected members of their community, the Corleonesi's *capi,* Leggio, Riina, Bernardo Provenzano and Leoluca Bagarella, all lived on the run for decades as fugitives of justice. Phantoms at the head of phantom armies, they were constantly moving, their whereabouts frequently as unknown to their fellow *mafiosi* as to the police. "The 'Corleonesi' are 'invisible targets,' " Di Cristina explained, "because they are almost all fugitives and run few serious risks with regard to their rivals or from the police."

Since they lived in society, the Palermo bosses tried to avoid spectacular, highly visible crimes, such as kidnappings or the murder of public officials, that would attract attention to themselves. They, too, killed when necessary, but preferred working behind the scenes with police and politicians rather than seeking direct confrontation. The "traditional" mafia accepted an occasional jail term as an occupational hazard (needed to help the state maintain face with public opinion) and used their powerful connections to win light sentences or early parole. The Corleonesi took a much more uncompromising attitude, moving quickly against anyone who tried to move against them. In 1977, they murdered Colonel

Giuseppe Russo of the *carabinieri* and the next year, Michele Reina, the president of the Christian Democratic Party in Palermo.

The traditional leaders of the mafia regarded this new strategy as totally counterproductive. But, as Giuseppe Di Cristina understood shortly before his own death, these killings had a double purpose: to intimidate law enforcement, and strengthen themselves at the expense of their rivals within Cosa Nostra. "Their criminal strategy, while crazy, has its rewards," Di Cristina said. "It provokes police activity but primarily against the 'old *mafiosi*' who are easy to identify; it causes their terrifying prestige to grow and undermines the prestige of the 'traditional' mafia and the principles on which it depends. It attracts to them, either through fear or through the appeal of such daring undertakings, new recruits and new forces." Di Cristina's own murder was a prime example. Instead of going after his real killers, police investigated Di Cristina's friend Salvatore Inzerillo, the mafia boss on whose territory he was killed and Stefano Bontate's closest ally on the Commission.[16]

Nineteen seventy-eight was a key year in the Corleonesi's drive to power. Not only did they order the assassination of important public figures, they began eliminating members of the "traditional" mafia in other parts of Sicily—Di Cristina and Giuseppe Calderone of Catania—who might have acted as support to Totò Riina's main rivals in Palermo.

With characteristic shrewdness, the Corleonesi were able to justify their actions by appealing to the traditional rules of Cosa Nostra. They had to kill Di Cristina, they said, because he had broken his vow of *omertà* by going to the police; but they omitted the fact that they had already tried to murder Di Cristina *before* he went to the police and that his secret meeting with the *carabinieri* was a direct result of this earlier assassination attempt. The Corleonesi always appeared to be playing by the rules when they were in fact making a mockery of them. Similarly, the Corleonesi used some infraction on the part of Gaetano Badalamenti not only to have him removed as head of the Commission but expelled entirely from Cosa Nostra.

But the Corleonesi were always careful to act through third parties. Giuseppe Calderone was not killed by Totò Riina's men but by Calderone's own underboss, Nitto Santapaola. The killing appeared to have local origins but Santapaola was an ally of Riina and furthered his overall strategy. With similar indirectness, Totò Riina installed Michele Greco, "the Pope," as the new head of the Commission in 1978. Greco gave the Commission a facade of neutrality behind which the Corleonesi effectively hid their expansionist aims. Contrary to appearances, Buscetta explained, "the Pope" was a mere figurehead. "Michele Greco, given his bland and weak personality, was the perfect person to become head of the Commission so as not to stand in the way of the designs of Riina," Buscetta explained.[17]

In episode after episode, "the Pope" gave his blessing to Riina's most blatant violations of mafia rules. "When the killing [of Colonel Giuseppe Russo] occurred, Bontate, who knew nothing about it, protested vigorously at a Commission meeting, but no one gave him satisfaction, by telling him who had committed the murder," Buscetta said. "Later, Michele Greco told Bontate that the Corleonesi had ordered the killing and that one of the actual killers was Pino (The Shoe) Greco. . . . But Michele Greco denied to Bontate that he knew about the killing beforehand even though one of his own men was used in the hit squad. . . . This is completely improbable and it is worth noting that no disciplinary action was taken by the Commission against either the Corleonesi or Pino Greco."

The same pattern repeated itself in 1979, with the assassination of Judge Cesare Terranova and police inspector Boris Giuliano. "I know for sure, having learned it from Salvatore Inzerillo, that [the killings] were decided by the Commission of Palermo, without the knowledge of Inzerillo or of Stefano Bontate or Rosario Riccobono," Buscetta said.

The period from Michele Greco's ascension to the head of the Commission in 1978 to the official outbreak of the mafia war in the spring of 1981 was a time of uneasy truce in which the Corleonesi continued to chip away at the power and prestige of Stefano Bontate and the "traditional" Palermo families. Buscetta had occasion to live through this phase firsthand when he was released from prison and broke his parole in June of 1980. He returned to Palermo, where he spent much of his time with his good friend Stefano Bontate. Buscetta was much closer to Bontate than to his own boss, Giuseppe "Pippo" Calò, and, at one point, Bontate had tried, unsuccessfully, to persuade Calò to let Buscetta switch fam-

ilies, joining Bontate's clan of Santa Maria di Gesù. But membership in a particular family, like membership in Cosa Nostra itself,
is an immutable commitment from which a "man of honor" can
be released only at death.

At a certain point while Buscetta was in Palermo, Calò sum-
moned him to Rome, where Calò had been living under an assumed name for many years. Buscetta was angry with Calò for
having abandoned him and his family during his eight years in
prison. Not only had Calò failed to offer financial assistance to
Buscetta's family (a standard mafia practice), another member of
their mafia family in prison informed Buscetta that he had been
suspended from Cosa Nostra (*posato*, literally "placed" or put
aside) for his "immoral" behavior in having left his first wife, and
having married three times. The mafia, while sanctioning murder,
heroin trafficking and extortion, remains—at least formally—extremely conservative on matters of social behavior. While it is
common for a mafia boss to keep a mistress, he must do so with
discretion, continuing to live with and showing respect for the
mother of his children. Suddenly, after years of neglect, Calò became extremely solicitous, assuring Buscetta that the story of his
"suspension" from Cosa Nostra had been a misunderstanding and
swearing that he did not know that Buscetta's family had financial
problems. He also used all means to convince Buscetta to stay in
Italy. "Calò . . . when I expressed my intention of returning to
Brazil, insisted strongly that I remain in Palermo, telling me that
there were lots of possibilities for making money, since the
restoration of the old 'historic center' of Palermo was being controlled by Vito Ciancimino, from Corleone [the former mayor and
commissioner of public works], who, in Calò's words, was 'in the
hands of Totò Riina.' "

On emerging from prison, Buscetta was struck by the seemingly
limitless wealth that the drug trade had created within Cosa Nostra. At the same time, he could see the storm clouds gathering over
Palermo as he became aware of the evident tensions among the
bosses of the Commission. Calò was clearly worried about the
growing conflicts within Cosa Nostra and wanted Buscetta to remain in Palermo so that he could use his status as a "gray emi-
nence" to make peace between the warring factions.

Calò had once been a close friend of Stefano Bontate but, perceiving the shift in power toward Totò Riina, had moved into what was clearly the winning camp. "Speaking of Calò, Bontate told me that he had become a complete slave of the Corleonesi and of Michele Greco, so much so that during the meetings of the Commission, when they expressed their opinions, he didn't even speak, merely nodding his head," Buscetta said.

Bontate was so frustrated he swore he would pull out a pistol and shoot Riina in front of the whole Commission. "I told him that it was extremely dangerous because he risked being killed by the other members of the Commission, who would be afraid that Bontate would turn his gun against them, too. He told me that he didn't care and that he preferred to die if it meant killing Riina. . . . I remained convinced that it was an error . . . and I remember telling Bontate that he was a lost man."

In an attempt to avoid a clan war, Buscetta arranged a secret meeting among Calò, Bontate and Salvatore Inzerillo in order to create a new alliance in the Commission to counterbalance the power of the Corleonesi. Despite an apparent agreement, the Commission continued to act in defiance of Bontate and Inzerillo.

When Captain Emanuele Basile was murdered in the spring of 1980, once again, Bontate and Inzerillo were taken completely by surprise. "The killing of Captain Basile was ordered by the Corleonesi . . . with the consent of the Commission, but without the knowledge, once again, of Inzerillo and Bontate. . . . This time the irritation of these two was greater than usual because one of the trio who committed the murder . . . was a member of the family of Ciaculli, so that it was impossible, as Michele Greco maintained, that he knew nothing about the killing."

Interestingly enough, as Buscetta explained, the murder of chief prosecutor Gaetano Costa was a response not so much to the antimafia work of Costa but to the killing of Basile. "Salvatore Inzerillo, entirely on his own initiative, in order to show that he could buck the Commission just like the Corleonesi, ordered the killing of . . . Gaetano Costa, who had signed the arrest warrants against Inzerillo's family. . . . I should point out, however, as Salvatore Inzerillo explained to me himself, he was not particularly angry at Costa for the arrest warrants, but intended to use that as an opportunity to . . . make a show of his own and his family's power in front of his enemies."

After the killing of Costa, Pippo Calò told Buscetta that "Salvatore Inzerillo was a baby for having Gaetano Costa killed out of pique and that Stefano Bontate was not what he used to be."

Foreseeing the coming disaster, Buscetta left Palermo for Brazil, where only a few months later he learned of the deaths of Stefano Bontate and Salvatore Inzerillo and of the slaughter of the faithful members of their families. Antonio Salamone, another member of the Commission who traveled between Brazil and Palermo, kept Buscetta abreast of developments in Sicily. Salamone described the brilliant trick Totò Riina used to catch Salvatore Inzerillo off guard. "Before the death of Stefano Bontate, Riina cynically entrusted Salvatore Inzerillo with a 50-kilo shipment of heroin. After [Bontate's] death, when Antonio Salamone warned . . . Inzerillo to be careful . . . he replied that he had nothing to worry about until after he had repaid Riina for the shipment. Instead, Riina went ahead and killed him before the payment."

In fact, Inzerillo's family was so taken in by this stratagem that they were convinced that the heroin money was the reason for their boss's murder. His brother, Santo Inzerillo, showed up at a peace meeting with a suitcase full of cash to make good the money owed on the heroin shipment. Totò Riina and his men took the cash but then strangled Inzerillo and the friend with whom he had come. "This shows that there was no conflict over drug trafficking and that the real source of conflict was the fact that Stefano Bontate and Salvatore Inzerillo were the only two people in a position to stand in the way of the hegemonic designs of the Corleonesi," Buscetta told Falcone.

Salamone provided Buscetta with details of the betrayals-within-betrayals that made up the so-called mafia war of 1981. After the deaths of Bontate and Inzerillo, the new head of Bontate's family invited several members of the family to a meeting to discuss the future of the family. Smelling a rat, some members, including Salvatore Contorno and Emanuele D'Agostino, skipped the meeting and tried to dissuade their friends from going. The ones who showed up were never seen again.

D'Agostino decided at that point to seek refuge with his good friend Rosario Riccobono, the boss of Partanna-Mondello. "Riccobono then killed D'Agostino and disposed of his body, making an ample show of his loyalty to the Corleonesi," Buscetta said.

"Salamone, commenting on the episode, said that D'Agostino had been smart not to trust . . . [the new head of his family] but foolish to trust Rosario Riccobono. . . . Riccobono then did the same thing to D'Agostino's son, drawing him into a trap by telling him to bring some clean clothes to the place where his father was hiding."

Before being killed, Emanuele D'Agostino told Riccobono that his old boss Stefano Bontate had intended to kill Totò Riina. "At this point, the Corleonesi cried victory, since they now had a perfect motive, after the fact, to justify their killings," Buscetta said.

By betraying his friends and providing Totò Riina with the perfect excuse for killing his rivals, Rosario Riccobono thought he had insured his own future. But surprisingly, he made the same mistake in trusting Riina that Emanuele D'Agostino had made in trusting Riccobono himself. At the end of 1982, Riccobono and his men were invited to a congenial Christmas barbecue at the estate of Michele Greco. After dozing off in an armchair for his habitual postprandial nap, Riccobono was awakened by a group of killers with a cord in their hands. "Saru [nickname for Rosario], your story ends here," they told Riccobono before strangling him. Simultaneously, the Corleonesi hunted down about twenty of Riccobono's men, eliminating in one stroke his entire entourage.[18]

When Gaetano Badalamenti went to visit Buscetta in Brazil in late 1982, he filled him in on the next round of Palermo mafia killings. Totò Riina's killers had even stooped to killing the young son of Salvatore Inzerillo, a boy barely sixteen years old. His executioner was the infamous Pino "the Shoe" Greco, who, although nominally Michele Greco's underboss, had become Totò Riina's favorite killer. "In describing the particular ferocity of Greco, the Shoe, Badalamenti told me that before killing Inzerillo's young son, he cut off his right arm, saying that now he would not be able to use it to kill Totò Riina."[19]

Badalamenti tried to persuade Buscetta to return to Palermo to lead the mafia families who wanted to strike back at the Corleonesi but Buscetta told him it was a lost cause. Nonetheless, Totò Riina got word of the meeting in Brazil and soon after Badalamenti's visit Buscetta's relatives in Palermo began to disappear.

As he fingered the killers in the great mafia war and revealed the names of those who had ordered the assassination of Palermo's "excellent cadavers," Buscetta insisted that, while his information was often secondhand, it was as rock solid as if he had witnessed the events himself because "men of honor" had an absolute obligation to tell the truth to other men of honor when talking about mafia business. The revelations of Stefano Bontate, Salvatore Inzerillo, Gaetano Badalamenti and Antonio Salamone "have the value of absolute truth," Buscetta insisted. "I realize that I am expressing a concept that is hard for anyone who is not Sicilian or who is not a *mafioso* to grasp. . . . A man of honor . . . must always tell the truth. Whoever breaks this rule, since he has the right not to speak, is guilty of a serious violation that is punishable even with death."

While many might have laughed at the notion of an obligation to always tell the truth within an organization where killing, stealing and cheating are the order of the day, Falcone had the wisdom to listen to Buscetta carefully. Clearly the current generation of Cosa Nostra had made a mockery of its "code of honor." The elaborate laws regulating members' behavior were an important source of internal strength that gave the mafia enormous advantages over other forms of organized crime and helped it to survive for 120 years. Men of honor were extremely disciplined criminals, who generally avoided gratuitous violence, often went to extreme lengths to protect their own kind, and never cooperated with police—all of which had made them extremely difficult to prosecute. "[The mafia] expresses a subculture which is the criminal extreme of certain values that, by themselves, are not bad: courage, friendship, respect for tradition," Falcone said in a 1986 interview.[20] Falcone was convinced that until the government took the mafia as seriously as it took itself, efforts to combat it would be doomed to failure. And so, rather than limiting himself to a discussion of specific crimes and criminals, Falcone drew Buscetta out on the more apparently "folkloristic" elements of mafia life.

"No one will ever find any written codes of the mafia, but its laws are as rigid as iron and are universally accepted," Buscetta said. "Similarly, no one will ever find membership lists but the bond that ties men of honor is stronger and more impenetrable than if it were written in any document. . . . In my opinion, one of the principal mistakes that has been made in the war against the mafia has been to ignore this reality that every man of honor knows very well."[21]

While modern scholars of the mafia had dismissed the idea of initiation rites as Hollywood fantasy, Buscetta confirmed their existence, as have all subsequent mafia witnesses. Buscetta's description of his own initiation rite matched accounts dating from the nineteenth century.

> The neophyte is brought . . . together with at least three "men of honor" of the family and the oldest member present warns him that "this House" is meant to protect the weak against the abuse of the powerful; he then pricks the finger of the initiate and spills his blood onto a sacred image. The image is placed in the hand of the initiate and lit on fire. The neophyte must withstand the pain of the burning, passing the image from hand to hand, until the image has been consumed, while swearing to keep faith with the principles of "Cosa Nostra," solemnly swearing that "may my flesh burn like this saint if I fail to keep my oath." This, more or less, was the initiation rite when I entered Cosa Nostra. I don't know whether it is still maintained.

The members of the local family look for new recruits among the toughest, smartest and most aggressive kids in their neighborhood. Before inducting new affiliates, the family assigns them various criminal tasks, and studies their behavior over a period of years. Potential members must be Sicilian and must not have any relatives in law enforcement. Cosa Nostra also excludes anyone whose father has been killed by a man of honor. The reason, Buscetta explained, was, once again, the firm obligation to tell the truth: the new member would naturally want to know who had killed his father and the organization would be faced with the choice of lying to him or creating an internal conflict. Under the circumstances, it was better to exclude him entirely.

Members are instructed to honor other men's wives, not to steal from or lie to other men of honor. There are strict prohibitions against killing women and children, prostitution and taking drugs, drinking to excess and "immoral" sexual behavior.

Because of the secrecy of Cosa Nostra the conditions under which a man of honor can reveal his identity to another *mafioso* is a delicate problem. As Buscetta explained, the two would have to be introduced by a third man of honor who knew them both as members of the organization who would say "Lui e' la stessa cosa" (He is the same thing) or "E' come te e come me" (He is like you and like me).

If a man of honor needs to contact a member of another family he should ask his own boss, who would then arrange an introduction between the two men. "This is an effective system for guaranteeing the secrecy of the mafia families," Buscetta explained. "In fact, the relations between different families are kept to the essential minimum."

While men of honor are bound to tell the truth, they are generally men of few words. "In conversation with another man of honor, one does not ask direct questions because that is a sign of deplorable curiosity that can be taken the wrong way," Buscetta explained. "You limit yourself to listening to what the other person has to say. Within the mafia, no one will give you a blow-by-blow description of a crime; it is enough, and one should never ask more, that a person makes it clear, even through his silence, of being the author of a certain crime. . . . With us, a gesture, a look, a wink of the eye is enough to understand exactly what happened and to know, consequently, how to behave with law enforcement. . . . To give you a banal example, if two *mafiosi* are stopped in a car and there is a pistol in the glove compartment, an exchange of glances between the two will be enough so that one of them will know to say nothing about the gun and the other to take responsibility for its possession."

One of the reasons that the relationship between Falcone and Buscetta worked so well was that Falcone, as a Sicilian, understood this language of gestures and indirect messages. "We understood one another without having to speak," Buscetta said after Falcone's death. "He had intuition and intelligence, honesty and the desire to work."[22] With Buscetta there was also a subtext, a subtle, nonverbal dialogue that moved—that ran parallel to their conversation. "I have the impression that our relationship was conducted in a kind of code," Falcone said.[23]

This subtext began in their first meeting. At the end of the session, Buscetta had mentioned casually that he was out of cigarettes. Falcone then offered him the open pack from which he had been smoking. Buscetta accepted. During their next encounter, Buscetta made clear that the episode of the cigarettes had been a kind of test. "I accepted your cigarettes because the pack was already open," he said. "I never would have taken a carton or even a few unopened packs because it would have been an attempt to humiliate me."

"Some might see something pathological in this ceremonious exchange, in this extreme attention to detail," Falcone wrote several years later, reflecting on the episode. "But someone who lives in constant danger needs to understand the meaning of even the most apparently irrelevant clues and to interpret them through a constant effort at decodification."[24]

Falcone knew automatically when to back off and when to push forward with a line of inquiry, when to break the tension with a joke and when to treat things with absolute seriousness. Falcone and Buscetta developed a remarkable synchrony. "When I told him something, you could see a light go on," Buscetta said. "It was a real pleasure to listen to his analyses of things; he never asked a superfluous question, never anything dumb. He was the only one who understood."[25]

Buscetta did not have the same respect for some of Falcone's colleagues at the Procura della Repubblica who generally attended the sessions. At one point, when Buscetta was telling the story of a mafia killing, a magistrate interrupted him and asked: Is it true you used to eat oysters and drink champagne when you were an inmate at Ucciardone prison? "No," Buscetta answered rapidly, shooting him a dirty look, and then continued telling Falcone his story. A few hours later, Buscetta asked the prosecutor, "Why, when I was talking about something as serious as a murder, would you ask such a frivolous question?"[26]

From time to time, during the daily marathon sessions that took place during the summer of 1984, Vincenzo Geraci of the Procura would begin nodding off to sleep. Geraci's fatigue was comprehensible: he was having to keep up with Falcone's breakneck pace, putting in days of twelve, fourteen, sixteen hours during the infernal heat of July and August. But Buscetta regarded Geraci's occasional dozing as a sign of disrespect. "I don't like that magistrate," Buscetta told Falcone privately. "I don't trust him."[27]

At another point, in the middle of August, when virtually all of Italy was on vacation, Falcone and Buscetta were continuing their deposition in a sweltering attic room, above the Rome police station. The window was open and they could hear music coming up from the apartments of the police officers who lived on the floor below. Increasingly irritated by the racket, Falcone asked a police officer there to ask the men to turn down the music. But nothing happened. Then, suddenly, despite the unbearable heat, Buscetta went over and closed the window. When Falcone asked him why, he said: "This way, Judge, if the men continue making noise, you will have to intervene and have them punished. If I close the window, we won't hear them and you won't have to intervene." Reflecting on the incident years later, Falcone found this a typically mafia and Sicilian form of reasoning: Avoid direct confrontation whenever possible, particularly if you are not sure of the outcome.[28]

Falcone was impressed by the enormous internal discipline that Buscetta and some of his comrades displayed. Buscetta spent three years living in close quarters in prison with another *mafioso* he intensely disliked who had killed one of his and Stefano Bontate's closest friends. But not only did Buscetta avoid showing him any animosity, he occasionally invited him to dinner in his cell. Buscetta knew that the man's elimination had already been decreed and that, in the meanwhile, he, Buscetta, must avoid doing anything that would arouse his suspicion. And sure enough, the day the *mafioso* left prison he was murdered.[29]

While frequently demonstrating incredible cruelty, men of honor were also capable of great acts of personal loyalty. For example, when Totò Riina was applying pressure to track down Buscetta in Brazil, he had turned to Buscetta's friend Antonio Salamone, knowing that Buscetta could be trapped only by someone he trusted. But Salamone suddenly returned to Italy and turned himself in to police rather than hand Buscetta over to his enemies.

Contrary to popular imagination, the mafia did not kill for pleasure and its members were not (with some exceptions) bloodthirsty psychotics. Murder was a last resort when other means had been tried and exhausted. A businessman who refused to pay for his "protection" would first receive a phone call, then perhaps have his car burned, and only if an escalating spiral of intimidation proved unsuccessful would the organization turn to violence. Moreover, Cosa Nostra's choice of methods was strictly pragmatic. Its preferred method was strangulation, not because it was painful but because it was silent and left no evidence. But to strangle your victim, it was necessary to be able to lure him into a trap. When that was impossible, they would use guns. They resorted to bombs, as in the case of Rocco Chinnici, not in order to make a loud, public statement, but because Chinnici was well protected and an armed attack might not work. "Men of honor are neither devils nor madmen," Falcone said. "They would not kill their father or mother for a gram of cocaine. They are men like us. . . . We must recognize that they resemble us."[30]

The *mafiosi* with whom Falcone dealt were, like himself, taciturn men used to keeping their feelings well hidden. They were skeptical students of mankind, unusually watchful observers, with remarkable memories for detail. Ironically, the *mafioso* and the mafia prosecutor—while enemies—were like mirror opposites, moving in the same world, interpreting the same signs and living with the constant presence of death. "If Falcone had been on the other side, he would have been a great *mafioso*," said Leonardo Guarnotta, Falcone's friend and colleague in the Palermo anti-mafia pool. The more time he spent with Buscetta and other mafia witnesses, the more Falcone recognized certain reflections of himself.[31]

"Aware of the malice and cunning of my fellow human beings, I observe them, analyze them and try to avoid low blows," Falcone wrote in 1991. "The *mafioso* is animated by the same skepticism about the human race. The Catholic Church teaches us 'Remember death, for you, too, shall die.' The unwritten catechism of the mafia teaches something similar: the constant risk of death . . . has taught them to live in a state of perennial alert. We are often amazed by the incredible quantity of detail the people of Cosa Nostra are able to recall. But when you live in constant fear of the worst no detail is too small. . . . Nothing is left to chance. The certain presence of death, in a moment, a week, a year, pervades their sense of the precariousness of every instant of their lives. . . ."[32]

Knowing men of the mafia had a profound influence on Falcone. "I learned to recognize humanity in even the apparently worst people and to have a real respect, not only outward respect, for the opinions of others. . . . The categorical imperative of the *mafiosi* to 'tell the truth' became a cardinal principle of my own personal ethic, at least in the most important relationships of my life. Strange as it may seem, the mafia taught me a lesson in morality."[33]

Telling the truth about mafia business was not simply a matter of chivalrous honor, it was a practical necessity in a world in which crossing the wrong person was often a matter of life and death. Creating a sense of solidarity among men of honor helped them maintain a solid wall toward everyone else. Some degree of transparency within the organization was important to maintaining its opacity to the outside world. Cosa Nostra's rules have considerable psychological importance as well: because most men of honor are not violent psychopaths, they must feel justified in their actions in order to commit particularly grisly crimes. Thus the arcane rationalizations used by the Corleonesi to explain the need to kill this or that person were not invented only to deceive their adversaries but also to fortify their own men in the belief that they were upholding the laws of Cosa Nostra rather than violating them.

Part of Totò Riina's success in demolishing his rivals lay in his willingness to overturn the traditional rules of Cosa Nostra. By keeping his own membership secret, and lying about his actions, Riina kept everyone else off balance. He took advantage of the growing, lucrative traffic in narcotics to undermine the traditional "family" structure of Cosa Nostra. Because drug trafficking was not considered mafia business, men of honor were free to invest in drug deals together with members of other families. Riina cultivated members of rival clans and pitted them against their own bosses, so that when it came time to kill Stefano Bontate and Salvatore Inzerillo, he could do so easily, with information from people close to the two bosses. These men would then take over the family leadership, short-circuiting any possible retaliation from the old clan.

While this strategy was devastatingly effective, it came at a price. By making a travesty of its traditional family loyalties, Totò Riina and the Corleonesi undermined the culture of internal solidarity and *omertà* that had protected Cosa Nostra so successfully from the outside. The survivors of the losing clans were reduced to living like cornered animals, watching helplessly as friends and relatives were murdered, and waiting for their own assassins.

Buscetta himself had lost a dozen relatives and virtually all of his friends in Cosa Nostra. There was nothing left for him but to commit suicide or cooperate with Falcone. Thus, with some justification, Buscetta could say that it was not he but Totò Riina who had betrayed Cosa Nostra, killing off its code of honor.

EIGHT

Buscetta's confessions revolutionized mafia prosecutions on both sides of the Atlantic. Not only did he name hundreds of mafiosi operating in Sicily, the United States and South America, but he made it possible to understand Cosa Nostra as a whole and to connect countless crimes in an intelligible pattern. "Before him, I had—we had—only a superficial understanding of the mafia phenomenon," Falcone later wrote. "With him we began to see inside it. He confirmed for us numerous ideas about the structure, recruitment techniques, and the functions of Cosa Nostra. But above all he gave us a broad, wide-ranging, global vision of the phenomenon. He gave us an interpretative key, a language and a code. He was for us like a language professor who allowed us to go among the Turks without having to try to communicate with our hands."[1]

The Palermo anti-mafia pool now had the necessary elements to put the entire organization of Cosa Nostra on trial, from the members of the Commission at its head to the lowliest neighborhood enforcer. With the law that Pio La Torre had died for (the Rognoni–La Torre law), which made it illegal to belong to the mafia, the prosecutors had a legal framework for the case. Buscetta had given them a map of the structure and the decision-making process of the organization. But it would be wrong to say that the maxi-trial of Palermo was based primarily on Buscetta's confessions. More than anything else, he provided a means of organizing the overwhelming amount of raw data that the group had already gathered over a period of years. The "family" relationships he described were corroborated by tens of thousands of financial records that Falcone had been collecting since starting work on the Spatola case in 1980. They now understood how the expansion of the heroin trade—which they had documented painstakingly through wiretaps, photographs, fingerprint analysis, bank records, drug seizures, and the confessions of numerous witnesses from New York and Palermo to Bangkok—was integral to the rise of the Corleonese mafia and its allies. They understood how the great mafia war of the early 1980s had been carefully orchestrated and how the long string of "excellent cadavers"— from the shooting of chief prosecutor Judge Cesare Terranova in 1979 to the car bombing of Rocco Chinnici in 1983—fit into that strategy.

Even the growing axis between Palermo and Catania that General Dalla Chiesa had begun to investigate, and that Falcone suspected had led to the general's death, was confirmed by Buscetta. He happened to be with the former head of the Commission, Gaetano Badalamenti, on the evening of September 3, 1982, when Brazilian television broadcast the news of the general's assassination. "Badalamenti, commenting on the event, said that it was certainly an act of bravado by the Corleonesi who were responding to the challenge to the mafia represented by Dalla Chiesa," Buscetta told Falcone. "He added that the Catanesi were certainly used to do the job, because they were closest to the Corleonesi . . . and since new faces who would not be recognized were needed to carry out the assassination in the center of Palermo." Badalamenti, Buscetta said, even confirmed Falcone's hunch that the boss of Catania, Nitto Santapaola, had provided the manpower for the Dalla Chiesa killing. "[Badalamenti] pointed out that the Catanesi were repaying the favor the Palermitans had done them through the murder of Alfio Ferlito."[2]

While Falcone was spending much of his time in Rome with Buscetta, the rest of the anti-mafia pool was busy trying to verify his accusations, checking them against the statements of other witnesses. For the most part, they matched to a remarkable degree.

Vincenzo Marsala, the son of the boss of the town of Vicari, who had begun to cooperate after his father's assassination in 1983, gave a description of the organization and its rituals that was identical to Buscetta's—even though the men were separated by more than twenty years in age and one was from the city, the other from the countryside.

Even the forms for introducing two men of honor and the obligation of telling the truth had been discussed by Marsala a year earlier. "When a man of honor introduces another man of honor to a third, he uses the phrase 'Questo e' la stessa cosa.' 'He is the same thing.' My father told me that there is an obligation to tell the truth among other men of honor."[3]

Moreover, after Buscetta's confession, the prosecutors in Palermo received the transcript of an old wiretap that Canadian police had made in 1974. While Buscetta could be accused of tailoring his confessions to please investigators, this was a private conversation between a Sicilian man of honor (Carmelo Cuffaro) and a mafia boss in Montreal (Paul Violi) about important changes in the organization in Sicily ten years before Buscetta's return to Italy. Cuffaro referred to a new member as having been "regularly made" *(regolarmente fatto)* and having become "the same," *lo stesso,* or "the same thing" *(la stessa cosa).* He used the term "Cosa Nostra," talked about the election of family "representatives," *capi-mandamento* (district leaders), and even mentioned that Giuseppe Calderone, then the boss of Catania, had been elected to the Commission.

Violi, who had been based in Canada for many years, confirmed Buscetta's statement that the organizations in Sicily and North America were strictly separated. He wanted to make clear that a *mafioso* from Sicily could not arrive in Canada and expect to enter the North American branch of Cosa Nostra immediately, but that he must expect to undergo a period of observation lasting five years before he can be considered for membership. He also insisted that if Cuffaro should come to North America he must not discuss the affairs of the Sicilian mafia with American *mafiosi.*[4]

A t a certain point during their discussions, Buscetta asked Falcone how he could keep all these names and dates straight in his head. "Don't worry," Falcone told him. "If I don't understand something, Dr. Borsellino will figure it out." On a few occasions, Falcone brought Borsellino to Rome to interrogate Buscetta. "He used Borsellino as a 'reality check,' " according to Richard Martin, the assistant U.S. attorney who was working parallel to Falcone and Borsellino on the Pizza Connection case in New York. " 'Paolo, am I on the right track, or is this a lot of baloney?' Borsellino was the prosecutor's prosecutor." [5]

The new anti-mafia "pool" had established a highly successful division of labor. Leonardo Guarnotta took over most of the work on the financial aspects of Cosa Nostra, taking advantage of the new law on seizing mafia assets. Giuseppe Di Lello worked on dozens of homicides and countless minor crimes that tied the hundreds of defendants to the criminal enterprise of Cosa Nostra. Borsellino worked on the numerous "excellent cadavers" from Boris Giuliano and Captain Emanuele Basile to Dr. Paolo Giaccone, on the activities of the clan of Filippo Marchese and the "family" of Corso dei Mille as well as on the drug trafficking activity of boss Pietro Vernengo. The anti-mafia pool of the Procura della Repubblica had its members following each line of inquiry, double-checking the work of the investigating magistrates in order to make sure their evidence would stand up in court. [6]

They worked frenetically translating Buscetta's revelations into concrete results before word of his cooperation leaked to the public or to someone within Cosa Nostra. The pool prepared arrest warrants for hundreds of people Buscetta had identified, pulling up old case files and police records to gather supporting evidence for the arrests.

By the end of September, they were getting ready to move, preparing an enormous dragnet for October 4 at dawn. But on the morning of September 29, Giovanni Falcone got a tip that the Italian newsmagazine *Panorama* was about to break the story of Buscetta's collaboration in its next issue. Suddenly, the pool had to accelerate its plans, making the arrests during the weekend before the magazine hit the newsstands.

Everyone dropped everything to prepare for 366 arrests. Falcone, Borsellino, Leonardo Guarnotta and Antonino Caponetto worked straight through the day and night, flanked by a team of clerks, secretaries and even drivers who helped print and copy the warrants. In its frenzy, the group had forgotten about the fourth member of the pool, Giuseppe Di Lello, who had been busy interrogating a witness at Ucciardone prison that day. In the middle of the night someone realized that he would have to sign the warrants and so Falcone called his house and woke him. At about three in the morning, the 366 signed warrants were ready for police inspector Ninni Cassarà, who had massed forces from all over Sicily to begin the early morning raid.[7]

Despite the haste and fear of leaks, the operation succeeded almost perfectly. Most of the 366 defendants were captured. Newspapers from one end of Italy to the other declared the raid an unqualified triumph in huge banner headlines. While the predictions of the mafia's imminent demise were to prove premature, there was no denying the operation's historic importance. It was the biggest anti-mafia initiative in more than twenty years and arguably the most successful.[8]

Buscetta's revelations had an equally clarifying effect for the American prosecutors working on similar cases in the United States. Since 1980, Louis Freeh (current director of the FBI) and Richard Martin, both assistant U.S. attorneys in New York's Southern District, had been trying to unravel the dense network of heroin traffickers operating between Palermo and New York. They had managed to make considerable progress using standard police methods—wiretaps, drug seizures, fingerprints, undercover operations—but Buscetta was a fundamental interpretative key. Before Buscetta, the American prosecutors had charged their defendants with drug trafficking but did not have the evidence to charge them with belonging to the mafia. "He helped us understand much better the evidence we already had," said Richard Martin. "While we always knew the Cosa Nostra was behind our organization, we didn't put the racketeering charge into our indictment until after Buscetta's revelations, until we had a witness who could say, 'This guy is a mafia member, that guy is a mafia member, the traffic is controlled by the mafia.' He gave us the basis for the RICO [Racketeer-Influenced and Corrupt Organizations Act] charge."[9]

Buscetta helped the Americans understand the division of labor between the Sicilian and American mafia. The New York prosecutors were surprised to discover that most of the twenty-two defendants in their case were not members of the American mob at all but belonged to the Sicilian mafia. Many of them owned property and maintained residences in the United States. The nephews of Gaetano Badalamenti operated pizzerias—and distributed heroin—out of small midwestern towns that were hardly known as centers of Italian-American organized crime. The Sicilians dominated the heroin trade, while the American mobsters received a cut for allowing the Sicilians to operate on their territory. "We had thought they were part of the 'Sicilian faction' of the Bonnano family, but Buscetta said no, that's impossible, you're either a member of the Sicilian mafia or of the U.S. mafia but not both," Martin recalled.

While it had once been possible to move back and forth between the American and Sicilian branches of Cosa Nostra, by the 1960s the two organizations were distinct. "It is absolutely out of the question that a Sicilian man of honor could become a member of the American Cosa Nostra at this time," Buscetta said. "By now the cultural differences between the two organizations are too great for there to be any organic ties between them."[10] The Americans admitted non-Sicilians and even sometimes non-Italians into their mafia and indulged in activities like prostitution on which the Sicilians frowned. The Italian-American community had become largely absorbed into the middle class, the sons of mafia bosses, who graduated from college, were not prepared to do all the dirty work of mafia business. The Americans had chosen to opt out of the dangerous business of importing drugs, content to let the Sicilians take it over in exchange for a share of the profits. With unemployment among the young in Sicily reaching 30 percent, Sicilian Cosa Nostra had an almost inexhaustible reservoir of hungry, desperate men who were prepared to kill, risking death or jail, for only a few hundred dollars. In the 1950s and 1960s the American mafia ran a network for bringing illegal Sicilian aliens into the United States. Many of them were brought in to work as cheap labor in pizza parlors that were being opened around the United States. Some of these businesses, in turn, had the double purpose of providing a natural channel for the distribution of heroin in the United States. The system had numerous advantages. Combining legal and illegal business provided an excellent cover for criminal activity, and the considerable cash flow of the pizza business could serve as a means of laundering drug money. It also provided a lucrative market for other mafia-controlled businesses in Italy. Manufacturers of cheese, olive oil and tomatoes could also be useful export vehicles for smuggling drugs into the United States. John Gambino, for instance, cousin of slain Palermo boss Salvatore Inzerillo and the mastermind of Michele Sindona's fake kidnapping, was discovered to be the owner of some 240 pizzerias which generated an estimated $200 million in legitimate business a year.[11]

For a long time, American law enforcement failed to see the connections in this broad network. When an undercover agent pointed out that the heroin in Pennsylvania was identical to that found on a Sicilian defendant arrested in New York, his superiors dismissed the link, referring to the Sicilian "as just another meatball."[12]

But the tough young Sicilians began to throw their weight around. Joe Pistone, an FBI agent who managed to infiltrate the Bonnano crime family in New York during the late 1970s, began to hear the American *mafiosi* complain about the growing power of the Sicilians, referred to with a mixture of contempt and fear as the "zips."

In a memoir of his experiences, Pistone quoted one member of the Bonnano family:

He said the zips were Sicilians brought into the country to distribute heroin and carry out hits for Carmine "Lilo" Galante. . . . They were set up in pizza parlors, where they received and distributed heroin, laundered money, and waited for other assignments from Galante. . . . The zips, he said, were clannish and secretive. . . . They were, he said, the meanest killers in the business. . . .[13]

But in 1979, Carmine Galante, the head of the Bonnano family, was murdered with the aid of his own Sicilian bodyguards, Cesare Bonventre and Baldo Amato. Another Sicilian *mafioso*, Salvatore Catalano, took over the family's heroin operations.

Catalano had a criminal record in Italy stretching back twenty years, but he was an unknown quantity to American law enforcement. The American FBI and Drug Enforcement Agency began to watch Catalano and his group very closely. In the early 1980s, as they developed the Pizza Connection case, they conducted thousands of hours of wiretaps and had a hundred agents working two shifts daily for eighteen months just following and watching gang members.

Eventually, they realized that the men they were tracking were part of an entirely independent operation, working in cooperation with American Cosa Nostra. The reason was simple, but of fundamental importance. "As for drug trafficking, at least in the period I lived in the U.S., there was a strict ban within the American Cosa Nostra against getting involved with dealing," Buscetta said. "All those who are involved in drug trafficking in the U.S.—like Giuseppe Ganci, Gaetano Mazzara, Salvatore Catalano and Giuseppe Bono—are all men of honor of the Sicilian Cosa Nostra."[14]

They now understood what Gaetano Badalamenti, the former head of the Commission, was saying when he was wiretapped speaking to his nephews in the United States about some non-Sicilian business partners in the heroin trade. "They need us, they don't have an import license. We have the license."[15]

Investigators were able to get their hands on the photographs of the lavish wedding that one of their chief defendants, Giuseppe Bono, held at the Hotel Pierre in 1980. Bono had spent nearly $5,000 photographing the event and his five hundred guests, creating a kind of photo album of the international drug trade. But American prosecutors could not identify all of those in attendance. Guests had flown in from Italy, Great Britain and Canada but, according to Buscetta, most were members of Sicilian Cosa Nostra. The seating arrangements corresponded to the mafia affiliations of the guests, with members of specific families grouped together at the same table.[16]

Understanding the division of labor between the two organizations helped clarify the power struggle that was going on within American Cosa Nostra. "He explained to us why it was that Sal Catalano, Baldo Amato and Cesare Bonventre participated in the murder of Carmine Galante," Richard Martin said. "Galante had been running this organization and had not been sharing the profits with the Commission. . . . With Buscetta's testimony, we were able to look back at some of our own evidence and . . . understand what was going on." Now American investigators grasped the importance of a meeting they had observed a few years earlier between Paul Castellano and Catalano and Ganci. At the time, it had seemed puzzling that the most powerful mafia boss in the United States, Castellano, the head of American Cosa Nostra's Commission, would bother with obscure figures like Catalano and Ganci. Now it was clear. Having gotten rid of Galante, the Sicilians would now deal directly with Castellano, the head of the American Commission, who wanted to make sure that the American mafia got its fair share of the profits from the Sicilian Connection.[17]

With Buscetta, the already warm relations between American and Italian law enforcement had gotten even closer. Martin, who spoke fluent Italian, was on the phone almost daily with Falcone, and Ninni Cassarà, Palermo's chief police investigator, was busy helping American prosecutors interpret the Sicilian dialect they were taping on their wiretaps. The two countries worked out a special agreement for sharing and protecting Buscetta. Although he had been extradited to Italy, Buscetta would be admitted to the U.S. Witness Protection Program, since Italy had none. In exchange for allowing the Italians to question Buscetta first, Italy did not pursue the extradition of Gaetano Badalamenti, who had been arrested in Spain in April 1984, letting the Americans bring him to the United States as one of the lead defendants in the Pizza Connection case. On October 3 of that year, the Italian minister of the interior, Oscar Luigi Scalfaro, met in Washington with Attorney General William French Smith to toast the success of the Buscetta operation and sign the new international agreement marking a new era of cooperation and the sharing of witnesses and information.[18]

I f the confessions of Buscetta were important to prosecutors, their significance was perhaps even greater for the men living inside the world of Cosa Nostra itself. A great precedent had been set: a mafia boss had broken the rule of *omertà* and had lived to tell the tale. The anti-mafia pool of Palermo had proven that it could protect its witnesses and could keep their secrets so that not a word trickled out. It sent a powerful message to the hundreds of *mafiosi* in Italian prisons, wondering when and if they would ever get out and how long they would live if they did. One of these was Salvatore ("Totuccio") Contorno. He had narrowly escaped one assassination attempt, and the Corleonesi had hunted down and killed a score of his relatives. As the loyal bodyguard of Stefano Bontate, he was a man marked for death. He had secretly passed on information about his enemies to police investigator Ninni Cassarà, but during two years in prison had steadfastly refused to cooperate any further. Clearly, Contorno still nursed hopes of revenge: when he was captured in Rome, he had three bulletproof automobiles, a stash of arms and was stalking the secret Rome residence of Pippo Calò (the boss of Buscetta's mafia family), whom Contorno blamed for the murder of Stefano Bontate.

But in the wake of Buscetta's confession, Contorno decided to follow suit. Some investigators say that Contorno even met secretly with Buscetta, falling to his knees and kissing Buscetta's hand. "Totuccio, you can talk, now," Buscetta supposedly told him.[19] Whether or not this scene took place, there is no question that Buscetta was a decisive influence: Contorno agreed to talk on September 30, the day after the news of Buscetta's cooperation became public. The next day, October 1, 1984, Falcone was back in Rome to take Contorno's statement. "I intend to collaborate with the justice system telling everything I know about Cosa Nostra . . . because I realize that it is nothing but a band of cowards and murderers," Contorno said at the beginning of the meeting.[20]

Salvatore Contorno was very different from Buscetta. While Buscetta was among the most intelligent members of Cosa Nostra, Contorno was a man of action. Buscetta was thoughtful, well spoken and fluent in several foreign languages; Contorno spoke only pure Sicilian dialect. When he eventually testified in court, translators were needed for the attorneys from northern Italy. Even chief prosecutor Antonio Caponetto, himself from the Sicilian city of Caltanissetta, had a hard time understanding Contorno's heavy

Palermo accent. Police inspector Gianni De Gennaro once asked Contorno what percent he had revealed to prosecutors of everything he knew about the mafia. Twenty, forty, sixty, eighty percent? "Twenty," Contorno answered. At that point, Buscetta, who was in the room, turned to Contorno and asked him, "Totuccio, do you know what a percent is?" and Contorno said, "No." "That's Contorno," recalled Antonio Manganelli, the head of the Servizio Centrale Operativo, one of the Italian police's chief anti-mafia units. "He is a person with an intuitive, animal-like instinct, an ability to smell danger and incredibly quick reflexes—which explains how he survived," Manganelli added.[21] While virtually all of Bontate's loyal soldiers fell into traps laid by their own friends, Contorno always managed to avoid them. He had even survived an ambush by eight to ten heavily armed *mafiosi*. He had spotted a few too many familiar faces as he was driving along one day with his ten-year-old son. When he noticed in the rearview mirror a high-power motorcycle pulling up he knew he was in real trouble. As super-killer Pino "the Shoe" Greco opened fire with his infamous Kalashnikov assault rifle from the back of the bike, Contorno—timing his move perfectly—ducked into the passenger's seat to protect his son without losing control of the car as the windshield shattered on top of them. When the motorcycle turned around for another pass, Contorno managed to pull the boy from the car, get out his gun and take cover in front of the automobile. Although armed with only a .38 caliber pistol against a Kalashnikov, he managed to ward off the second attack, hitting Greco as he charged forward on the motorcycle firing his rifle. "I am certain I hit him in the chest because as he fell backward, the machine gun pointed upward, hitting the shutters and the wall on the second floor of the building behind me," Contorno told Falcone. "Seeing Greco fall, I realized it was time to escape and I made a run for it on foot. . . . Later, I learned that Greco was not wounded because he was wearing a bulletproof vest. In fact, my cousin, Nino Grado, told me he had seen him at the beach in a bathing suit showing no signs of having any wounds."[22]

Although Contorno did not have the historic knowledge and global vision of the mafia that Buscetta possessed, he had much more recent and specific knowledge of the Palermo mafia up to the time of his arrest in 1982, enabling police to issue some one hundred and twenty new arrest warrants. Contorno gave first accounts of many of the same events of the Palermo mafia war that Buscetta had heard secondhand from fellow bosses Antonio Salamone and Gaetano Badalamenti.[23]

Contorno was also able to provide information that was to prove instrumental in the Pizza Connection case in the United States. He had been present at a farmhouse in Bagheria (outside of Palermo) when a group of *mafiosi* from New York had come to test the quality of a heroin shipment. "I saw packages of cellophane containing white powder and I saw something boiling on the stove and smelled an intense acid odor. . . . [Emanuele] D'Agostino . . . explained to me that the merchandise was destined for several different buyers but was being shipped at one time. He told me that to distinguish the various shipments . . . the packages themselves were marked, either with pencil or with little cuts at the bottom of the package. . . . A few days later, there was news that police had seized a shipment of 40 kilos of heroin in Milan and D'Agostino told me that it was the same shipment."[24]

Although the Italians arrested in this bust had been convicted by Falcone in the Spatola case, U.S. prosecutors were not able to win their case against the American defendants. Contorno's testimony offered a potential breakthrough.

"Falcone then flew to Milan and got the seized heroin shipment out of storage and, sure enough, the cellophane packages were marked up just as Contorno had described," said Richard Martin.[25] This was the missing piece to the puzzle. By putting together American and Italian evidence, prosecutors could now document every crucial moment of the heroin trafficking circuit. An undercover agent had discussed the shipment with mafia bosses (Salvatore Inzerillo, Rosario and Joe Gambino) in New York, and had traveled with other defendants to take possession of the shipment in Milan, where the drugs had been seized. Now, they were able to trace the shipment all the way back to its refinery in Sicily, with the *mafiosi* from New York conferring with their Sicilian counterparts. Contorno was able to identify the "Americans" as Salvatore Catalano, Giuseppe Ganci and three other Pizza Connection defendants. In 1980, Italian police had photographed them meeting with Sicilian *mafiosi* but hadn't known who they were. The Americans' original case against the Gambino family had resulted in acquittals because they had lacked evidence of the Italian half of the deal. Now, armed with Contorno's confession and the telltale marks on the cellophane bags of heroin, they could revive the case as part of the larger Pizza Connection conspiracy.

NINE

In the wake of Buscetta's revelations in the fall of 1984, Ralph Jones, the U.S. consul general in Palermo, reflected on the possible political fallout from the blitz, sending off a top-secret memorandum to the embassy in Rome and the State Department in Washington.

> Magistrates in Palermo have issued 366 arrest warrants against *mafiosi* of every type . . . based in large part on the unprecedented confessions of the mafia boss Tommaso Buscetta. . . . The arrest warrants struck exclusively members of the military arm of the mafia. . . . No politicians were arrested. An indictment was issued against the former mayor of Palermo, Vito Ciancimino (Christian Democrat), who is the puppeteer who maneuvers various members of the city council. . . . The PCI (Partito Comunista Italiano) may try to play the "mafia card" against Foreign Minister Giulio Andreotti, whose faction, which has for some time tried to cover its left flank by cooperating with the PCI in the regional government, is considered by many the most closely tied to the mafia on the entire Sicilian political scene. . . .[1]

Although it was only a small first step, the indictment of Vito Ciancimino opened up the Pandora's box of mafia and politics.

Suspicions had surrounded Ciancimino for more than twenty years, but no one had ever taken action against him, or any of the other major politicians in "odor of mafia." He had been the commissioner of public works during the infamous Sack of Palermo, when Salvatore Lima had been mayor. The parliament's anti-mafia commission had dedicated some seventy pages to documenting his sinister rise from his father's barbershop in Corleone to the pinnacle of power in Palermo. Friendships with both government ministers in Rome and local *mafiosi* had proved a lucrative combination for Ciancimino, who had accumulated a suspiciously large fortune during his political career. Rumors of his mafia ties were so persistent and widespread that when he became mayor in 1970 it became a national scandal and he was forced to resign after only a few months. Ciancimino maintained a low profile, but his power inside municipal government remained notorious. He was said to control several city agencies, placing relatives, political cronies and mafia friends in key jobs. A nephew helped run the department that bought water from the private wells of Michele Greco, "the Pope," and other mafia chieftains. When municipal employees were arrested for serious crimes, their jobs would be waiting for them when they returned from prison.[2]

The indictment of Ciancimino immediately raised questions about other Palermo politicians, in particular about Salvatore Lima. Both men had started as acolytes of Amintore Fanfani, the most successful Christian Democratic politician of the late 1950s and early 1960s. They rarely appeared in public, made speeches or held political rallies, and yet, at election time, votes materialized for them and the candidates they sponsored as if by magic.

While both men exercised power behind the scenes, they had different styles and talents. Ciancimino was a crude man with blunt, rough manners that reflected his humble origins in Corleone. He enjoyed flexing his muscles, bragging that nothing got done at City Hall without his say-so. And he was not above using his sinister reputation to intimidate his adversaries.

Lima, by contrast, was a smoother and more polished character, who had succeeded (to some extent) in distancing himself from Palermo, becoming a member of the national parliament and then of the European parliament in Strasburg. With his tall, elegant bearing and his distinguished-looking silver hair, Lima moved among the most powerful men on the national and international scene. While Ciancimino understood only the simple quid pro quo of Palermo politics, Lima played on a much larger field, weaving alliances, balancing delicate interests, and building a potent political machine across Sicily. And he was able to leverage his power in Sicily to gain a role in national politics, first as part of the Fanfani "faction" and then in the Andreotti "faction" within the Christian Democratic Party.[3]

In the Balkanized world of Italian postwar politics, everything from the town council of impoverished villages to the formation of the national governments has been characterized by factionalism, coalitions and horse trading. Not only were there negotiations and alliances among the dozen principal parties, many of the individual parties themselves were divided up into factions, which fought among themselves over the division of power, money and patronage jobs. As the largest single party, the Christian Democrats had split into at least five or six different factions, which frequently warred among themselves to build up their own political fiefdoms. Power within the party (and therefore in the government) was determined by the number of party "membership cards" each faction controlled. In a modern version of Gogol's *Dead Souls,* many party membership cards were made out to dead or nonexistent people, who nonetheless helped determine the outcome of party congresses, where major decisions were taken, strategic alliances made and important resources and jobs divvied up. Salvatore Lima's faction controlled some 25 percent of the Christian Democratic membership in Sicily, according to Giorgio Galli, author of a history of the party.[4] When Lima decided to hitch his wagon to Andreotti's rising star, it was an important moment for both men's careers. Lima's electoral machine greatly increased Andreotti's muscle within the party, and the Sicilian politician, sensitive to matters of prestige, wanted to make sure his importance was acknowledged publicly. When he formally joined the Andreotti faction in 1964, he insisted on a public show of respect commensurate with his power. "If I come with Andreotti, I don't want to come by myself, but with my colonels, lieutenants, infantry and flags," Lima told Andreotti's right-hand man, Franco Evangelisti. "And when he appeared at Andreotti's office in parliament, he arrived at the head of an army," Evangelisti recalled in a 1992 interview.[5]

The move paid off for both men. Lima entered parliament in 1968 and Andreotti became prime minister in 1972 and remained the pivotal figure in the party for the next twenty years. Lima rose along with his mentor and was even named undersecretary of finance. Like Andreotti himself, Lima was skillful in brushing off accusations of mafia ties with witty and learned remarks: "Dante wrote: In church with saints and in the tavern with sinners," he told reporters once. "Man lives with the society he finds around him. Certainly, here in Sicily the risk of certain contacts is greater. People who do not live with the mafia risk nothing, he who has it at home runs that risk," he said.[6] But rumors of his mafia ties dogged him: Lima's name was mentioned 163 times in a multivolume report of the parliament's anti-mafia commission.[7] When his party made him an undersecretary of finance, an important economist resigned in protest. Lima could not aspire to the highest levels of public office, he would have to remain in a secondary role as an adviser, albeit an adviser to Andreotti, the most powerful man in the country.

Lima never forgot that the source of his power was Sicily and he remained intensely involved in island politics. Even after becoming a member of the European parliament in Strasburg, he spent much of his time keeping the peace among the various members of the Andreotti faction in Sicily, picking candidates for mayor and city council, mediating disputes, and organizing Andreotti's frequent campaign trips to Sicily. In the mid-1970s, he succeeded in bringing the troublesome Ciancimino under the Andreotti tent. Although he never became a member of the prime minister's inner circle, Ciancimino threw his support behind Andreotti at party congresses between 1976 and 1983. Ciancimino supposedly controlled only 3 percent of the Christian Democratic vote in Sicily but he continued to hold clout in Palermo, where he could count on 17 percent of the party membership. "In the early 1960s, before Lima, the Andreotti faction accounted for less than 10 percent of the DC's membership, but in the late 1970s it rose as high as 15 percent," Galli said.[8]

In the early 1980s Andreotti men occupied the most important posts in Sicily: Mario D'Acquisto was president of the Sicilian Region. And Nello Martellucci, handpicked by Lima, was mayor of Palermo. But the assassination of General Dalla Chiesa in 1982 shook things up. Both D'Acquisto and Martellucci, accused of failing to support the general, were forced to resign. Pressure was growing to "reform" the party in Sicily and banish the mafia specter that always haunted it. In 1983, Ciancimino formally withdrew from the party, but Ciancimino's banishment proved more apparent than real. Members of Ciancimino's local faction continued running for office and occupied key positions. His men controlled four of the sixteen principal city agencies and many seats on the city council. The Christian Democrats had a slim majority on the city council, forty-one of the eighty seats, and Ciancimino could blackmail the majority by threatening to withdraw his votes at any moment.[9]

In April 1983, Salvatore Lima suggested that a woman medical doctor named Elda Pucci become mayor, giving a new, clean face to the Palermo Christian Democrats. But when Pucci tried to exercise real power by opening up the big city contracts for the maintenance of the streets, sewers and public lighting to public bidding, she suddenly found herself undermined by forces within her own party.[10]

The disgrace of Palermo's city contracts had become so obvious that it could no longer be ignored. Quite literally, the system was leaking before everyone's eyes. About 40 percent of the city's water supply was (and is) lost through holes in the old, rusted pipes and water was generally available only every other day. The city of Milan, by contrast, lost only 6 percent of its water, and the national average was 15 percent. When the water did arrive, its metallic content made it unsafe for drinking. For these substandard services, Palermo paid three or four times more than other major Italian cities. It paid nearly three times more for lighting than the city of Turin, even though Turin had almost three times as many streetlights and Palermo's dimly lit streets were dangerous to walk at night. Rome—hardly a model of northern European efficiency—spent 32 billion lire (about $40 million) a year maintaining its streets and sewers; Palermo spent 59 billion lire (about $70 million) even though it was about a quarter of the size.[11] Like the city's leaky pipes, Palermo was losing tens of millions of dollars a year in public contracts, siphoned off through no-show jobs, kickbacks, corruption and inefficiency. Count Arturo Cassina had controlled the street and sewer contracts for thirty years, and since he owed his monopoly to politicians and *mafiosi* rather than to open competition, he had little incentive to improve services.

When Mayor Pucci's proposal was shot down on the city council, she resigned, leaving Salvatore Lima and the Christian Democrats to look for a new mayor. In 1984, they turned to a party insider, Giuseppe Insalaco, who appeared to be a far more malleable choice. Insalaco had grown up within the Palermo city machine and his name was not free from the odor of corruption and mafia ties. But Insalaco was to prove a major surprise (and disappointment) to those who had chosen him. Years of bending to the will of the local potentates had caused Insalaco to accumulate a deep well of silent, pent-up resentment against his political masters, which flooded as soon as he became mayor. One of his first acts in office was to plaster the city with anti-mafia posters commemorating the assassination of Pio La Torre, the Communist leader murdered in April 1982. "Now, they'll see who Giuseppe Insalaco *really* is," he told a young council member, Leoluca Orlando, shortly after his selection as mayor.[12] But Insalaco's rebellion ran aground, just as Pucci's had, when he tried to press forward with the reform of the city contracts. He began to receive anonymous letters, threatening phone calls, and when he spoke again with Orlando after a couple of months in office, his tone had changed. "I'm afraid, I'm afraid," he said privately. "I've never seen a man age so much in a few months," ex-mayor Elda Pucci said in an interview that year. "I think in the end he was afraid of meeting a bad end. . . . And the fact that his government fell on the question of the city contracts is a confirmation that in Palermo it's impossible to remain in power without the consensus of certain 'power groups' outside the institutions." When Pucci was asked if she was referring to the mafia, she said: "I'll leave you to draw that conclusion," availing herself of the discretion that is common among Sicilian politicians.[13]

With government after government falling, the Christian Democrats tried another reformer: Leoluca Orlando, protégé of Piersanti Mattarella, the president of the Sicilian Region who had been assassinated in 1980 after he had tried to clean up local contracts. But Orlando's government fell even before he took office. He had demanded a secret vote to make sure that he enjoyed the genuine support of his own party and, sure enough, he failed to win a majority, sabotaged by the anti-reform forces. "Who does he think he is?" Ciancimino reportedly said of Orlando. "Does he think he can be mayor of Palermo without even giving me a phone call?" The party then turned again to Nello Martellucci, the Andreotti man who had resigned as mayor after Dalla Chiesa's assassination in 1982. In the fall of 1984 Palermo was back where it had started.[14]

It was in this atmosphere of local political crisis that the Ciancimino indictment came down in October 1984. Buscetta had said clearly what many had long suspected but generally only whispered behind closed doors: "Ciancimino is in the hands of Totò Riina." When Buscetta left prison in 1980, his boss, Pippo Calò, had urged him to remain in Palermo, saying with Ciancimino's help they would make a lot of money from the restoration of the old center of the city. On top of this, the prosecutors had seized some 10 billion lire (about $12 million) in assets they believed Ciancimino had come by dishonestly.[15]

In the wake of the Ciancimino indictment, two recent mayors of Palermo, Pucci and Insalaco, and the current mayor, Martellucci, were called before the anti-mafia commission in Rome to testify about Ciancimino and mafia infiltration of the city administration. Insalaco referred to Ciancimino as "the Lord of the contracts," while Pucci described him as "the most disturbing and polluting element of Palermo life." Martellucci was more evasive. He performed a complex verbal tap dance, denying the influence of the mafia in city life, while, at the same time, acknowledging the need for reform. When pressed to be specific, he said: "*Mafiosi* exist but I haven't seen them." Martellucci may not have seen the *mafiosi,* but they evidently had seen him. Someone detonated a bomb at his Palermo villa as a warning. The same thing had happened to Mayor Pucci. And a few days after their testimony in Rome, someone set fire to Mayor Insalaco's car in Palermo.[16]

In press interviews, the former mayors were even more explicit about the political situation in Palermo. "Certainly, the mafia exists . . . you breathe it, you feel it," Insalaco said. "It has given precise messages; it has killed a whole series of politicians and magistrates. . . . It has great influence and has determined important government decisions."[17]

"When I accepted the job, I didn't know I was being used," Pucci said. "For Lima and Ciancimino I was supposed to last a few months and go home. I was supposed to save the face of the DC [Democrazia Cristiana] after the polemics over the death of Dalla Chiesa. I knew I would fall as soon as I addressed the problem of the government contracts. . . .

"The [Christian Democratic] party no longer exists . . . the only party members are phantoms in the hands of the same old men, who, in order to preserve their own power, have destroyed the party. It is an internecine war of all against all. . . . The parties have turned into reservoirs of votes. And then there is the responsibility of Rome, which has always shown little interest in the problems of the South in general and of Sicily in particular. . . . After all, for years the state has delegated even the business of collecting taxes to private citizens, to the Salvo family as in the era of the Bourbon kings. . . . Democracy does not exist in Sicily."[18]

Asked about the mafia, Pucci made reference to something called "the third level," a level of politicians close to the mafia above the military arm of Cosa Nostra. The concept was a misappropriation of a term Giovanni Falcone had invented in an essay he had written with the Milanese prosecutor Giuliano Turone in 1982. Falcone and Turone had said that there were three levels of mafia crimes: the first level was made up of ordinary mafia business: extortion, smuggling, drug trafficking; the second level consisted of the killings committed within the mafia or among those who do business with it. The "third level" of crimes were killings with larger, political ramifications, decided at the very highest levels of Cosa Nostra: the assassination of important government officials. Falcone and Turone had said nothing about a cabal of politicians who pulled the strings of the mafia but many Italians began to use the term this way.

"As long as the state of Sicily does not perform its own role, the 'third level' will continue to run the political class," Pucci said. "The 'third level' is that which gives a single family the control of Sicilian agriculture. I will even say it openly: I don't know if the Salvos are *mafiosi*. But I know they enjoy great political protection."

As the American consul general in Palermo had predicted, with the Buscetta arrests a lot of dirt was coming out from under the carpet. The fact that Buscetta had mentioned only one politician in his confessions created pressure to intensify that element of the investigation. "The only thing that doesn't convince us about Tommaso Buscetta's extremely important confessions is his total silence about who pulls the strings of mafia power, about the 'third level' of the mafia," declared the head of the Communist Party in Sicily, Luigi Colajanni, to the Rome newspaper *La Repubblica*. "How is it possible that a boss of his caliber knows nothing about who is behind the Corleonesi and the Grecos?"[19] The consul general had guessed correctly: the Communist Party had begun, as he put it, "to play the mafia card."

The revelations in Palermo coincided with a series of equally embarrassing developments elsewhere. Michele Sindona had just been extradited from the United States to Italy and was about to go on trial for murder. A parliamentary commission released a report concluding that the Italian secret services had a whole "parallel service," composed exclusively of members of Licio Gelli's secret P2 Masonic Lodge. Only a few days after the 366 arrest warrants in Palermo, the parliament in Rome was scheduled to vote on whether the government should demand the resignation of Foreign Minister Giulio Andreotti, because of his handling of the Sindona affair.

Andreotti's salvation came from a somewhat unexpected direction: the Communists. When the issue came before the Chamber of Deputies, the Communist delegation abstained from the vote.[20] While the PCI (Partito Comunista Italiano) thundered publicly against Andreotti and the mafia's political power in Sicily, the underlying reality was not quite so simple. After all, Andreotti was one of the protagonists of the "historic compromise," the rapprochement between the Communists and the Christian Democrats. The Communists had been Andreotti's silent partners in the so-called governments of national solidarity that ruled between 1978 and 1980. Even afterward, Andreotti remained the PCI's principal interlocutor within the government.

Although this mixing of Left and Right seems paradoxical, it is typical of Italian history. From the unification of Italy in 1870, Italian conservatives have excelled in what the Italians call *trasformismo* (transformism), the ability to co-opt political opposition and "transform" it into a government force. "We must change everything—in order that nothing change," declared the aristocratic hero in the great Sicilian novel *The Leopard,* distilling the essence of *trasformismo.*[21] The Christian Democrats were masters of this political art. When they first came to power after World War II, Italy was in pieces and on the brink of renewed civil war: Fascists and Communists kept their guns well oiled beneath their beds should they be needed; the Christian Democrats moved ably between the two extremes, as occasion demanded, without ever losing their balance. Governments came and went, falling at the rate of more than one a year, but the Christian Democrats remained firmly in control. It is a testament to their supreme political skill that with less than 40 percent of the vote, they managed to dominate every government for almost fifty years. They added or dropped coalition allies as circumstances dictated, often playing one force off against another. Even the appearance of dangerous instability had its use: a nervous electorate, fearful of plunging the nation into chaos, ensured that the Christian Democrats remained Italy's first party. But the anarchy was superficial: in the musical chairs of Italian politics, the same group of party leaders traded ministries, moving in and out of government for more than fifty years. Amintore Fanfani was prime minister for the first time in 1954 and for the sixth time in 1987. But the symbol of the Christian Democrats' permanent government was Andreotti: he had played an important role in Italy's first postwar government in 1946 and had remained at the center of power ever since, occupying virtually every important government post.

The Christian Democrats' success depended on their ability to remain acutely sensitive to change and to listen carefully to the rumblings of public opinion. In the 1960s, the Christian Democrats invited the Socialist Party to join the government. The move worried the United States, but it proved a political masterstroke, dividing the Italian Left, and strengthening the DC. These center-left governments acceded to many of the Socialists' demands, and built the foundations of Italy's modern welfare state. Rather than being threatened by these changes, the Christian Democrats understood that they could turn them to their own advantage. The new array of government services—state-run factories, public works projects, national health care, welfare, unemployment and disability benefits—could all be used by the patronage system. The greatly expanded public sector created hundreds of thousands of jobs for party followers and billions of dollars to distribute to friendly businessmen, a portion of which could be "kicked back" to finance the party itself. After a decade of center-left government, the DC was still firmly in power and the Socialists—tarnished by their close association with the government—were in pieces. No longer a credible alternative to the DC, the Socialists' share of the vote had dropped to a mere 9 percent nationally by the mid-1970s.[22]

With the historic compromise, the Christian Democrats did to the Communists in the 1970s what they had done to the Socialists in the 1960s. The Christian Democrats were able to govern without their usual allies (the socialist, republican, social-democratic and liberal parties) because the Communists agreed to abstain from all confidence votes that might cause the government to fall. The Communists did not obtain a single government ministry for their support. But they hoped to gain political respectability with Italy's jittery middle class and wielded considerable indirect influence on government policy. In order to keep their silent partner happy, the Christian Democrats further expanded the welfare state. The government made it virtually impossible to fire anyone in Italy, increased the wages of state employees, kept open or expanded failing state industries, sponsored more public works projects and made Italian pensions the most generous in Europe. In 1970, state spending accounted for only 30 percent of the gross national product; by the late 1980s it had swollen to 52 percent. To help pay for its spending spree, the Italian treasury kept printing more money, sending inflation up to nearly 20 percent.[23]

By removing their opposition, the Communists legitimized the Christian Democratic patronage state. Rather than eliminating the traditional "division of the spoils" system, they were happy to settle for a relatively small piece of the pie. The Communists got their own public television network, just as the Socialists had before them. Now Communists would sit next to Christian Democrats and Socialists on the board of directors of public banks or state-owned companies. While the other parties gave contracts to friendly businessmen who would pay them bribes, the Communists (at least in some instances) tried to make sure that a certain number of government contracts went to Communist "cooperatives," worker-managed businesses sponsored by the party. Eager to show they were "responsible" enough to be trusted with power, the Communists decided to work within the system rather than denounce it.

But the strategy backfired. Voters who wanted to change the system, not expand it, punished the Communists at the polls. In 1976, when the "historic compromise" was born, the Communists had been breathing down the Christian Democrats' necks with 35 percent of the vote; by 1980, they had slipped below 30 percent. As a result, they withdrew their support from the government and returned to the wilderness of the opposition. Meanwhile, the Christian Democrats had actually increased to 38 percent.[24]

When asked by an impertinent critic whether the many years in power had "worn out" the DC, Giulio Andreotti cleverly replied: "Power wears out those who don't have it."[25]

G iovanni Falcone knew that Tommaso Buscetta had not told the whole truth about a number of things. Given his legal position, this was almost inevitable. Not only were Italian prosecutors unable to offer reduced sentences in exchange for cooperation, they were required to prosecute witnesses for any crimes they admitted to. Unless Buscetta wanted to spend the rest of his life in Italian prisons, he had to be careful about what he said. It is not surprising, therefore, that he denied most of the charges that had been leveled against him during the previous thirty years. He told prosecutors he had never killed anyone. Once he was safely hidden in the United States, however, he admitted to his Italian biographer that he had participated in several mafia killings during his early years in Cosa Nostra. He acknowledged having smuggled tobacco (a crime for which he had already served time) but denied having been a cocaine or heroin trafficker.[26]

Buscetta insisted that his status within Cosa Nostra was largely due to what he called his *ascendente,* his personal charisma, and the wisdom and good judgment accumulated over decades of experience on three continents.

Unfortunately, my strong and proud personality has created around me the legend of an international drug trafficker and of a ruthless and violent mafia boss, which does not correspond to reality. What is most incredible is that this myth, along with influencing the press, has influenced the criminal world as well, so that inside prison I was regarded with a mixture of fear and respect. My own reserved manner was mistaken in that world for mafia power derived from crimes that I had, in fact, never committed. It was perfectly useless for me . . . to try to convince people that I was not the monster that many imagined . . . when I protested my innocence, people would simply laugh.[27]

This explanation was not as fanciful as it might seem. Within the world of Cosa Nostra, the perception of power is power, which is why *mafiosi* are obsessed with the problems of "reputation" and "prestige." In Buscetta's case, it was hard to judge the source of his unquestionable prestige within Cosa Nostra.

On the one hand, Buscetta seemed to have all the trappings of a major boss when he was arrested in Brazil. His family operated a massive 65,000-acre ranch in the Brazilian countryside and he had luxury apartments in both Rio de Janeiro and São Paolo. His apartment in Rio was in the same building as that of Antonio Bardellino, a gangster, who by Buscetta's own admission was a member of a special group of Neapolitan *mafiosi* admitted to the Sicilian Cosa Nostra to direct the traffic in tobacco and heroin. But Buscetta insisted that his proximity to Bardellino was simply coincidence. His ranch, he said, belonged to his father-in-law and cost practically nothing: the Brazilian government was giving away vast tracts of land in the Amazon valley to encourage development of the area.[28]

"We didn't find evidence that Buscetta—at least in the period before his arrest—was trafficking in drugs," said Gianni De Gennaro, the police official who worked most closely with him. "A big drug trafficker doesn't have problems paying his lawyer, and we found evidence that Buscetta's wife was pawning her jewels to pay his lawyer. Ko Bak Kin—the big drug trafficker from Thailand—never had problems like this—always the best lawyers, always well paid."[29]

Since Buscetta was in prison between 1973 and 1980, it is entirely possible that he had not reestablished himself in the drug trade in the relatively brief span before being rearrested in 1983. It is unlikely, however, that Buscetta's standing in the mafia rested entirely on his charisma and sound judgment.

Buscetta also tended to downplay the criminal roles of his close friends, like Stefano Bontate, while the Palermo prosecutors had ample evidence to the contrary. Similarly, Falcone knew that Buscetta was not telling everything he knew about the relationship between mafia and politics. The few references he made to politics were vague but highly suggestive. There was, for example, his enigmatic account of his conversation with Gaetano Badalamenti on the assassination of General Dalla Chiesa. Badalamenti had said that "some politician had used the mafia to get rid of the troublesome presence of the general." Buscetta had also said that the boss of his own family, Pippo Calò, "was certainly mixed up in the death of the banker [Roberto] Calvi." (When Calvi's body was found hanging from Blackfriars Bridge in London, many suspected murder. Later witnesses have testified that Calvi served as a major money launderer for the Corleonesi faction of Cosa Nostra, as Michele Sindona had performed this role for the old mafia families such as Bontate and Inzerillo.)[30]

Buscetta refused, however, to elaborate on these relationships. He repeatedly denied, for example, knowing the Salvo cousins, even though wiretapped phone conversations clearly showed that Nino Salvo wanted to smuggle Buscetta into Italy during the great mafia war. He also denied—against all evidence—that he had been in Italy in 1970 together with several major mafia bosses attending what had all the appearances of being a Cosa Nostra summit. Privately, Buscetta let Falcone know that there was much he couldn't tell him yet. The Italian state—or rather a few isolated representatives of the state—had just begun to combat the mafia. He wanted to see how far the government was prepared to go before entrusting it with his darkest secrets.

Buscetta seemed to take heart from the successful handling of Salvatore Contorno's confessions. On October 25, 1984, Saint Crispin's feast day, Italian police issued 127 arrest warrants based on Contorno's testimony, the second major blow to the mafia in less than a month. Then on November 3, the prosecutors ordered the arrest of Vito Ciancimino. Until then he had only been under indictment.[31]

When Falcone and Paolo Borsellino went back to Rome a week later, Buscetta began to open up a little more. "Although I continue to have my doubts about the real will of the state to combat the mafia, I have decided to reveal a part of what I know, while reserving the rest for a later time," Buscetta said at the beginning of the session of November 10, 1984.

> The cousins Ignazio and Nino Salvo are "men of honor" of the family of Salemi and were presented to me as such by Stefano Bontate, when I came to Palermo in 1980. The friendship between Bontate and the Salvos was very close and, as I observed, they saw one another frequently. . . . The Salvos' role inside Cosa Nostra is modest but their political importance is enormous. They have direct relationships with well-known members of parliament, some of them from Palermo, whose names I would prefer not to reveal. . . . I also met with Nino Salvo in Rome. Salvo had to come to Rome for questioning by a prosecutor and since I was in Rome at the time, staying with Pippo Calò, I met with him and with a member of parliament whom I hadn't seen in a number of years. The meeting took place in the lobby of a hotel during the summer of 1980, perhaps in September. . . .[32]

To back up his claims, Buscetta revealed that he and his current wife, children and father-in-law had spent the entire Christmas and New Year holidays as the guests of the Salvos in Palermo—confirmed by travel records showing that the Salvos had rented a private plane for the Buscetta family holiday. They were given one of the Salvos' villas on a property near the enormous Zagarella Hotel complex. Buscetta was able to describe the layout of the property and of the house they stayed in, leaving little doubt that he had actually been there. "Both Nino and Ignazio Salvo came to see me in the villa . . . and New Year's Eve dinner was brought to us from the Zagarella Hotel, by an employee of Nino Salvo, custodian of the villa, who lived in a little house nearby."

Buscetta's revelations about the Salvos helped shed important light on how the mafia indirectly controlled Palermo's city contracts. "Through the mediation of the Salvos, [Mayor Nello] Martellucci agreed to let Ciancimino handle the restoration of the historic center of Palermo, Stefano Bontate told me. When, subsequently, a bomb was detonated in Martellucci's villa, Bontate was particularly upset, because he didn't understand what more Ciancimino and the Corleonesi could possibly want after this previous agreement." Buscetta said he did not think that Bontate knew Mayor Martellucci personally and that all direct contacts were handled by the Salvo cousins.

On November 12, 1984, Falcone ordered the arrest of Nino and Ignazio Salvo, the heads of perhaps the richest and most powerful family of Sicily, and the men suspected of being Cosa Nostra's ambassadors in the halls of power.

T he defection of two major figures, Buscetta and Contorno, were not blows that the mafia could allow to go unanswered. After a lull in violence of several months, in early October 1984 the mafia killed representatives of the Badalamenti and Mineo clans, "losing" families associated with Buscetta and his friends. And then in a gruesome show of force, eight men were found murdered on October 18, in a horse stable in Palermo's Piazza Scaffa. The largest group killing in Palermo history, it was instantly compared to the famous Saint Valentine's Day massacre in the Chicago of Al Capone. The motive was not clear: investigators suspected it was related either to the lucrative world of clandestine horse racing or to the active black market in butchering and selling the meat of stolen horses. But Falcone and Borsellino suspected that a killing of these dimensions at such a delicate moment must have been sanctioned by the Commission and must have had a larger purpose than merely punishing an infraction of mafia rules.

Paolo Borsellino was assigned the Piazza Scaffa massacre case. The killing had occurred in the squalid slums of Corso dei Mille, territory of the bloodthirsty boss Filippo Marchese, whom Borsellino had been investigating for years. He went to the fetid stable, where stalls were strewn with the brains of some of the victims who had been shot in the head at close range with shotguns. The sound of repeated shotgun blasts must have been heard because news of the massacre had been circulating for hours before police were alerted the next morning. In fact, when officers arrived, they found the father of one of the victims already on the scene, trying to cart off his son's badly mutilated corpse. Clearly, *omertà* was still powerful in Palermo. Rather than reporting his son's murder to the police, the father was trying to remove evidence of the crime.[33]

Two weeks later, the mafia struck again. Leonardo Vitale, who had been released recently from the insane asylum where he had been sent after becoming the first modern mafia witness, was shot and killed after attending Sunday Mass with his mother.[34] The mafia could not strike at Buscetta and Contorno, but it could send a clear message. It had been eleven years since Vitale had first walked into the Palermo police station offering to reveal what he knew of the mafia. The Italian state had long forgotten about Vitale but the mafia had waited patiently, showing that its death sentences can be postponed but not commuted.

Despite Vitale's pathetic death, Falcone and Borsellino's investigations did not seem to miss a beat. Only four days after Vitale's murder, Vincenzo Marsala, an underused mafia witness who had not been questioned by prosecutors in over a year, started talking again. Previously, Marsala had only talked—or been asked—about the mafia of his rural town of Vicari and about the death of his father, a local boss. As it turned out, Marsala had quite a lot to say about mafia and politics. A member of the Vicari mafia family (Aurelio Ocelli) "used to brag about his friendship with Vito Ciancimino and Salvo Lima, for whom he collected votes," Marsala testified. "He would gather votes in Vicari and the neighboring towns. It was well known that Ocelli was friends with Vito Ciancimino and it was because of these friendships that he was admitted to the mafia."[35]

In a later session, Marsala explained that Cosa Nostra had rules as specific for political behavior as it had for other areas of mafia life:

> When it comes to national and local elections in Sicily, the mafia follows precise rules. . . . From the time I began to speak of these things with my father, the only party we supported were the Christian Democrats, because its representatives were those who gave the greatest protection to the mafia. I remember that Peppe Marsala [the *capo-mandamento* of Vicari] always supported Salvo Lima and I know from having learned it from my father, that the whole organization supported other men of the

DC, such as [Mario] D'Acquisto, [Vincenzo] Carollo, Fasino. The fundamental rule was that it was allowed to campaign publicly only for the Christian Democrats . . . although you could privately support candidates of other parties to thank them for favors they had performed, but on a purely personal basis, not through open campaigning. . . . It was strictly forbidden to vote for or support either the Communists or the Fascists.

Marsala said he had even driven his father to the house of Mario D'Acquisto, the president of the Sicilian Region and a prominent member of the Andreotti faction in Sicily. His father had had his driver's license revoked—a common measure taken against suspected *mafiosi*—and turned to D'Acquisto to have it reinstated. "I believe my father got his license back, although, at a later time, the police took it away again."

At the same time that Marsala was talking about Salvatore Lima and Mario D'Acquisto, Buscetta indicated to Judge Falcone that he was prepared to take another step forward. He asked, however, that Falcone bring Antonino Caponetto, the head of the investigative office, to hear what he had to say and that Vincenzo Geraci, the assistant prosecutor for the Procura della Repubblica, not be present.

When Caponetto and Falcone visited Buscetta in his Rome hideaway, the *mafioso* prepared them coffee. "Now I know why you're called 'Caponetto,' " Buscetta said, jokingly. (Caponetto literally means "clean head" in Italian.) It was a double pun, playing both on the fact that Caponetto was bald and that the "head" of the investigative office was "clean" of any suspicion of corruption.[36]

When they had finished their coffee, Buscetta launched into an incredible story about a failed right-wing coup d'état. In 1970, at the height of the left-wing protest movement, an Italian general and member of the nobility, Prince Junio Valerio Borghese, had organized a neo-fascist plot. The basic outlines of the story were well known. The so-called Borghese coup had always seemed like a comic opera: Borghese tried to use a group of "forest rangers" to take over the government and it had failed miserably. But Buscetta added a curious chapter to the tale. Prince Borghese had tried (and ultimately failed) to recruit the mafia for his plot. Not long before the failed coup, Buscetta and Salvatore Greco (Cichiteddu, "Little Bird")—the head of the Commission in the 1960s—were stopped by Italian police at a routine police roadblock while traveling under false passports. They were with Giuseppe Calderone, the head of the Catania mafia, and Giuseppe Di Cristina, the boss of Riesi. Buscetta had always denied that he was indeed the man detained by Milan police for carrying the false Canadian passport made out to Adalberto Barbieri. Now, suddenly, he reversed course.

> About twenty days before being stopped in Milan, I got a telephone call in New York from Salvatore Greco ("Cichiteddu"), who was living then in Peru, under the name of Renato Caruso Martinez. He told me we needed to go to Italy right away for something very important, which, obviously, he didn't explain over the phone. We made an appointment to meet in Zurich, and I accepted the invitation, even though I was a fugitive in Italy at the time, because of the importance of the person who had asked me. . . .
>
> We went right away to Catania, where we stayed in the house of Giuseppe Calderone. . . . We met with Calderone and Giuseppe Di Cristina and learned that Prince Junio Valerio Borghese was organizing an anti-Communist coup d'état. . . . Prince Borghese wanted Cosa Nostra to supply armed support in Sicily to put down any eventual resistance. . . . The coup was clearly of fascist origin, which worried both Salvatore Greco and me; but both Calderone and Di Cristina were enthusiastic. Moreover, certain sectors of the government parties and other institutions were prepared to lend their support.[37]

The approach, Buscetta said, had been made through Sicilian Freemasons with close ties to the mafia. In exchange for Cosa Nostra's support, Borghese was prepared to offer an amnesty for its members still in prison. Calderone and Di Cristina then met personally with Borghese in Rome, where they were joined by Greco and Buscetta. The foursome then drove to Milan to meet with Gaetano Badalamenti. "During the trip to Milan, we learned from Calderone and Di Cristina that Borghese wanted the *mafiosi* to wear a green ribbon or some distinctive mark during the coup, which created serious concerns. Even more incredible was his demand that we give him a list of the *mafiosi,* something no mafia boss would ever consent to. Badalamenti shared our concerns and we informed Calderone that we would not participate, or would take a neutral position, in what was being prepared."

In explaining why he had not discussed this episode before, Buscetta told Falcone and Caponetto, "I was afraid—and I still am afraid—that my statements may compromise the war against the mafia, which the state has always talked about, but has begun seriously only very recently . . . of which, for the moment, I see only the first timid signs. I therefore ask you to understand that if I don't tell everything that I know it is to avoid creating too traumatic an upheaval that may jeopardize your own investigations."

When the prosecutors tried to push him, Buscetta replied: "Don't ask any more about it, because I am not sure that the state could handle the reaction to what I have to say on this subject. . . . If I were to talk about this, I'm not sure I would be safe even in America."[38]

Seeing that the recent murders in Palermo had not stopped the new mafia witnesses, Cosa Nostra upped the stakes. On December 23, 1984, Italian railway train 904 traveling between Naples and Milan was blown up by a bomb, killing sixteen people and wounding two hundred others. Investigators later determined that the attack was planned by Pippo Calò (Buscetta's boss), and carried out by Calò's friends in organized crime and neo-fascist circles in Rome. The terrorist action was apparently designed to divert attention from the confessions of Buscetta and Contorno and the growing campaign against the mafia.[39]

TEN

After the confessions of Tommaso Buscetta and Salvatore Contorno, preparation for the maxi-trial of Palermo became a national priority. The government appropriated the money to build a massive new tribunal specifically for the trial, overseen by Liliana Ferraro, whose work in Palermo had come a long way since she had first procured a new desk for Giovanni Falcone. Built in the shadow of Ucciardone prison, the new maxi-courtroom, known as the *aula-bunker* or "bunker-hall," would be the ultimate in high-tech gargantuan courthouse construction. A single massive courtroom, the bunker-hall is nearly the size of a sports stadium. Thirty huge steel cages for several hundred defendants are built in a semicircle into the back wall facing the dais in the front where the judge sits. With bright green wall-to-wall carpeting, it looks like the world's largest pool table. In the middle, there are dozens of tables where as many as a thousand lawyers and witnesses can sit. On a balcony above is an enormous gallery with another thousand or more seats for members of the press and the public. The bunker is constructed of slabs of reinforced concrete, built to withstand bazooka fire or a missile attack. It is surrounded by barbed wire and an army tank stands guard day and night outside the front door. An enormous computerized filing system allows lawyers to locate documents quickly among hundreds of thousands of pages of evidence. The building bristles with high-tech security devices, metal detectors, electronic monitors, alarms and private television cameras. Justified paranoia dominated the construction process as the government tried to exclude mafia-linked companies, who might sabotage the building by planting bombs or listening devices or providing logistical information for an eventual military assault. For the opening of the trial, 3,000 armed soldiers would be posted outside the bunker-hall.[1]

With nearly five hundred defendants scheduled for trial—perhaps as much as 10 percent of the membership of Cosa Nostra and many of its most important leaders—the government had to be ready for anything.

Security for the members of the anti-mafia pool also increased to new levels of caution. Police motorcades with blaring sirens cleared the streets when the prosecutors passed on their way to and from work. "No parking" zones were established in front of their houses to avoid the kind of car bomb that had killed chief prosecutor Rocco Chinnici. A helicopter shadowed the movements of Giovanni Falcone, in order to spot any suspicious activity around his house or office. A special military plane stood ready at the Palermo airport, at the prosecutors' disposal, so that they could avoid the security risk of taking commercial flights when they needed to travel to question witnesses.

The prosecutors, who were working twelve to fourteen hours a day, limited their movements as much as possible. Falcone, who loved to swim, gave up his regular trips to the pool. Throughout his life, Falcone oscillated between periods when he was trim and fit and others when he was pudgy and overweight. In 1985 his paunch and jowls grew heavy during months in which he rarely left his windowless bunker and saw the sky only for fleeting moments getting in and out of his bulletproof car. But Falcone, a man of sedentary habits, suffered from this life of deprivation less than others; he was never happier than when he was working well and he seemed to relish the long days spent at his desk, devouring and making order from mountains of documents, as classical music played in the background.

Borsellino felt the loss of freedom more keenly and in his rare moments at home he would occasionally allow himself sudden, mad breaches of security. Telling his bodyguards that he would not be needing them for the next several hours, he would suddenly emerge from the garage of his apartment building on his son's *motorino,* wearing blue jeans, his face hidden under a crash helmet and visor. Few would suspect that the man gunning the engine of his motorbike throughout the streets of Palermo was a distinguished and heavily protected magistrate. Borsellino figured that such sudden and unexpected moves were probably less dangerous than his habitual trips to and from the office.

The mood of the city, as anticipation of the maxi-trial built, swung back and forth between widespread skepticism and wild euphoria. As work started on the bunker-hall courthouse, some people made ironic comments: "Do we really need this?" "Why don't they spend the money on another hospital?" But there were also signs of growing support. After police issued 127 arrest warrants due to the confessions of Salvatore Contorno, some twenty thousand students held a mass rally to demonstrate their solidarity with the Palermo police. "A demonstration like this shows that a lot of things in Palermo are really changing, that people's attitude toward the police is not what it once was," said Ninni Cassarà, deputy head of the investigative squad.[2]

For the first time, a genuine anti-mafia culture was developing in Palermo. New civic anti-mafia groups were springing up. The family members of mafia victims formed their own extremely active group, Il Coordinamento Anti-mafia (The Anti-mafia Network). Many local parish priests were speaking out against the mafia in their sermons or trying to create alternatives for young people in the poorest neighborhoods where the mafia did most of its recruiting. The local Jesuit research center became a rallying point for growing political opposition to the mafia. After decades of ambiguity, the Catholic Church was beginning to take a clear stand against the mafia.

In the spring of 1985, the Christian Democrats lost substantial ground in local elections, slipping from more than 46 to 37 percent of the vote in Palermo.[3] To suit the new anti-mafia climate, the DC made Leoluca Orlando, a maverick Catholic reformer (close to the Palermo Jesuits), the new mayor of the city. In a place where government officials had long been hesitant to pronounce the word "mafia," Orlando never missed an occasion to inveigh against Cosa Nostra and to render homage to its victims. Although he was from a prominent Palermo family (and there was debate about his lawyer father's possible ties to the mafia), Orlando had an effective populist touch. He visited the poorest, most run-down sections of town and opened up the ornate rooms of city hall during the evening for use by citizens groups. A university professor who had studied jurisprudence in Germany, Orlando promised to make Palermo a great European capital once again. He paid his respects to the anti-mafia prosecutors and frequently expressed his public support for them. Under Orlando's leadership, the city government took its place beside the prosecution in the maxi-trial as a "friend of the court." For the first time, the prosecutors felt they had friends in power. The Orlando experiment was dubbed the "Palermo Spring"—echoing the brief and giddy season of political freedom in Czechoslovakia in 1968, known as "Prague Spring."[4]

"The people are beginning to root for us," Paolo Borsellino told Falcone as he felt the mood of the city change. Falcone, imbued with a deep Sicilian pessimism, was not so sure: "They're standing at the window, waiting to see who wins the bullfight."

Although it became fashionable to make public professions of anti-mafia commitment, there were many subtle (and some not-so-subtle) forms of resistance to the new spirit of the city. A group of neighbors in Falcone's building wrote a public letter printed in the *Giornale di Sicilia* complaining of the possible damage to their property should the magistrate be assassinated on the premises. "Falcone was very bitter about this letter," his boss, Antonino Caponetto, recalled. "These people were more worried about their property than about Giovanni's life."[5]

The strength of the mafia depends on a degree of popular consensus that goes well beyond the 5,000 or 6,000 "made" members of Cosa Nostra. Some estimate that between 100,000 and 200,000 Sicilian families (in an island of 5 million people) depend directly on some form of illegal activity sanctioned by the mafia; traffickers in drugs, underground lottery tickets, contraband cigarettes, bootlegged audiotapes and videotapes, even the ubiquitous pushcart peddlers selling bread without a license. Moreover, billions of dollars of drug money was being recycled into hundreds of apparently legitimate businesses: construction companies, res-

taurants, clothing stores, supermarkets. And much of this was
trickling down to people who had little or nothing to do with the
mafia, creating a kind of "gray zone" that provided a certain passive support for the city's criminal class. Palermo (like many other
poor southern Italian cities) had gotten fat off the mafia economy
of the 1970s and 1980s. Although, officially, it continued to rank
among the poorest Italian cities in terms of family income and unemployment, Palermo had quickly taken its place among the highest in per capita consumption. The center of Palermo was now
crowded with designer clothing shops, Armani, Fendi, Benetton,
and traffic was crammed with Alfa Romeos, Ferraris and Mer-
cedes-Benz. Of course, shopkeepers had to pay protection money,
but they were making money as never before. And while the mafia
war, with its hundreds of corpses, provided a terrifying spectacle,
almost all the victims were criminals. In general, the only legitimate businessmen killed were those brave or foolish enough to
stand up to mafia power.[6]

This "gray zone" of society, which regarded the war on the
mafia with hostility or indifference, found its voice in the principal
Palermo newspaper, *Giornale di Sicilia*. The paper always seemed
to find room for letters of protest or criticism of the anti-mafia
pool, and yet never saw fit to grant an interview to Leoluca Orlando during his first term as mayor of the city. In April 1985, the
newspaper gave prominent play to a letter from another neighbor
of Giovanni Falcone, Patrizia Santoro, proposing that the anti-
mafia prosecutors be moved to a kind of ghetto outside the city in
order to guarantee the peace and quiet of ordinary citizens: "Every
day, morning, noon and night I am continually 'assaulted' by the
deafening sirens of the cars escorting the judges. Now, I ask,
shouldn't it be possible for someone take an afternoon nap or
at least enjoy a television program in peace, given that even with
the windows closed, the noise of the sirens is overwhelming?" Ms.
Santoro suggested that the "distinguished gentlemen" of the anti-
mafia pool be packed off to "villas in the periphery of the city so
as to ensure the tranquillity of ordinary worker-citizens and . . . to
guarantee our safety in the case of an assassination, in which we
might be involved for no reason (as in the Chinnici bombing)."[7]

That the *Giornale di Sicilia* should express hostility to the anti-
mafia pool is not especially surprising: one of its major investors is

a member of the Costanzo family of Catania, one of the Four Horsemen of the Apocalypse whom the Palermo prosecutors had targeted for their ties to the mafia.

But the members of the anti-mafia pool paid relatively little attention to the world around them. "We were so isolated in our bunkerized lives that we were not especially aware of what was happening outside," said Antonino Caponetto. "We got the oxygen we needed from Rome for those two years, with Martinazzoli as minister of justice, Rognoni and Scalfaro at the Ministry of Interior and with [Liliana] Ferraro, without whom we would never have made it to the maxi-trial."[8]

Falcone, already a tireless worker, seemed to turn up his level of intensity another few notches. "He could work twelve, fourteen, sixteen hours a day, seven days a week, month after month," said Domenico Signorino of the Procura della Repubblica. "His capacity for work was almost frightening. Those of us who worked with him would take turns because we couldn't maintain that rhythm for long. The only one who could keep up with him was Paolo Borsellino."[9]

The "pool" met every Monday and many evenings to compare notes and share information. Sometimes, during the meetings, Falcone and Borsellino would spar in heated but friendly competition, arguing over whether a certain defendant was a member of this or that mafia family. Both of them, who had been filling hundreds of notebooks for years, had encyclopedic memories and knew the entire structure and genealogy of most of Sicily's mafia clans backward and forward. When other prosecutors were confronted with a name they didn't recognize, they would simply call Falcone or Borsellino. "If I didn't know who somebody was," said Gianni De Gennarro, "I would pick up the phone and call Giovanni and he would say right away: 'X is the brother-in-law of Y who is a soldier in such-and-such a mafia family and owns a clothing store together with Z, who was convicted five years ago for the following crimes.' "[10] Caponetto said that the only person who could sometimes outdo Falcone in his memory for precise detail and arcane mafia facts was Borsellino.[11]

That year, prosecutors in Palermo made an astonishing 3,064 bank requests for financial data on mafia suspects. (In Naples, a city three times the size of Palermo, only 479 were made.) "It was an exciting time, almost every day there would be a new discovery, a new witness or a bank record that would turn up," said Ignazio De Francisci, who joined the pool in early 1985.[12]

There was a great deal of camaraderie among the members of the pool. Both Falcone and Borsellino were fond of joking and clowning around, often as a way of relieving the tension of their work. Falcone was especially fond of plays on words and bad puns. When friends would call him on the phone, beginning the conversation by giving their names, "Franco, here," Falcone would respond, "No, Franco's not here." When he rode the elevator in the Palace of Justice Falcone never tired of asking unsuspecting colleagues "How many people can fit in this elevator?" They would answer "four," noting the sign that said: "Capienza Quattro Persone." (Capacity Four People). Falcone would say, "No, five. You forgot 'Enza,' pointing to the word *capienza* in the sign. In Sicilian dialect the word *capi* means "enter" or "get in" and "Enza" is a woman's name and so *Capienza,* Falcone would explain, really means "Get in Enza," so the capacity is four people plus Enza. "He had this 'demented' kind of humor that usually involved word play," said Leonardo Guarnotta of the anti-mafia pool. Similarly, Falcone would frequently refer to their boss, not as "Caponetto" but by the synonym *"Testa pulita,"* "Cleanhead." "Have you seen Cleanhead? Cleanhead would like to talk to you."[13]

They would all tease Borsellino about his strong Palermo accent. He had particular trouble with the hard *tr* sound in Italian, slurring it so that it sounded like a soft *ch*. "Say 'quattro' (four)" they would tell him, and he would obey with good nature; and when he said "quachro" they would all break out in laughter.[14]

A certain amount of gallows humor found its way into their banter, as the prosecutors sought to exorcise the thought of death that accompanied their work. In the middle of a conversation, Borsellino would suddenly say to Falcone: "By the way, Giovanni, when are you going to give me a key to your safe deposit box?" "Why should I?" Falcone asked. "So I can get your stuff out after they kill you." At the end of a long day, the members of the pool would amuse themselves by composing mock obituaries for one another.[15]

As Buscetta had predicted, Falcone had become a celebrity, the symbol of the war against the mafia, his picture regularly in the national newspapers. His reserved, Sicilian manner—with his dark beard and dark eyes—had taken on a legendary aura. "He was like a mysterious Arab," said Judge Stefano Racheli, a prosecutor from Rome who met Falcone in that period. "Falcone's principal quality was that you never knew exactly what he was driving at but you never doubted that he knew exactly where he was heading."[16]

John Costanzo, a narcotics investigator with the American Drug Enforcement Agency (DEA), had a similar sensation watching Falcone interrogate a witness in New York. "Falcone arrived to question a certain witness, and he had maybe three simple, precise questions," Costanzo said. "None of us, including the witness, understood the significance of the questions, but they were obviously pieces that fit into some much larger puzzle Falcone had in his head. He got his answers and left."[17]

Ignazio De Francisci, one of two young prosecutors who joined the anti-mafia pool in 1985 to help handle the growing workload, would sometimes attend Falcone's questioning of witnesses just to watch him work. "Falcone was an unbeatable fencer," said De Francisci, "I will never forget the first interrogation of Michele Greco. Initially, I was wondering why we were wasting so much time. Falcone was allowing him to talk on and on about a boat trip he once took with a chief prosecutor of Palermo, with whom he had discussed a question of land. I didn't understand. Then by the third session, I understood that this served as evidence to show the relationship of collusion between the mafia and a part of the judiciary. This was his great ability: to lead the defendant where he wanted, without the other being aware of it."[18]

During interrogations, Falcone developed an elaborate personal routine that became a part of his professional persona. Extremely finicky and precise, he invariably traveled with various pads of papers and numerous expensive fountain pens with different colored inks, which he would lay out in a neat row. He would use different colors of ink for different kinds of information and wrote carefully in elegant handwriting. His knowledge of the various Sicilian mafia families was such that he could quickly sniff out whether a witness was telling the truth or knew what he or she was talking about. His reserved, severe manner, extreme meticulousness and remarkable memory for detail conveyed the impression that it was better to be forthcoming than to try to pull the wool over his eyes.

Borsellino was also extremely able in dealing with witnesses but for somewhat different reasons. Beyond the obvious prerequisites of a reputation of incorruptibility and a prodigious grasp of the mafia problem, Borsellino's easygoing manner, his humor and extreme sense of humanity worked in his favor. Witnesses instinctively trusted him and opened themselves to him because they sensed that he respected them and was genuinely interested in their lives. He developed a strong relationship with Pietra Lo Verso, the widow of one of the victims of the Piazza Scaffa massacre—the multiple murder of eight men in a Palermo stable. When it became known in the neighborhood that she was cooperating with prosecutors, the family butcher shop was deserted by its clients and went into bankruptcy. When Borsellino heard that Mrs. Lo Verso had pawned her own jewelry to make ends meet, he used his own money to get them out of hock.[19]

Borsellino was also instrumental in getting the most out of Vincenzo Sinagra, an important witness who had begun talking in 1983 but who had only been interrogated a few times. If Buscetta had provided a glimpse into life within the mafia at its highest levels, Sinagra offered a view of day-to-day life of a low-level mafia killer. Sinagra had not been formally initiated into the mafia; he had been recruited for a variety of dirty jobs when extra manpower was needed during the great mafia war of 1981–82. But with Sinagra's help, investigators discovered the horrors of the so-called Room of Death, a squalid apartment near Piazza Sant' Erasmo, where the boss Filippo Marchese tortured and murdered his victims.

Sinagra's experience was probably not too different from many young mafia recruits in Palermo. He grew up in the slums of Corso dei Mille, the son of a fisherman, who had trouble feeding his wife and their fourteen children. Sinagra began his criminal career with a few small thefts before attempting a couple of larger burglaries with a friend. At one point, however, they had the misfortune of robbing someone with close ties to the mafia. Sinagra's partner then compounded his error by showing up in the neighborhood with fancy clothes and a new motorbike, making it obvious to local *mafiosi* who had pulled off the heist. This might have led to instant death, but Sinagra had a cousin in the mafia, also named Vincenzo Sinagra, nicknamed "Tempesta" (Tempest) for his violent power. Tempest approached Vincenzo and told him he had to make a choice: leave Palermo, work for the mafia or die. Vincenzo decided to remain in Palermo, and ran errands for Filippo Marchese, firebombing stores in order to intimidate shopkeepers into paying protection, committing murders or getting rid of bodies. An indication of how cheap life in Palermo was at the time—Vincenzo was paid as little as $200 or $300 a month. "But my cousin Vincenzo Sinagra (Tempest) told me after the mafia war there would be plenty of money and I would be taken care of economically," Sinagra later testified.[20]

The routine of killing was almost always the same: the victims would be lured into the fetid apartment at Piazza Sant' Erasmo, to a room with crumbling plaster, a naked light bulb and a table with a couple of chairs. A sickly chemical odor crept into the air from the next room. When the victims appeared, Sinagra and one of his cousins would grab them and tie them to a chair. The boss, Filippo Marchese, would then arrive to interrogate the victims, sometimes taking notes at the table. When the interrogation was over, the victim would be strangled. It was not easy work. It often took two men holding either ends of the rope about ten minutes, with one or two others to hold the victim still. As low man on the totem pole, it was generally Vincenzo's job to hold the feet and get rid of the body. Strangulation was reserved for the boss.

"Although he was head of the family, Marchese personally strangled most of the victims himself, often for the most insignificant reasons," Sinagra testified. "[Marchese] was a bloody-minded character and gave the impression of enjoying killing people and demanded that no one betray any emotion at the spectacle."

After the killing was done, they generally dipped the bodies of their victims in vats of powerful acid stored in the next room, which released a foul, noxious odor as it ate away at the corpses. Sometimes, the acid was impure and the bodies would not dissolve completely. At that point, Vincenzo and his cousin would dispose of the remains by rowing out into the bay of Palermo in a little fishing boat and dropping the partially dissolved body parts overboard in a thick plastic garbage bag, weighted down with stones.

Sometimes there was no acid at all, and so they would resort to a technique of disposal known as *incapramento,* meaning literally "en-goatment." Police were often puzzled when they found bodies in the trunks of cars, with the hands and feet tied behind the back and a cord attaching them to the neck, like the bodies of slaughtered goats. Some investigators imagined that these corpses were the victims of a particularly excruciating kind of ritual killing. Vincenzo explained that these victims were strangled normally and tied up afterward in the "goat" formation for purely practical reasons. "Contrary to what you imagine and what the newspapers have written, these people are *incapratettati* (en-goated) not as means of slow suffocation but because it is the easiest means of getting the body to fit comfortably into the trunk of a car or into a bag," he said. "It is important to tie up the victim immediately after the person is dead before the body stiffens."

Sinagra led Borsellino over the familiar terrain of the great mafia war of 1981–82, but from a ground's-eye perspective, providing precise descriptions of specific murders, identifying victims, assassins, the motive for the killings. Since the bodies of most victims had been destroyed, Sinagra was able to turn many unsolved "missing persons" cases into murder indictments. (Some 160 suspected *mafiosi* had "disappeared" during the mafia war of 1981–82.)[21] While Buscetta and Contorno had heard through the mafia grapevine that this or that person had been murdered, Sinagra had actually seen it happen. He took Borsellino to the scene of the crimes and to the places where the bodies had been disposed of.

Sinagra described the death of Antonio Rugnetta, a contraband cigarette trader, who was one of the many victims of the manhunt for Salvatore Contorno. Although Sinagra did not know who they were talking about, he remembered clearly Rugnetta's interrogation at the hands of Marchese. He kept asking for someone called "Curiano" or "Curiolano della Floresta," which prosecutors recognized as the nickname of Contorno, "Coriolanus of the Forest." "Believe me," Rugnetta had begged, "if I could tell you where he was hiding, I would tell you." When they realized they would not get anything useful out of Rugnetta, Marchese, together with his good friend, Pino "the Shoe" Greco, strangled him. Also present at the killing was Pietro Vernengo, one of Marchese's closest aides and a major heroin trafficker whom Borsellino had been trying to nail.[22]

Two of the bodies that Sinagra helped "en-goat" were the ones found in the trunk of the car in the area outside Palermo known as the "triangle of death" shortly before the killing of General Dalla Chiesa. An anonymous caller had alerted the *carabinieri* saying, "Operation Carlo Alberto is almost complete." Sinagra had overheard Marchese and his band discussing early plans to murder Dalla Chiesa. The murder took place September 3, 1982, three weeks after Sinagra's arrest.

Sinagra had also heard about a plan to kill Giovanni Falcone. "I know, because my cousin Vincenzo (Tempest) told me that Filippo Marchese, speaking of Judge Falcone, said he was 'busting our balls,' and would have to be killed for going after people he shouldn't." His brutal and violent ways did not prevent Marchese from having friends in high places. "Marchese has informants, both in the investigative unit of the police and in the first police district as well as at the Palace of Justice," Sinagra said. "Basically, he always knows everything." Someone had tipped Marchese off about Ninni Cassarà's top secret report of July 1982 on the mafia war, known as "the report on Michele Greco + 161," and the boss warned his men not to sleep at home for a while.

Sinagra's short, unhappy career in the mafia came to an end on August 11, 1982, after only about a year. Sinagra had been a mediocre *mafioso* who often let his emotions get the better of him. Filippo Marchese had once reproached him when he allowed a sense of horror to show on his face as he watched the boss strangle a murder victim. Vincenzo had been arrested the very first time he had been given a leading role in a hit squad because of his nervousness. Vincenzo was supposed to lure a neighborhood friend (Diego Fatta) into a trap so that he and his cousin Tempest could shoot him at close range. But when the critical moment arrived, Vincenzo's pistol misfired and Tempest had to do the job. Overcome by the emotion of helping to kill a friend, Vincenzo carelessly left his gun in the getaway car so that when police arrested him later that day they had him red-handed.

For almost a year, Sinagra (together with both his accomplices) feigned insanity, growing a long beard and repeating over and over that he wanted to go fishing. But Vincenzo was even a failure at being a madman. He began to crack under the pressure of having to maintain his role and decided to talk.

Unlike virtually all the early mafia witnesses, Sinagra admitted to all his worst crimes, and even asked the forgiveness of the families of his victims.

By the time Borsellino met him, Sinagra had been moved to a prison on the Italian mainland, where it would be more difficult for the mafia to kill him. When word spread about the gruesome murders in the Room of Death, Sinagra was placed in an isolation cell and regarded with stark terror. Moreover, his family in Palermo, afraid of being punished for Vincenzo's decision to talk, had cut off all ties with him. Borsellino saw that despite his violent life, Vincenzo was actually a gentle-natured person who had become trapped in the life of the Palermo clans. He took an interest in his situation and tried to relieve his isolation. "I know you are not a violent person," Borsellino told him. "I wouldn't hesitate to put my youngest daughter in the same cell with you," Sinagra recalled.[23] When Vincenzo, who spoke only Sicilian dialect and had only the most rudimentary schooling, showed signs of wanting to educate himself, Borsellino brought him his children's old school books. Sinagra, in turn, helped Borsellino solve a murder that he had long investigated: that of Dr. Paolo Giaccone, the forensic pathologist who had identified the fingerprints of Filippo Marchese's nephew (Giuseppe Marchese) on the getaway car of the Christmas Massacre committed in Bagheria in 1981. Giaccone had been shot on August 11, 1982, the same day that Sinagra was arrested for the murder of his friend Diego Fatta.

"My cousin Vincenzo [Tempest] told me . . . the same day I was arrested, that Salvatore Rotolo [another member of the Marchese band] had killed a man at a hospital, probably a doctor, who had identified the fingerprints of Pippo [Giuseppe] Marchese from the scene of a killing," Sinagra said. "[Tempest] told me this in order to boost my spirits in preparation for the killing of Diego Fatta, which, in fact, we committed a few hours later."[24]

With his usually precise memory, Sinagra recalled that Dr. Giaccone's assassin, Salvatore Rotolo, had a kind of nervous tic that kept his face contorted in an almost permanent grin. One of the eyewitnesses to Dr. Giaccone's murder had noted that one of the killers was grinning as he ran from the scene.[25]

At the time, Rotolo was one of the 221 mafia fugitives that police in Palermo were trying to track down.[26] But here, too, there was progress. The Palermo "fugitive squad" under the direction of Beppe Montana, a young police officer, had started to make some headway in the last two years. In 1983, he discovered a large arsenal used by Filippo Marchese and Michele Greco, including machine guns, sawed-off shotguns and dozens of .38 caliber pistols. In the spring of 1984, he arrested Giovanni Falcone's childhood Ping-Pong partner, Tommaso Spadaro, the so-called King of the Kalsa, trafficker in heroin and contraband cigarettes. (Spadaro was found at his home in Palermo, where, evidently, no one had thought to look for him before.) In 1985, police in Rome had finally arrested Pippo Calò, Buscetta's boss, and one of the members of the Commission. And in the summer of 1985, Montana's men finally found Salvatore Rotolo, Dr. Paolo Giaccone's killer.[27]

Borsellino took an instant liking to Montana. Like the best Palermo policemen, he went way beyond the call of duty, using his own means and time to make up for the police department's scandalous lack of resources. Ninni Cassarà and Montana often moved around Palermo pursuing dangerous criminals on their own motor scooters or in their own little economy cars because the government claimed it didn't have money to provide them with bulletproof cars. Montana and Borsellino both loved the sea and they talked about the little boats they both kept near Palermo and took out for an occasional Sunday holiday. Montana sometimes used his boat to cruise the Sicilian coast looking for houses where mafia fugitives might be hiding. In the summer of 1985 he had rented a little seaside cottage so that he could explore an area he suspected was honeycombed with mafia hideouts.[28]

On July 25, Montana and his men led a successful operation arresting eight mafia fugitives, including the boss of Prizzi (a town near Palermo), Tommaso Canella, ally and business partner of Michele Greco, "the Pope." Three days later, on a Sunday, Montana took his girlfriend and a couple of friends out in his little boat, but when he returned at the end of the day, two killers were lying in wait for him. After he docked the boat at the marina of Porticello, they fired four shots from a .38 caliber pistol, killing Montana on the spot.[29]

Shortly after the murder, Paolo Borsellino arrived at the scene with police investigator Ninni Cassarà—both good friends of Montana. Borsellino stared at the body of the young police agent, small and fragile in his bathing suit, lying in a pool of his own blood on the dock. As they drove back to Palermo, Borsellino found Cassarà completely changed by the killing. "Years of work together had created an affectionate friendship between us, further cemented by a trip for work we had taken together in Brazil in 1984," Borsellino recalled. "I had come to appreciate his extraordinary humanity . . . his pureness of soul, almost like a child's, that radiated from his intelligent, honest face. Suddenly, this same Ninni Cassarà, always light-hearted and optimistic like all people who are pure of heart, suddenly said to me as he dropped me at my house after the terrible visit with the corpse of Montana . . . 'Let's face it, we are walking cadavers.' " Then Cassarà drove back to his office to resume his work.[30]

The Palermo police immediately started a veritable manhunt for Montana's killers. An eyewitness recalled the first numbers of the license plates of the white Peugeot in which Montana's killers had fled the scene of the crime. Starting a massive search of some 10,000 cars with those same numbers, investigators gradually came up with a suspect: Salvatore Marino, the twenty-five-year-old son of a fisherman from the neighborhood of Piazza Sant' Erasmo (near the Room of Death). Witnesses had seen Marino at the Porticello Marina the afternoon of the murder and when they searched his house, they found a shirt with blood on it and 34 million lire (about $30,000) wrapped in a copy of a newspaper dated Sunday, July 28, the day of the crime.[31]

But what had started as a promising break in the case quickly turned to tragedy. In the course of fifteen hours of nonstop interrogations, police began to beat Marino and forced him to drink salt water, in an effort to make him reveal the names of his accomplices. By four o'clock on the morning of August 2, the suspect had been reduced to an unconscious, bloody pulp and was pronounced dead on arrival at the hospital. The police compounded the situation by trying to lie about their crime, claiming the victim had drowned. The cover-up collapsed almost immediately: there were human teeth marks found on the suspect's arm.[32] On August 4, 1985, Marino's family carried the coffin with the victim's bruised and battered body across the city in a procession inveighing against the "police murderers." The following day, Minister of the Interior Oscar Luigi Scalfaro (the current Italian president) ordered the immediate transfer of three senior police officials, including Francesco Pellegrino, the head of the Palermo investigative office. The considerable goodwill that the Palermo police had built up over years of patient and dangerous work dissipated almost overnight.[33]

Ninni Cassarà remained barricaded in his office after Beppe Montana's murder, rarely leaving to eat and sleep. In response to the atmosphere of extreme tension and imminent danger, he varied his schedule and sometimes even spent the night at the office. One of Cassarà's assistants, twenty-three-year-old Roberto Antiochia, gave up his vacation to remain in the August heat of Palermo to help protect his boss.

At about three o'clock on the afternoon of August 6, Cassarà unexpectedly picked up his office phone and told his wife, Laura, that he would be arriving at home shortly. When Cassarà arrived in a bulletproof Alfa Romeo with three bodyguards, an enormous mafia hit squad of as many as fifteen men lay in wait for them. Demonstrating their complete control of the streets, the *mafiosi* had occupied the entire building across from Cassarà's apartment without attracting the attention of any concerned citizens. Laura Cassarà, who had the habit of scanning the street for trouble whenever her husband arrived, stepped out on her apartment balcony just in time to watch him shot down in a veritable Armaggeddon of machine-gun fire. After the killers had fired some two hundred shots, Cassarà and Antiochia were dead. A second bodyguard, Giovanni Lercara, was badly wounded, while Cassarà's driver, Natale Mondo, had miraculously survived by crawling underneath the car.[34]

In the confusion and anguish of those days, some wondered whether the entire sequence of events—from the murder of Montana, to the killing of Salvatore Marino and the assassination of Cassarà—hadn't been carefully orchestrated. Perhaps a mole in the police department had pushed Salvatore Marino over the edge in order to eliminate a dangerous potential witness, discredit the police and provide the excuse for killing Ninni Cassarà. It is more likely, however, that Marino's death was a simple case of police officers losing control in a blind fury against the man they blamed for the death of a friend and colleague. But the ten days from July 28 to August 6 couldn't have gone better for the mafia if the whole thing had been planned. The police chief, Giuseppe Montesano, was transferred; and the head of the investigative division, Francesco Pellegrino, and ten other police officials were charged with the murder of Salvatore Marino. The team of able investigators that had been slowly and painfully reconstructed after the assassinations of Boris Giuliano and Emanuele Basile was wiped out by the murders of Montana and Cassarà and the Marino affair. In this period of extreme tension, the traditional rivalry between the police and the *carabinieri* reached the point where all cooperation between the two police corps broke down. The Palermo police nearly rioted when Minister of the Interior Oscar Luigi Scalfaro arrived for the funerals of Cassarà and Antiochia, and had to be restrained by the *carabinieri* assigned to the minister's protection.

But if Salvatore Marino's death was probably a fatal mistake, the killing of Cassarà had more deeply disturbing implications. His movements had been so irregular in that period that someone from inside the police station almost certainly alerted the mafia to Cassarà's imminent arrival. It was highly unlikely that a squad of fifteen hit men was camped out for days on end in front of his apartment waiting for the moment when he would finally return home. (Mafia witnesses later testified that several members of the Commission were present to oversee and celebrate the killing of Cassarà.)

Vincenzo Sinagra had said specifically that his boss, Filippo Marchese, had an informant on Cassarà's investigative unit. And Buscetta had told Falcone about another possible mole in law enforcement: Bruno Contrada, who had once headed the investigative unit and had gone on to become an important member of the Italian secret services.

Suspicions, instead, centered on Ninni Cassarà's driver, Natale Mondo, guilty of having survived the assassination unharmed. Eventually Mondo was completely exonerated, only to be murdered by the mafia at a later date.

The death of Cassarà hit Falcone especially hard. The two had worked in almost perfect synchrony for years and had become close friends. Of all the "excellent cadavers" Falcone had seen since returning to Palermo in 1978, Cassarà's was the hardest to accept. Young, intelligent, university-educated, totally honest and completely dedicated, Cassarà represented the promise of a different future for Sicily. His death, and the completely inadequate support and protection he had received, represented the betrayal of that promise. The judges were comparatively well guarded, but the mafia understood quite shrewdly that it could strike at them by hitting the police. Without an effective police team to capture defendants, the judges would have no one to prosecute and further investigations would be paralyzed.

Although the Cassarà murder appeared to be a direct retaliation for the killing of mafia suspect Salvatore Marino, Falcone understood that it fit into the logic of a broad counteroffensive. "The maxi-trial is at the center of the mafia's strategy," he said. "The mafia does not accept the idea of being put on trial by the state. . . . The mafia understood how dangerous the investigative unit had become in sniffing out the hiding places of the mafia fugitives. Therefore, according to their calculation, the investigative unit must not be allowed to keep moving up the ladder and bring its work to a successful conclusion. It's useless to conduct investigations, and perhaps even to hold maxi-trials, if we are not able to arrest the fugitives."[35] While police had been able to arrest some members of the Commission (Pippo Calò, Mariano Agate), several of the most important leaders, including the "beasts" of Corleone Salvatore Riina and Bernardo Provenzano, remained at large.

The killings had a sobering effect on a public that had become inebriated with the euphoria of the maxi-trial. "At the beginning of the summer of 1985 it was not uncommon to hear people talking of the defeat of the mafia," Borsellino reflected in a speech he made the following year. "With the killings of Montana, Cassarà and Antiochia, Cosa Nostra demonstrated clearly that its structure was very much intact and that . . . it was capable of translating its most terrible decisions into the bloodiest action."[36]

A few days after the funeral of Ninni Cassarà, police arrived in the middle of the night at the houses of Giovanni Falcone and Paolo Borsellino, telling the magistrates to pack their bags immediately. The two prosecutors were taken directly to the airport, where a secret military airplane waited to remove them to an unknown destination. Police investigators believed that the mafia was about to carry out a plan to assassinate the two prosecutors before they were able to finish writing up the massive document in which they detailed the evidence for the maxi-trial. It wasn't until the plane landed that Falcone and Borsellino discovered that they had arrived on Asinara, the Alcatraz of Italy, a remote island prison off the coast of Sardinia where some of the most dangerous criminals were held in almost total isolation. The magistrates were told they would have to stay at Asinara in quarters provided by the prison director for about two months. Borsellino's wife and children, Falcone's fiancée, Francesca Morvillo, herself a magistrate in Palermo, and Francesca's mother were all evacuated to Asinara as well. The move was a telling indication of the upside-down nature of life in Sicily on the eve of the maxi-trial: mafia fugitives moved freely about Palermo while government prosecutors had to live in prison for their own protection.[37]

ELEVEN

The Falcones and Borsellinos spent an extended summer vacation from the middle of August 1985 until mid-September on the island-prison of Asinara. For Paolo Borsellino's younger children, Manfredi and Fiammetta, it was an exciting adventure. They had the run of the island; the sea air was fresh and the water clean. They had dozens of police guards as companions for their games and when they went in the water to swim, police motorboats followed their every move. They didn't fully grasp the reasons for their sudden evacuation to this island paradise. "For Manfredi [who was twelve years old at the time], it was a perfect vacation," says Borsellino's sister, Rita. "But Lucia, who was a little older [fifteen] and understood more, suffered much more." All of a sudden, she stopped eating and began rapidly losing weight, developing a serious case of anorexia. The Borsellinos were convinced that it was a reaction to the terror created by the shadow that had crept over her father's life.[1]

The two prosecutors worked hard trying to finish their work getting the maxi-trial ready, receiving occasional visits from friends and colleagues. When they left the island thirty-three days after their arrival, Falcone and Borsellino, to their surprise, were presented with a bill for room and board. Alternately amused and irritated, Borsellino kept the receipt as a memento.

Falcone and Borsellino were nearly finished with the maxi-in-dictment by the time they returned to Palermo in late September, and on November 8, 1985, it was complete: 8,607 pages in forty volumes, plus appendices of 4,000 pages, including documents and photographs, laying out evidence against 475 defendants.[2]

Given the fears that the prosecutors might be killed before com-pleting the work, the mere act of depositing the enormous docu-ment was itself a triumph. Although the general outline and various pieces of evidence were well known, the full scope of the case in its finished form made a powerful impression. The maxi-indictment, the bulk of which was written by Falcone himself, is a truly magisterial document: a great historical saga with the sweep of a Tolstoian novel. It opens: "This is the trial of the mafia orga-nization called 'Cosa Nostra,' . . . which, with violence and intim-idation, has sowed, and continues to sow, death and terror." Like the great historical novel of Sicilian life, *The Leopard* by Giuseppe di Lampedusa, it is a lucid diagnosis of a diseased society. The in-dictment traces the decadence of the old Sicilian aristocratic fami-lies, whose power and land are gradually eroded by the emerging mafia bosses.[3]

The symbol of the new order was Michele Greco, "the Pope," who appropriated the fortune of his noble landlord, the count of Tagliavia—as the indictment demonstrates, step by step. First, the Grecos rented a large estate with several villas and a lucrative cit-rus farm for little more than a thousand dollars a month. Then, mysteriously, the Grecos succeeded in getting their rent cut by more than half. In desperate need of cash, the aristocrats tried to put the land up for sale. Only one buyer stepped forward, offering to pay more than $1 million (in 1974 money) and putting down a down payment of 150 million lire (about $200,000). But then, the buyer, despite being one of Palermo's leading real estate develop-ers, pulled out of the deal, forfeiting his deposit, claiming he had mistaken his calculations and didn't have the means to complete the sale. The highly attractive property remained on the market without a single bid for several years until members of Greco's mafia family bought it for a fraction of the original price. By squeezing the landowner and scaring away all other potential buy-ers, the Grecos were able to take over two vast tracts of prime real estate for a laughably low sum. Acting as intermediary in the transaction was Luigi Gioia, a Palermo lawyer and Christian Democratic member of the national parliament—guarantor of the passage from the *ancien régime* to the new.[4]

The prosecutors then scrupulously documented the way in which the Greco clan consolidated its hold on the surrounding area, eventually establishing a reign of terror over their territory. During the great mafia war of the 1980s, "the Pope's" cousin and chief killer, Pino "the Shoe" Greco, literally evacuated the neighborhood around his house after learning of a plot to kill him. On receiving death threats, dozens of residents simply picked up and moved, abandoning their homes and businesses.

Like any historic saga, the maxi-indictment has a cast of thousands, including small-time Palermo hoods, Neapolitan contrabandists, ruthless bosses, terrified victims, courageous witnesses, opportunistic businessmen, dishonest bank clerks, corrupt politicians, and ambiguous government ministers. There are an infinite number of plots and subplots: drug shipments, kidnappings, murders, real estate deals, government contracts, complex financial transactions, rigged laws and suspicious electoral campaigns, friendships, alliances, betrayals and betrayals-within-betrayals.

But despite the myriad characters, there are a few clear underlying themes: the growth of the heroin trade, the rise of the Corleonesi and the increasing violence of life within Cosa Nostra. The prosecution showed how the old routes of the contraband cigarette trade were converted to the more lucrative traffic in narcotics, how the Corleonesi used the heroin trade to infiltrate other families and gradually eliminate all their rivals. The indictment provided a vast organizational map of Cosa Nostra, based on the testimony not only of Tommaso Buscetta and Salvatore Contorno, but also of several other witnesses, living and dead, corroborated by hundreds of phone wiretaps and financial transactions.

There was, as well, the parallel story of the government's failure to respond to the threat. The indictment documented the mistakes and missed opportunities of the Palermo Palace of Justice during the lost decade of the 1970s, when government inertia or outright collusion allowed the mafia to grow to unheard-of levels of power. It told the tragic, little-known stories of the early proto-mafia witnesses, Leonardo Vitale and Giuseppe Di Cristina, who had confided their secrets to police in 1973 and 1978, respectively, and had both been murdered. Falcone quoted from the moving, stream-of-consciousness confessions of Vitale, in the middle of his religious/mystical crisis: "I have been made a fool of by life, by the evil that rained on me from the time I was a child. . . . My sin is having been born into a mafia family and of having lived in a society where everyone is a *mafioso* and is respected for it, while those who are not are treated with contempt."[5]

There are heroes, as well as villains, in particular the long string of courageous investigators who died fighting the mafia during a time of indifference. In the chapters on the murders of police inspectors Boris Giuliano, Emanuele Basile and Calogero Zucchetto, Paolo Borsellino wrote: "The lack of complete knowledge and of a lucid, global strategy against the mafia phenomenon did not prevent several individuals, animated by remarkable zeal and keen awareness . . . from conducting numerous effective investigations against various criminal groups. . . . Unfortunately, these initiatives had little follow-up in the courts; they took place in virtual isolation and in a climate of general skepticism, at a time when the 'Pax Mafiosa' had generated the pernicious notion that there was no powerful criminal organization pulling the strings of the most potent criminal enterprises. . . ."[6]

The prosecutors also paid homage to the magistrate who had planted the first seed of the maxi-trial. "It is important to remember that this investigation was begun more than three years ago by Chief Prosecutor Rocco Chinnici, who invested all his civic passion into it, at the cost of his own life."[7]

Although no politicians were among the defendants, the maxi-indictment explained how deeply the mafia had dug its claws into the body of Sicilian life. It contained a lucid analysis of the mafia system of power in Sicily: the empire of the Salvo family and its vast influence in the Sicilian parliament; the businessmen of Catania, known as "The Four Horsemen of the Apocalypse" and their integral relations with the local mafia and with politicians in Rome; the disturbing political background to the assassination of General Dalla Chiesa and the role of the Andreotti faction in Sicily.

These connections were documented carefully and dispassionately in order to build an unassailable wall of evidence. But occasionally Falcone (who wrote this section) allowed flashes of bitter irony and moral indignation to pierce the surface of his sober ac- count. When investigating the mafia of Catania Falcone had found photographs of a party showing the mayor and members of the city council in merry revelry with Nitto Santapaola, the notorious *capo-mafia* who, at the time, was conducting a bloody clan war in the streets of the city. There is an element of black comedy in the juxtaposition of the photographs and the evasive, unconvincing testimony of Catania's leading citizens. One picture featured Santa- paola in the friendly embrace of Salvatore Lo Turco, a member of the Sicilian parliament's anti-mafia commission. Trying to explain himself, Lo Turco told Falcone, "Santapaola won me over with his gentlemanly air and good manners."[8]

Appreciating its historic importance, two different publishers printed excerpted editions of the maxi-indictment. In the intro- duction to one of them, journalist Corrado Stajano wrote: "The forty volumes and 8,607 pages of the indictment are an essential X ray of Italy today . . . the contradictions of which are hard to grasp if you don't take the mafia into account . . . its legal and il- legal business activities, the power of its wealth and its relation- ships with those who profit from it, its complicity with people in government, its organizational structure and military power, its internecine wars of hegemony, and its political assassinations, but also of its language and customs. . . . For the first time since the unification of Italy . . . we have a reconstruction of the [mafia] phenomenon in all its complexity."[9]

Less than two weeks after depositing the maxi-indictment, the Palermo prosecutors were again hit by tragedy. On November 21, 1985, one of the police cars escorting Paolo Borsellino spun out of control and killed two high school students waiting at a bus stop. Out of his mind with grief and guilt, Borsellino kept vigil at the hospital where a third child clung to life by a thread. "He wept for two days straight," Borsellino's mother said. "He didn't want to talk to anyone and he even considered quitting the magistrature," said his sister, Rita. "We tried to explain to him it wasn't his fault, it wasn't even his car. . . . He loved kids and felt as if he had killed his own children. Perhaps the only thing that pulled him out of it was that he was able to help one of the kids who remained in a coma for several days. He went every day and talked to him. Also he felt the affection of the parents of the victims—especially from the mother of the girl who died, Giuditta. The girl was her only child . . . but she would hug Paolo every time she saw him, which helped him a lot."[10]

In his desperation, Borsellino called his friend and boss, Antonino Caponetto, who was taking a hard-earned vacation in Florence after the completion of the maxi-indictment. Although Borsellino didn't ask for it, Caponetto understood that Borsellino needed help. He cut short his vacation and returned immediately to Palermo. "He was destroyed," Caponetto recalled. Until the end of his life, Borsellino would frequently remember the episode with tears in his eyes, telling Caponetto: "If you knew how often I think of that act of friendship . . . and of how much good it did me."[11]

Meanwhile, the Palermo newspaper, *Giornale di Sicilia,* tried to exploit the political potential of the death of the two children, using it to attack Borsellino and the anti-mafia pool. But the schoolmates of the dead children responded with remarkable maturity and judgment, writing to protest the shameful press campaign and expressing their support for the judges who were risking their lives each day for the future of the city.

The episode, in some ways, set the tone for the growing battle for the hearts and minds of Palermo before the opening of the maxi-trial.

As the trial of the bosses actually became a reality, forces anxious to maintain the status quo in Sicily stepped up efforts to undermine the case by any means possible. In fact, *Giornale di Sicilia* took every opportunity to raise doubts about the value of the maxi-trial, moving from the articles about the noisy sirens of the anti-mafia judges to ones about the cost and size of the maxi-trial, and, finally, to expressions of concern about the "criminalization" of Sicilian society and the risks to the Italian system of justice if the word of confessed criminals should be used to put respected citizens in prison. In the past, the newspaper had never shown much interest in the problem of civil liberties. It had taken, for example, the hard line in crushing left-wing terrorism, favoring greater police powers, pretrial incarceration without bail, reduced sentences for terrorist witnesses and even the return of the death penalty, which, in Italy, is a position popular only on the far right. But suddenly it demonstrated an unusually sensitive concern that the fragile rights of the defendant might be trampled by the mastodonic maxi-trial.[12]

Prominent political figures were quoted warning against a hasty rush to judgment and the "climate of suspicion." And the owner of *Giornale di Sicilia* stated his belief that "the mafia, today, is outside the world of political power . . . I don't believe that there are organic ties between politics and mafia, just as one can't say that every corrupt public official is necessarily a *mafioso*."[13]

At the same time, the paper fired one of its top mafia reporters, Francesco La Licata, considered to be close to the anti-mafia pool, while an editor with close ties to the Salvo cousins, defendants in the maxi-trial, was promoted—a situation that provoked a strike from its editorial staff.

While the press campaign against the maxi-trial was in full swing, a series of demonstrations were organized to protest the arrest of former mayor Vito Ciancimino and the elimination of patronage jobs in city contracts. Unemployed workers marched through the city, shouting "Long live the mafia!" or "At least with Ciancimino, there were jobs!" The timing of the protests, coming just before the opening of the maxi-trial, seemed carefully orchestrated.[14]

Unexpectedly, the archbishop of Palermo, Cardinal Salvatore Pappalardo, added his voice to the chorus. Historically, the Sicilian Church had been reluctant to do anything to upset the local Christian Democrat power structure, but Pappalardo had begun condemning the mafia in no uncertain terms. In his impassioned homily on the death of General Dalla Chiesa, he had appeared to point his finger at the government, when he compared Palermo to the city of Sagunto, abandoned by ancient Rome as it was overrun by the barbarians. But with the advent of the maxi-trial, the archbishop appeared to reverse himself. "Palermo is not Sagunto, and never will be," he said at a well-attended press conference. "It is a city with its problems, like many others. . . . The Church . . . does not have a position on this big trial. The Church hopes that it can clear up some cloudy horizons, but it is also worried that holding such a large trial will attract too much attention to Sicily. . . . Why do you pay so much attention to this [mafia] question? In my work as bishop it represents perhaps only two percent of my work. . . . The mafia kills fewer people than abortion." He denied having said that members of the mafia should be automatically excommunicated from the Church and even seemed to lend support to the pro-mafia demonstrations taking place when he said, "Many of today's problems are due to unemployment."[15] The archbishop even published an article in *Giornale di Sicilia* in which he appeared to implicitly criticize the trial when he wrote: "It's much better to construct something good than to denounce evil." As if it were possible to "construct something good" without first freeing Sicily from the stranglehold of the mafia.[16]

When a group of Palermo students held a rally on the eve of the trial to express support for the prosecutors, the newspaper reacted as if democracy in Italy were in danger: "Let no one think they can influence the proceeding with political pressure, marches and mass protests, which are the stuff of summary trials of certain Mediterranean dictatorships."[17]

The day the trial opened, while most Italian newspapers ran headlines like THE MAFIA BEHIND BARS, the *Giornale di Sicilia* featured a strange, ambiguous invitation to end all discussion of the case: SILENCE, THE COURT ENTERS! The newspaper took the rather unusual position that it would refrain from editorial interpretation during the course of the trial. "We want to faithfully document what takes place, without commentary," the editors wrote. And for much of the trial, it ran two competing columns, headed: "Mafia" and "Anti-mafia"—as if journalistic objectivity required maintaining a position equidistant between the mafia and its prosecutors.[18]

B efore it even began, the maxi-trial got off to a somewhat rocky start. None of the criminal court judges in Palermo was prepared to try the case. Although the jurists all had plausible-sounding reasons, many people suspected that the judges had retreated in stark terror. It was not until someone from Palermo's civil court, Alfonso Giordano, stepped into the breach, that the maxi-trial found its judge. Giordano would be flanked by two other judges on a three-man panel, in case something happened to him during the long trial. A tiny man, with a balding, disorderly head of red hair and a high-pitched, almost falsetto voice, Giordano seemed an unlikely hero.

The case opened on February 16, 1986, in a wild, spectacular fashion. More than six hundred members of the press from around the world attended the first sessions, sitting on bright green seats together with hundreds of citizens in the enormous, stadium-like gallery that overlooked the vast octagonal courtroom, facing the raised dais of the judges. Like the orchestra at an opera, hundreds of lawyers crowded the tables on the bright green carpet floor. Along the back and sides of the courtroom, as in a zoo, thirty cages held the hundreds of accused *mafiosi,* while hundreds of *carabinieri,* carrying machine guns, stood on the other side of the bars, watching the defendants.

The defense immediately tried to derail the case by demanding that Judge Giordano step down, a request he promptly refused. The lawyers may have hoped to rattle him into lashing out against the defense in such a way that the case could be overturned on appeal, but Giordano never lost his balance and managed to convey a sense of being firm but fair.

Judge Giordano would need his patience. As the trial began, the defendants immediately tried to turn it into a circus. Some interrupted the court to demand water and cigarettes. One removed his clothes and threw a shoe at his lawyer.[19] Another, taking *omertà* to new extremes, literally stapled his mouth shut, indicating with hand gestures that he would slit his throat if a written statement of his was not read aloud to the court. Vincenzo Sinagra's cousin, Tempest, still feigning madness, began screaming unintelligibly during the proceedings. Even though he was confined to a straitjacket, he fought like a bull against the small army of agents who tried to carry him from the courtroom, demonstrating how he had earned his nickname. Luciano Leggio, the old boss of Corleone, insisted that it was impossible for the defendants to follow the trial with police guards watching their every move. Giordano never lost his cool during these antics, and yet never allowed the trial to spin out of control. He tried carefully to sort out the reasonable requests from the unreasonable ones. By the end of the trial, he had won almost universal praise for his careful, judicious manner.[20]

As the case bogged down in more than a month of procedural

squabbling without the prosecution presenting its star witnesses, some began to wonder whether the ex-*mafiosi* would actually dare to testify at trial. Then, at the beginning of April, a court attendant announced: "Your honor, Tommaso Buscetta is at the disposal of the court."

Buscetta's arrival electrified the audience and long lines formed outside the bunker-hall with members of the public eager to hear the testimony.

"You could tell the importance of certain *mafiosi* by how much noise the defendants made when they testified: if someone insignificant took the stand, the *mafiosi* would continue talking among themselves, ignoring the witness, but if someone who counted was talking there would be silence," said government prosecutor Giuseppe Ayala. "When Buscetta testified you could hear a fly buzz."[21]

Even a hardened skeptic like novelist Leonardo Sciascia was impressed by Buscetta's authoritative bearing and clear and careful narration. "Buscetta speaks with a firm, calm voice, never loses his composure, no matter what the question," Sciascia wrote. "He knew what he wanted to say and what he didn't want to say, had thought about it, had measured his words, was sharp and precise." Buscetta held the stand for a full week, with the nightly news broadcasting the day's highlights and *Radio Radicale* broadcasting the hearings from gavel to gavel.[22]

In his testimony Buscetta repeated what he had already told Falcone in his many depositions. He described the structure of Cosa Nostra, the first mafia war of the 1960s, the formation of the Commission, the growing tension between the traditional families and the Corleonesi, the mafia war of the 1980s. Again, he minimized his own criminal past and that of his friends, and was evasive on the topic of mafia and politics, for which he received much criticism. He didn't remember the name of the member of parliament he had met with in 1980 nor did he remember which politicians the Salvo family was close to.

And yet there were glimpses of this world of complicity. There was a memorable exchange when one of the defense lawyers asked Buscetta about the mafia's role in Michele Sindona's fake kidnapping in Sicily in 1979.

LAWYER: What did [Stefano] Bontate tell you about his relations with Sindona?

BUSCETTA: That Sindona was crazy, he wanted to start a revolution in Italy, something that didn't interest Stefano Bontate, and so he told him to forget it.

LAWYER: But Sindona talked to him about a revolution. Wasn't Bontate worried about being the keeper of such a secret?

BUSCETTA: The secrets of Sindona are like a feather compared to the secrets that Bontate had.[23]

Some of the major bosses, such as Pippo Calò and Luciano Leggio, tried to shake Buscetta's testimony by challenging him directly—something the Italian court system allows. Accused and accuser were seated side by side in front of the judges' dais offering their competing versions of reality.

The tension between Buscetta and Calò, lifelong friends turned worst enemies, made for high courtroom drama. Buscetta said that he was the one who initiated Calò into the mafia, while Calò went on to become the boss of Buscetta's "family."

Like an old couple in a vicious divorce suit, Buscetta and Calò traded insults and accusations, slinging mud at each other. "Unfortunately, he's always had this idea of himself as some kind of superman," Calò said, "this vanity of letting people know his name is Buscetta. . . ." "He's a liar . . ." Buscetta replied. "You're vain, you've always had that vice," Calò said.[24]

Calò complained of Buscetta's immoral conduct, of his abandoning his first wife and children, remarrying twice and even having an affair with a Mexican ballerina. Playing the role of the concerned family friend, Calò told about how one of Buscetta's brothers, with whom Calò had been in prison, complained constantly about Buscetta's shirking his family responsibilities. "[Buscetta's brother] came to see me in Rome . . . and told me with tears in his eyes: 'Look what Masino has done, he's gone again, leaving me with one son in prison and the other on drugs.' "[25] At that point, Buscetta lit into Calò: "The only true thing he has said in this court is that he and my brother were very close friends, what he's forgetting, in this moment, is that he sat at the table, together with the rest of the Commission, when they decided the death of my brother and his son." Then turning to Calò, Buscetta said: "Hypocrite. . . . You had my entire family murdered: my brother-in-law, my sons, my son-in-law, my cousins. Why didn't you have me killed?" To which, with an air of menace, Calò replied: "Don't worry."[26]

Calò insisted that Buscetta's anger toward him stemmed from an incident in 1980, when Calò said he would not allow Buscetta and his Brazilian wife to stay indefinitely at Calò's Roman hideout.

Buscetta, always sensitive to any allusion to his many marriages and his dubious morality, shot back at Calò: "You would never have the balls to tell me to get out, you don't have the balls!" To which Calò replied: "And I'm the *mafioso*? Look who's talking!"[27]

Buscetta then accused Calò of the murder of a member of his own mafia family (Giovanni, in Sicilian Giannuzzu, Lallicata), whose only sin was having been too close to exiled boss Gaetano Badalamenti.

CALÒ: You're always the same, telling your lies . . .
BUSCETTA: You call them lies . . . Giannuzzu, Giannuzzu Lallicata, you killed him with your own hands. . . . You and I talked about it. . . . You and I."

Calò then turned to Judge Giordano and said: "I gave Mr. Buscetta hospitality and took him in when he was a fugitive, let him sleep at my house, and look how he thanks me . . ."[28]

While this vicious round of mudslinging may have tarnished Buscetta's image as the noble and unflappable "man of honor," the obvious intimacy between Buscetta and Calò created the overwhelming impression that they were both major players in the life of Cosa Nostra. Calò found himself in the classic bind of organized crime defendants: they need to smear the witnesses as amoral criminals, but cannot avoid having a certain amount of the tar sticking, by association, to their own hands.

The confrontation between Luciano Leggio and Buscetta produced a paradoxical situation in which witness and defendant appeared to exchange roles. Buscetta claimed never to have met Leggio, while the boss of Corleone insisted that they knew one another well. "Buscetta has said he doesn't know me . . . telling a lie. . . . He met with me, not once, but several times. . . ."[29] Leggio went on to describe how he had gotten rich off the black market during and after World War II, how he had met Buscetta frequently during the 1960s, generally in the company of Salvatore Greco, Cichiteddu (the alleged head of the Commission at the time). He acknowledged knowing all the major bosses of the period, referring deferentially to *"Don* Paolino Bontate" and his son Stefano Bontate, Gaetano Badalamenti and Totò Riina—"I have great affection for him . . . because he was a cellmate of mine, together with one of his brothers. . . ."

Describing Buscetta as a ruthless schemer, Leggio indicated that Buscetta played an underhanded role in the mafia war of the 1960s, trying to depose the boss of his own "family," Angelo La Barbera, by pitting him against the powerful Grecos. To make his point, Leggio invoked the words of La Barbera himself, whose clan was indeed wiped out in the conflict. Leggio testified that he had interceded on La Barbera's behalf, putting in a good word for La Barbera with Salvatore Greco (Cichiteddu), with whom the La Barberas were at war. "I acted as ambassador [to Cichiteddu] for that good soul, Angelo La Barbera. . . . I have heard it said that I was his enemy. . . . I have never been anyone's enemy . . . the proof is that when we were in prison together, Angelo La Barbera came to my cell and asked, 'You have to do me a favor.' . . . [La Barbera] knew of my friendship with Cichiteddu and with the Greco family . . . [he told me] 'You have to tell Cichiteddu not to listen to a word that Buscetta tells him. . . . He's a worm . . . a double-crossing troublemaker . . . he is the reason for all my troubles. . . .' This is what La Barbera told me, and I passed it on, as ambassador to Totò [Salvatore Greco]." Even if one chose to believe this characterization of Buscetta as "a worm," Leggio's account confirmed the fact that Buscetta was a key player in the mafia of the 1960s, enlarging, if anything, his role and placing him on close terms with Leggio and the other bosses of the period. By depicting Salvatore Greco (Cichiteddu) as a kind of head of state receiving ambassadorial missions, Leggio gave further weight to Buscetta's contention that he was the head of the Commission at the time.[30]

The centerpiece of Leggio's defense was the story of the failed Borghese coup d'état of 1970, in which he portrayed himself as a patriot and a political victim. His life sentence for murder, Leggio insisted, was punishment for his having turned down the neo-Fascists' request for mafia help in their failed attempt, led by Prince Junio Valerio Borghese, to overturn democracy. "My conviction is political," he told the court. In Leggio's version of the Borghese coup, Buscetta and Salvatore Greco (Cichiteddu) were in favor of helping the neo-Fascists and traveled together from America to push the project. The plan was for the mafia to carry out a series of terrorist bombings and assassinations, providing the justification for the right-wing coup. But Leggio said he vetoed the idea. Buscetta's hatred for Leggio and the Corleonesi, the old boss said, stemmed from this episode. "Buscetta considers me the man who destroyed his dreams of glory," Leggio said. Buscetta had hoped, he said, to be able to return to Italy under the new regime and make a fortune from "government contracts, logistical supplies, arms, contraband. In short there were hundreds of millions of dollars at stake . . . and he hoped to get the lion's share."[31]

Leggio's account provided an interesting twist to the Borghese coup, which may help explain Buscetta's evasiveness on the subject and his reluctance to admit knowing the boss of Corleone. But as a defense, Leggio's strategy backfired. He evidently hoped to take the court by surprise by talking about the coup d'état. He had not calculated the possibility that Buscetta had already anticipated his move, by telling the same story to Falcone in deposition. "The public prosecutor, who had a copy of Buscetta's deposition, informed Leggio and he was stunned," wrote Antonino Caponetto in his memoirs. "Buscetta had understood that sooner or later Leggio would have pulled out that story and . . . so he beat him to the punch."[32]

Leggio's testimony had the unintended effect of strengthening Buscetta's credibility: while they both slanted the story to their own advantage, the important facts were identical. Leggio had implicitly validated the existence of the Commission: in both stories, all the alleged top bosses, Leggio, Greco, Gaetano Badalamenti, Giuseppe Calderone and Giuseppe Di Cristina, discussed the decision like the heads of a collective government. Leggio's story also made clear his own dominant role in Cosa Nostra at that time. He had a hard time explaining to the court why the success of the coup hinged on his approval, if, as he contended, he had no role in the mafia, or if there were no such thing as the mafia. "They turned to you to carry out a coup d'état because of your notoriety, because of your name?" Judge Giordano asked Leggio. "A myth has been created around me, naturally. . . . They wanted my [approval] because there was this myth. So they wanted this myth."[33]

After Leggio, the jury and the public got a look at Michele Greco, "the Pope" who had been captured during the course of the trial after spending four years in hiding. Greco, supposedly elected head of the Commission in 1978, portrayed himself as a hardworking, successful citrus farmer, ruined by libelous anonymous letters and because the notoriety of his cousin Salvatore "Cichiteddu" Greco had made the Greco name synonymous with mafia. At the same time, "the Pope" bragged of his many friends in the Palermo aristocracy and the Palermo magistrature and described the idyllic life he led on the grand Favarella estate he had acquired from the count of Tagliavia. "So many respectable and illustrious personages have visited us. . . . You remember His Excellency [Emanuele] Pili [a former chief prosecutor of Palermo]. . . ." Greco went on to name a long list of high-ranking officials in the police and the *carabinieri,* who had the keys to and free rein of the estate. Other frequent guests, as Greco was forced to admit, were notorious mafia bosses, such as Paolino Bontate and his son, Stefano, and Salvatore "Cichiteddu" Greco. But they came not for meetings of the so-called Commission but because they were passionate hunters, eager to shoot quail and rabbits in Favarella's vast hunting reserve. "Poor Stefano [Bontate] came over often," Greco said. "Stefano had a great passion for hunting and for hunting dogs. . . . We were together on the Holy Friday, just days before his misfortune," he said. Bontate's "misfortune" was being murdered in the spring of 1981.[34]

Salvatore Contorno presented another side of mafia life. Unlike Buscetta, Contorno was comparatively candid about his own crimes, which included murder, drug trafficking and contraband. Contorno insisted in speaking in a Palermo street jargon that even many Sicilians had trouble following. An expert in local dialects from the University of Catania was brought in to act as interpreter as Contorno described his life within Cosa Nostra. If Buscetta had seen the world outside the mafia, Contorno clearly knew no other reality than Cosa Nostra. Contorno appeared to be an unrepentant *mafioso* using the arms of the law now that he could no longer fire his .38 caliber pistol. When the rabble inside the defendants' cages jeered at him, he hurled insults back at them. When a lawyer asked him how he defined a killer, Contorno replied: "A good kid, someone who counts." Contorno, Sciascia wrote, lived inside the world of Cosa Nostra "the way the rest of us live inside our own skin, as if the mafia were a state into which you were born and always remained a citizen of."[35]

Contorno's criminal credentials were impeccable. He had a long police record before becoming a witness. And when he was captured in Rome in 1982, investigators found two bulletproof cars, several weapons, tens of thousands of dollars in cash, some heroin, and 140 kilos (290 pounds) of hashish in his possession.[36] He was stalking Pippo Calò, whom he held responsible for the death of Contorno's boss, Stefano Bontate. "Too bad I didn't succeed," he told the court at the maxi-trial.[37]

From direct experience, Contorno could identify specific drug shipments, and, as a result, was highly credible when he described a heroin laboratory on Michele Greco's Favarella estate: "The door was open and I could smell the odor, they were working the drugs," he testified.[38] But with Favarella being used increasingly for meetings of the Commission and the hiding of mafia fugitives, the refinery was considered too great a risk. "There was too much confusion, too many cops around, so they moved the lab," Contorno testified.[39]

With his more direct, up-to-date knowledge of Cosa Nostra, Contorno was able to stand up, turn around and identify some 150 of the *mafiosi* sitting behind him in the cages.

All in all there were more than one thousand witnesses, for both prosecution and defense. There was Ko Bak Kin, the drug trafficker from Thailand, who acknowledged his role in numerous heroin shipments to Palermo, and Vincenzo Sinagra, who described the horrors of the Room of Death. His testimony was crucial in winning numerous murder convictions, including his own: a twenty-one-year term, which he is still serving.

Even when things didn't go as the prosecution planned, the overwhelming impression confirmed the anti-mafia pool's vision of the case. For example, when a local newspaper printed a story that the defendant Vincenzo Buffa might be cooperating with prosecutors, the women in his family provided a chilling public display of Sicilian *omertà*. Seven women, Buffa's wife, eldest daughter, and five sisters, all began shouting in a kind of Greek chorus: "Enzo is not a witness. He hasn't talked and he won't talk." Despite orders from Judge Giordano to remain silent, the women, shouting in the direction of the defendants' cages, had to be physically removed from the bunker-hall.[40]

The trial was comparatively free of political revelations. The ministers of the government, such as Giulio Andreotti, succeeded in giving their testimony in Rome, out of the public eye. Andreotti denied having had the conversations that General Alberto Dalla Chiesa had noted in his diary, saying the general must have confused Andreotti's name with someone else's. The attorney for the Dalla Chiesa family tried to have Andreotti brought up on charges of perjury but, being a case of a dead man's word against that of a living foreign minister, nothing came of the matter.

Nino Salvo had died of cancer in a Swiss hospital just before the trial began, but his cousin, Ignazio Salvo, testified. In painting his family as victims of the mafia rather than *mafiosi,* he fully confirmed the powerful role of the mafia in the economic and political life of Sicily. Less than a decade after many had insisted that the mafia did not exist, here was Ignazio Salvo, one of the richest and most powerful businessmen in Sicily, offering a description of the mafia's power that coincided closely with that of the prosecution.

> For many years, the state's complete absence from the war against the mafia and the almost endless instances of complicity and collusion have left the defenseless citizens in the hands of the mafia organizations. One has no choice but to try to survive by avoiding the dangers to his own family, particularly if one's own business activity puts one in regular contact with these organizations. I have never been a *mafioso* but I am one of the many businessmen who in order to survive has had to come to terms with the enemies of society.[41]

TWELVE

The period of the maxi-trial—from February 1986 to December 1987—was a time of great and genuine achievements and serious, but less visible setbacks. While the trial held center stage, a number of more subtle developments began to whittle away at the foundations of the anti-mafia pool of Palermo.

The fact that the maxi-trial unfolded in a climate of respect for the law, that the defendants were given every opportunity to plead their cause, was in itself a triumph of civilization. That all of Italy could listen each night to the stories of men like Buscetta and Contorno, comprehend the horror of the mafia through Vincenzo Sinagra's tales of the Room of Death, and see mythical figures like Luciano Leggio and Michele Greco "the Pope," cut down to size as mere ordinary mortals, provided an invaluable education for a nation that had only recently begun to grapple with the mafia problem.

"Public opinion now knows the names of the people who shoot and kill and the names of those who deal in heroin," Paolo Borsellino said in an interview at the time of the trial. "It's not nothing, but it's not everything," Borsellino added, cautioning against the risk of seeing the maxi-trial as the "defeat" of the mafia. "Unfortunately, these people are still extremely dangerous," he said. "The bitter truth became obvious last summer when the mafia showed its terrible firepower," he said, referring to the assassinations of Ninni Cassarà and Beppe Montana. "In less than a week, it decapitated the entire investigative squad of the Palermo police. . . . Also, there is a troubling statistic: one-third of the defendants in the maxi-trial are fugitives, and three-quarters of the important bosses and the hit men responsible for the most serious crimes are at large."[1]

Behind the scenes, during the course of the trial, the anti-mafia pool continued its investigative work. Before the maxi-trial was even half finished, the group had completed preparing the evidence for another maxi-trial, the second in a planned series of four. "Maxi-two," as it was called, was much smaller than the first: the evidence was contained in five volumes of about 1,400 pages and involved eighty defendants. While the first trial, maxi-one, had concentrated on Palermo, maxi-two dealt with the mafia of the surrounding countryside. As Vincenzo Marsala, the son of the former boss of the town of Vicari, told Giovanni Falcone: "The truth is, Judge, you have to use an iron fist with the mafia and if you don't start with the countryside, you will never uproot this noxious weed. The countryside is the great reservoir of manpower for the mafia, allowing it to continually find fresh blood for its membership."[2]

Along with the professional accomplishments, it was also a time of great personal happiness for Giovanni Falcone. On a spring day in May 1986, he and Court of Appeals Judge Francesca Morvillo interrupted their working day at the Palermo Palace of Justice, sneaked off to City Hall and got married. They invited only a handful of close friends and were married personally by Mayor Leoluca Orlando. "That day he really seemed happy," said secretary Barbara Sanzo. "He came back to the office and he couldn't help showing off his ring." Around the time of his marriage, Falcone shaved off his beard, leaving an elegant mustache. He started swimming again and lost the weight he had gained in the previous couple of years. "Suddenly, he looked ten years younger," Sanzo recalled.[3]

Giovanni Falcone and Francesca Morvillo had a great deal in common. They were both from Palermo; they both had serious, shy, introverted natures and both had been outstanding students of the law. Francesca was a highly respected magistrate, in her own right, from a family of magistrates. Both of them were veterans of disastrous youthful marriages, something that deepened their appreciation of the happiness they had found together. Francesca was affectionate, demonstrative and solicitous with Giovanni. " 'The Sweet Francesca,' Paolo called her," said Rita Borsellino, his sister. "That's how I remember her even as a girl— we were in junior high school together."

But there was much more to Francesca Morvillo than sweetness. While obeying the outward forms of the good Sicilian wife, she was an independent-minded woman who understood her husband's work and had her own career and intellectual interests. "I think this 'Sweet Francesca' stuff has been overdone," said Pasqua Seminara, a good friend and fellow magistrate in the Palermo Palace of Justice. "Francesca did have a sweet nature, but she was not the classic 'good wife' who stayed at home, waiting for her important husband to return. She was an excellent criminal lawyer. . . . She had her own life, a strong personality and a decisive character. . . . Giovanni had great respect for her opinions." When Falcone was away, or working late, Francesca would go on her own or with friends to plays, concerts and movies.

"It was not a conventional marriage, it was an intelligent marriage," said Judge Francesco Lo Voi, who together with Judge Seminara, his wife, socialized often with Giovanni and Francesca. Falcone traveled half of the time and when he was in Palermo, he often worked until late at night. "It was not made of the little experiences of everyday life. But they were very fond of each other. . . . I don't think Giovanni ever took a trip without bringing a present for Francesca and I don't think Francesca ever went shopping without getting something for Giovanni."

The couple decided against having a family. Falcone was worried about not having enough time for children as well as exposing them to the restrictions and dangers of his bulletproof existence. "You're supposed to bring children into the world, not orphans," Falcone said, half jokingly.

With maxi-one in court and the indictment of maxi-two complete, Paolo Borsellino decided to leave the anti-mafia pool, putting his name in as a candidate to become chief prosecutor of Marsala, a city on the western coast of Sicily about an hour and a half's drive from Palermo.

There were many reasons for Borsellino's move. With the investigative work into the first two maxi-trials completed, a certain cycle of work had ended. Three bright young prosecutors—Giaocchino Natoli, Giacomo Conte and Ignazio De Francisci—had been added to the pool and trained to take over part of the workload. But the maxi-trials had concentrated on Palermo and the small towns around it, while the power of the mafia in the rest of Sicily remained uncontested. Borsellino saw the move to Marsala as "missionary" work, bringing the approach of the anti-mafia pool to other offices on the island. Borsellino also felt, inevitably, a desire to be his own boss, to go out on his own, friends have said. As long as he stayed in Palermo, he would be considered a satellite in the orbit of Giovanni Falcone, who, by the sheer force of his personality, reputation and intellect, became the center of gravity of every major investigation. Now, Borsellino would have a chance to be the head of his own office and apply what he knew, albeit in a small provincial city.

Another factor, according to some, was a desire to escape the accumulated pressures of five very long years on the front line in Palermo. The intense glare of the spotlight focused on the capital had taken its toll on his family, living in constant anxiety about whether he would return each night. His daughter, Lucia, was reduced to skin and bones from anorexia nervosa, weighing under eighty pounds, and Borsellino felt that his leaving Palermo might relieve the pressure on the family.

Borsellino's good friend and colleague Vincenzo Geraci played a critical role in getting him the Marsala job. Part of the anti-mafia pool at the Procura della Repubblica of Palermo, Geraci was elected to the Italian judiciary's governing body in early 1986 in order to give the judges of Palermo a voice in Rome. Along with working closely together, Borsellino and Geraci were close personal friends and their families were part of the same small social circle. Both men were conservative politically and both were part of the same judicial "current."

Like everything else in Italian life, the judiciary is divided up along political lines, with each "current" electing its representatives to the Consiglio Superiore della Magistratura (CSM). Despite their generic, interchangeable, nonpolitical names, Magistratura Indipendente (Independent Magistrature), Unità per la Costituzione (Unity for the Constitution) and Magistratura Democratica (Democratic Magistrature), all three groups had clear political orientations. Both Borsellino and Geraci were members of Independent Magistrature, a conservative group that represented everyone from Christian Democrats to members of the far right. Falcone was a member of the center-left group, Unity for the Constitution, while Democratic Magistrature was associated with the Italian Communist Party and other smaller, left-wing parties.

Because of Geraci's work on the maxi-trial and other cases, some magistrates in Palermo broke with their usual political "current" to support his candidacy, believing he would bring a greater understanding of the war on the mafia. "People on the Council often failed to understand many things because they had no direct understanding of the [mafia] problem," said Giuseppe Ayala, who argued the maxi-trial in court and who, like Falcone, was a member of the centrist judicial current. "When Vincenzo Geraci presented his candidacy for the CSM . . . I felt that we should support him, breaking with the idea of the currents, even though I had some personal reservations about him. . . . Here, finally, was someone who was one of us and who understood our problems. . . . Giovanni [Falcone] said to me: 'So you've decided to support him?' 'Yes, and I am going to try to convince my friends to do so, too,' I told him. To which he said: 'I will never vote for him.' "[4]

Falcone and Geraci had worked closely on a number of cases, but a certain friction had developed between them. Geraci was an unusually intelligent and ambitious prosecutor who resented the attention that was focused almost exclusively on Falcone. Tensions had grown during the handling of Buscetta: "I don't like that magistrate," the witness told Falcone, speaking of Geraci.

But when the position of Procuratore della Repubblica of Marsala came up, Geraci had fought for his friend Borsellino. To win the battle Geraci had to challenge the rigid seniority system that dominated judicial appointments. The seniority system—that great leveler—was backed by an unusual coalition. Along with mediocrities of every political stripe, who expected to rise effortlessly and automatically, the seniority system also had the support of the Italian Left, which argued that, while arbitrary, the system was, at least, equitable. Many on the Left worried that once seniority was abandoned, political criteria would come to the fore, allowing the parties in power to dominate the nominating process.

Geraci was able to push the Borsellino nomination through. The task was made easier by the fact that the principal competitors had no background in mafia cases and only one or two years' more seniority.

The month after the Consiglio approved Borsellino's transfer to Marsala, police in Palermo arrested Vincenzo Puccio, one of Captain Emanuele Basile's three killers, whom Borsellino had spent years prosecuting. A few months later, a second killer, Giuseppe Madonia, was also captured, along with his father, Francesco Madonia, the powerful boss of Palermo's Resuttana neighborhood. After several trials, appeals, and retrials, the murder convictions of the infamous trio Puccio, Madonia and Bonnano had finally been upheld by Italy's highest court—in absentia. Now, finally, the killers would actually have to serve their life sentences. It seemed a good note on which to leave Palermo.

Just three months after Borsellino moved to Marsala, however, a stunning attack on his selection appeared on January 10, 1987, in one of the country's most respected newspapers, the Milan daily *Corriere della Sera,* written by none other than novelist Leonardo Sciascia. Entitled "Anti-mafia professionals," the article said that the war on the mafia had become "an instrument of power" and a quick ticket to success in Sicily. Sciascia chose as his principal targets Mayor Leoluca Orlando and Paolo Borsellino. About Orlando, he wrote:

> Let us take the example of a mayor who, either out of conviction or calculation, appears—in television interviews, at conferences, symposia and school meetings—as an anti-mafia leader. Even if he dedicates all his time to these appearances and has no time to dedicate to the problems of . . . the city he administers (. . . from the lack of water to the abundance of garbage) . . . anyone who, however timidly, dares to reproach his lack of administrative zeal . . . runs the risk of being branded as a *mafioso.*[5]

Sciascia went on to attack Borsellino's recent promotion and concluded the article with this biting sentence: "Nothing is better to advance your judicial career in Sicily than to have taken part in some mafia trials."[6]

For millions of Italians, including Falcone and Borsellino themselves, who had grown up on Sciascia's novels, the article was an ugly shock. Sciascia was not only Sicily's greatest living writer, he had written brilliant denunciations of the mafia at a time when Sicilian politicians insisted that the mafia did not exist. Now that the majority of Sicilians had come around to Sciascia's point of view, he had turned against them with a vengeance.

What accounted for this bizarre about-face? Part of the reason probably lay in Sciascia's anti-conformist, gadfly temperament. Sciascia was used to swimming against the current and now that the prevailing tide was anti-mafia he felt the need to maintain an independent critical stance against what he perceived as the risks of a new conformism. From the beginning of his career, Sciascia was obsessed with the problem of justice and the dangers of the arbitrary power of the judiciary, from the Spanish Inquisition in Sicily to the show trials of Stalin and Mussolini. Sciascia became a vocal champion of Enzo Tortora, an Italian television host, arrested in 1983 and wrongly accused of dealing drugs in the course of an investigation into organized crime in Naples. Prosecutors had Tortora held at length in prison without bail on the word of a pair of highly suspect criminals, with virtually no corroborating evidence. Tortora's career was destroyed and he died of cancer while fighting a bruising judicial battle trying to exonerate himself.

Sciascia was right to be alarmed by the Tortora case, but he was wrong to blame the judges of Palermo for the sins of their colleagues in Naples. Falcone and Borsellino had investigated the Salvo cousins for nearly three years before finally indicting them and did so only when they had the testimony of two different witnesses, and ample corroborating physical evidence in the form of wiretapped conversations and financial records. Even then, the witnesses were released on bail and allowed to defend themselves from the comfort of their homes.

Moreover, Sciascia had wrongly bunched together the two very different figures of Orlando and Borsellino. It was legitimate to demand of a politician like Orlando that his fiery speeches be followed by concrete results. There was a risk that rhetoric replace action in the war against the mafia. But Borsellino had been working quietly in the trenches for twenty years, grinding out indictments and convictions long before there was anything fashionable about fighting the mafia. Given the number of Palermo prosecutors recently murdered—Cesare Terranova, Gaetano Costa and Rocco Chinnici—there was something grotesque in Sciascia's suggestion that combating the mafia was an easy shortcut to success. Becoming Procuratore of Marsala was hardly the road to fame and fortune. Borsellino was, in fact, moving from the spotlight in Palermo to a difficult job in a dull, provincial town at considerable personal and financial sacrifice. Because his family remained in Palermo, Borsellino had to maintain two residences, living in a small apartment above the Marsala police station during the week, and commuting home on weekends. Borsellino's only sin, even in Sciascia's misguided article, was in having been judged the most qualified candidate for the job. Sciascia never made clear why he considered the old-boy network of the judicial system a bulwark of democracy.

In response to the many attacks on his article, Sciascia admitted that he knew absolutely nothing about Paolo Borsellino, and that certain friends had passed on some documents about his recent promotion. Sciascia, who was old and in failing health, did not bother to check whether there was substance to the charges. Sciascia later apologized to Borsellino, privately, for unfairly singling him out for criticism. "They talked it over and Sciascia asked Paolo to forgive his mistake," said Rita Borsellino. " 'I can't be mad at Sciascia because he's too great,' Paolo said. 'I grew up on his books.' Sciascia was badly advised in this business, he was manipulated."[7]

In this period, Sciascia had many friends in the Radical and Socialist parties, both of which, for different reasons, were beginning to wage a battle to drastically reduce the powers of the Italian judiciary. The Radical Party had always been in the forefront of the battle for civil rights in Italy, and after the successful drives for the right to divorce and abortion, it was looking for a new issue to galvanize its forces. The Socialist Party had its own reasons for wanting to declaw the Italian judiciary: under the direction of Bettino Craxi (who became party secretary in 1976), the Socialists were busy turning the Italian system of government bribery into an exact science. In all likelihood, it was one of his political friends who had tried to set Sciascia against Borsellino and the anti-mafia pool.

Shortly after the Sciascia article, Giovanni Falcone boarded a plane with Mayor Leoluca Orlando on a vacation trip to the Soviet Union. Both of them saw the article as a bad omen. "When the rain comes, you can suddenly see all the snails' horns," Orlando said to Falcone, repeating an old Sicilian proverb.[8]

In fact, Sciascia's article gave ideological respectability to those who wanted to attack the judges. Hack politicians, slick mafia lawyers, even neighborhood enforcers, people who had never before read a word of the Sicilian novelist, declared themselves lovers of Sciascia. "Salvo Lima and [Mario] D'Acquisto [leaders of the Andreotti faction in Palermo] became *Sciasciani,*" wrote Saverio Lodato, Palermo correspondent for the Communist daily *L'Unità* . . . "and how many Sciascia lovers in the Palace of Justice! . . . There were all the do-nothing judges . . . who had never written an indictment or a sentence of any substance. . . . Those who seemed shocked when a journalist would mention possible connections between mafia and politics. . . . All those wig-wearing magistrates who repeat the litany that 'the prosecutor is never against anyone.' They could almost taste the promotions that were around the corner now that the seniority system, with Sciascia's help, had come back into fashion. . . . There were even the neighborhood tough guys on their powerful Kawasaki and BMW motorcycles [commonly used for mafia hits] who proclaimed that they 'agreed with the writer.' "[9]

Giornale di Sicilia jumped on the bandwagon, declaring that "The show-business anti-mafia campaign is . . . on its last legs, its cards have been laid on the table."[10]

The members of the anti-mafia pool could feel the climate around them change. Even before the maxi-trial began, the prosecutors were afraid that the public and the political world were placing too much importance on it. "The press seemed to say that . . . the fate of the mafia depended on this trial. . . . Perhaps

Sicily would free itself of the scourge, perhaps the mafia will be destroyed," Borsellino told the journalist Luca Rossi. "But it was an attitude we didn't like, that alarmed us. Because the more weight was placed on the trial, the less energy was going toward new investigations. . . . You don't defeat the mafia with a single trial. . . . You fight the mafia by continuing to work."[11] The maxi-trial was not even over and people were acting as if the war against the mafia had been won. Already in August 1986, Antonino Caponetto sounded a note of alarm in an interview with the Rome newspaper *Il Messaggero*. "For months I have not heard a member of the government or a prominent politician pronounce the word 'mafia,' " he said. "I hope that if it is absent from their speech, that this problem . . . remains, at least, in their thoughts."[12]

That same summer, the sociologist and mafia expert Pino Arlacchi resigned from his position as consultant to the parliament's anti-mafia commission, saying that "the activity of the commission has virtually come to a halt." It appeared that now that the maxi-trial was under way, there was no reason for the rest of the government to continue busying itself with the mafia problem. Arlacchi was also troubled by another development: the nomination of Christian Democratic senator Claudio Vitalone to the position of vice president of the anti-mafia commission. Senator Vitalone was a former prosecutor, but he was also a close adviser to Giulio Andreotti, and a magistrate with an extremely checkered record. Vitalone had been denied promotion by the Consiglio Superiore della Magistratura because of unprofessional conduct as an assistant prosecutor in Rome. Vitalone was accused of having tried to monopolize (and sometimes sandbag) sensitive political cases, introducing other prosecutors to his friends in power, and of trying to squash a criminal investigation into an alleged fraud committed by his own brother. Given the persistent rumors about the Andreotti faction's mafia ties in Sicily, putting Claudio Vitalone at the head of the anti-mafia commission was a little like letting a fox guard the chicken coop.[13]

The general lowering of the defenses was reinforced by an almost total lack of violence in Palermo. With the maxi-trial, murder had taken a holiday in Palermo. After some 150 murders a year during the height of the great mafia war, death had gone on vacation: there was an average of just thirty-three murders a year in Palermo in 1985, 1986 and 1987, only a portion of which involved organized crime.[14] Many in the general public mistook this for weakness on the part of the mafia—an interpretation belied by the ferociously efficient killings of police investigators Beppe Montana and Ninni Cassarà. For those who knew the mafia well, the ban on killing indicated anything but weakness. It was a sign of its extraordinary control of the city: Cosa Nostra could turn the level of violence in Palermo up or down like a thermostat, depending on whether they wanted the climate to be hot or cool. At a time when a jury sat each day judging 460 suspected *mafiosi* in the bunker-hall, it was clearly not a moment for shootings in the streets of Palermo. Since the number of mafia killings is usually a sign of internal conflict, their almost total lack was a good indication that the leaders of Cosa Nostra continued to reign supreme.

During this new time of Pax Mafiosa Falcone and Borsellino again had the disturbing sensation that they had lost their grasp of what was going on within the closed universe of Cosa Nostra. No new major witnesses had come forward since Salvatore Contorno's decision to collaborate in October 1984, and Contorno's information dated from the time before his arrest in March 1982. Buscetta's knowledge of Cosa Nostra was even more outdated, since he had left Palermo for Brazil just after New Year's in 1981. The slaughter of Buscetta's and Contorno's friends and relatives, the killing of Leonardo Vitale and others had stemmed the tide of mafia defections. Like everyone else in Sicily, potential witnesses appeared to be waiting, waiting for the outcome of the maxi-trial before deciding whether the war against the mafia was real or just for show.

Based on information from the early 1980s, prosecutors had assumed that Luciano Leggio of Corleone and Michele "the Pope" Greco were the most powerful figures in Cosa Nostra. But both were now in prison, Leggio since 1974, Greco since 1986. Meanwhile, there were rumblings that suggested seismic shifts within the leadership of Cosa Nostra. There were rumors that Filippo Marchese, the brutal boss of the Room of Death, had been strangled and eliminated in much the same way that he had dispatched so many of his victims. There were rumors that Michele Greco's right-hand man, Pino "the Shoe" Greco, had met a similar fate. On September 29, 1987, another of Michele Greco's super-killers,

Mario Prestifilippo, was shot down on the streets of Bagheria as he was riding a motorcycle from one hiding place to another.[15] This appeared to confirm the impression that someone within the mafia was intent on consolidating power, getting rid of dangerous young rivals and weakening Michele Greco. In 1984, Buscetta had told Falcone: "Michele Greco, given his bland and weak personality, was the perfect person to become head of the Commission so as not to stand in the way of the designs of Riina."[16] Evidently, now that he was in prison, Greco had outlived his usefulness. Buscetta believed that Riina was acting on the will of Luciano Leggio, who remained the "boss of bosses." But after twelve years in prison, it was hard to imagine that Leggio was pulling all the strings. Suspicions turned, once again, to his mysterious lieutenants, "the Beasts," Riina and Bernardo Provenzano, neither of whom had been seen in almost twenty years.

Police had nearly captured Riina several times, always arriving a moment too late. They had discovered the apartment where he had evidently been living with his wife, Antonietta Bagarella, the younger sister of well-known *mafiosi* from Corleone (Calogero Bagarella, killed in a 1969 shootout, and Leoluca Bagarella, suspected of having murdered police inspector Boris Giuliano). Police also found invitations to the Riina wedding, celebrated in a church in Palermo in 1974. The ceremony was performed by the mafia priest Agostino Coppola (cousin of the Italian-American gangster Frankie "Three Fingers" Coppola), who had been defrocked for his role in a kidnapping. The couple had four children, all of whom were delivered in the same Palermo hospital and registered dutifully under their real names. Clearly, the boss was living right under the noses of investigators in Palermo, presumably with the protection and complicity of many, many people. The last photograph that police had of Riina dated from the 1970s. Showing Riina smiling for the camera like any other tourist among the pigeons of St. Mark's Square in Venice, the picture became a mocking symbol of the impunity of the mafia.[17]

But the Palermo police were unlikely to catch Riina any time soon. The department had still not recovered from the assassinations of their top investigators Beppe Montana and Ninni Cassarà, and the mass transfers that followed the killing of mafia suspect Salvatore Marino. When they found the body of the notorious mafia killer Mario Prestifilippo in late 1987, the newly arrived officers at the Palermo police had no idea who the victim was even though his criminal career had been documented for years. The historical memory of the department had been wiped out and it was now groping in the dark.

A s the maxi-trial moved into its final phase, politics began to intrude more and more into the mafia prosecutions of Palermo.

In March 1987, the nearly four-year reign of socialist prime minister Bettino Craxi came to an end. For six years, the Christian Democrats had shared power by letting leaders from other parties head the government. First, Giovanni Spadolini from the tiny but respected Republican Party had been made prime minister. But when it became clear that the visibility and prestige of the office had caused his party to nearly double its vote from 3 to 6 percent, the Socialists and Christian Democrats torpedoed his government. Craxi then got his turn and began to emerge as the strongman of Italian politics. After four years, the Christian Democrats had decided they had had enough of building up Craxi's career at their own expense. They were, after all, the largest party in parliament and had gallantly sat on the sidelines for long enough. The elderly Amintore Fanfani, who had first been prime minister in 1954, became prime minister again (for the sixth time) in April 1987. But his government lasted only ten days before it, too, was sabotaged by the warring factions of the coalition. The squabbling among the five parties of the government coalition was beyond remedy. President Francesco Cossiga had no choice but to dissolve parliament and call for national elections in June.

The parliamentary vote was only one of two major elections scheduled. The Socialists and the small, opposition Radical Party had gathered enough signatures to hold a national referendum to reduce the power of the Italian judiciary. Stimulated by the ordeal of television host Enzo Tortora and other travesties of justice, the referendum sought to hold magistrates responsible for their mistakes. A judge or a prosecutor could be sued personally for damages if he or she wrongly arrested or imprisoned an innocent citizen. There was much that needed reforming in Italy's legal system: clear rules for speedy arraignments and bail hearings after arrest, limits on the use of pretrial incarceration; but the referendum, with its emphasis on punishing prosecutors, seemed to be aimed less at reform than intimidation.

The attack on the judiciary became a central component of the Socialists' campaign strategy for the political elections held in June. Bettino Craxi had created his political fortune on a clever mix of "conservative" and "liberal" issues. He tried hard to distinguish himself from the Communist Party by making his party a staunch supporter of NATO and friend of the United States and by taking a hard line against inflation and limiting workers' wage increases. But he wanted to maintain a certain left-wing appeal by seeming liberal on social issues such as abortion, divorce and civil rights. By attacking the judges, Craxi appeared to be standing up for defendants' rights.

But there was more to the campaign than public relations. The magistrature represented a serious obstacle to Craxi's ambitious drive to power. In 1976, he had taken over a battered, disoriented party on the brink of extinction that had dwindled from 25 percent to a mere 9 percent of the vote. Next to the shrewder and tougher Communists and Christian Democrats, the Italian Socialists seemed woolly-headed, idealistic losers. Craxi was determined to change all of that. When his party reentered the government in 1980, he decided to increase its strength by adopting the old Christian Democratic patronage system but infusing it with aggressive new energy. The Christian Democrats had been slowly building their empire for nearly forty years. Craxi had to make up for lost time.[18]

"Bring in votes and money" was the watchword of the day. These were the marching orders Craxi gave to party member Valerio Bitetto when Bitetto was appointed in 1980 to sit on the board of directors of ENEL, Italy's national electric company. ENEL was one of the country's massive state industries, which could be looted to finance the party's pharaonic election campaigns. Bitetto would steer energy contracts to "friendly" businesses, who would kick back a percentage of the money to the party. Bitetto found nothing unusual about Craxi's instructions, as he told prosecutors when the lid blew off the system in 1992. "I was no ingenue, I knew how the world worked," he later testified. "If a party had little money it would have few votes. . . . ENEL was under Christian Democratic domination and the Socialist Party was cut out of the big deals. We had to roll up our sleeves and get to work."[19]

Craxi brought new economic realism to the Italian government, but somewhere along the way he and his party completely lost track of whatever ideals may have originally animated them. "At the beginning of the 1980s with the triumph of Reaganism and the failure of social democracy, Craxi's old ideals collapsed and were replaced by the new values of success, extreme competitiveness and a passion for money," explained a former close friend and Socialist, Carlo Ripa di Meana.

With the rapacity of guests who have come late to the banquet, the Socialists set about trying to place their men in all the key spots in government, industry, banking, transportation, real estate, art, theater, journalism. They created fiefdoms, divvied up jobs, apartments and women, threw lavish parties, sponsored symposia and cultural initiatives. At every turn, the theme was the same: "Bring in votes and money." As they tasted power, the new generation of socialist leaders lived like Ottoman pashas, traveling with enormous entourages of flunkies, bagmen, pretty girls and hangers-on.

Although the Italian judiciary had never distinguished itself for vigilance in the area of political corruption, the Socialists had reason to fear that some zealous prosecutor might try to rain on their parade. Already in the early 1980s magistrates had stumbled on many of the scandals that would eventually bring the system down some ten years later, but they had been effectively squelched. There were several ways of derailing corruption investigations. The most successful was parliamentary immunity, which was finally lifted only in 1993. The system worked so well that, before 1992, only one government minister was ever prosecuted for corruption.

The institution of parliamentary immunity created the perfect Catch-22: prosecutors were not allowed to investigate members of parliament without the permission of parliament, which rejected the overwhelming majority of cases on grounds of insufficient evidence. And yet, if prosecutors tried to muster the necessary evidence, they risked being sanctioned for violating parliamentary immunity. This, in fact, is what happened to Judge Carlo Palermo, a young magistrate operating in the northeastern city of Trento.

Pursuing an investigation into arms and drugs trafficking from Eastern Europe to Sicily, he stumbled on an enormous bribery scandal. Financiers of the Italian Socialist Party were involved in skimming money from contracts they helped arrange between "friendly" Italian companies and the government of Argentina. The trail of evidence led to socialist minister Gianni De Michelis and Prime Minister Craxi himself. (The charges went beyond mere graft: there were indications that the Socialists had arranged for the sale of military equipment to the Argentines during the war with Britain over the Falkland Islands—which helped explain Craxi's reluctance to condemn Argentina, and support Italy's British ally.) When Judge Carlo Palermo sent the incriminating evidence to the parliamentary commission to seek permission to continue his investigation, Craxi mounted an aggressive counteroffensive, accusing Palermo of violating his parliamentary immunity. Soon it was Palermo and not Craxi who was under investigation—his career in jeopardy. The parliament turned down Judge Palermo's request to pursue the corruption case, while disciplinary hearings were called to consider whether the magistrate should be stripped of his position.

(It is worth noting that a member of the parliamentary commission that refused to waive Craxi's immunity was Senator Claudio Vitalone—one of Giulio Andreotti's men. Craxi had voted against demanding the resignation of Andreotti for his relations with Michele Sindona and now the Andreotti faction was returning the favor to Craxi, in his hour of need.)

Carlo Palermo's story did not end there. He asked to be transferred to Trapani, Sicily, to take the place of his friend Giangiacomo Ciaccio Montalto, who had been murdered by the mafia in January 1983. Because Judge Palermo's arms and drugs case had had a strong Sicilian component, the two magistrates had worked closely together. Palermo continued to pursue the case in Sicily and he contributed to the investigation that led to the discovery of Europe's largest heroin refinery, in the small town of Alcamo, Sicily. But on April 3, 1985, he narrowly escaped assassination. Palermo's car was destroyed by a bomb placed on the highway, but he survived. The full force of the explosion was absorbed by a passing car, carrying a woman and her two small children, who were all killed. The mafia appeared to be behind the attack, but many people wondered whether it was Judge Palermo's corruption investigation that provoked the attempt on his life. Judge Palermo's brush with death did not prevent the Socialists from pursuing disciplinary sanctions against him. Judge Palermo, in fact, finally resigned his prosecutorial post, taking a desk job at the Justice Ministry in Rome.[20]

Aside from the shield of parliamentary immunity, there were other strategies for short-circuiting corruption investigations. In 1984, judges in Milan discovered the existence of a massive "slush fund" of Italy's largest state-owned holding company, IRI, used to disperse some 300 billion lire (more than $350 million) to fund election campaigns, Catholic political groups, and Christian Democratic and Socialist newspapers. The Procura della Repubblica of Rome opened its own investigation, creating a jurisdictional conflict. And—as had happened with the investigation into the secret P2 Masonic Lodge—Italy's Supreme Court (La Corte Suprema di Cassazione) intervened in favor of Rome. The investigation petered out without leading to major indictments. In 1987, when the case had slept in the Rome prosecutors' office for two years, there were calls for a parliamentary investigation, but the governing parties were able to beat back the measure. The Rome Procura became a kind of "Bermuda triangle" that politically sensitive investigations entered, never to emerge. At one point in 1985 some forty-six assistant prosecutors demanded that their boss resign, protesting that he had intervened to influence or sandbag numerous delicate political cases.[21]

Despite the malleability of some judicial districts, the major political parties had good reason to fear a strong, independent, aggressive magistrature. And so the electoral campaign of 1987 was heavily conditioned by the broadside attack on the judges. While the Tortora case in Naples was the example everyone cited, Palermo, strangely enough, became the center of the electoral campaign. The two leaders of the referendum to punish prosecutors— Marco Pannella of the Radical Party and Socialist leader Claudio Martelli, the "dauphin" of Bettino Craxi—both decided to run for parliament from Palermo. (In Italy, before recent electoral reform, members of parliament could run from more than one district simultaneously.) To many, the campaign appeared to be a subtle, and sometimes not-so-subtle, attack against the Palermo anti-mafia pool. Pushing the theme of defendants' rights, the Radical Party openly courted the criminal world, sponsoring membership drives in prisons across Italy. In desperate need of funds, the Radicals announced that unless they received contributions from ten thousand new members, their party would have to disband. The party had surprisingly little difficulty meeting its goal, receiving contributions from convicted murderers and organized crime figures. The campaign was a great success at Ucciardone prison in Palermo, where even Luciano Leggio, the boss of Corleone, asked for a Radical Party card. Radical leader Marco Pannella, known for his sense of political theater (in a later stunt, he got porno star Cicciolina elected to parliament), defended his decision to grant membership to convicted bosses. "We Radicals cannot deny these requests," he said. "We pose no preconditions on our members."[22]

To many *mafiosi*, the Socialists and Radicals had proved more helpful than their old friends in the Christian Democratic Party. One telling instance occurred during the maxi-trial. The defense attorneys came up with a legal ploy that nearly derailed the trial. Citing an old and almost unknown law, they demanded that every word of testimony heard in the case be read back aloud in court—something that would have quite literally doubled the length of the two-year trial. This colossal stalling tactic might have resulted in a mistrial, since it was unclear how many jurors would have lasted through this kind of legal filibuster. A coalition of Christian Democrats and Communists came together to strike the law from the books, saving the maxi-trial. Both the Socialists and Radicals opposed the measure, citing concern for civil rights.

Both Pannella and Martelli, the leaders of the anti-judges campaign, did remarkably well in Palermo. Martelli gathered some 117,000 votes, and the Socialist Party nearly doubled its electorate in Palermo, climbing from 9.8 percent to 16.4 percent. The Radical Party, whose presence had been almost too small to count in Sicily, collected 2.3 percent. The Socialists overtook the Communists in Palermo for the first time in recent memory, while the Christian Democrats slid down to their lowest total in years, 35.2 percent. A decade of spasmodic efforts at reform in Sicily had cost the Christian Democrats 10 percent of the vote. A district-by-district analysis revealed that the Socialists and Radicals were concentrated in areas of so-called high-density mafia vote.[23]

Shortly after the election, Mayor Leoluca Orlando denounced the fact that the Socialists had courted the mafia vote, creating a local government crisis. The Socialist Party resigned from the city government in indignation, forcing Orlando to form an "anomalous" coalition that included the Christian Democrats, the Communists and a small Catholic reform group called "The City of Man." Orlando's idea was to form a "fusion" government that cut across traditional party lines and united all the groups committed to a program of government reform and the fight against the mafia. This combination—in defiance of the national alliance between Socialists and Christian Democrats—was seen as a particular threat to the Socialists, who never lost an opportunity to attack the government in Palermo.[24]

Unfortunately, the war against the mafia became confused with this larger power struggle, so that political opponents lashed out at Orlando and the anti-mafia pool indiscriminately. Claudio Martelli, the vice secretary of the Socialists, referred to the Orlando coalition as "a shadow government of magistrates and Jesuits."[25]

After the elections, a new national government was formed that reflected the new hostility toward the magistrature. The previous government, formed in 1983 in the wake of the Dalla Chiesa and Chinnici killings, had provided the foundation for the maxi-trial. The anti-mafia pool had a receptive ear and received concrete help from its ministers of justice and interior. These men were replaced in July 1987 by ministers whose anti-mafia credentials were far more suspect. The new minister of the interior (the nation's top law enforcement position) was Amintore Fanfani, whose local supporters in Sicily once included questionable figures such as Vito Ciancimino and Salvatore Lima. The new minister of justice was Giuliano Vassalli, one of the leaders of the campaign to limit the powers of the judiciary. Although a respected jurist, Vassalli had invested much of his energy recently in attacking the use of *pentiti*, criminals turned government witnesses. By choosing him, the government made clear that it would block the legislation that mafia prosecutors were calling for: a witness protection program and the ability to negotiate with criminals to win their cooperation.

These reversals in Rome were felt immediately in Palermo.

"With this changing of the guard, everything stopped," said Antonino Caponetto, the head of the investigative office. "Before, we
got anything we wanted: Xerox machines, computers, airplanes,
the helicopter to protect Falcone. Suddenly it all stopped."[26]

The prosecutors of the anti-mafia pool did their best to ignore
the changing political climate, hoping that if they kept up their
work it would prove a passing storm. In August 1987, they finished the indictment for the third maxi-trial, sticking to their plan
of doing a major new trial each year. The latest case used new evidence—like the discovery in 1985 of the massive heroin refinery
in the town of Alcamo (near Palermo)—to pursue the Sicilian network of international drug trafficking.

Although the group maintained its impressive work rhythm, it
missed the presence of Paolo Borsellino. "Without Paolo, the distance between Falcone and the rest of us grew," said Ignazio De
Francisci, the youngest member of the group. "Borsellino had the
professional and personal experience to go head-to-head with Falcone as an equal. At the same time, he was more approachable,
down-to-earth, more similar to us and so he acted as a kind of
bridge between us and Falcone. . . . I remember once Paolo gave
me an important piece of advice in dealing with Falcone. He told
me: 'Don't challenge him directly in front of other people at a
meeting. If you have a disagreement with him, go to him the next
day privately.' And in fact, Falcone would be very open and flexi-
ble. . . . Borsellino also offered a kind of middle ground between
the insane work tempo of Falcone and our more normal pace. . . .
But we managed to move forward preparing the work for both
maxi-two and maxi-three."[27]

The campaign against the judges intensified throughout the fall
of 1987, in anticipation of the national referendum on the judiciary scheduled for November. Some claimed that the Italian magistrature was a political instrument of the Italian Communist
Party—the "judicial road to Communism," it was called. Conservative papers even portrayed the anti-mafia pool of Palermo as a
hotbed of left-wing power. The pool had gone to great lengths to
avoid this perception by making sure that its members came from
all points of the political spectrum. When the group added three
prosecutors in 1985, one, Giacomo Conte, was a man of the left;
another, Giaocchino Natoli, was a centrist; and the third, Ignazio

De Francisci, was a political conservative. They wanted to make clear that the pool's only goal was to combat the mafia. This did not prevent some newspapers from taking liberties with the truth. One even portrayed the scholarly, moderate De Francisci as a wild-eyed student radical. "I was an A-student, who couldn't stand demonstrations . . . I've always voted Christian Democrat," De Francisci said.[28]

But the campaign against the judges worked. The Socialists' success in the parliamentary elections in June was capped by an equally satisfying triumph in the November referendum: magistrates could now be sued for damages for their errors in judgment.

While the nation was voting on the judicial referendum, the jury in the maxi-trial retired to consider its verdict. And so from the middle of November to the middle of December, Palermo waited.

At seven-thirty in the evening on December 16, 1987, Judge Alfonso Giordano called the court to order and began to read the verdicts, a process that, given the size of the case, took an hour and a half. Before a stunned court, Giordano inflicted guilty verdicts on 344 defendants, for a total of 2,665 years. Not only were hundreds of mafia "soldiers" found guilty, the court handed down nineteen life sentences for many of the most important bosses in Sicily: Michele Greco, "the Pope"; Francesco Madonia; and, in absentia, Salvatore Riina and Bernardo Provenzano. For the first time in history, the court had accepted the fact that Cosa Nostra was a hierarchical organization, governed by a "Commission," in which different families frequently acted in concert. Several of the killers of the Room of Death received life sentences: Vincenzo "the Tempest" Sinagra and his brother Antonio, and Salvatore Rotolo. In many cases the mafia had been swifter in exacting justice than the court: Rosario Riccobono, Filippo Marchese, and Giuseppe "the Shoe" Greco had all disappeared, while Mario Prestifilippo had been shot and killed before the verdict.

The court showed mercy toward the prosecution's star witnesses, Tommaso Buscetta and Salvatore Contorno, sentenced to three and six years, respectively. Vincenzo Sinagra, whose frank and precise testimony was fundamental to convicting the operators of the Room of Death, was repaid for his candor with a hefty twenty-one-year sentence.

Despite the accusations of being a judicial monstrosity, the maxi-trial proved highly efficient: it had taken twenty-two months from beginning to end, only six more months than the Pizza Connection trial in New York, the largest drug conspiracy case in U.S. history, which had only twenty-two defendants. The Palermo court also managed—contrary to the predictions of civil libertarians—to discriminate carefully among the hundreds of defendants: 114 defendants were let off for insufficient evidence. The court found that Luciano Leggio could not be held responsible for the decisions of the Commission during his years in prison. Giuseppe Calò was acquitted for several crimes committed in Palermo while he was in Rome, but sentenced to twenty-three years in prison on other counts. "We did not convict anyone simply on the word of government witnesses," Judge Giordano explained in an interview after the verdict.

The mafia, however, was not so lenient: one of the acquitted, Antonio Ciulla was murdered within an hour of being released. Despite testimony from five different witnesses, including Buscetta and Contorno, that Ciulla was a mafia heroin dealer operating out of northern Italy, the court acquitted him because of a lack of corroborating evidence. Ciulla bought pastries and champagne after leaving Ucciardone prison, but his assassins reached him before he made it home to celebrate. He was the first of at least eighteen defendants acquitted at the maxi-trial who were later executed by the mafia.[29]

THIRTEEN

The verdict of the maxi-trial of Palermo was, in many ways, the end of an era. Antonino Caponetto, Chinnici's successor, now sixty-eight years old, decided it was time to leave Palermo. He had spent four and a half years living like a prisoner in a military barracks and was anxious to get back to his family in Florence, where he could spend the final two years of his career before retirement. Before putting in his request for a transfer, however, Caponetto wanted to be sure that the anti-mafia pool would remain in good hands. Giovanni Falcone was the obvious candidate for the job and Caponetto wanted to be sure that the Consiglio Superiore della Magistratura felt the same way. Caponetto knew that there was some resistance and hostility toward Falcone and the anti-mafia pool, but he felt it would be very difficult, in the wake of the triumph of the maxi-trial, for people in Rome to justify denying Falcone the job.

There were six candidates for the position as head of the investigative office, all of them with greater seniority than Falcone. But the judicial Council, after the nomination of Paolo Borsellino as chief prosecutor of Marsala, had indicated that merit was as important as seniority in making appointments. In terms of qualifications, particularly with regard to mafia investigations, none of the five other candidates could be reasonably compared to Falcone.

With the decision expected by mid-January, the various candidates began jockeying for position. "Giovanni never had many influential friends in the Palace of Justice in Palermo or in Rome," Caponetto later wrote. "The fact that Falcone was head and shoulders above the others created around him a climate of incomprehension, rivalry, jealousy, little envies." One of the rival candidates to head the investigative office, Marcantonio Motisi, threatened to resign from the magistrature if Falcone got the job. Motisi had several years' seniority over Falcone, was already an assistant chief prosecutor, and could not stand the idea of working for someone who should, by his lights, be his inferior.[1]

On January 12, 1988, the politicking and in-fighting at the Palace of Justice was interrupted by the renewal of mafia violence. Giuseppe Insalaco, the former mayor of Palermo who had tried to clean up the area of city contracts, was assassinated. The parabola of Insalaco's strange career encompassed all the contradictions of Palermo: a creature of a corrupt political system, he had turned against the machine during his brief stint as mayor in 1984 and was finally destroyed by it. In the final months of his life, Insalaco had actually become a fugitive of justice, accused of having embezzled money from a clinic for deaf-mutes of which he had been a trustee. Although there may have been some merit to the accusations, it is probably not a coincidence that they surfaced, in the form of anonymous letters, at the time Insalaco was threatening to open up Palermo's system of assigning its city contracts. Insalaco had been blackmailed, threatened, had his car burned and, now that the moratorium on violence observed during the maxi-trial had lapsed, he had been murdered.[2]

On the day of Insalaco's funeral (January 14, 1988), the mafia settled another old score. Natale Mondo—the police officer who had narrowly escaped death when his boss, Ninni Cassarà, was assassinated in 1985—was shot and killed in Palermo. Mondo, who had been suspected of having betrayed Cassarà, had been transferred and then eventually absolved. Now, with the picture of his corpse in all the newspapers, he at last received the full public exoneration he had wanted.[3]

Just a few days after Mondo's death, a third bombshell hit Palermo: police found a kind of political "last will and testament" in which Mayor Insalaco, from beyond the grave, fired a parting shot at his enemies, making troubling accusations against many of the city's most important politicians. Two national newspapers, *La Repubblica* and *L'Unità,* had obtained copies and, on January 17, 1988, began publishing them in full. As Insalaco was running both from the police and his mafia assassins, he committed some of his secrets and suspicions to paper in a strange series of documents. One of them, called "The Two Faces of Palermo," was a list of the good and evil rulers of the city. There were fifteen names on the list of evil rulers: aside from the usual suspects like Vito Ciancimino and Nino and Ignazio Salvo, there were a number of political heavyweights: the Republican Party leader and government minister Aristide Gunnella; the brothers Giovanni and Luigi Gioia (both Christian Democratic members of parliament); Salvatore Lima; and former prime minister Giulio Andreotti.[4]

In a long memoir, or diary, Insalaco told the story of his legal difficulties and of the attempts to threaten and blackmail him. He described meetings with local politicians who promised or threatened to use their friendships in the magistrature to squelch or reactivate the investigation into Insalaco's alleged wrongdoing. He told of a tense encounter with Republican Party leader Gunnella over the reassignment of city contracts: Insalaco interpreted Gunnella's tone as a direct threat and decided to send his children away from Sicily. The former mayor also talked about the secret power of a mysterious confraternity, The Knights of the Holy Sepulcher, a religious order dating from the Middle Ages. Although it was not clear what purpose a crusading order served in late-twentieth-century Palermo, the fact that the order was headed by Count Arturo Cassina, the king of city contracts, suggested aims other than the guarding of Christ's tomb. As Insalaco pointed out, several people on his list of the evil rulers of Palermo, including Procuratore della Repubblica Vincenzo Pajno and police agent Bruno Contrada, were "knights" of the Holy Sepulcher. Insalaco's dislike of Pajno may have stemmed from the criminal charges filed against him, while suspicions about Contrada had persisted for years. In 1984, Tommaso Buscetta had warned Giovanni Falcone that Contrada may have been in collusion with the mafia during his days as head of the Investigative Squad of the Palermo police.

This had not prevented Contrada from going on to become one of the highest officials in the Italian secret services.

The assassinations of Insalaco and Mondo and the revelations of the former mayor served as sobering evidence that the mafia was anything but dead after the maxi-trial and reminded some people of how much was at stake in the nomination of the new head of the investigative office at the Palace of Justice. Would the "hidden powers" of Palermo, of which Insalaco wrote, influence the selection of the new chief prosecutor?

A few weeks before the final vote, scheduled for January 19, 1988, a subcommittee of the Consiglio Superiore della Magistratura (CSM) in Rome had narrowed the six candidates down to two, Falcone and Antonino Meli, a sixty-eight-year-old appellate court judge from Caltanissetta. At the end of a long career, Meli wanted to return to Palermo, where his family lived, and had applied for three different positions.

Meli appeared to have little other than his seniority in his favor. He had had a long, unblemished career, but his background was not particularly well suited to the Palermo job. He had been primarily a trial judge, had little experience with the mafia and had never worked as an investigative magistrate. Perhaps most serious, he was sixty-eight years old, only two years from obligatory retirement. With the anti-mafia pool in the middle of a series of complex investigations, it seemed a poor idea to hand the office to someone who would have to leave the job just as they were beginning to master it.

But the Council in Rome, although it was supposed to be dedicated to the impartial administration of justice, represented specific interests. Twenty members were elected directly by their fellow magistrates, the great majority of whom were more interested in protecting their careers than in the war on the mafia in Palermo and had a strong personal stake in protecting the seniority system. The other ten were picked directly by the parliament, using the same division-of-the-spoils system that governed everything else: four seats went to the Christian Democrats, three to the Communists, two to the Socialists and the remaining spot to one of the smaller government parties.

The Council's subcommittee on appointments took a preliminary vote in which it favored Meli over Falcone by a margin of three to two. When Caponetto spoke with some members of the Council, he was troubled by the bureaucratic mentality he found even among some who were sympathetic to Falcone's candidacy. "If we make Falcone a chief prosecutor today, in ten years he'll be on the Supreme Court," said Giuseppe Borrè, a left-wing magistrate, who was worried about the possible ripple effect the decision might have on accepted career paths and civil service rankings.[5]

It seemed preposterous that the Council would hold Falcone's "youth" against him. After all, he was forty-eight years old, at a time when long experience and youthful energy had blended to bring him to the height of his powers. His American counterpart, Rudolph Giuliani, had become the number three man at the U.S. Justice Department while in his mid-thirties, and, at the age of thirty-nine, was made U.S. attorney of the Southern District of New York, the country's most important federal district, at the head of an army of prosecutors and federal agencies. Falcone, by contrast, with nearly twenty-five years of experience, still occupied the humble rank of assistant prosecutor.

With Falcone's nomination apparently in jeopardy, Caponetto drew up a telegram withdrawing his request for transfer. He did not want to see four and a half years of work go up in smoke and preferred to hang on in Palermo for the last two years before his retirement in order that his group could continue its work. Caponetto kept the telegram ready should it be needed. The game, however, still seemed wide open, with many members of the Council undecided. Every day, as their hopes rose and fell with each passing rumor, Caponetto and Falcone debated whether or not to send the telegram. One evening when things looked particularly bleak, they agreed that Caponetto should revoke his transfer. But the next morning, as Caponetto was about to wire the judicial Council, Falcone arrived in his office with a happy, confident air. "Nino, rip up that telegram," Falcone said.[6] During the previous evening, Falcone had received assurances that his selection was all but certain.

Caponetto ripped up the telegram but remained somewhat doubtful. He had learned from years of experience that Falcone was a strange mixture of skepticism and naïveté. As a prosecutor, Falcone was a pessimistic realist, who could smell prevarication immediately and quickly strip away a witness's layers of deception. But in his own life, Falcone could be remarkably ingenuous. "Outside of his work, he was a person of astonishing candor and simplicity, with an unlimited faith in the promises other people gave him," Caponetto later wrote.[7]

On the afternoon of January 19, 1988, the day the CSM met, Falcone had carefully prepared a list of all of the members of the panel. In ink, he wrote the names of those certain to support Meli on one side and those who had committed to support him on the other side. In the middle, he wrote the names of the undecided voters in pencil. As the evening wore on, he received periodic updates on the progress of the debate. Names were checked off, and moved from column to column. By the end of the long evening, even some of those whose names he had written in ink under his own name had had to be crossed out and moved to the other side. At about nine-thirty in the evening came the final tally: 14 votes for Antonino Meli, 10 for Falcone. Five members abstained.

As he left the office after the long evening, a crowd of reporters was waiting outside the Palace of Justice. Despite the galling defeat, he reacted with characteristic, unflinching self-control. "We will continue work as before," he said. "I will remain in my job and I have no comments to make."[8] But early the next morning, when he arrived punctually at the office, he was still clutching the piece of paper with the names on it. And with obvious bitterness, he handed it to Caponetto. "In that note you can see the traces of the agony he suffered that night, in the form of all the names crossed out and moved," Caponetto wrote. "In the end it was two names that changed columns that made the difference."[9]

One of the decisive last-minute switches was that of Vincenzo Geraci, who, according to Caponetto, had promised Falcone his support on the morning of the vote. As the only mafia prosecutor on the panel, Geraci's vote was highly influential. Coming from a friend and colleague, Geraci's behavior seemed like a stab in the back. Paolo Borsellino felt so strongly about it that he broke off relations with Geraci. Their very close friendship turned almost overnight into powerful enmity.

But the movement to stop Giovanni Falcone went far beyond Geraci. "It was a complex orchestration," said Giuseppe Di Lello, another of the founding members of the pool. "I think it is a mistake to demonize one person, Geraci. . . . There were many people who wanted to stop Falcone because he upset many different equi-libria."[10]

Although some believe that the "plot" to stop Falcone was hatched in political circles in Rome and Sicily, it was carried out quite willingly by Falcone's own colleagues in the Palermo Palace of Justice, who acted out of a variety of motives in which professional jealousy, personal dislike, well-intentioned but shortsighted principle and bureaucratic rigidity mingled with the darker forces of personal ambition and outside political influence into a powerful mixture. Working in the bunkerized offices of the investigative office, Caponetto and Falcone had limited contact with the legions of faceless magistrates that filled the cavernous marble spaces of the Palermo Palace of Justice. They had avoided the judicial politics to which some magistrates dedicated more time than to their cases. They had tried to pay as little attention as possible to the buzz of courthouse gossip and the sarcasm of the black-robed figures who crowded its seemingly innumerable corridors.

The skepticism that greeted Falcone's bank investigations at the time of the Spatola case had not been dispelled by his subsequent successes. On the contrary, his achievements were salt in his critics' wounds. When important government officials—the minister of justice, the minister of the interior, even the president of the Republic—arrived in Palermo, the first person they sought out in the crowd was Giovanni Falcone, walking past and appearing not to notice far more senior magistrates, the appellate judges, the chief prosecutors, even the president of the tribunal. The police escorts and the dark blue bulletproof Alfa Romeos of the anti-mafia prosecutors had become status symbols in Palermo. Judges had begun to fight over them, and now everyone wanted protection and resented not having it, even magistrates who had never put themselves in the line of fire.

"The principal characteristic of magistrates is professional envy," said Ignazio De Francisci, the youngest member of the anti-mafia pool. "Even at my level, there was envy: a colleague wanted a bodyguard and told me it wasn't fair that only we had them, he, too, had investigated the Marchese family. But what he didn't say was that he had let them off. . . . In Palermo, career is everything. People die of heartbreak over it. Vanity and power. With maybe vanity being the more important of the two. . . . The magistrature is a professional caste, with its leaders, its factions and alliances, its gangsterish power bases. . . . The Consiglio Superiore della Magistratura is the expression of that soft underbelly that hates Falcone, the expression of the bureaucracy."[11]

The campaign to stop Falcone was won by a series of behind-the-scenes maneuvers made long before the decisive vote. The first move was to persuade Antonino Meli to push for the job as chief of the investigative office. Originally, Meli had applied for three different openings and hoped to become president of the tribunal. Meli, in fact, was the most senior candidate for that job, a more prestigious but less demanding position, which many considered better suited to a sixty-eight-year-old judge on the edge of retirement. Meli, in fact, withdrew his candidacy for the investigative office in order to make clear his preference for the job of president of the tribunal. But his withdrawal almost assured Falcone's victory. The other candidates, although more senior, were much closer in age and experience to Falcone. Because the CSM, led by Vincenzo Geraci himself, had preferred Paolo Borsellino to an older magistrate as chief prosecutor of Marsala on the grounds of his superior qualifications, it would have been close to impossible to reject Falcone for someone with only a few years more experience. Meli, on the other hand, was twenty years older than Falcone, with sixteen years more experience as a magistrate. Rejecting him created a serious institutional problem, completely overturning the seniority system.

Just before the final decision, Meli suddenly reapplied for the job as head of the investigative office and at the same time withdrew his name for consideration as president of the tribunal. This set up an either/or choice for the CSM between Meli and Falcone, without the possibility of offering Meli another position as a compromise. According to several members of the CSM, this conflict was artfully staged by Geraci and Umberto Marconi, another member of the judicial panel. "Geraci and Marconi let Meli know through their respective channels in Palermo that if he didn't withdraw his nomination for president of the tribunal, he wouldn't get either of the two positions," said Vito D'Ambrosio, a member of the CSM at the time and now a prosecutor on Italy's highest court in Rome. "[Meli], who was a basically honest but naive type . . . allowed himself to be talked into it. . . . There was a very precise choreography. Although [Geraci and Marconi] have never admitted it, they have never denied it."[12]

Although he did not name names, Antonino Meli himself admitted making the move out of "friendship" after being approached by other senior magistrates who did not want to see themselves leapfrogged over by Falcone. "They will never admit it, but one thing is certain," said De Francisci of the anti-mafia pool. "Meli did not go to the investigative office on his own initiative. Someone put him there."[13]

Once the showdown between Meli and Falcone had been arranged, there was still the problem of convincing a majority to support Meli. Despite the disparity in age, there were still a lot of judges who were prepared to back Falcone and several others who were waiting to see how certain key members would vote. Vincenzo Geraci played an extremely active—and highly duplicitous—role in convincing his own judicial current to back Meli, according to Stefano Racheli, a member of the same group within the CSM, Independent Magistrature, the conservative, Christian Democrat faction.

Geraci apparently hoped to abstain from the vote while, at the same time, convincing his group to unanimously support Meli. "He wanted to be the behind-the-scenes architect without appearing that way in public," said Judge Racheli. But some members were uncertain or leaning toward Falcone, but were prepared to vote for Meli if a clear majority of the group did so. "Geraci said, 'I am going to abstain since I am from Palermo, it's better for me to remain impartial.' . . . But Marcello Maddalena, another member of our group, and a very decent person, said he would vote for Falcone, unless everyone opposed the nomination. . . . 'If you abstain,' he told Geraci, 'then there is no group discipline and I will feel free to vote for Falcone,' which would have ruined Geraci's whole plan. . . . Instead Vincenzo Geraci was forced to abandon his appearance of neutrality and vote against Falcone. . . . And he was not at all happy about that."[14]

Independent Magistrature was only one of the three groups on the Council. The majority of Falcone's own faction, Unity for the Constitution, also voted down his nomination. "One of the leading opponents was Umberto Marconi, a member of my and Falcone's faction," said Judge Vito D'Ambrosio, who participated in all of the group's discussions about the vote. "Marconi opposed Falcone because his electorate consisted of mediocre magistrates who did not want to see Falcone rewarded for his merits. . . . They wanted to protect their own careers."

But Falcone could still have been elected had the left wing rallied behind him. Despite the passionate defense of one of their leaders, Giancarlo Caselli, the majority of the group voted for Meli. They were particularly worried by the chronological abyss between Meli and Falcone. If the CSM had total discretion to ignore seniority, they feared, the council might begin to reject candidates on political grounds. In the end, they fell into the trap presented by those who had convinced Meli to push for the investigative office. "They were very shortsighted, and we all paid the price," said Giuseppe Di Lello, of the anti-mafia pool, himself a member of Democratic Magistrature.[15]

But the suspense continued until the vote on the night of January 19, 1988, held at the CSM's fascist era headquarters in Palazzo dei Marescialli. The debate that preceded the vote was highly dramatic, containing some of the highest and lowest moments in the recent history of the Italian judiciary.

Meli's supporters were careful not to utter a word of criticism of Falcone, but took covert potshots at him through the frequent use of what had become commonly understood code words in the campaign against the judges. Umberto Marconi inveighed against "personality cults" and "distorted protagonism." Judge Sergio Letizia announced that he "did not believe in geniuses or supermen." Another magistrate, Sebastiano Suraci, warned against "the danger of encouraging, certainly not in Dr. Falcone himself, attitudes of exasperated personalism, inspired by the desire for rapid career advancement."[16]

In a bizarre leap of circuitous logic many of the magistrates argued that Falcone should be rejected precisely because he was exceptional. "The best signal the Council could send the country in its war against the mafia is not to give this position to Dr. Falcone, and thereby show that Dr. Falcone is not the only magistrate in Italy capable of fighting the mafia phenomenon," declared Judge Antonio Bonajuto.

A year of public debate that started with Sciascia's article on the "anti-mafia professionals" and ended with the referendum against the judges had clearly taken its toll. Some of the panelists referred openly to both the Sciascia article and the referendum, others simply used the rhetorical ammunition supplied by those debates in explaining their decision to vote against Falcone.

Umberto Marconi repeated some of the Socialist Party rhetoric about the danger of "power bases within and without the judiciary," and reminded the panel of the political context of the vote: "An entire Nation is waiting, and waiting not just for the law on the civil punishment of judges; the public's expectations are directed toward the Government . . . toward the Parliament and toward the political parties. Yes, the parties."

In his somewhat veiled speech, Marconi conjured a specter hanging over the Italian judiciary, suggesting that the political parties would drastically reduce the judiciary's powers if the CSM didn't act to clip the wings of its boldest magistrates, like Falcone, eliminating the so-called centers of power like the anti-mafia pool of Palermo.

Judge Stefano Racheli tried to bring the discussion back to the immediate problem at hand, choosing the best person to head the investigative office of Palermo, a point that seemed to have gotten lost in the discussion. "I remind everyone here that this is our sole task at the present moment," he said. None of Antonino Meli's own supporters had even tried to argue that he was the more qualified candidate. "I don't want to cast aspersion on anyone," he continued, "but I think it's important to make two brief observations: the magistrate proposed by the Commission [Meli] is on the brink of retirement and has never (I repeat, never) worked as an investigating prosecutor. . . . Having seniority and an unblemished career is not enough to become the head of the investigative office of Palermo."

Giancarlo Caselli, the only member of the left-wing group Democratic Magistrature to support Falcone, attacked the "abstractness" of the debate on seniority, which had barely touched on the problem of the mafia. He reminded the panel of the "centrality of the investigative office of Palermo and the quantum leap" made by the anti-mafia pool after decades of impunity for Cosa Nostra and of indifference, failure and even complicity on the part of the Sicilian magistrature.

With bitter irony, he denounced the hypocrisy of the discussion of judicial "protagonism." "The story of protagonism is a bit like the story of women when they wore the veil. Then all women were beautiful, but when the veil fell, people began to note the differences. The same thing has happened with the magistrature. When none of the magistrates made 'trouble,' . . . they were all great. But when some judges began to take a clear stand, to give signs of life and try to reestablish the rule of law, to do things that were unthinkable previously, suddenly they are accused of 'protagonism.' . . . This, while there are judges who retreated from the front lines . . . and who risk nothing. And no one criticizes them. . . . But it is inconceivable, and somewhat scandalous, to speak of privilege when talking about the prosecutors in Palermo who operate in the conditions that are known to all of us."

Some members of the CSM had pointed out that Meli had a reputation for his mercurial temper and his violent reaction to criticism, which had led him to become involved in a bitter public feud with a colleague in Caltanissetta whom he had sued. Moreover, his behavior during the nomination process had been somewhat disturbing: his sudden withdrawal and equally sudden reinstatement of his candidacy and the fact that he had bristled fiercely when some on the Council had questioned his lack of prosecutorial experience. "His continual impulsiveness would not seem to be an ideal character," CSM panelist Massimo Brutti had pointed out.

Finally, at the end of the debate, Vincenzo Geraci took the floor to deliver a speech of extraordinary eloquence meant to convey the impression of a man racked by a Hamlet-like inner torment, torn between the loyalty to his good friend Giovanni Falcone and his overarching sense of duty to the law.

Nothing can erase in me, who has stood at his side in dramatic and emotionally wrenching experiences, the awareness of the merits of Giovanni Falcone in the war against the mafia. With some discomfort I am forced to relive moments from my own life that have remained impressed on me of that small band—they called us, with sarcasm, the "samurai"—that threw itself generously . . . at enormous personal sacrifice and risk of life in combatting the barbarism of the mafia at a time when the streets of Palermo were, as they are again today, literally paved with corpses and the principal representatives of the state on the island were assassinated one after the other. . . . I feel the moral obligation to give my own personal testimony that Giovanni was the best of us all and I consider it my own exalted and unique privilege to have worked beside him, who has written pages of civic redemption in the book of the history, not just of the judiciary, but of our country. . . .

I hope you will allow me to express my own, personal, unspeakable torment during this entire proceeding and the inextricable dilemma in which I find myself caught. On the one hand, the celebrated talents of Falcone and the personal and professional ties that have bound me to him for years induce me to favor him in this choice, but there is an obstacle posed by the personality of Meli, who has always demonstrated his high and silent sense of duty, even in faraway and dramatic times when he was deported to several Nazi concentration camps in Poland and Germany, where he remained prisoner of war for two years. . . . In such a condition, I ask you to understand how much suffering and humility it takes for me to give my vote in favor of the Commission's proposal [in favor of Meli].

Geraci's speech remains one of the finest rhetorical tributes to Giovanni Falcone and would be genuinely moving if one did not know how hard Geraci had worked behind the scenes to torpedo his colleague's nomination. The lyricism of the speech, delivered as he was sinking Falcone's hopes, made his betrayal seem even more chilling. In the wake of Falcone's assassination in May 1992, Borsellino made an emotional public speech at the Palermo public library in which he referred to Geraci's actions that night: "Giovanni Falcone began to die on January 19, 1988, when he was betrayed by a Judas."[17]

Geraci has insisted that he has been made the scapegoat for a collective decision. "People have chosen to attack me because I'm a convenient lightning rod and this helps them avoid attacking the Communists and the left-wing members of the Commission who voted against Falcone on this and other occasions," he said. "After all I was only one of thirty members of the committee."[18]

But magistrates close to Giovanni Falcone insist that Geraci must be held to a different standard. "Geraci's behavior really surprised us," said Leonardo Guarnotta, one of the four original members of the anti-mafia pool. "We had worked closely together, he knew all our problems. He knew very well that if they nominated Meli or someone other than Giovanni the office would be unable to continue working as it had up until that time. . . . He has said that Meli was a gentleman and no one has ever questioned that. But he was not the right man for the job and someone like Vincenzo Geraci could not but know that. If he hadn't known our situation so well, I might believe he was in good faith. But because of his experience and intelligence, I don't believe he was in good faith at all."

Geraci insists that his objections to Falcone were on important, long-standing differences of legal philosophy. "I was one of those who was concerned about the size of the maxi-trial," he said. "The reasons for the conflict with Falcone stem from the fact that I told him I was against having a trial for 500 people." It is true that the Procura della Repubblica recommended reducing the number of defendants to 350. But this seems like a specious attempt at a posteriori self-justification. If Geraci had these philosophical objections to the maxi-trial approach he never expressed them during the debate at the CSM at which Falcone's nomination was considered. Moreover, the days of the 500-defendant trials were already over. The anti-mafia pool had itself reduced the scope of its biggest trials: both maxi-two and maxi-three involved fewer than a hundred defendants. The original maxi-trial had been a unique event, necessary to establish the legal precedent against Cosa Nostra by demonstrating its organization in all its ramifications.

If Geraci's objections to Falcone were on matters of legal principle, it is not clear why he needed to hide his real intentions: pretending to support Falcone (or to be undecided) in public, while working energetically against his candidacy in private. "Geraci had a larger political mission, of blocking, delegitimating and dismantling the anti-mafia pool, which can only have come from a lucid political plan," said Judge D'Ambrosio. "Geraci was notoriously close to the Andreotti faction in Sicily." Some have written that Geraci had ambitions of running with the Christian Democrats for a seat in the Italian Senate. Geraci has denied the charge and, in fact, has never run for political office.

But the hostility toward Falcone did not begin and end with Vincenzo Geraci. The resistance to Falcone was shared by several capable, honest judges in the anti-mafia pool of the Procura della Repubblica. The situation was aggravated by the peculiar structure of the Italian judiciary of that period: there were separate prosecutors' offices, the investigative office and the Procura, that worked on the same cases. But, by law, the investigative office took the lead in the development of witnesses and the discovery of evidence, while the magistrates of the Procura were reduced to the more passive role of checking and critically examining the evidence the investigators produced. Magistrates like Vincenzo Geraci, Giusto Sciacchitano and Alberto Di Pisa were generally silent while Giovanni Falcone questioned witnesses like Tommaso Buscetta and Salvatore Contorno. The charismatic personality of Falcone further accentuated the imbalance between the two offices. "I used to tell my colleagues, you have to face the fact that Falcone is the engine," Giuseppe Ayala, the public prosecutor in the maxi-trial, recalled. "Someone else can be the wheels, and even the steering wheel but we're not going anywhere without the engine." But many of these magistrates, who had worked diligently on mafia cases for as long as or longer than Falcone, were jealous of the recognition he had received.

"Geraci, Di Pisa, Sciacchitano and several others could never accept the fact that when you are playing soccer with a world champion center-forward you have to give him the ball if you want your team to win," said De Francisci. "These people were convinced they were just as good as Falcone, maybe better." The magistrates of the Procura were among Vincenzo Geraci's closest friends, and looked on with mixed feelings at the prospect of Giovanni Falcone achieving increased power.

But the envy of his peers, by itself, would not have been enough to doom Falcone's candidacy. "This vote was part of a much larger game," said Leonardo Guarnotta of the anti-mafia pool. "Remember that the Socialists, particularly Craxi and Martelli, unleashed a violent campaign against us."

"The interests of the magistrature, which wanted to maintain the status quo and the seniority system, coincided perfectly with the interests of the political class, which feared Falcone," said Giuseppe Ayala. "For different reasons they came together on one point: Giovanni Falcone must not get the nomination."

While Giovanni Falcone refused to make any public comments

on the nomination, Antonino Caponetto, on the eve of his departure from Palermo and close to retirement, protested loudly. "At a moment when the mafia has begun to kill again, we needed an innovative and courageous decision that would have guaranteed continuity in the prosecution of mafia investigations," he said the day after the CSM decision. "I would have thought that for the sake of the war against the mafia . . . people might have put aside less noble interests. . . . Evidently, I was mistaken. In Sicily these signals have great weight." In disgust, Caponetto resigned from the National Association of Magistrates. In fact, the Meli-Falcone battle was so fierce that it split the entire Italian judiciary. Hundreds of magistrates from across Italy—including Falcone and several members of the CSM—resigned from their traditional judicial "factions" and formed a fourth group of their own.

A few days after his rejection, Giovanni Falcone had dinner in Rome with several members of the Consiglio Superiore della Magistratura at the home of Judge Stefano Racheli, one of the panel members who had left his judicial faction in protest over the vote. Falcone was in an extremely gloomy mood, wondering about how his public humiliation would be interpreted in Palermo. "I am a dead man," Falcone said. He was acutely aware of the dangers of political isolation in the war on the mafia, recalling what General Dalla Chiesa had said shortly before his death: "I've understood the new rules of the game: they kill the man in power when this fatal combination has come about: he has become too dangerous but he can be killed because he is isolated." The victory in the maxi-trial had proved again how dangerous Falcone was, while the rejection that came on its heels showed how deeply isolated he was. "I'm a dead man," he repeated.

FOURTEEN

Shaking off his initial despair, Falcone responded to defeat in characteristic fashion, by reimmersing himself in his work. For Falcone, work was a refuge, a kind of narcotic drug, his friends and colleagues have said. And he was quietly preparing his biggest coup since the revelations of Tommaso Buscetta in the fall of 1984.

The long, three-year drought in major mafia witnesses had come to an end the previous spring when Antonino Calderone had decided to talk. Falcone had been on Calderone's track since 1981, when (during the Spatola case) he had followed the money trail from a drug deal to a bank account in Calderone's wife's name. Afterward, Buscetta had indicated that Calderone's older brother, Giuseppe, had been a member of the Commission—a fact that was corroborated by a wire-tapped phone conversation between two *mafiosi*.

Antonino Calderone had been arrested by French police in Nice, where he, his wife and children had been living under false names, running a Laundromat. The Calderones were among the big losers in the recent mafia war; Calderone's older brother, Giuseppe, had been murdered in 1978, and Antonino Calderone was forced to flee Sicily in 1983 in fear for his life. As he sat in the Nice prison, he became convinced that he was about to be killed by other Sicilian inmates. Suddenly, he began screaming for a prison guard. He demanded to talk to the head of the prison and said he wanted to speak with Judge Giovanni Falcone. They moved Calderone to an insane asylum for his own protection and on April 9, 1987, Falcone—together with police investigator Antonio Manganelli and French prosecutor Michel Debaq—sat face to face with Calderone in a Marseilles prison. After an initial refusal to talk, Calderone suddenly said: "I know a lot about the mafia, because I am a member of it." Once he started, Calderone talked for almost a year.[1]

While previous witnesses had all been from the capital of Palermo, Calderone described the mafia's grip on Catania, Sicily's second-largest city, located on the east coast of the island, at the foot of volcanic Mount Etna. Before the 1980s, when the level of violence in Catania began to match Palermo's, many believed that the mafia was confined to western Sicily and that Catania—which once bragged of being the Milan of the south—was free of the phenomenon. As Calderone revealed, Cosa Nostra in Catania dates back at least to the fascist period. Calderone's own family was a history of the Catanese mafia in miniature. One of his uncles had helped found the city's first mafia family in 1925 and had been prosecuted by Mussolini's "Iron Prefect," Cesare Mori. Another uncle had helped the mafia get back on its feet after World War II, organizing the black market in contraband tobacco. In the 1960s, Calderone's older brother, Giuseppe, known as Pippo, became the head of the Catania family, while Antonino Calderone himself had been the underboss of the family.

The Calderones were good friends with the "traditional" mafia bosses, Stefano Bontate, Salvatore Inzerillo and Giuseppe Di Cristina, wiped out in the mafia war of the 1980s. It was hardly coincidental that Pippo Calderone was murdered in 1978 only a few months after Di Cristina. The struggle for power in Catania and other provincial cities in the late 1970s was an important prelude to the great mafia war of Palermo of the 1980s. Totò Riina and the Corleonesi were stripping away the layers of support for their ultimate target, Stefano Bontate, by getting rid of his allies elsewhere on the island.

Totò Riina's chief ally in Catania was Nitto Santapaola, who had been a close friend and protégé of the Calderones. Santapaola was the underboss of the Catania family and became the head in 1975 when Pippo Calderone was elevated to the Commission. While the elder Calderone was acting as mafia diplomat, Santapaola was taking care of business at home, making millions in heroin smuggling, establishing himself as the chief enforcer for the leading Catania businessmen and increasing his military strength by carefully building a private army that was loyal exclusively to him, much as Riina had done.

Antonino Calderone was different from Buscetta and Contorno. While they expressed no regret for their crimes, Calderone seemed to suffer from genuine remorse. He began to scream and writhe in agony on the floor as he told of his participation in the murder of several teenage boys, suspected of having snatched the purse of the mother of Nitto Santapaola. Falcone and Manganelli had to have prison guards restrain Calderone for fear he would smash his head on the ground.

As the brother of a Commission member, Calderone was in a strong position to testify about the workings of the organization and he confirmed the essential role of the mafia's governing body in the major assassinations of the 1970s and 1980s.

In fact, although from the other end of Sicily, Calderone was the first mafia witness to provide extensive firsthand accounts of the leaders of the Corleonese mafia. Describing Luciano Leggio, Calderone said: "He liked to kill. He had a way of looking at people that could frighten anyone, even us *mafiosi*. The smallest thing set him off, and then a strange light would appear in his eyes that created silence around him. When you were in his company you had to be careful about how you spoke. The wrong tone of voice, a misconstrued word, and all of a sudden that silence. Everything would instantly be hushed, uneasy, and you could smell death in the air."[2]

Calderone's account of Leggio's successors, Totò Riina and Bernardo Provenzano, was in some ways even more chilling. "The Corleone bosses were not educated at all, but they were cunning and diabolical," Calderone said. "They were both clever and ferocious, a rare combination in Cosa Nostra." He described Bernardo Provenzano as a killing machine. "My brother used to call him *u tratturi,* 'the Tractor' [in Sicilian] because of his capacity for slaughter." But Riina, who was called (but not to his face) *u curtu,* the Short One, was even more dangerous. "Totò Riina was unbelievably ignorant, but he had intuition and intelligence and was difficult to fathom and very hard to predict," Calderone said. "And at the same time he was savage. His philosophy was that if someone's finger hurt, it was better to cut off his whole arm just to make sure." He followed the simple code of the brutal, ancient world of the Sicilian countryside where force is the only law and there is no contradiction between personal kindness and extreme ferocity. Riina was soft-spoken, highly persuasive, and often highly sentimental. He cried when recalling how his mother had been too poor to visit him in prison on the mainland in the 1960s. And Calderone described him as a dedicated father and faithful husband: "I don't want any other women than my Ninnetta," he told Calderone, adding, "And if they don't let me marry her, I'll have to kill some people."[3]

But with Riina you never knew what was genuine and what was play-acting. Calderone described the surreal scene of a mafia banquet honoring his dead brother, held by the men who had had him killed. Riina gave an impassioned eulogy describing Pippo Calderone as a great peacemaker that reduced many in the crowd of hardened *mafiosi* to tears, even though they had reason to suspect that Riina himself had given his blessing to the assassination. Riina's admiration for Calderone may have been sincere: he regretted having to have him killed, the way the president of a company regrets having to lay off a valued employee during a time of economic difficulty.

More than any other witness, Calderone testified about the important relationship between the mafia and the Knights of Labor of Catania. The Calderones had acted as the "enforcers" for the Costanzo family, the chief builders of the city, and made sure that their company had no problems when it worked elsewhere in Sicily. When Pippo Calderone was killed, his place on the Costanzo payroll was taken by Nitto Santapaola. The Catanese mafia had blown up the construction sites of rival companies and even murdered a competitor of the Costanzo company. Calderone also bolstered Falcone's conviction that the Catanese had played a vital role in the assassination of General Dalla Chiesa. At one point, Gino Costanzo took Calderone aside and launched into a tirade about the danger represented by Dalla Chiesa: "What are our Palmeritans doing? Sleeping? Don't they realize the situation is serious?" In recounting the incident, Calderone commented: "If he expressed himself like that to me, who at that time counted for almost zero within Cosa Nostra . . . one can only imagine what he was saying to the bosses of the Catania families."[4]

The Costanzos, according to Calderone, had also helped provide an alibi for Nitto Santapaola at the time of the killing of his rival Alfio Ferlito (the "payoff" for Catania's help in the Dalla Chiesa assassination). Santapaola and his family were staying at the Costanzos' luxury hotel complex at Perla Ionica in the company of a colonel of the *carabinieri* when the murder took place. Gino Costanzo had invited the colonel to stay for free at the hotel, so that, if needed, this accommodating law enforcement officer could be forced to confirm Santapaola's story.[5]

Perhaps the greatest novelty in Calderone's confession was his openness about the collusion between the mafia and members of the Italian government. He described how he and his brother prepared elaborate gifts each year at Christmas for the leading judges, prosecutors and politicians of the city. Calderone explained how the leading Catania businessmen kept important officials in their pockets by giving them rent-free apartments. The Catanese mafia was generally able to learn about arrest warrants before they were issued and sometimes have particular names crossed off the list.

This helped explain why there had been no major mafia prosecutions or corruption investigations in Catania. Top prosecutors had been transferred (but not kicked out of the magistrature) for bending the law in favor of the Knights of Labor. The Catania police had released Nitto Santapaola after only a few routine questions when his bulletproof car had been found at the scene of a vicious shoot-out in which several people had been killed. Moreover, they continued to grant him a license to bear arms, despite his well-known criminal record. (Not surprisingly, no prosecutors or police officers had been assassinated in Catania.)

When the *mafiosi* of Catania needed a false passport for foreign travel, they turned to their member of parliament in Rome, Giuseppe Lupis, of the small Social Democratic Party. Someone in Lupis's office, Calderone testified, would obtain a passport from the German embassy in Rome, bypassing the Italian authorities who tried to restrict the travel of convicted criminals. This helped explain why Lupis became one of the top vote-getters in the city.[6]

"Politicians would always come to us, because we control lots and lots of votes," Calderone told Falcone. "To give you an idea, figure that each 'man of honor,' between friends and relatives, disposes of at least 40 to 50 votes. There are about 1,500 to 2,000 men of honor in Palermo. Multiply by fifty and you get a nice block of 75,000 to 100,000 votes to steer toward friendly candidates and parties."[7]

The large number of seats in the Italian parliament (945—one for roughly every 40,000 voters) has meant that a candidate can win with only several thousand votes. The existence of at least twelve major parties and Italy's old proportional system made it even easier to manipulate results with well-placed blocks of votes. While the mafia had generally chosen to support the most powerful party, the Christian Democrats, the proportional system made it, at times, particularly rewarding to back a candidate of one of the smaller parties. In the elections of 1968, Giuseppe Lupis (whom Calderone accused of running the mafia's "passport office") was able to carry three seats in parliament for his tiny Social Democratic Party on the strength of only 34,000 votes. In those same elections two Christian Democratic candidates with more than 25,000 votes failed to get elected, while Aristide Gunnella of the Republican Party won a seat in parliament with only 12,000 votes.[8]

According to Antonino Calderone, *Onorevole* Gunnella owed some of his good fortune to the mafia and to his friendship with Giuseppe Di Cristina, the boss of Riesi, killed in 1978. "The example of the Di Cristina family is classic," he said. "They were the bosses of the Riesi mafia for three generations . . . they supported the Democrazia Cristiana, they were all DC." Di Cristina's brother was even the Christian Democrat mayor of the town. "But when the scandal of all these *mafiosi* in the Sicilian DC broke out, Giuseppe Di Cristina . . . was kicked out of his party and put under house arrest. He then abandoned the DC and went with Gunnella. . . ." Despite Di Cristina's criminal record, Gunnella gave the boss a job with the Sicilian state-owned mining company that Gunnella headed.[9]

Gunnella eventually consolidated his electoral position, controlling about 30,000 votes, making him a formidable power within his own tiny party. Despite the hue and cry created by his relationship with Di Cristina, Gunnella was repeatedly defended by Republican Party leader Ugo La Malfa. Although considered a man of great personal integrity, La Malfa evidently decided that his party could not do without one of its top vote-getters. Rather than expelling Gunnella from the party, La Malfa made him vice secretary and a minister of the government.[10]

Calderone had met Gunnella and a host of other important Sicilian politicians. Some had actually been introduced to him "ritually" as members of Cosa Nostra, but had now vanished from the political scene.

But perhaps Calderone's most explosive revelation involved Salvatore Lima, Giulio Andreotti's chief lieutenant in Sicily, the Salvo cousins and the transfer of Francesco Cipolla, a diligent, zealous police official in Catania. "We tried to have him transferred using our own connections in Catania, but we didn't succeed," Calderone said. "We decided finally to go to Palermo and see the Salvos. . . . Those were different times. With today's mentality, they would simply eliminate an investigator like Cipolla without wasting time and money over transfers. . . ." When Pippo and Antonino met with the Salvo cousins in their office in Palermo, their conclusion was immediate: 'For this we need *Salvino.*' That is Salvo Lima, the parliamentarian." The Calderones met with Lima in the Rome office of another Palermo business, in the company of Nino Salvo. Lima listened carefully and promised to look into the matter. "Later the Salvos told Pippo that the minister of the interior of the period had told Lima to be a little patient because Cipolla was going to leave Catania anyway, because he asked to be transferred near his wife, who was a schoolteacher."[11]

Throughout much of the second half of 1987, Falcone flew once a week to Marseilles to talk to Calderone, taking some 1,000 pages of deposition. Police began sifting carefully through Calderone's statements and found him to be a remarkably accurate witness. "We checked more than 800 details from Calderone's depositions," said Antonio Manganelli, the police agent responsible for handling Calderone.[12]

In January and February 1988, Manganelli and Falcone were scrambling to prepare arrest warrants for a mass roundup based on Calderone's confessions. Among other reasons, they wanted to move in early March before Antonino Meli took over the investigative office so that the complex transfer of power did not affect the rapid completion of the operation.

Before proceeding with arrests, however, Falcone wanted to pursue the political avenue indicated by Calderone. He thought that perhaps Calderone's revelations might persuade Tommaso Buscetta to tell what he knew about mafia and politics. Falcone had good reason to believe that Buscetta, like Calderone, knew *Onorevole* Salvatore Lima. Buscetta had been most active in Cosa Nostra in Palermo in the early 1960s when Lima was mayor. He was thought to have used his influence at City Hall to obtain building licenses for friendly real estate developers.

In the wake of Calderone's disclosures Falcone flew in February 1988 to a secret location in the United States, where Buscetta was in hiding. Falcone told Buscetta about Calderone's testimony regarding Lima. He prodded him to be more frank about a mysterious meeting Buscetta said he had had in a Rome hotel in 1980 with Nino Salvo and a certain member of parliament, whose name he had refused to reveal. But Buscetta was unmovable:

> Since I decided to collaborate with the justice system of my own free will, I have told you on several occasions that I would talk about the relation between mafia and politics only when the time was ripe. From what I have seen so far, I must say, with some bitterness, that there is a persistent lack of a serious desire to combat the mafia on the part of the state. There are so many episodes, including recent ones I have read about in the newspapers. It would be foolish for us to touch this subject, which is the crucial knot of the mafia problem, when many of the people of whom I would have to speak have not left the political scene. Therefore, I do not intend to confirm or deny whether I met with Lima in Rome or whether I know him at all, for the reasons I have explained.[13]

Buscetta, referring to recent events in the newspapers, had read the writing on the wall in Falcone's recent rejection. If Falcone did not have political clout in Rome to become the head of a thirteen-man office in Palermo, it was crazy to think that he could mount an investigation against members of parliament and people at the highest level of government.

T he first sign that life in the investigative office of Palermo was going to change became evident almost immediately, even before its new chief, Antonino Meli, took office. In late January and early February, while Caponetto was still nominally in charge, all the investigating magistrates received two stern memoranda generated by Marcantonio Motisi, the deputy chief of the office. Making clear that he was acting at Meli's behest, Motisi complained that many prosecutors were not handling enough cases, and referred cryptically to a possible "reign of terror" if magistrates failed to meet their statistical goals. This raised the specter that the office was returning to the bureaucratic management of the past, in which prosecutors were judged primarily by the quantity and not the quality of their cases. Falcone's detractors had tried to use statistics against him when he began dedicating so much time to the Spatola case in 1980, but he had received support from his bosses, first Rocco Chinnici and then Caponetto. Now the bureaucrats were back in power and seemingly eager to take their revenge.[14]

On March 9, 1988, police across Sicily issued some 160 arrest warrants based on the testimony of Antonino Calderone. It was the swan song of the Caponetto era and the last major operation generated by the anti-mafia pool he had created in 1983.

Five days later, Caponetto bid farewell to his colleagues at a ceremony to welcome his successor, Meli, to Palermo. During the ceremony, Caponetto noticed tears running down Giovanni Falcone's cheeks. It was the first time Caponetto had ever seen Falcone, normally a model of self-control, express so much emotion.[15]

The senior judges of the Palace of Justice "wanted to say good-bye to Caponetto at the same moment as we welcomed Meli in order to create a sense of continuity and harmony," as Antonio Palmieri, the president of the tribunal, would later testify. "I made a conciliatory speech, urging everyone to put the past behind them and to move forward together. Caponetto responded in the same spirit . . . the only voice out of tune was Meli . . . who, when he spoke, could not help sounding a polemical note . . . recalling the events that preceded his nomination."[16]

Antonino Meli, a proud and stubborn man, thin-skinned, with a prickly character, was still smoldering over some of the things that had been said during the debate over his nomination. He found it unforgivable that even many of his own supporters had said that "seniority" was the only reason to prefer him to Giovanni Falcone, while others had pronounced him unfit for the job of chief prosecutor. "As if I had spent forty years just warming a seat!" he said. While it was true he had never done investigative work, he had been a trial judge in mafia cases and had even sentenced Michele Greco, "the Pope," to life in prison for the assassination of chief prosecutor Rocco Chinnici.

That Meli arrived in Palermo in an angry, resentful mood was not entirely accidental. Someone threw gasoline on the fire by sending him nasty anonymous letters that succeeded in making his blood boil. "The Freemasons elected you," said one of two letters he received. "You are a shit and you should return to the shit you came from." Members of the anti-mafia pool received anonymous letters all the time and did their best to ignore them. They were generally from criminals trying to intimidate or unnerve prosecutors, or throw investigations off the track. But Meli reacted with redoubled fury at his new colleagues—probably just as the anonymous letter writer hoped he would. While it is inconceivable that the prosecutors in the anti-mafia pool would waste their time writing anonymous letters, let alone ones as vulgar and scurrilous as this, Meli seemed convinced that they were responsible. Still fuming over the letters months later, he said: "I have good reasons to believe that this letter did not come from Rome or from Milan, or from Turin, but from nearby, very nearby."[17]

Just days after Meli's arrival at the investigative office, the new head of the Procura della Repubblica, Salvatore Curti Giardina, had two journalists arrested for publishing extracts of the confessions of Calderone. Curti Giardina was another beneficiary of the renewed emphasis on seniority, one of the many magistrates who had gradually drifted to the top through sheer longevity and decades of steering close to the shore. The newspapermen, Attilio Bolzoni of *La Repubblica* and Saverio Lodato of *L'Unità* (both left-wing publications), had gotten hold of the depositions and given prominence to Calderone's accusations against major political figures. Republican leader Aristide Gunnella, one of those mentioned, was furious and threatened legal action. Curti Giardina, instead of having Gunnella investigated for his alleged mafia ties, took the rather extreme step of arresting the two journalists. Particularly disturbing to many prosecutors was that Curti Giardina had gone beyond merely accusing them of revealing confidential documents; he charged the journalists with "theft," adopting the highly questionable legal argument that they had stolen government property by using a government Xerox machine to copy the documents. This more serious charge enabled Curti Giardina to hold the journalists at Ucciardone prison for six days, a rather draconian response to a news story.[18]

Rather than dismissing the case against the journalists, Meli assigned it to his faithful deputy, Marcantonio Motisi, who pursued it with vigor. Within a few weeks of the arrival of their new boss, the members of the anti-mafia pool found themselves being treated as suspects in one of their own office's investigations. Motisi called in Falcone and the others for questioning. Even Borsellino, who had been in Marsala for more than a year, was deposed. When Borsellino arrived, Meli said to him jokingly, "Now, watch out you don't leave in handcuffs." Despite their reputations as "protagonists" the members of the anti-mafia pool had always maintained a rather cautious distance from the press and did not have a reputation as leakers. More than anyone, they were acutely aware of the damage that publicity could do to a delicate mafia investigation, and their major operations had succeeded in part because the office had managed to prevent word getting out about the collaboration of witnesses Buscetta, Contorno and Calderone. When he was deposed in the Bolzoni-Lodato "theft" case, Falcone did not like the drift of the questions, full of insinuation and innuendo. All of a sudden, he was being treated like a criminal defendant.[19]

Meanwhile, the atmosphere of openness and collegiality in the investigative office quickly became closed and hierarchical. Meli remained barricaded behind his desk and never ventured out to the other prosecutors' offices. "The prevailing attitude is 'I'm the boss and you're the subordinate,' " noted the president of the Court, Palmieri, observing Meli and his staff.[20]

Chief prosecutor Meli arrived promptly at the office each morning but rarely returned after lunch. While this is the normal routine of Italian state employees, the anti-mafia pool also worked in the afternoons and often into the night. After all the controversy, Meli clearly wanted to avoid the appearance of interfering with the anti-mafia pool, but seemed to have taken it to the extreme of ignoring its work altogether.[21] "We might have expected . . . that he might at least call a meeting for an exchange of views, to discuss the enormous problems of how to manage these trials, but nothing of the kind has occurred," Falcone said later that year.[22]

Shortly before leaving Palermo, Antonino Caponetto had assigned case number 1817, the maxi-trial and all its offspring, to Giovanni Falcone so that the case would not founder during the time of transition. The case, which was known collectively as the "container" trial, officially included all the work on the Cosa Nostra organization, but was then broken off into manageable sections, maxi-one, two, and three. The Calderone material was supposed to form the basis of maxi-four. Now that Meli was in Palermo, Falcone and the pool felt that it was important for their new boss to familiarize himself with the case and eventually, as Caponetto had, take over its overall direction while delegating the day-to-day work to the pool.

Meli seemed inclined to agree, but then an unexpected event got in the way. In a police blitz that flowed from Calderone's confessions, police arrested a relation of the new chief prosecutor, the father-in-law of Meli's son. Although the connection between the two men was not close, it proved a public embarrassment for Meli. He was furious when stories about the arrest appeared in the newspapers, with his photograph and a headline about a "relative of the chief prosecutor arrested." Although many papers carried the story, Meli saw signs of a vicious plot against him, reinforced by the fact that among the offending journalists was Attilio Bolzoni of *La Repubblica,* one of those arrested and jailed for printing the Calderone confessions. Meli was used to working in the sleepy provincial city of Caltanissetta and was unprepared for the media glare and inevitable criticism that come with working on high-profile cases of national significance. Again, he was convinced that his misfortunes were orchestrated by the members of his staff who had opposed his arrival. In a sudden fit of pique, he refused to assume direction of case 1817.

Although he refused to hold meetings or study the papers of the maxi-trial, Meli began, however, to assert his authority in the assignment of cases. During the formation of the anti-mafia pool a set of specific protocols had been worked out and approved by the Consiglio Superiore della Magistratura that created a clear division of labor in the Palermo investigative office. All mafia cases were to be assigned to the pool and, since the nature of some crimes was unclear, there was constant dialogue between the prosecutors to help sort things out. Meli was unaware of this system and quickly began to turn it upside down. Without consulting anyone, he distributed the new cases that arrived on his desk according to his own lights and sometimes seemingly at random. When a suspect in an important mafia case was killed he assigned the investigation to a prosecutor outside of the "pool." When a jeweler, whom Falcone had investigated for laundering drug money in the Spatola case, was kidnapped, it was treated as an ordinary criminal case. Having no experience with Palermo mafia trials, Meli did not recognize the names of defendants and had no way of distinguishing a crime of passion from a mafia hit. But that did not stop him from making the decisions on his own, without asking for guidance.

Falcone and members of the pool would wait for weeks expecting the papers on a certain crime to arrive from the Procura della Repubblica only to discover that the case had been assigned to someone else. Frequently, they would learn what had happened only when the other prosecutor, equally perplexed, would come to them and ask why he or she had been assigned an obvious mafia case.

When Falcone and the members of the pool asked if they could at least obtain copies of the evidence to see if it had any bearing on their own cases, Meli turned down their request. He said the pool might be able to see part of the material, if it could first identify which portions of the evidence related directly to their own cases without, however, being able to look through the documentation beforehand. This was completely contrary to the spirit of sharing information that had prevailed during the Caponetto period. Moreover, it posed a serious practical problem. The anti-mafia pool kept the only central data bank on mafia prosecutions and painstakingly entered evidence from all important new cases into a computer. Meli did not seem to understand that it was this global view of the phenomenon that had been the key to the pool's success.

In this growing atmosphere of mutual incomprehension, the members of the pool and their new boss began communicating primarily by letter. Although Giovanni Falcone continued his practice of visiting the chief prosecutor most mornings to keep him up-to-date on the latest developments in his work and Meli said that Falcone's behavior was extremely cordial, there were no meetings in which to discuss larger problems. The pool wrote elaborately polite and formal letters expressing its concerns about the handling of mafia cases; and Meli, in turn, responded in equally polite and formal terms, expressing his disagreement.

The seemingly arbitrary assignment of mafia cases was soon followed by an equally disturbing new development. A flood of new cases that were clearly not mafia-related: pickpocket, purse snatching and prostitution cases, check-kiting, marital assault and burglary prosecutions began to arrive on the desk of Giovanni Falcone and the members of his group. This, too, was against the rules that had been worked out. The members of the pool had always handled a certain number of ordinary criminal cases to help out with the office's large caseload, but they had done so voluntarily, on a limited basis, in consultation with chief prosecutor Caponetto. Suddenly, they began to receive dozens of old cases together with reproachful memos about the office's large backlog, urging them to increase productivity. Many of these old files, by Meli's own admission, involved petty crimes for which there was no evidence and no suspects: but, in the bureaucratic conception of jurisprudence, "finishing" cases improved office productivity— even if it meant closing the case "against unknown suspects" or prematurely aborting a complex investigation.

"Chief prosecutor Meli, often, very often, asks me to finish cases, but some investigations take the time that they take, like some of the political cases, such as the assassination of [President of the Region Piersanti] Mattarella." Falcone said. "Gradually, a conflict between two different judicial philosophies emerged: a bureaucratic-administrative-hierarchical kind of management and one whose goal is getting results from investigations." "Falcone never gave up on cases," said Giuseppe Di Lello, one of the original members of the pool. "There were suspects he had followed for years. He never gave up searching for bank records, adding new pieces of evidence."[23]

After having initially refused to involve himself in the central mafia investigation, Meli suddenly reversed his position and announced that he would now take command. Not only would he continue giving the pool non-mafia cases, he announced that he was adding three new investigating magistrates to the anti-mafia pool. "In the past, the addition of every new member had been the fruit of extended reflection and discussions between the pool and the chief prosecutor," Borsellino said.[24] The pool was not a machine with fungible parts but a delicate mechanism that required a high degree of compatibility and mutual commitment. Many prosecutors were unsuited to its work, not because they were not capable but because their lives did not permit them to travel frequently or work long evenings. Some, with small children or sick family members, could not drop everything at a moment's notice and fly to Brussels or Istanbul or work until 2 A.M. to finish urgent arrest warrants. Moreover, while Meli insisted that he was simply "expanding" or "reinforcing" the pool, in reality he was changing its whole *modus operandi*. The original premise of the pool was to have a group of prosecutors who would dedicate themselves exclusively, or almost exclusively, to organized crime investigations and who would work together, each staying abreast of the other's work. But now the anti-mafia prosecutors were spending greater and greater amounts of time on non-mafia cases. And numerous individual cases were being parceled out throughout the office to people who were not familiar with the more than one million pages of documents generated by the mafia pool over the previous five years. Cases were now assigned to one or two prosecutors, while the other members of the pool were excluded. In short, the office was returning to its old management style: all prosecutors would do a little of everything and each would pursue his or her own cases in isolation from the rest.

Meli seemed to think the anti-mafia magistrates were spoiled prima donnas, used to picking and choosing their cases and carrying a lighter load than the others. But, even by Meli's narrow statistical standards, the members of the pool were among the "most productive" in the office. In the final six months of 1987 before Meli's arrival, Giuseppe Di Lello and Leonardo Guarnotta had finished ninety-nine and eighty-five cases, respectively, including the massive documentation of the third maxi-trial and other highly complex mafia investigations. Their caseload was, in fact, greater than that of many of the prosecutors who handled only the more straightforward criminal cases, including those prosecutors who were now being imposed on the anti-mafia pool. Falcone himself, despite handling the massive Calderone investigation almost single-handedly, had some sixty other cases in his docket.[25]

While chief prosecutor Meli was revamping the anti-mafia pool, he still had not found the time to read the evidence the group had produced during the last four years. He told members of the pool that he was waiting for the summer vacation in August to study the indictment of the first maxi-trial. But maxis one and two were already over, the third was in court and the pool was trying, with increasing difficulty, to prepare the fourth.[26]

FIFTEEN

From the moment of his arrival in Marsala in August 1986, Paolo Borsellino plunged into a new world. Although Marsala was only about eighty miles (120 kilometers) from Palermo, Borsellino moved from the comparatively well-equipped anti-mafia pool to a sleepy provincial office in almost complete disarray. There was only one assistant prosecutor in the office and he was scheduled to leave in a few months, having asked for (and obtained) a transfer. "I *am* the Procura of Marsala," Borsellino told people jokingly, referring to his skeleton crew. The office was responsible for all criminal prosecutions in a substantial geographical area that extended well beyond the city of Marsala, including the important center of Mazara del Vallo, the largest fishing port in Italy, and several towns in the interior that are considered important centers of mafia activity. Borsellino's office was supposed to have eight prosecutors, but it was hard to fill the jobs: like many smaller southern Italian cities, Marsala was viewed as a hardship post reserved for novice magistrates who scored poorly on their entrance exams and had to accept whatever positions were open. In fact, the replacement for his one departing assistant was a kid straight out of law school, Diego Cavalliero.[1]

"I wasn't able to be of much help in those first months—it was my first job," said Cavalliero. "We started, like a couple of manual laborers, to dust off and go through hundreds of back cases. We worked twelve hours a day and often on weekends. . . . He had an incredible stamina for work. I used to call him 'ass of stone,' because he remained seated at his desk for days on end, devouring paper. But he also had a remarkable capacity for seeing the crucial points of a case right away and cutting through to the essential."

Marsala is not an easy place for outsiders, especially mafia prosecutors who have to be unusually careful in choosing their friends and accepting invitations. "It is a very closed city," said Cavalliero. "After the stores close at eight in the evening you don't even see a dog on the streets. It's not like Palermo, where people are milling about the piazzas at all hours. . . . The entire social life of the city takes place behind closed doors, among little groups of friends that have known one another a lifetime. There are tight-knit social clubs, groups that get together to play cards, Freemason lodges. I can remember Paolo Borsellino going out in the evening twice in the two years we overlapped in Marsala. . . . He had to be very careful. There are a lot of people in these places who want to be able to brag to their friends, 'I know the chief prosecutor. I'll talk to him for you.' "

At one point, it looked as if the office would receive a second assistant prosecutor, another novice. "He was a very sweet-natured kid from Rome," said Cavalliero. "When he arrived, he asked where are the theaters in Marsala? where are the movie theaters? where are the concerts? Paolo and I looked at each other and smiled. This kid expected to find in Marsala the things he was used to having in Rome. The boy burst into tears and left Marsala. For us who were living far from home it was a very difficult life. . . . Our only amusement was to leave the office at about ten o'clock at night and eat something at Paolo's little one-room apartment above the police station, for which he had to pay a normal rent. He would cook and I would wash the dishes. He wasn't a very good cook and so I would try to get him to go out to dinner. This was Borsellino's 'reward' for being an 'anti-mafia professional.' "

During his two and a half years in Marsala, Cavalliero almost became a kind of adoptive member of the Borsellino family, often spending his weekends with them in Palermo. "Paolo even brought me *caffè-latte* in bed," Cavalliero recalled. "He was a serious, practicing Catholic, not just at Mass on Sunday, but in all the little things between Monday and Saturday. He was always the person people turned to with their problems. If someone needed to find an apartment, they called Paolo, if they couldn't get their telephone installed, they called Paolo. His door was almost always open."

Borsellino made his presence felt in his work, as well. Shortly after arriving in late 1986, he and his bodyguards happened by chance upon the scene of a mafia hit in driving to work. A pair of killers on a motorbike whipped through traffic and shot a man in a car, a butcher who evidently had refused to buy his meat from the "right" source. Borsellino told his bodyguards to trail the motorbike and they managed to trace it back to a garage. After calling for police backup, they raided the garage, which turned out to be an important headquarters of the local mafia. "They arrested nine or ten people," said Calogero Germanà, a police official who worked closely with Borsellino during that period. "It was a beautiful operation. They nailed the heart of the Marsala mafia."[2]

Investigations into the local mafia were extremely difficult. Palermo seemed like an open, civic-minded city when compared to the suffocating *omertà* of the countryside around Marsala. Diego Cavalliero recalled going to the scene of a murder in the town of Salemi that had gone unreported for many days and perhaps weeks. "A corpse had been left in the back of a truck and under the sun in this enclosed space the body decomposed rapidly and began to give off a terrible stink," he said. "The truck was in a parking lot, with people walking by it every day. But no one reported the body until the smell became so bad that the workers picking grapes in a nearby field couldn't work any longer because of the stench. That's *omertà*!"[3]

Although Marsala was the largest city in the area, the capital of the local mafia was actually Mazara del Vallo. The home of thousands of fishing boats, large and small, it was the natural conduit for all kinds of commerce, legal and illegal. Contraband cigarettes, hashish and heroin moved in and out among the throng of fishing boats that shuttled between Sicily and North Africa. "If you tried to put a drug-sniffing dog in the port of Mazara he would go crazy," said Diego Cavalliero. "The smells of the fishing port were so many and so powerful that a dog with a highly developed ol-factory sense would become completely confused."

Mazara del Vallo was the fiefdom of mafia boss Mariano Agate, who had already been convicted in the maxi-trial of Palermo. Far more than just another local boss, Agate was the *capo-mandamento* (district leader) of the entire area and a member of the Commission. And while he was still in prison at this time, his men were reportedly still firmly in command. The Mazarese mafia appeared to be closely allied with the Corleonesi. "Although Corleone is near Palermo, it is an agricultural area, and so the Coreleonesi, like Totò Riina, have greater affinities with the leaders of the rural mafia than with the city bosses of Palermo," said Calogero Germanà, who was chief of police of Mazara del Vallo during Borsellino's first years in Marsala. "The ties between Corleone and Mazara del Vallo are very close. Gaetano Riina, the brother of Totò Riina, lives in Mazara." (One of the false sets of identification papers under which Totò Riina traveled during his fugitive life had been procured in Mazara. "That gives you an idea of how close the ties were," said Germanà.)[4]

Germanà and the local commander of the *carabinieri* had been carefully gathering information on the mafia of Mazara del Vallo for years. By applying his experience of the Palermo anti-mafia pool, Borsellino was able to translate their evidence into a major prosecution. "Borsellino gave us, in effect, a new investigative methodology," said Germanà. "His idea was to strike at the top of the organization and freeze the people with decision-making power. He had a global vision that we may have lacked."

In late 1987, Germanà and Borsellino prepared indictments against some seventy-two defendants, including arrest warrants for the fourteen most dangerous suspects. On a somewhat smaller scale, the case was a kind of "maxi-trial" of the mafia of Mazara del Vallo. The methods of the Palermo anti-mafia pool were bearing fruit across Sicily and not just in Marsala. Prosecutors in the Sicilian cities of Messina and Agrigento had mounted important maxi-trials of their own, receiving important backup support from the prosecutors in Palermo.

By March of 1988, Borsellino had finished drafting the five volumes of evidence against the mafia of Mazara—just as Falcone was overseeing the Calderone operation and Antonino Meli was taking over the investigative office of Palermo.

Consistent with Borsellino's and Falcone's ideas about Palermo acting as a kind of clearinghouse for information about Cosa Nostra, Borsellino sent a copy of the voluminous evidence in the Mazara case to the new chief of the investigative office. Because of the organic ties between the "family" of Commission member Mariano Agate and the Palermo mafia, portions of Borsellino's case fit with existing evidence of the ongoing "container" trial of Cosa Nostra. This did not mean, as some have suggested, that the anti-mafia pool had a monopoly on prosecuting all mafia cases. Rather, the idea was for provincial prosecutors to try defendants for local crimes and for Palermo to handle the broader racketeering charges that implicated the organization of Cosa Nostra, charges that needed to be understood in a larger context.

Not long after sending his lengthy brief to Palermo, Borsellino was surprised to find it back on his desk. Chief prosecutor Meli had returned it immediately, without saying a word to Giovanni Falcone, who, having talked with Borsellino, was expecting the papers. Borsellino, thinking it must be an oversight, sent the thick volumes of evidence back to Meli, with an explanatory letter. But again, the packet came back immediately, this time with a curt note saying that the case was outside the jurisdiction of Palermo.[5]

Although he had been in Marsala for a year and a half, Borsellino had been following developments in Palermo closely. He talked often with his friends in the anti-mafia pool on the phone and stopped by his old office frequently when he returned home to Palermo on weekends. He felt the chill that had come over the office, heard the growing complaints of his colleagues and saw the structure of the pool being gradually broken down. And now, as Borsellino experienced directly, Meli was sending back evidence from other parts of Sicily without so much as a word to Falcone. Whether or not he was aware of it, Meli was overruling the court finding in the maxi-trial that had established that the mafia was a unified organization with its center in Palermo. It seemed to Borsellino, as to his former colleagues, that the anti-mafia pool was being dismantled piece by piece.

Moreover, the situation in Palermo seemed to be part of a wider counterrevolution designed to undo eight years of steady progress in mafia prosecutions. In April, the government chose as its new minister of the interior, Antonio Gava, a Christian Democratic power broker from Naples, widely suspected of close ties with the Neapolitan Camorra. One of Gava's political deputies, Ciro Cirillo, had been ransomed from terrorist kidnappers in 1981 with the help of the Camorra, and many believed that Gava was deeply involved in the secret negotiations that had led to his release. While the rumors about Gava were unproven, apparently no one in the government seemed particularly troubled by the possibility that the nation's chief law enforcement officer might be linked to organized crime.[6]

In Rome the Italian parliament was not keeping pace with the magistrature in providing support for the war on the mafia. The Socialist minister of justice, Giuliano Vassalli, was vehemently opposed to any law establishing a witness protection program, saying that it would be dangerous to create the illusion that the Italian government could protect the families of witnesses when in fact it could not. There was also total resistance to offering reduced sentences to *mafiosi* who turned state's evidence. Moreover, the Italian parliament had passed a series of highly liberal civil rights laws that worked at cross purposes with complex mafia prosecutions. A 1984 statute dictated that all criminal defendants had to be released from jail within two years of their original arrest, even in the middle of trial, regardless of their criminal records or the chances of their fleeing. Major mafia cases, because of the mass of evidence and the constitutional guarantees for defendants, took a long time to prosecute, and not just in Italy. The Pizza Connection case in the United States took some three years from indictment to conviction and involved only twenty-two defendants. A special law had to be passed in the middle of the Palermo maxi-trial to prevent most of the defendants from going free. But less than a year after their conviction, most of the defendants were already on the loose, obtaining bail pending appeal or benefiting from one of any number of legal loopholes.[7]

A 1986 law offered generous sentence reductions and prison furloughs for "model prisoners." Convicted criminals could leave prison for six weeks a year and qualify for "semi-liberty," leaving prison by day to attend jobs on the outside, returning to sleep in their cells at night. While these humanitarian measures may have helped rehabilitate some, hundreds of *mafiosi* took advantage of them and skipped town entirely. "In the last half of 1988, 2,992 convicted prisoners out on furlough or daytime permits disappeared," wrote the American journalist Claire Sterling. "Half the fugitives were ranking *mafiosi* convicted for murder, theft, kidnapping, and drug-trafficking." One of them was a member of the Commission of Cosa Nostra.[8]

Moreover, some of the appellate courts in Sicily and in Rome seemed dead set on overturning the growing number of mafia convictions being generated at the trial level. Like Borsellino's own Basile case, many prosecutions bounced around from court to court, being retried a half-dozen times, with the defendants going free and disappearing. (In Italy there is no restriction on trying a defendant again for the same offense.) Most disturbing of all was the trend on Italy's Supreme Court, which seemed to overturn every mafia conviction it encountered. In a strange quirk of fate, all organized crime cases had become the almost exclusive province of one rather enigmatic judge, Corrado Carnevale— known as *l'ammazza-sentenze,* "the sentence-killer." Although Italy's Supreme Court is divided into several sections, it was decided that all organized crime cases should be heard by the "first section" of the Supreme Court, of which Carnevale, the sentence-killer, was president.

Considered by some a "fifth column" of the mafia, by others, a judicial purist, the only thing certain about Carnevale is that in case after case, he set free convicted *mafiosi,* frequently on the most slender of technicalities. Mistakes in form, mistakes in filing dates and other seemingly superficial errors led to the undoing of major prosecutions. While invoking the principle of a strict application of the law, Carnevale appeared at times to step over the line into extreme judicial activism: he frequently entered into the merits of the evidence itself, seeming to substitute himself for judge and jury. In some instances, he decided that witnesses the jury had chosen to believe were not credible. He overturned, for example, the conviction of Michele Greco, "the Pope," and his men for the assassination of Judge Rocco Chinnici, deciding not to believe the testimony of the Lebanese informant Bou Ghebel Ghassan, who had spoken to some of Greco's men both before and after the bombing. He threw out convictions in another case on the grounds that certain "cryptic" wiretapped conversations were not clearly talking about drugs, choosing to ignore well-established evidence that traffickers almost always spoke in code, referring to "shirts" and "suits" instead of heroin or cocaine. He freed 100 of the 120 convicted members of a vast ring of criminals from Catania operating out of the northern city of Turin, twenty-six of whom had been sentenced to life in prison. He released Commission member Antonio Salamone, despite his conviction at the maxi-trial, in consideration of his advanced age and fragile health. Neither age nor illness prevented Salamone from promptly disappearing, returning, it is believed, to his riches in Brazil.[9] Like Homer's Penelope in the *Odyssey*, who unraveled by night the same tapestry she diligently wove by day, the "sentence-killer" began pulling at the threads of the enormous fabric of the Cosa Nostra trial that the anti-mafia pool in Palermo had painstakingly stitched together.

At the same time, there appeared to be a virtual collapse of the investigative capacity of the Palermo police, who had still not recovered from the 1985 assassinations of Ninni Cassarà and Beppe Montana, and the mass transfers and arrests of officers after the torture and killing of murder suspect Salvatore Marino. The department had entered a downward spiral of murder, suspicion and betrayal. Transfer followed transfer and the new arrivals seemed to stay only a month or two. In the summer of 1988, yet another head of the Investigative Squad was transferred, blamed for the murder of officer Natale Mondo earlier that year by placing him in excessive danger through an undercover operation. At the same time, the head of the Palermo homicide squad, Francesco Accordino, was suddenly transferred, after having received a death threat—from a phone within the police department itself. Although Accordino resisted being transferred, he was sent to work as a postal inspector in Reggio Calabria. The new head of the police Investigative Squad announced that he planned to work for the "normalization" of the situation in Palermo; but to many, normalization looked like the gradual erasure of the department's historic memory.[10]

Realizing that he was in a freer position than his friends in Palermo, Borsellino decided to speak out. If Falcone protested, it would be interpreted both as insubordination on the part of an assistant prosecutor against his boss and a self-interested attempt to undermine and replace his rival, Meli. Borsellino had accepted an invitation to speak on July 16, 1988, at a symposium in Agrigento on the war against the mafia.

Departing from the convention observed by most magistrates of sticking to vague generalities in public speeches, Borsellino issued a stinging indictment of the backsliding in the war on the mafia, denouncing the undermining of the anti-mafia pool and the complete paralysis of the Palermo police. The organizer of the event, Giuseppe Arnone, a political activist in Agrigento, was so enthusiastic about Borsellino's speech that he asked if he could borrow Borsellino's notes and give them to the local Sicilian newspapers. Interestingly, neither the *Giornale di Sicilia* of Palermo nor *La Sicilia* of Catania printed stories about the speech. But a couple of days later, Borsellino got requests for an interview from Attilio Bolzoni of the Rome paper *La Repubblica* and Saverio Lodato of the Communist daily *L'Unità,* the two journalists who had been arrested for breaking the story about Antonino Calderone's confessions. Far from backing away from his public remarks, Borsellino sounded the alarm in a joint interview that created a national scandal overnight:

> They have taken the control of the main anti-mafia investigations away from Giovanni Falcone. Police investigations have remained stalled for years. The Investigative Squad has never been rebuilt [after the murder of Ninni Cassarà]. . . . The last police report worthy of that name dates from 1982, the dossier [written by Cassarà] on Michele Greco + 161. Since then we have no comprehensive picture of the Palermo mafia. . . . I send material to the chief prosecutor of Palermo and, to my great surprise, it is returned to me. I have the impression that there is a maneuver afoot to dismantle the anti-mafia pool. . . .
>
> Up until recently all the anti-mafia investigations, because of the unity of Cosa Nostra, were centralized in Palermo. . . . Now, instead, the cases are being dispersed in a thousand directions. "Everybody must work on everything" is the official explanation. But it is not convincing. . . . I have the unpleasant sensation that someone wants to move backwards. . . .[11]

Because no news about the deteriorating situation in Palermo had seeped out from the highly private investigative office, the Italian public was stunned. The president of the Republic,

Francesco Cossiga, called the Consiglio Superiore della Magistratura (CSM) into emergency session, demanding an immediate inquiry into the troubles in Palermo. The members of the judicial panel who had already scattered for the summer returned from vacation and called for a battery of hearings, including some fourteen magistrates from Palermo.

When he was later asked by friends why he had taken this audacious public stand, Borsellino replied: "I was sorry to see the pool die and I felt if it were to die, it should happen in public."

Certainly, the hearings held on July 30 and 31 took place in the glare of the national spotlight; the battle of Palermo had moved from the corridors of the Palace of Justice to the front page of all the principal newspapers. But, on a personal level, Borsellino risked a professional lynching. Within the closed caste of the magistrature, one did not air criticisms in the press. The proper thing for Borsellino to have done, many said, was to file a formal complaint with the CSM—forgetting that it was the judicial council, with its choice of Antonino Meli over Giovanni Falcone, that was principally responsible for the situation in Palermo. Many magistrates wanted Borsellino brought up on disciplinary charges, and stripped of his position as chief prosecutor of Marsala. "Not one of Borsellino's statements corresponds to the truth," Meli told the press, opening the possibility of a lawsuit for libel.[12]

Meli was convinced, as were others in Palermo, that Borsellino's actions had been carefully orchestrated in concert with Falcone and the pool to get him out of the way. In fact, Falcone was caught off balance by Borsellino's impetuous move. "Giovanni was not prepared for and not altogether pleased with what Borsellino had done," said Liliana Ferraro, a friend and colleague of both men at the Ministry of Justice.[13] Throughout his career Falcone always preferred quiet compromise, studiously avoiding major head-to-head confrontations, particularly ones like this from which he might emerge badly bloodied and bruised. But now that the situation had been blown wide open, Falcone had no choice but to meet the challenge straight-on. Realizing that Borsellino's career was in jeopardy and that they both risked being placed on trial by the CSM, Falcone decided to raise the stakes of the game, by handing in his letter of resignation on July 30, 1988, the morning the CSM convened its session.

For the last several years that I have worked on organized crime investigations, I have tolerated in silence the inevitable accusations of "protagonism" and professional misconduct. Believing that I was performing a useful service, I was happy to be able to do my job and felt that this was simply one of the many inconveniences connected to this kind of work. I was sure that the public trials of these cases would eventually demonstrate, as has in fact happened, that the investigations in which I participated were conducted with an absolute respect for the law. When the question arose of substituting the chief prosecutor of the investigative office of Palermo, Doctor Caponetto, I put forward my candidacy, believing it was the only way to guarantee the continuity of our work. . . . Again on that occasion, I was forced to listen to scurrilous libels and a denigratory campaign of unheard-of baseness, to which I did not respond, believing, perhaps mistakenly, that my role imposed silence upon me. But now the situation is profoundly changed, and my reserve has no longer any reason to be. What I feared would happen has taken place: the investigations into the mafia have bogged down, and that delicate mechanism known as the anti-mafia pool . . . has stalled. Paolo Borsellino, by whose friendship I am honored, has demonstrated once again his sense of the state and his own courage, by publicly denouncing omissions and inertia in the war on the mafia that are there for anyone with eyes to see. In response, an unworthy campaign has been launched to distort the profound moral value of his gesture, reducing everything to a squabble between "factions" of magistrates. . . .[14]

During two days of marathon hearings, some fourteen Palermo magistrates trooped before the judicial council. The great majority of the witnesses confirmed Borsellino's description of the state of affairs in Palermo. "If we want to go right to the origin of the conflict, it lies in the heavily contested nomination of Meli as chief of the investigative office," said Carmelo Conti, the president of the Palermo Court of Appeals. "Not that Meli is not a person of total integrity . . . but because Meli undoubtedly has a rather thorny and authoritarian character, which is the direct opposite of his predecessor, Caponetto . . . the other prosecutors, Falcone above all, are disoriented by this new approach. . . . And this new climate makes it unlivable not only for the prosecutors, but for the citizens of Palermo, who feel lost and without any guide or certainty."[15]

The president of the tribunal, Antonio Palmieri, testified that the chief prosecutor had blithely ignored the assignment system that had been set up to regulate the investigative office and had changed the nature of the pool. The chief judges produced statistics demonstrating that rather than being slackers who avoided doing their fair share of work, the members were already among the most "productive" prosecutors in Palermo. (Four members of the pool were among the five prosecutors with the heaviest caseloads.) Case after case was discussed in which Meli had taken mafia investigations away from the anti-mafia pool. Witnesses confirmed that the chief prosecutor had never held staff meetings or visited the offices of other prosecutors to discuss their needs and problems.

When Meli testified on the afternoon of July 30, 1988, he gave ample proof of what Chief Justice Conti had described as his "thorny and authoritarian character" and the spiral of paranoia into which he had descended after his nomination. Meli appeared to have become psychologically unhinged by the events of the previous eight months: "I arrived [in Palermo] after a controversy that has destroyed me," he said. "They said that Falcone was a great professional—and I am the first to acknowledge it, always, always—and for me, seniority, as if I had spent forty years 'warming a seat!'" Meli seemed to shake with anger as he talked about the obscene anonymous letters that he had received and as he described the objections to his taking control of the "container" mafia trial. "This trial was not supposed to end up in such unworthy hands, such unworthy hands—that they were unworthy, was made clear publicly by Dr. Caponetto—in such unworthy hands!" He explained that there was a "plan of destabilization" of the Palace of Justice in Palermo that had begun with the anonymous letters, proceeded with the publication of the articles about the arrest of his in-law in a mafia raid and culminated in Borsellino's interview. "I arrived at the investigative office with these anonymous letters calling me a shit and then these things happen. . . . They say that this latest business of Borsellino is part of the plan of destabilization."[16]

The hearings made painfully clear what some had already realized before Meli's nomination: that Meli's quick-tempered, litigious and unpredictable character made him unusually ill-equipped to occupy a hot seat like that of chief prosecutor of Palermo.

But the people who were supposed to mediate the Palermo conflict were the ones who had helped create it by choosing Meli in the first place. For the CSM to condemn Meli and accept Borsellino's diagnosis would be to condemn itself. In fact, Meli played on this situation in repeated appeals to the panel: "When Borsellino has the gall to talk about bad choices, he is criticizing you, as well as the decision you made, censoring and offending you, as well. . . . In other words, gentlemen, [Borsellino] should worry about being chief prosecutor of Marsala. . . . and not come here and criticize Palermo, continuing to talk about bad choices. . . . In short, I'm fed up, let's speak frankly, I am really fed up, tired, nauseated."

Giovanni Falcone tried to depersonalize the controversy, saying that the fundamental differences between himself and his boss on dozens of individual cases and on the handling of mafia cases in general had led to an impasse. "There is nothing personal in this matter, the relations between the chief prosecutor and myself could not be more cordial; we see one another daily and I believe we have both acted in good faith. But things have developed in such a way that those of us who are involved in these investigations find ourselves in a kind of stalemate. We are returning to the bureaucratic/administrative management of mafia cases which was one of the main causes of the failures of past years and past decades."[17]

Perhaps inevitably, the debate over the "Borsellino affair" split the Council more or less along the same lines of division that had formed during the original Meli-Falcone battle. The majority that had voted for Meli tended to defend its choice and those who had voted for Falcone tended to defend Borsellino. As a result, Borsellino found himself in a sometimes hostile, star chamber tribunal, with his career on the line. Rather than discussing the merits of Borsellino's public observations, many of the panelists tried to focus on Borsellino's decision to discuss judicial business in the press. Judge Sergio Letizia, who had voted against Giovanni Falcone, accused Borsellino of violating his friends' confidences by making the problems of the anti-mafia pool public. "And so . . . after having had private conversations with your colleagues, you believe it was proper to make them public and even make them the object of a newspaper interview?"

Borsellino held his ground without losing his balance. "I did not betray my colleagues' confidences, I stated my own convictions based on conversations with my colleagues. . . . I raised an issue that I felt was important to raise, at a round table discussion about the state of mafia investigations. Either we speak in riddles and code, talking about 'a drop in tension' . . . so that people don't understand what we're talking about or we confront these problems in a concrete manner, citing real facts and putting the scalpel right into the wound, saying: 'The central office for mafia investigations is no longer working.' . . . I don't see why public opinion shouldn't be informed about these problems; rather, it is dangerous when public opinion is not informed about them."[18]

Although the lengthy hearings were held in closed session, there was nothing to prevent individual members from discussing them in public. Day after day, the Palermo Palace of Justice was front-page news, with journalists swarming around the CSM hoping to pick up details of the hearings. "We all understood that the battle was being fought in the realm of public opinion," said CSM member Vito D'Ambrosio. "Conservative journalists were crowded into [Vincenzo] Geraci's office and left-wing journalists in mine."[19] While most of the press appeared to pull for Falcone and Borsellino, the influential conservative paper *Giornale* attacked them viciously, portraying them as the agents of a Communist plot. "The Communists want to control the anti-mafia movement and so they support the protagonist-magistrates of the Falcone faction," the paper wrote as the hearings began. "Conquering the Palace of Justice of Palermo, the Italian Communist Party will become untouchable," it continued the following day.[20]

After the end of the hearings, virtually the entire judicial Council stayed up all night on August 4, 1988, furiously debating what to do about the Palermo situation. Because Borsellino had started the controversy and had questioned the wisdom of the Council itself, the mood was not favorable to him. The bad feeling generated by the earlier Meli-Falcone battle was intensified by the latest controversy. "Geraci was furious with Borsellino, he wanted Borsellino's head on a platter," said D'Ambrosio. "Things got very tense. At a certain point, I said something very harsh to Geraci like: 'You are not going to have Borsellino's head, and if you do, I will have yours.' "[21]

The question was not whether to censure Borsellino but how. During the course of a stormy all-night session, the Council finally worked out a compromise that rejected Borsellino's criticisms of the Palermo office but that acknowledged his good faith in making them. "This is the best we could do," D'Ambrosio said. "Those of us who were friends of Falcone wanted to make sure that he was not destroyed by this business. And we were able to pass a statement that expressed full support for Falcone and appreciation for his work." The document urged Falcone and Meli to patch up their differences, stressing that the chief prosecutor should try to be more sensitive to the needs of the anti-mafia pool.

Falcone was under overwhelming pressure to withdraw his resignation and, in reality, had little choice. Any request for a transfer would have to be approved by the CSM itself, which made clear it wanted him to remain in Palermo. And having said that the problem was not personal but professional, Falcone had to satisfy himself with a vague promise from all sides that everyone should overcome their differences and make a renewed effort to work together. The crisis had left Falcone weaker and more exposed than ever. Despite the words of extravagant praise, the hearings had clearly shown that he had lost control of his investigations and that the anti-mafia pool was being dismantled against his will. He had not even been allowed to resign. Moreover, by drawing him into a bitter public controversy, (justly or unjustly) the battle diminished his status as an impartial figure who stood above the fray. Now, as the Palace of Justice in Palermo was commonly referred to as "the Poison Palace," he appeared increasingly as simply one of several players in a complex power struggle.

The tepid compromise of the CSM was accompanied, almost simultaneously, by another slap in the face for Falcone. On August 5, the cabinet of ministers announced that it had chosen a new High Commissioner for anti-mafia affairs (the position that General Dalla Chiesa had hoped to occupy), Domenico Sica, a Rome prosecutor who had been active in the fight against terrorism. Moreover, they announced that the new High Commissioner would have new special powers, far beyond anything that General Dalla Chiesa had dreamed of: the power to authorize wiretaps, the power to coordinate investigations throughout southern Italy. People in the government let it be known that they had been considering Falcone for the job but decided against him because they did not want to appear to be taking sides in the Palermo controversy.

"Borsellino ruined Falcone's chances for becoming High Commissioner," said Vincenzo Geraci. "That would have been the perfect job for him, because he was really an investigator, not a judge."[22]

"Like many things that Vincenzo Geraci says, it is, because he is clever, near the truth, without being the truth," said Judge D'Ambrosio.[23] Falcone believed that the story about his almost being made High Commissioner was a total fiction: no one had even contacted him to ask whether he would be interested in the job. When the Borsellino case erupted, the government rushed to make its announcement; the controversy provided the government with the perfect excuse for again denying Falcone a job for which most people concurred he was the most qualified candidate. Domenico Sica, the new High Commissioner, was an intelligent and capable magistrate, but he had never prosecuted mafia cases. He was believed, however, to have powerful friends in the Socialist Party and Falcone had none. It is highly doubtful that the government had any intention of giving Falcone so much power.

SIXTEEN

That Giovanni Falcone's image had been sullied by the continuous "Palermo controversy" was evident in the cynical interpretation some gave of his decision not to resign. The conservative newpaper *Il Giornale* insinuated that Falcone was staying in Palermo to protect the skeletons in his closet—an outrageous, unsubstantiated charge probably no one would have dared make a year earlier. "Falcone had a precise motive for agreeing to this latest compromise," the article said. "Giovanni Falcone perhaps fears that . . . the cover will come off the secrets of 'his' pool."[1] Falcone was damned no matter what he did: if he had insisted on resigning, he would have been branded as a prima donna who refused to work under someone else; and in agreeing to go forward he was accused of a sinister cover-up.

The bosses of Cosa Nostra had a rather different view of the power struggle in Palermo.

On September 20, 1988, a few days after Giovanni Falcone withdrew his resignation, American agents tapping the phone of the Café Giardino in Brooklyn recorded a conversation (in Sicilian dialect) between Joe Gambino and an anonymous caller who had just returned from Palermo.

GAMBINO: What did he [Giovanni Falcone] do? Did he resign?
ANONYMOUS: No, they smoothed things over and he withdrew his resignation. He's gone back to where he was to do what he was doing before.
GAMBINO: Shit![2]

The anonymous caller then consoled Gambino by filling him in on the latest details of Italian politics, in particular about the reforms of the Italian criminal code designed to greatly limit the power of judges to arrest and hold defendants in jail.

ANONYMOUS: Now they've approved the new law, now they can't prosecute as they did in the past. . . . They can't arrest people when they want. Before they do, they have to have solid proof, they have to convict first and arrest later.
GAMBINO: Oh, so it's like here, in America.
ANONYMOUS: No, it's better, much better. Now those bastards, the magistrates and cops, can't even dream of arresting anyone the way they do now!
GAMBINO: The cops will take it up the ass! And that other one who has come back [Falcone] won't be able to do anything either? . . . They'll all take it up the ass!
ANONYMOUS: Yeah, they'll take it in the ass.

Three days later, Joe Gambino received more news from Italy from a second unknown caller. The conversation again focused on the new penal code, the law to hold prosecutors legally responsible for their mistakes, and the vigorous efforts of Socialist minister of justice Giuliano Vassalli to punish prosecutors in Calabria whom he felt had overstepped the bounds of propriety in prosecution of the mafia.

GAMBINO: They tell me that the new code has been passed in Italy.
ANONYMOUS: It's better than the American law . . . the evidence has to be overwhelming . . . and the prosecutors are responsible . . . The prosecutors can go fuck themselves. Vassalli has put them on trial . . . He's telling the prosecutors: Keep to the straight-and-narrow, you bastards . . .
GAMBINO: Yeah, but with these new laws they won't be able to do anything.
ANONYMOUS: They'll go pick beans.[3]

While the Italian public was further disoriented by twisted conspiracy theories about Falcone, the bosses of Cosa Nostra demonstrated, once again, their lucid, clear-eyed grasp of reality. While
severely disappointed that Falcone had withdrawn his resignation,
they observed correctly that he would have a difficult time getting
anything done in such an unfavorable political climate.

In fact, as soon as Falcone returned to work in Palermo in September 1988, the same problems that had provoked his resignation in July cropped up again. Prosecutors in Termini Imerese, a
small town half an hour away on the northwestern coast of Sicily,
had sent evidence to Palermo gathered on several defendants fingered by the new mafia witness Antonino Calderone. The prosecutors assumed that Palermo would want to use the material in
the case Falcone was building from Calderone's revelations. But
Antonino Meli sent back the evidence, insisting that the case be
prosecuted locally. Just as he had with Paolo Borsellino six
months earlier, Meli took this action without consulting the members of the anti-mafia pool. Never mind that Termini Imerese was
entirely unprepared to handle such a case—there were only two
investigative magistrates in town, with a backlog of nearly two
thousand cases and only one assistant prosecutor in the Procura
della Repubblica to handle the trial work. The office had hardly
any experience in mafia cases. The local police force, whether because of inadequate means or intimidation, had failed to generate
a single report on mafia activity in the area in some nine years,
even though Termini Imerese was reputed to be a major hideout
for mafia fugitives.[4]

When they learned of Meli's decision, the anti-mafia prosecutors warned that it would bring "extremely serious damage to various investigations under way," in a letter of protest to the
president of the Palermo tribunal. "After decades of fragmented
investigations, dispersed in a thousand directions with completely
disappointing results, it was the merit of the late chief prosecutor
Rocco Chinnici to have intuited the unity of the mafia and to have
begun directing investigations that took account of that reality. . . ." Meli's decision, they wrote, "erases with a single swipe
of the sponge, proven evidence gathered through enormous sacrifice, and sometimes loss of life, by many magistrates and investigators and throws us back to the time when everything was

scattered in the labyrinth of numerous different trials each treated with myopic, bureaucratic vision."[5]

Because of the irreconcilable differences between the anti-mafia pool and Antonino Meli, the jurisdictional battle over the Calderone case went to Italy's Supreme Court, or rather to the first section of the Supreme Court, presided over by Corrado Carnevale, the "sentence-killer."

The mafia appeared to take advantage of the paralysis of the justice system by taking the offensive once again. On September 14, retired Sicilian judge Alberto Giacomelli was murdered near his home in Trapani. On September 25, 1988, mafia assassins attacked the car of Judge Antonio Saetta, killing him and his mentally retarded son, Stefano, as they were returning to Palermo after a weekend in the country. A member of the Palermo Court of Appeals, Judge Saetta was scheduled to hear the appeal of the original maxi-trial. Saetta had shown himself tough and incorruptible in past trials. He had convicted the three killers of Captain Emanuele Basile and upheld the verdict against Michele Greco, "the Pope," for the assassination of Rocco Chinnici—before Carnevale, the "sentence-killer," threw both cases out.[6]

The following day, another group of killers murdered Mauro Rostagno, a former student radical who had started a drug rehabilitation center in Sicily and who had made the error of courageously denouncing mafia drug traffickers on local television.

On September 27, Giuseppe Lombardo, the brother-in-law of mafia witness Salvatore Contorno, was shot and killed in Palermo; he was approximately the thirtieth relative or close friend of Contorno's to have been eliminated. The next day, still another group of killers rang the doorbell of mafia boss Giovanni Bontate and his wife, and murdered them in their home. Despite his conviction in the maxi-trial, Bontate had been released from prison due to a herniated disk in his back. Although he had been spared during the first mafia war by allying himself with the Corleonesi against his older brother, Stefano, Giovanni Bontate had now been removed from the scene in some further consolidation of power taking place within Cosa Nostra.[7]

Reactions to the latest series of killings varied. "These are deaths foretold," Paolo Borsellino said, addressing a meeting of magistrates in Palermo on the day of Bontate's murder. "We are faced with a new criminal threat that will bring other deaths, perhaps other excellent cadavers. We are in a climate like that which preceded the death of Dalla Chiesa. Cosa Nostra is striking at judges like Giacomelli and Saetta and at journalists like Rostagno, people who are in the front line of the battle but who are left alone, like the general killed six years ago."

The president of the Palermo Court of Appeals, Carmelo Conti, was even more extreme. "The war is lost, there is no hope. There's no point in fooling ourselves, the state has abandoned us."

But Antonio Gava, the minister of the interior with alleged ties to the Neapolitan Camorra, saw reasons for optimism in the current crime wave: "These forms of greater violence are signs that the mafia perceives that the state is making a greater effort to combat it."

A few days later, when Antonino Calderone, the latest big mafia witness, took the stand in a Palermo court, he announced he was not going to testify. "I don't feel protected," he said.

Another witness, Salvatore Contorno, in hiding in the United States, announced that he, too, was refusing to cooperate any further. "I have realized that the [Italian] state does not want to destroy the mafia," he said in an interview with the newsweekly *Europeo*. "While I continue to live as a fugitive, in fear for my life, the people I denounced are leaving prison . . . on who knows what kind of legal technicalities. It's not worth the risk."[8]

In a stark evaluation of the situation, the new High Commissioner for anti-mafia affairs, Domenico Sica, told the parliament that the Italian government had effectively lost control of much of the southern third of the country. "In many parts of Sicily, Calabria and Campania the domination of the territory by organized crime groups is absolute," he said.[9]

At the same time, in November 1988, Antonino Meli chose to begin a new counteroffensive against Giovanni Falcone and the anti-mafia pool. Meeting with several members of the parliament's anti-mafia commission who were visiting Palermo, Meli complained that Falcone and the pool were afraid of arresting the Knights of Labor of Catania—Carmelo and Pasquale Costanzo, denounced by Antonino Calderone. Immediately, a Socialist member of the anti-mafia commission spoke publicly of "disturbing facts and interests that some want to cover up."[10] It was more than a little ironic that Meli, who had argued that Palermo did not have jurisdiction over most of the defendants in the Calderone investigation, should now be faulting Falcone for not arresting defendants on the other end of Sicily. But, immediately, the "Costanzo case" was front-page news, with accusations that Falcone was going easy on the Knights of Labor—whom Falcone had been the first to investigate. Meli was called to Rome to testify before the parliament's anti-mafia commission, where he intensified his vituperative attacks against his own staff. "I find myself . . . with six untouchable prosecutors and with all these trials piling up every day and in deference to the decision of the CSM I can't assign them to the pool in order not to create bad feelings. . . . I bow down before my colleague Falcone—who wouldn't recognize his enormous merits? I would build a gold statue of Falcone. But they're not all Falcone. The proportion is like ten to one, or two, three at the most. None of them rate more than a three."[11]

Despite his statement about wanting to build a gold statue of Giovanni Falcone, Meli repeated his accusations about Falcone's refusal to arrest the Costanzo brothers. It was a severe breach of legal ethics for Meli to discuss an ongoing investigation, but the accusation put Falcone's integrity and reputation in question. Without even hearing any evidence, some members of the Consiglio Superiore della Magistratura demanded that both Meli and Falcone be transferred from Palermo.[12]

According to members of the anti-mafia pool Meli simply failed to understand Falcone's strategy, which involved trying to maneuver the Costanzos into becoming government witnesses: "I was present during the deposition of the Costanzos," said Ignazio De Francisci of the anti-mafia pool. "[Falcone] had a strategy of great breadth . . . he was trying to get Costanzo, who was on the verge of being indicted, to become a witness . . . by not arresting him but letting him smell the odor of prison . . . and Costanzo gave signs of opening up. . . . Then along comes Meli, says that Falcone is trying to protect Costanzo and says we must arrest the Costanzos."[13]

Falcone's decision not to have the Costanzo brothers arrested immediately was very much in keeping with his traditional prudence and scrupulousness as a prosecutor. He had resisted arresting the Salvo cousins in 1983, when his old boss, Rocco Chinnici, was chomping at the bit. He waited until the following year when he had two witnesses prepared to testify that they were actually members of Cosa Nostra and he had enough evidence to win a conviction in court. Falcone understood that because he was carrying out a judicial revolution, he needed to be sure of having extremely strong cases. Thousands of defense lawyers, judges, and politicians were waiting to pounce on the anti-mafia pool and discredit it for making a false step, arresting someone on flimsy evidence. After all, the maxi-trial had clearly established that you could not convict someone simply on the word of a mafia witness and Falcone had relatively little on the Costanzos beyond the testimony of Calderone. Moreover, Calderone had not accused the Costanzos of being members of Cosa Nostra (as was the case of the Salvo cousins), he had merely said that they had benefited through their close association with *mafiosi*. They were in the somewhat ambiguous position between victim and victimizer and, at the very least, Falcone wanted more evidence before clapping them in jail. Another prosecutor, Carlo Palermo, had already indicted the Costanzos and failed miserably. They had been acquitted and apparently vindicated, claiming to be victims of prosecutorial overreaching, while Palermo, after narrowly escaping assassination, ended up fighting off disciplinary charges that effectively ended his prosecutorial career.[14]

"Falcone believed, as with the Salvos, that when you aim high, you have to be absolutely certain you will hit the target or it will come back at you, with even greater force, like a boomerang," said Judge Vito D'Ambrosio. "Sure you can arrest the Costanzos without solid proof, and then when they are acquitted not only will they destroy you, they will destroy your work. . . . This professional caution on Giovanni's part was mistaken by a stupid man like Meli, a person of genuinely limited intelligence, for a form of fear or collusion. For other people, it was a good opportunity to discredit Falcone. Many different interests converged in wanting to discredit Falcone."[15]

Now the same people who had railed against the abuse of judicial power and clamored for a law to hold prosecutors responsible for their errors were trying to crucify Falcone for failing to arrest someone for insufficient evidence. Because there was no substance to the charges against Falcone, the case blew over, but contributed once again to the atmosphere of confusion in the war against the mafia and to erode Falcone's prestige.

Just as the "Costanzo case" was dying down, on November 23, 1988, Italy's highest court delivered another blow to the anti-mafia pool. In the jurisdictional battle raised by the Calderone investigation, the court ruled in Antonino Meli's favor, ordering that the prosecution of Cosa Nostra should be scattered among the various local offices throughout Sicily rather than be concentrated in Palermo. The ruling, however, went way beyond the individual case, it threatened the legal premise of the maxi-trial and directly challenged the pool's conception of the mafia itself. "[Mafia families] are autonomous in their nature and operate without any dependence on hierarchical links to the Commission," the court wrote. The mafia is "a plurality of criminal associations, often in contrast with one another which, while adopting common mafia methods and structures, have a wide sphere of decision-making power."[16] The section of the court, headed by Corrado Carnevale, the "sentence-killer," simply acted as if the last eight years of mafia cases did not exist. "There was not a shred of evidence that supported this thesis and thousands of pages of trial testimony that directly contradicted it," said Giuseppe Ayala, the public prosecutor at the maxi-trial.[17]

On the strength of this decision, Antonino Meli was able to carve up the Calderone case among twelve different local Sicilian prosecutors' offices. Most of these towns had none of the resources to handle cases of this size and complexity. More than a few of them, like Enna and Termini Imerese, had only one assistant prosecutor to perform all the trial work for the entire district.[18] Not surprisingly, soon all but 11 of the 160 defendants in the Calderone investigation were out of jail.[19]

Looking at Antonino Meli's tenure at Palermo's investigative office from the outside it would seem that he had set out deliberately to sabotage the war against the mafia, but even Meli's harshest critics have never questioned his good faith. "Meli was a gentleman," said Giuseppe Ayala. "But he was an old magistrate on the brink of retirement who understood nothing about the mafia, had no ideas, or had extremely dated, old-fashioned ideas."[20] Underneath the Falcone-Meli struggle were two radically different visions of the role of the magistrate. Technically, in the Italian legal system there is no clear separation between prosecutors and trial judges—both are, theoretically, "judges." In this scheme, the "investigative magistrate" (which, until 1989, was called the *giudice istruttore*), was a strange hybrid creature who, on the one hand, had vast powers of inquiry and, at the same time, was supposed to "judge" his own evidence with serene impartiality. Some magistrates interpreted the need for impartiality as limiting the *giudice istruttore* to the purely passive job of evaluating the documentation presented by the police. Other magistrates, like Falcone, felt that the law imposed on them a positive obligation to "investigate" the case in order to be able to judge who should stand trial for a given crime. While, in places like Sicily, the passive interpretation of the law happened to harmonize well with a laissez-faire attitude toward the mafia, it was also a point of pride among magistrates who saw themselves as blindly weighing the scales of justice. In attacking Falcone, Meli undoubtedly felt he was upholding the traditional role of the magistrate and that, even though this might disrupt specific mafia investigations, the judge's job was to obediently apply the law—whatever the consequences. The Italian system is driven by laws rather than by court precedent, and therefore, theoretically, nothing is allowed unless it is specifically sanctioned by law. The Anglo-Saxon system based on precedent has a strong element of trial and error: in the United States, prosecutors are free to try a new legal strategy, which becomes law if the courts uphold it. "Falcone was an innovator, he had an extremely American, pragmatic approach," said John Costanzo, station chief of the U.S. Drug Enforcement Administration in Rome.[21] Meli undoubtedly felt he was performing a public service by clipping Falcone's wings, while, at same time, satisfying his wounded pride and the need to assert his own authority. It also coincided with other interests. Although not a knowing accomplice in a plot to destroy the anti-mafia pool, Meli may have been a pawn in a larger game. "He was certainly egged on by others against Falcone, so that he felt that everything Falcone did was wrong," said Ayala. "He was a useful instrument in a plan that was directed by others, inside and outside the magistrature."

Three days after the Italian Supreme Court scattered the Calderone case to the four winds, on November 26, 1988, Meli and Falcone signed a kind of truce in the offices of Carmelo Conti, the president of the Palermo Court of Appeals. In this document, Falcone agreed to accept Meli's right to make the final decisions on the overall direction of mafia cases; in exchange, Meli acknowledged the anti-mafia pool's right to run their day-to-day operation.[22]

Already battered and bruised by a year of public controversy, Falcone was particularly reluctant to turn the office upside down again—especially in light of the Supreme Court's decision. Moreover, an extremely delicate investigation he had worked on for three years was about to break. The case had special interest for Falcone because it involved many of the defendants of the Spatola case who were already back on the street and into the heroin trade after their convictions in 1982. It showed clearly that some of the "losing" families in the mafia war had been allowed back into the fold in order to handle the lucrative and dangerous drug trade. Involving groups in different parts of Sicily and the United States, the case directly contradicted the Italian Supreme Court's contention that the mafia was simply a loose association of independent criminal bands.

The first hint that the losing families were attempting a comeback surfaced in a wiretap made in March 1985, which captured a desperate appeal made by Rosario Spatola in Palermo to his cousin John Gambino in Brooklyn, New York. Spatola, who had been one of Palermo's chief real estate dealers and the friend of members of parliament, was in dire straits. He had been sent to prison for his involvement in the Spatola-Inzerillo-Gambino heroin ring and, while he was away, much of his mafia (and blood) family, including its boss, Salvatore Inzerillo, had been hunted down and murdered. Afraid for his life, flat broke and desperate, he called Gambino to see if he could get back into the heroin game. Interestingly, Spatola and Gambino call each other *compare,* "godfather," the term Sicilians reserve for friends who have witnessed the christening of each other's children. Unlike the other term for "godfather," *padrino,* used by an inferior toward a superior, *compare* is generally used by *mafiosi* of roughly equal status who are close.

SPATOLA: *Compare*, I wanted to tell you something, I am here without a license, without a job, things are tight . . .
GAMBINO: It's tight for all of us, we're in a bad way . . .

SPATOLA: There's no money, and the situation is hell. I don't know, with all these trials, where it's going to end. . . . Do you have troubles there, too?

GAMBINO: So far, no. *Compare*, let's hope we don't lose on every front.

SPATOLA: *Compare*, help me now!

GAMBINO: I'll do everything I can, but it's difficult because they [the Corleonesi] have everything in their hands, understand?[23]

When Spatola speaks of having no "license" he is probably referring to the permission to deal drugs from the Corleonesi. Gambino indicates that he cannot act on his own, without the okay of the Corleonesi, who have "everything in their hands." When the mafia war broke out in 1981, John Gambino reportedly flew from New York to Palermo to get instructions from the Corleonesi. He was told to kill all the members of the losing families who tried to flee to the United States. And in a sign that mafia family ties are often stronger than blood ties, the U.S. mafia is believed to have killed Gambino's cousin Pietro Inzerillo, brother of Salvatore Inzerillo, whose body was found in New Jersey with dollar bills stuffed in his mouth and around his genitals. But sometime after 1985, now that the Inzerillos and Spatolas no longer represented a serious threat, the Corleonesi apparently decided to let them back into business, allowing them to exploit their excellent international connections. Italian police noticed that many of the Inzerillos who had fled for their lives from Palermo in 1981 began drifting back to the city, and were living openly and occupying positions of prestige within their old neighborhood—something they could not do if they were still under a death sentence from the Corleonesi.

The Inzerillos and Spatolas were not only operating out of Palermo but also out of Torretta, the little town nearby where Rosario Spatola had hidden Michele Sindona during his fake kidnapping of 1979. In 1986, Italian police discovered that ordinary housewives from Torretta were being used as "mules" to carry drugs between Sicily and the United States. One middle-aged woman from Torretta was arrested at the Palermo airport when police spotted her dousing herself with unusually generous amounts of Chanel No. 5 perfume in an effort to evade drug-sniffing dogs.

When they searched her, they found a stash of heroin in her underwear. As they began to pay more attention to the town of Torretta, police even found gold faucets in some peasant cottages.[24] "The whole town was in on it," said Gianni De Gennaro, the police official who coordinated the Italian end of the investigation.[25]

As they dug deeper, investigators discovered that the Inzerillos in Italy were back in regular contact with their relatives in the United States and Latin America. Among other things, the different branches of the family had created a network to ship heroin from Italy to Santo Domingo in the Dominican Republic inside wine bottles, which would then be imported into the United States. "We own the Dominican Republic," one of the defendants was overheard saying. Running the operation in Santo Domingo was Tommaso Inzerillo, who was wiretapped talking with his cousin, Francesco Inzerillo in Italy. In one conversation, Francesco Inzerillo was careful to warn his cousin that while they were back in business, the Corleonesi were still in charge. At one point, he says explicitly, "*U curtu* (the Short One) from Corleone [Totò Riina] has everything in his hands." Another novelty of the case was that, among other things, the Sicilian Cosa Nostra was bringing cocaine back into Europe, sometimes in direct exchange for heroin. This was a good indication that the Sicilian and American mafias were in contact with the Colombia cocaine cartels. Having already saturated the flourishing American cocaine market, the Colombians were looking to expand in Europe and the Sicilians were helping them reach the wealthy northern Italian markets of Milan and Bologna.

In order to break the ring, the United States and Italy mounted another major joint operation. As in the Pizza Connection case, Falcone again worked closely with Rudolph Giuliani and, in particular, Louis Freeh in New York. Meanwhile, another veteran of the Pizza Connection team, Richard Martin, was acting as coordinator, having become the Justice Department liaison in the U.S. embassy in Rome. The operation was called "Iron Tower," after the name of the town Torretta, which means "little tower" in Italian. The operation assumed major proportions as investigators found members of the Spatola-Inzerillo-Gambino network operating not just in Torretta, Palermo and New York, but also New Jersey, Pennsylvania, Virginia, Florida, California and Latin

America. Once again, many of the American representatives were dealing heroin out of pizza parlors. The nerve center of the operation appeared to be the Café Giardino, the Brooklyn restaurant where the brothers John and Joe Gambino held court.

Early on the morning of December 1, 1988, police on both sides of the Atlantic were ready to move. When undercover cops entered the Gambinos' Café Giardino, at 2:00 A.M., a party was in full swing. "This is your last dance, folks," police said as they started their raid. Seventy-five suspects were arrested in the United States, while Italian police, led by Gianni De Gennaro, working in close cooperation with Falcone, made 133 arrests.[26]

SEVENTEEN

Giovanni Falcone was able to savor the satisfaction of Operation Iron Tower for only a short while. The "armistice" he had worked out with chief prosecutor Antonino Meli in November 1988 began to fall apart almost immediately. The two most politically radical members of the pool, Giuseppe Di Lello and Giacomo Conte, refused to sign the agreement. They believed that Falcone had conceded too much to Meli and that it was a mistake to continue investigations of which they had lost overall control. It was necessary, they felt, to make a loud public break with Meli.

"We saw there was no way to oppose Meli within institutional parameters," said Giuseppe Di Lello. "Falcone wanted to compromise, but . . . I felt we needed to denounce Meli publicly, in open conflict. Falcone felt the damages would be greater than the benefits."[1]

Falcone now found himself checked and blocked from above by his boss and challenged by his own colleagues from within the pool. In conversations with friends, Falcone jokingly referred to his younger colleagues, Di Lello and Conte, as the Ayatollahs. Magistrates with a more overtly political orientation, Di Lello and Conte were (in Falcone's view) intransigent purists, who felt it was more important to wage a battle of principle even if it meant disrupting ongoing investigations. Because the problem was political, they argued, one had to act politically. By being forced to work with one hand tied behind their backs they felt they were lending legitimacy to a government that wanted to appear to fight the mafia without really doing so. Falcone felt it was better to fight the mafia with one hand than not to fight it at all. "Falcone was very pragmatic," said Judge Vito D'Ambrosio, "he tried to adapt himself to situations in order to create the best conditions in which to be able to do his job."[2]

Given the unfavorable decisions of the Italian Supreme Court and of the Consiglio Superiore della Magistratura, Falcone felt the "truce" was the only way to save what he could of his mafia cases and to prevent the work of the pool from coming to a dead halt. Falcone was also aware of the feelings of his American colleagues, who urged him to continue. "Without the Italian pool, the mafia will win," Louis Freeh said at the time. "Dismantling the Italian group would create insoluble problems for us here. . . . The mafia has been destabilized in both countries, but it isn't finished. This is the critical moment for both of us. Without the Italian pool, we would be paralyzed too."[3]

By late January 1989, Conte and Di Lello, after refusing any compromise, were expelled from the pool by Meli. "[Falcone] saw their departure as a moment of clarification, almost of liberation," said Judge D'Ambrosio. "He was being attacked from within the pool and, at the same time, was having to mediate with Meli. . . . He said: 'Let Meli do what he wants, as long he lets me work.' He believed that he could work in such a way that Meli wouldn't even understand what he was doing. 'As long as he doesn't throw a wrench in the works.' "[4]

"[Falcone] didn't want to abandon his cases, particularly the big 'container' trial," said Di Lello. "He was coherent in his own beliefs. He was a man of iron loyalty to the institutions, and he did not want to undermine those institutions. . . . He didn't underestimate [the political dimension] of the problem, but he believed that the political dimension [of the mafia] would succumb through constant, patient investigative work by the judiciary, when just the opposite was true. The political dimension was stronger . . . the investigations had stalled at [Vito] Ciancimino and the Salvo cousins. . . ."

In these difficult conditions, the anti-mafia pool hobbled forward during 1989. "The maxi-trials were blocked, but we did some smaller but quite important trials, like Iron Tower and other international drug cases, which we did either individually or working in groups of two or three," said Ignazio De Francisci. But it became increasingly evident throughout 1989 that they were losing the war. Having had their wings clipped, it was impossible for a handful of prosecutors to make more than a small dent in such a vast and complex problem, if the other organs of the state, the police, the courts, the parliament, the national government did not do their part.

During its heyday, from 1983 to 1986, when the anti-mafia pool in Palermo had the energetic backing of sympathetic ministers in Rome, it had made a demonstrable difference. The concerted government crackdown not only dramatically lowered the murder rate, it clearly disrupted the drug trade. By 1985, when the pool was at the height of its powers, the number of deaths by drug overdose in Italy was cut by nearly half, dropping from 398 to 242, and remained low (at 292) in 1986. But with the change of government in 1987, the war against the mafia stalled. The number of deaths by overdose jumped immediately to 542 in 1987 and, after the pool began to disintegrate in 1988, drug-related deaths skyrocketed to nearly three times previous levels (reaching 809 in 1988 and 951 in 1989). It was "an indication of the clear relationship between the weakening of the anti-mafia efforts and the widening problem of drug addiction," as a later report of the anti-mafia commission put it.[5]

While the Italian state retreated, organized crime groups throughout Italy advanced, spreading to parts of Sicily and southern Italy where they had been absent and tightening their grip on areas where they had not been particularly strong. Places like Catania and Reggio Calabria replaced Palermo as the murder capitals of Italy. Puglia, the region which was always held up in public as an oasis of industry and progress in the Italian South, was clearly under siege. Crimes of intimidation like murder, arson and the dynamiting of stores and work sites had all doubled in five years, telltale signs that criminal groups were taking over the economy. The situation was even worse in the regions traditionally afflicted by organized crime: Sicily, Calabria and Campania, where murder and other serious crimes went up by 50 percent from their already high levels. And in the midst of this crime wave in southern Italy, the number of people arrested actually fell by half between 1984 and 1989, from 31,254 to 15,678—sending a clear message that it was indeed possible to get away with murder—and a host of other crimes. Even more disheartening was the fact that as crimes increased, the number of criminal suspects denounced to police actually went down. In other words, as the reign of the mafia grew, ordinary citizens were increasingly afraid to report the crimes of which they were victims.

Thanks to the leniency of the Italian courts, by early 1989, only 60 of the 342 defendants convicted at the maxi-trial were still in jail.[6] And many of those did not appear to be suffering overmuch. The most important bosses of the Commission spent months at a time, not at Ucciardone prison, but in the hotel-like conditions of Palermo's Ospedale Civico (Civic Hospital). Pippo Calò, Francesco Madonia, Salvatore Montalto and Bernardo Brusca— all Commission members convicted at the maxi-trial—were among ten major bosses in a special pavilion of the hospital. Along with these ten were two common criminals, whose duty it was to serve the *mafiosi*. As in prison, all their food was brought in daily from the outside. Calò was in the Palermo hospital for nearly two full years, with a diagnosis of asthma. Others were there only for tests, which took months at a time. Giuseppe Ayala, the public prosecutor in the maxi-trial, challenged this system by having the defendants examined by doctors from Milan, who found them to be in perfect health. But a Palermo court asked a second opinion of Sicilian doctors, who confirmed their mysterious illnesses.[7] The director of the Ospedale Civico was Giuseppe Lima, brother of Salvatore Lima, the member of parliament suspected of mafia ties. Although providing comfortable housing for the mafia's Commission, the hospital's medical services were atrocious. Tens of millions of dollars were poured into the Ospedale Civico for expensive equipment that was never even taken out of its boxes—allegedly bought for the kickbacks from suppliers— while many basic hospital services were nowhere in evidence. (When the hospital's CAT scan machine went back into operation it was announced in the newspaper as an exceptional event.)[8]

Whether through lack of government resources, or demoralization, many prosecutors simply stopped pursuing mafia crimes.

Falcone and the prosecutors in Palermo had begun bank searches and attempts to freeze the mafia's financial assets in the early 1980s, and in 1984 alone, prosecutors throughout Italy initiated 2,586 financial checks in order to confiscate criminal assets. By 1988 the number had dropped to 619. (In some regions, the efforts had stopped almost entirely. In Calabria bank searches dropped from 1,432 in 1984 to a mere 24 in 1988—this at a time when the number of murders went from 105 to 222, major robberies almost tripled from 143 to 406 and arson cases jumped from 265 to 362. Even when prosecutors succeeded in confiscating mafia assets, the criminals often regained control of them. When mafia-owned property was put up for public auction— apartments, businesses, automobiles or boats—no one would dare bid on them, so that, in the end, someone close to the owner would be able to buy them back for a small fraction of their real value. "In this way, the assets return to the *mafioso* from whom they were confiscated," said Antonio Palmieri, president of the Palermo Supreme Court, in April 1989.[9]

There were signs that judges were being effectively intimidated as well. In early 1989, Gianfranco Riggio, president of the Criminal Court of Agrigento, suddenly withdrew from his new job on the staff of the High Commissioner for anti-mafia affairs. Riggio had played an important role in the highly successful maxi-trial of Agrigento. The judge then confirmed the rumors that members of his family had been threatened. Although Riggio was widely criticized for his abdication, by publicly acknowledging the threat he was surely more courageous than most. Dozens, perhaps hundreds, accepted threats or bribes in silence and complicity.[10]

There were other signs of counterrevolution in Palermo. After arresting journalists in 1988 for publishing politically sensitive documents, in 1989 the Procuratore della Repubblica, Salvatore Curti Giardina, went a step further, censoring one of his own prosecutors. When assistant prosecutor Alberto Di Pisa submitted an evidentiary report for the trial of former mayor Vito Ciancimino, Curti Giardina simply removed the twenty-page section treating Ciancimino's dealings with other major political figures such as Salvatore Lima and Giovanni Gioia, arguing that it was irrelevant.[11]

The lack of a witness protection program had more or less put an end to the phenomenon of mafia witnesses. Stefano Calzetta, an important second-tier witness in the maxi-trial, now tried to retract his testimony on appeal. "I hit my head and lost my memory," he said. Unprotected and penniless, Calzetta was virtually homeless, spending his days in the public gardens of Piazza della Vittoria in Palermo, in front of the police station, figuring that he was less likely to be assassinated there than elsewhere in the city. Salvatore Contorno, unable to adapt to life in the United States and struggling to maintain his large family on the modest stipend of the American witness protection program, preferred to take his chances in Italy despite the lack of security or financial support.[12]

On May 26, 1989, during the raid of a mafia hideout near Palermo, police were surprised to find themselves face to face with Contorno, among the members of the criminal band of his cousin, Gaetano Grado, a *mafioso* and drug trafficker who had been convicted at the maxi-trial. Driven by a need for money and (perhaps) a desire for revenge, Contorno appeared to have returned to a life of crime. Almost for the first time since the mafia war of 1981–82, several prominent members of the winning families had been assassinated and police suspected that the Grado hideout might have something to do with it. When investigators swept in, with a police helicopter hovering overhead, they found numerous weapons, including a sawed-off shotgun near where Contorno was sleeping. The "Contorno case" seemed a clear illustration of the failure of Italy's effort (or lack of effort) to protect and provide alternative lives for their mafia witnesses.[13]

Someone, not surprisingly, saw something more sinister in the return of "Totuccio" Contorno. On June 5, 1989, an invisible hand mailed the first of five anonymous letters, written on Ministry of the Interior stationery, to various government offices in Palermo and Rome. The letters accused Falcone, together with other prosecutors and police investigators, of having arranged for Contorno to return to Sicily so that he would wage war against Totò Riina and the Corleonese mafia. Word of the letters drifted back to Falcone, but, having been the object of hundreds of such anonymous attacks over the years, he did his best to ignore them.[14]

Although he continued to work hard, Falcone was, to an extent, biding his time during the spring of 1989. With the overhaul of the Italian penal code, the investigative office where he had worked for the past nine years would soon cease to exist. As a part of the reform of the legal system, virtually all prosecutorial and investigative powers would be concentrated in the Procura della Repubblica. While the new arrangement might, in the long term, simplify and strengthen the system, in the short term it posed a practical problem for Falcone. To make room for him, the Palermo court created a position for a third deputy Procuratore della Repubblica in the new, expanded prosecutor's office. Falcone put his name up for the job in February. That same month, he gave a long, conciliatory interview to the right-wing Catholic magazine *Il Sabato* (The Sabbath), presenting an overly reassuring picture of the state of mafia investigations in Palermo. "I think that the drop in intensity that followed the end of the maxi-trial has been overcome. . . . Now that pause, the period of slowdown, is over and we are beginning to work with a good level of intensity." Falcone also appeared to downplay the importance of the investigations into mafia and politics.[15] To those who knew the deteriorating situation in Palermo, Falcone seemed determined to overcome his image—in some conservative circles—as a dangerous Jacobin, that had contributed to his past defeats. Nonetheless, his job request lay dormant for five months at the Consiglio Superiore della Magistratura.

With no major new witnesses and unable to conduct maxi-trials, Falcone concentrated on international drug trafficking cases, like Operation Iron Tower. Prosecuting the drug trade was one way to attack Cosa Nostra's vital interests without running into complex political or jurisdictional problems. No longer able to count on much help at home, Falcone could use the resources and professionalism of police and magistrates outside of Sicily. After the death of Ninni Cassarà, Falcone worked most closely with Gianni De Gennaro and Antonio Manganelli at Criminalpol in Rome, men whom he trusted fully and who had the centralized resources to act on a large scale.

Foreign cooperation had become even more important than before. In order to minimize detection in Sicily, Cosa Nostra was no longer refining morphine base into heroin in Sicily; it was buying the drugs pure at their source and avoiding large transfers of money by exchanging heroin directly for cocaine. The days when you could track major drug deals simply by checking local savings accounts were long gone. As law enforcement increased its pressures, criminal groups had become more and more expert in laundering money overseas, enlisting apparently legitimate businessmen to move money between Switzerland, Hong Kong, and the Bahamas. "We are chasing something that is always moving more quickly than we are," Falcone said in an interview with the newsweekly *L'Espresso*. "It reminds me of the famous saying 'Money has the heart of a rabbit and the legs of a hare.' "[16] Switzerland, and in particular, its Italian-speaking canton, Ticino—just an hour's drive from Milan—had become an especially attractive haven. The scale of the traffic was enormous. Two Sicilian traffickers in one of Falcone's cases purchased a total of two tons of Turkish heroin for a total of $55 million dollars, using Switzerland as their financial base.[17]

While traditionally resistant to any breach of banking secrecy, the Swiss had begun to wake up to the dangers of attracting mafia clients and had become increasingly cooperative in criminal investigations. Falcone established a particularly fruitful collaboration with Carla Del Ponte and Claudio Lehman, Italian-speaking magistrates in Lugano, on numerous major drug cases. In mid-June of 1989, Falcone's Swiss colleagues came to Palermo to continue their work together. On Monday evening, June 19, Falcone organized a dinner for them, inviting a handful of Palermo colleagues. The following day, he invited them to the beach house he and Francesca had rented in the town of Addaura, along the coast only a few miles from the city. The plan was to work in Palermo in the morning and then drive out to Addaura sometime after two o'-clock for a late lunch and a swim. But work went later than expected and the plan fell through. At the end of the day Falcone drove out to the beach house to spend the night. As he was shaving the next morning, a member of his security team suddenly came into the bathroom and said, "We have to leave right away. I've found a bomb."

The vigilant bodyguard had surveyed the beach below Falcone's rented house and spotted an Adidas sports bag, seemingly forgotten on the rocks below. Becoming suspicious, but careful not to lift it, he peered inside and noticed electric wires. It was a bomb with fifty-eight sticks of plastic explosives, powerful enough to kill anyone within ten or twenty yards. The bomb was extremely sophisticated, with two different detonation devices: a remote-control receiver and a manual device that would have caused the package to explode if anyone had picked it up. It was later ascertained that a crucial part of the detonator was missing, suggesting, perhaps, that the killers had defused the bomb when they realized that Falcone would not be going to the beach that day, but left the package figuring that they could reactivate the bomb should he remain in Addaura the following day. Falcone and his police escort returned to Palermo immediately.

Falcone had been threatened hundreds of times. Early in his career, he had been held hostage in a prison riot in Trapani, and an inmate at Ucciardone prison had tried to kill him in 1981. He had received an endless stream of menacing letters and phone calls, drawings of coffins, fake obituaries and even a photograph of himself with his murdered colleagues Rocco Chinnici and Ninni Cassarà with his birth and presumed death date written on them. He always forwarded these documents on to the proper authorities and learned to ignore them. He was accustomed even to the threats of mafia bosses. "If I were you," one of them had told him, "I would take my bodyguards into the bathroom with me when I peed." But the bomb frightened him in a way nothing else ever had. The letters, drawings and menacing remarks were part of psychological warfare. The real threats came, like this, without notice, catching you completely unprepared.[18]

What was perhaps most frightening to Falcone was that this bomb had all the earmarks of an inside job. He had gone to the beach only twice all year and no one would have planted the bomb on the off chance that he would have gone for a swim in the middle of a Tuesday afternoon. Whoever placed the bomb knew that he had invited his Swiss friends for lunch and a swim that afternoon. It was surely not an accident that the bomb would have killed not just himself but the magistrates who were helping him find the keys to the mafia's financial stronghold in Switzerland. Again, their presence in Palermo was known to only a few people, and all of them were in law enforcement.[19]

Falcone was even more unnerved when the first phone call he received after returning to Palermo was from Giulio Andreotti, the Christian Democratic politician. Although Andreotti expressed his sympathies over the bomb incident, the call struck Falcone as peculiar. The two men did not know one another well and Andreotti, at that moment, was foreign minister, an office with little connection to the war against the mafia. He could not help thinking of something a *mafioso* he had interrogated years before had told him: "If you want to know who committed or ordered a killing, look and see who sends the first wreath of flowers to the funeral."[20] The phone call may have been a genuine act of solidarity, but the suspicions Falcone confided to a few close friends tell us something about Falcone's state of mind after the attack. Falcone's friends had never seen him or his wife, Francesca, so upset. "Francesca was so shaken by the assassination attempt, that out of shock, she lost her voice for forty-eight hours," said Judge Francesco Lo Voi. But in some parts of Palermo, people made light of the incident. "The tendency was to minimize it," Falcone said in a later interview. "In the usual Palermo social circles people said: 'What assassination attempt? When the mafia decides to kill, it never misses. It's just a warning.' . . . Indicative of the atmosphere of the time was a conversation I had with a journalist, who said to me: 'Judge, I have two questions, one serious, the second, not. Let's start with the less serious one: what's the story with this assassination attempt?' "[21]

After learning of the attack, Falcone's rivals for the post of deputy chief prosecutor of the Procura della Repubblica withdrew their candidacies and a week after the Addaura incident, the Consiglio Superiore della Magistratura finally approved Falcone's job transfer. The episode prompted ironic comments from the local courthouse wits that perhaps Falcone himself had planted the bomb as a publicity stunt.

Seeing Falcone three weeks after the discovery of the bomb the journalist Saverio Lodato said he seemed like a man who "had attended his own funeral and didn't like what he saw." The attempt to belittle the danger he faced was part of the character assassination that seemed always to accompany real assassinations in Sicily. When Judge Ciaccio Montalto of Trapani was murdered, people spread the malicious rumor that his wife had been having an affair and that his death must have been a crime of passion. When General Dalla Chiesa was killed, some people ridiculed him for his efforts in Palermo, almost blaming him for his own death. "I see the same mechanism that preceded the death of General

Dalla Chiesa," Falcone told Lodato. "The script is the same. You only need eyes to see it."

Falcone said openly that he believed that the assassination attempt involved not just Cosa Nostra but people in the government. "We are dealing with extremely refined minds who are trying to guide certain actions of the mafia," he told Lodato. "There are perhaps points of convergence between the heads of Cosa Nostra and occult centers of power that have other interests. I have the impression that this is the most likely hypothesis if one wants to understand the reasons that drove someone to try to kill me."[22]

As Falcone analyzed the circumstances of his own near-death, his mind returned to the campaign of anonymous letters that had preceded the bomb. He now saw the denigratory letters as preparing the psychological terrain for his death. While most anonymous letters were crude and amateurish, the letters that preceded the Addaura bomb were highly sophisticated, demonstrating a detailed knowledge of current mafia investigations and of the handling of Salvatore Contorno, the mafia witness who had been rearrested near Palermo in May 1989.

The author of the anonymous letters knew, for example, that Contorno had reentered Italy in November 1988 and that the next month Giovanni Falcone and Leonardo Guarnotta of the anti-mafia pool traveled to Rome to take his deposition. The letter writer knew that Gianni De Gennaro, the police investigator who handled Contorno, had intervened personally with the courts so that Contorno could report to him by phone instead of having to come in person to the Criminalpol offices each week. While this was clearly a security measure taken for Contorno's protection, the poison-pen author interpreted it as part of a grand design to let Contorno return to Sicily as a hired killer. The letter even cited the clauses in the Italian criminal code that could be used to prosecute Falcone and De Gennaro as accomplices in murder. The author appeared to be someone directly involved in the Contorno case, perhaps even a magistrate.

De Gennaro, and the heads of Criminalpol in Rome, were perfectly aware that Contorno would go to Palermo to try to strike back at the Corleonesi and to flush out and kill Totò Riina, [one of the letters said]. De Gennaro flew to Palermo to discuss his project with prosecutors, in particular, Falcone, [Giuseppe] Ayala and [Pietro] Giammanco [both of the Procura della Repubblica], who posed no objection. The positive conclusion of this operation interested Falcone in particular, who was waiting to be nominated deputy Procuratore della Repubblica and to strike a blow against the High Commissioner [for anti-mafia affairs Domenico] Sica whom he does not like and also to do a favor for his Communist friends. . . . All these men should be considered responsible for the murders committed by Contorno, genuine state-sponsored killings. . . .[23]

The idea was, on its face, preposterous. Why would the police send Contorno to Palermo only to embarrass themselves by arresting him, in compromising circumstances, a short while later? Moreover, why would a killing spree of Salvatore Contorno help Giovanni Falcone become deputy chief prosecutor of Palermo, or "strike a blow against the High Commissioner Sica," or be a favor to "[Falcone's] Communist friends"? Despite these obvious weaknesses, the letters mixed enough genuine fact with fantasy to provide ammunition for partisans in the cause against Falcone and his colleagues.

"We all thought that [the letters and the bomb] were part of a single strategy," said Antonio Manganelli, a Criminalpol official who worked closely with Falcone and De Gennaro at the time. "It is preferable to kill a representative of the state after having discredited him, which also reduces the possible tensions within the mafia itself. If you can say Manganelli is a thief, it provides a justification for the people who kill him and softens the reaction to the crime. Perhaps that particular moment was chosen because for the first time Falcone appeared before the public not as the symbol of the war against the mafia but as a possible manipulator of witnesses, a prosecutor who had overstepped his bounds, and done something illegal. . . . This appeals to a kind of collective Sicilian public tribunal which has an old unwritten rule according to which they can't touch you as long as you are only doing your duty . . . but if you play dirty anything is justified. If Falcone is not a courageous magistrate, but a manipulator of government witnesses, then anything can happen to him."[24]

"In order to clear the way for the perpetrators two preconditions were necessary: a context and information," Falcone said in another interview at the time. "For months people have been saying, Falcone is over the hill. . . . Falcone hasn't made any progress since Buscetta, he is a judicial archaeologist, chasing the shadows of a mafia that no longer exists. . . . He's maneuvering to advance his career. . . . Falcone is a man of the Christian Democrats. . . . Falcone is a fifth column of the Communists. This intense subterranean work has the objective of making me appear in government circles as an untrustworthy prosecutor. . . . People in good faith . . . have begun to doubt, suspect. . . . These plague sowers, anonymous letter-writers opened cracks in my armor in order to discredit me, isolate me, damage my prestige. . . . And this is a precondition that the mafia knows how to evaluate—and create—before carrying out a crime against a representative of the state. The mafia is thinking about the impact of the crime, and planning what will happen afterwards."[25]

Privately, to a handful of trusted friends, Falcone shared his suspicions about who might have given the mafia the information about Falcone's plans to swim at Addaura on June 19, 1989. "He told me in no uncertain terms that he suspected Bruno Contrada," said Ignazio De Francisci, his colleague in the anti-mafia pool. Contrada, who had succeeded the slain Boris Giuliano as head of the Investigative Squad of the Palermo police, had been the object of rumor for years. Already in 1981, the chief of police did not trust Contrada: he had sent him to quell a nonexistent prison riot to keep him in the dark about an important police raid in the Spatola case. In 1984, Buscetta had warned Falcone about Contrada; the mafia boss Rosario Riccobono had told Buscetta in 1980 that Buscetta could safely hide in his territory of Partanna-Mondello without fear of being bothered by police. When Buscetta had asked his friend Stefano Bontate about this, Bontate had replied that Riccobono enjoyed special protection because of his close ties to Contrada. This was not sufficient evidence to make a case against Contrada but it might have been enough to convince his superiors to keep Contrada away from delicate mafia cases. Instead, he went on to become one of the chief investigators of the High Commissioner for anti-mafia affairs and was subsequently promoted to a highly sensitive post in the Italian secret services, which had become active in mafia investigations. "No one ever said 'Contrada you go to work for the police in Bolzano or Trieste [in northern Italy]," said De Francisci. "He was always there, and, in my opinion, not by accident. It served somebody's interests. . . ."[26]

Although Falcone mentioned Contrada to De Francisci and other friends, he never elaborated on the reasons for his suspicions. One theory that surfaced, however, involved Falcone's most recent Swiss investigation involving the mafia money launderer Oliviero Tognoli, the financial arm of Leonardo Greco, the boss of Bagheria. Tognoli had allegedly managed to acquire 200 kilos of pure gold with drug profits and reportedly kept numerous Swiss bank accounts for his friends in Sicily. Although an international warrant for his arrest was issued in 1984, he was not captured until 1989. Tognoli admitted to Falcone and Swiss magistrate Carla Del Ponte that he had eluded capture with Contrada's help (according to Del Ponte's own testimony in 1994). The bomb at Falcone's house in Addaura might perhaps have been designed to prevent Contrada's collusion from becoming public. But after the bomb's discovery, Tognoli changed his story and refused to make an official denunciation of Contrada.[27]

Although the assassination attempt had failed, the anonymous letters began to explode in the months that followed like a series of well-planted time bombs. In late June, the invisible hand dropped three copies of another anonymous letter into the mail, addressed to two leaders of the Communist Party and to Giampaolo Pansa, a left-wing journalist. This time the exclusive object of the attack was Giovanni Falcone.

Illustrious gentlemen, giovanni falcone, to use a euphemism, has been leading you by the tail, passing himself off as an anti-mafia champion while showing himself to be a squalid opportunist.

If you haven't understood yet, falcone has decided to distance himself from the Communist Party, attributing, as he has confided to friends, all his misfortunes (rejection as chief of the investigative office and rejection as High commissioner [for anti-mafia affairs]) to his closeness to that party, closeness, as he now maintains, that has discredited him to the outside world and created the opposition of other political forces, in particular the Christian Democrats and the Socialists, which are the parties that count today.

It is enough to read Falcone's interview with the magazine "Il Sabato," where, among other things, he claims that the pool still exists [a demonstrable falsehood], that the relations between mafia and politics are vague and not criminally actionable, that the "Third Level" does not exist, that there has been no drop in intensity in the war on the mafia, that prosecutors are not "against" anyone. . . . The truth is that Falcone, having to move to the Procura della Repubblica of Palermo dominated by people connected to the Lima-Andreotti group, and having no other possibilities, has decided to subordinate himself to those in the Procura who wield power in the interest of the Christian Democrats of Lima and Andreotti and in order to maintain his role of anti-mafia prosecutor (no longer very credible) will no longer investigate (and couldn't) into the Third Level (which doesn't exist, anyway) on the connection between the mafia and Christian Democratic politicians, and the complicity between mafia and business. . . . Falcone has sold out in order to get the job of deputy chief prosecutor. . . . But Falcone knows that you eventually have to pay all I.O.U.'s and that the collectors arrive punctually at the proper moment, in the middle of the investigation into the Third Level, Salvo Lima will remind him of his debt and Falcone will have to pay up.

In July, another letter followed, written, apparently, by a different hand. "I have belonged to the mafia for some time but I am tired. The dynamite set for Falcone wasn't put by the mafia, but by our people because Falcone asked us . . . his career was at stake for a promotion."[28]

By declaring himself a *mafioso*, by making obvious grammatical errors, by telling a patently absurd story, the author of this letter appeared determined not to be believed. Surely the mafia was too intelligent to take open credit for a letter—which could be a clever way of disguising its genuine authorship. Or perhaps this new letter was an attempt by the earlier anonymous author—clearly an educated person with a legal background—to throw police off the scent. The only certain thing is that someone or several people were playing an elaborate game, adding layer upon layer of disinformation.

The writing of anonymous letters is a common Italian vice, particularly in Sicily, where faith in obtaining justice through normal channels is in especially short supply. The first anti-mafia commission of the 1960s reportedly received some 40,000 anonymous letters and in 1989 the High Commissioner for anti-mafia affairs had a whole office dedicated to analyzing, cataloging and filing anonymous letters. Every once in a while, they provided vital information. But most of them—products of small-town rivalries, personal jealousies and professional feuds—ended up gathering dust in the archives.[29]

The letters written against Giovanni Falcone and his closest collaborators did not die a quiet death. Because of their possible connection to the Addaura bomb, because their author might himself be a mafia investigator and because everything connected to Falcone excited the Italian press, stories began to appear about the mysterious figure who was acting behind the scenes. He was even given a name, "The Raven," an Italian term for an anonymous letter writer. Because of the letters' denigratory content, Falcone's rivals may have seen a useful opportunity to further discredit him. Four of the letters had been sent, significantly, to Domenico Sica, the High Commissioner for anti-mafia affairs, a rival of Falcone. One of the clear purposes of the letters, in fact, was to foment ill will between Sica and Falcone.[30]

Sica's experience as High Commissioner had been somewhat frustrating. In typical fashion, while the Italian parliament had given him, on paper, vast but poorly defined powers to fight the mafia, they had yet to translate into reality. He was still largely dependent on the magistrates and police forces who had already been working on mafia cases, and it was not clear what, if any, authority he had over them. He was a magistrate without the power of prosecution, a policeman without a police force. The *carabinieri* in Palermo and the Criminalpol in Rome continued to work primarily with Falcone, whom they already knew well. Sica had, however, the power to question witnesses in any case that interested him and he began reinterrogating many of the mafia witnesses whom Falcone had already developed, producing largely redundant results. At one point, someone on Sica's staff let it be known that Sica was leaving for the United States to question Gaetano Badalamenti, the former head of the Commission who had been convicted in the American Pizza Connection trial. Stories that appeared in the press implied clearly that the old boss of Cosa Nostra was ready to "turn." But when Sica arrived to question Badalamenti at his U.S. prison, he found him anything but talkative. "Why did you publish the news of that meeting? Were you trying to get all my relatives killed?" Badalamenti said angrily in a later court appearance.[31] Falcone had been quietly working for five years to try to bring Badalamenti around, and the boss had begun to give a few cautious signs of opening up, something Sica apparently did not know about. His desire to compete with Falcone and a love of publicity had burned Badalamenti as a possible witness. As the first anniversary of his appointment approached, Sica found himself increasingly under attack as members of parliament began to question his effectiveness.

Sica decided personally to direct the investigation into the bomb at Addaura and the mystery of the anonymous letters. Normally, all cases involving the Palermo Palace of Justice were handled by the prosecutor's office in Caltanissetta, but the evening the Addaura bomb was discovered Sica flew to Palermo and took charge. "Sica wanted to appear to be the protagonist in the struggle against the mafia," said Judge Vito D'Ambrosio. Sica had now put himself in the position of being the arbiter of the fate and reputation of Falcone and all the other key mafia investigators.[32]

Sica was convinced that the letters could only have been written by a prosecutor in Palermo. As he and his staff began asking about possible suspects, one name kept coming up: Alberto Di Pisa, a member of the anti-mafia pool in the Procura della Repubblica. While Di Pisa had an excellent record as an intransigent, hardworking prosecutor, he also had the reputation, in the courthouse grapevine, of being a strange personality who did strange things. A female secretary at the courthouse had complained that she had been bothered by Di Pisa and suspected him of writing her unsigned letters. Di Pisa was also believed to have been behind several anonymous calls to the wife of a colleague, informing her that her husband was having an affair. "Di Pisa has a rather closed, confrontational and dark character, but he is a magistrate who has enjoyed complete faith in his professional activity, so much so that he was part of the anti-mafia pool," said Vincenzo Pajno, his former boss.[33] From the very beginning he had been one of the several magistrates in the Procura who had worked side by side with Falcone and Borsellino on the maxi-trial and virtually all of the major mafia cases of the last decade. It seemed hard to believe that such a magistrate would lend himself to such a squalid game.

Nonetheless, Di Pisa was also the first person several of his colleagues thought of as they speculated about the identity of the so-called Raven. He had a rancorous and difficult disposition and privately resented Falcone. He had been prosecuting mafia cases in Palermo longer than Falcone and had received only a fraction of the attention. In particular, Di Pisa expressed grave misgivings about the Contorno affair, which matched surprisingly with the contents of the anonymous letters. And he was among the handful of people who knew the intimate details of the Contorno arrest. He even looked the part of "the Raven," with his thick mane of jet-black hair and the morose and somber demeanor of an undertaker.

One of the things that made Di Pisa the most obvious and, at the same time, improbable choice was the fact that one of the people with whom the magistrate had shared his theories about Contorno's "secret mission" in Sicily was none other than High Commissioner Sica himself. In fact Di Pisa had developed a relationship with the High Commissioner that was so close he was considered by many to be "Sica's man" at the Palermo Palace of Justice. This deepened what began to be referred to as "the mystery of the Raven." Why would Di Pisa send anonymous letters to a person who would immediately suspect him? Why would Sica go out of his way to lead an investigation that would lead to the unmasking and disgrace of a friend and useful ally?

Whatever the case, on July 7, 1989, High Commissioner Sica invited Alberto Di Pisa to his office in Rome, offered him a glass of mineral water and then, after he left, called in technicians from the Italian secret services to take Di Pisa's fingerprints from the glass and from a desktop on which Di Pisa had drummed his fingers nervously during their conversation. Six days later, when he saw Giovanni Falcone in Rome, Sica told him that an analysis of the fingerprints had revealed that Di Pisa was, indeed, the anonymous letter writer.

But then the plot thickened, creating a "mystery within the mystery." On July 15, a member of the High Commissioner's staff, former magistrate Francesco Misiani, telephoned Falcone in

Palermo, saying that the identification of Di Pisa as "the Raven" had been premature because of a misunderstanding. The fingerprint taken from the anonymous letter was "compatible" with Di Pisa's but the print on the letter was too fragmentary to say they were "identical." After having informed the highest authorities, including the president of the Republic, that "the Raven" had been captured, the High Commissioner was forced to phone them all up and backtrack—just as Di Pisa's name was beginning to circulate in the press. This sudden about-face enraged Falcone and aroused his suspicions. "Any moderately well-trained technician knows that an analysis that says two fingerprints are 'compatible' with one another means absolutely nothing: it's like saying that two people are the same height," Falcone later said. Either Sica had made a colossal blunder or he and his staff were trying to cover up for their friend Di Pisa. "All this will generate suspicion, rumors—all hell will break loose—people will suspect that they have done this to help Di Pisa. If he is guilty they have done him a favor, and if he is innocent they have irremediably damaged his reputation," Falcone said.[34]

On July 20, as was predictable, the story broke that High Commissioner Sica had determined that "the Raven" of Palermo was mafia prosecutor Alberto Di Pisa. This then stimulated denials and the story of the inconclusive fingerprint test, which, as Falcone predicted, generated confusion and suspicion in all quarters.

That same evening, with his career on the line, High Commissioner Sica and his closest aides went to the laboratories of the Italian secret services outside Rome and oversaw a series of experiments to enhance the legibility of the fingerprint on the anonymous letter. They decided to try an experimental technique that involved treating the print with a fluorescent chemical; the fingerprint was then photographed and enlarged. A single fingerprint has twenty-five "characteristic" points to it, at least sixteen of which must be visible in order to determine their identity. Only eight "characteristic" points were left of the print fragment on the anonymous letter; but after being "enhanced" in the laboratory, suddenly at least eighteen points were now clearly legible. And the technicians agreed that the print did indeed belong to Alberto Di Pisa. There was only one problem: the enhancement technique removed almost all that was left of the original fingerprint, leaving

High Commissioner Sica with only the photograph of the print as evidence. After having spent most of the night at the secret service laboratories, Sica issued a press release on the morning of July 21 stating that Albert Di Pisa was indeed the anonymous letter writer. The evidence was then sent to the prosecutors in Caltanissetta, who, several days later, began criminal proceedings.[35]

But rather than putting an end to the case of "the Raven," the identification of Alberto Di Pisa turned out to be the beginning of another lengthy, painful drama that would cripple the anti-mafia front for many months. The parliament's anti-mafia commission called a parade of Palermo magistrates to testify in special hearings. The same parade then trooped through the halls of the Consiglio Superiore della Magistratura (CSM), which needed to determine whether to transfer or suspend Di Pisa as he prepared to go on trial.

Appearing before the CSM in the summer and fall of 1989, Alberto Di Pisa chose to defend himself by going on the offensive: attacking the agents of the Criminalpol, the anti-mafia pool, and, above all, Giovanni Falcone. While insisting that he did not write the anonymous letters, he not only endorsed most of their contents but upped the ante by making new and grave accusations against his colleagues. Not only did he harbor suspicions that Salvatore Contorno might have been sent to Sicily with the complicity of the police and magistrature, he insisted that the handling of mafia witnesses had been riddled with improprieties since Tommaso Buscetta began cooperating in 1984. Painting himself as a "dissident" among anti-mafia prosecutors he embarked on a bold but risky defensive strategy. Because he had always openly voiced his doubts, he argued, "I would have to be either crazy or stupid to write anonymous letters on this subject since I would be the first person people would suspect."[36]

Di Pisa's testimony was full, however, of inconsistencies. While expressing grave reservations about Falcone's integrity, he also pointed out that he had been the first person to congratulate Falcone when he was recently named deputy chief prosecutor. "In our work, my personal relations with Falcone have always been normal, of collaboration and cooperation, although, on a professional level, there were always differences, for example, on the handling of witnesses."

Di Pisa seemed to feel that cooperating witnesses should be treated exactly like any other criminal defendant. While this might make sense in an abstract, purely hypothetical realm, it ignored the simple facts of the real world. It was impossible to win the co-operation of witnesses like Buscetta and Contorno without establishing some kind of relationship of trust. These men were putting their lives on the line and needed to feel they could count on the prosecutors they worked with. Because there was no formal witness protection program, prosecutors had to take a direct interest in the security of the witnesses' family. Moreover, the episodes that Di Pisa cited as examples of excessive familiarity between Falcone and his witnesses were so tame as to seem ridiculous. Falcone and Borsellino, he said, once brought the Sicilian pastry, cannoli, to either Buscetta or Contorno. Gianni De Gennaro had once disguised Buscetta in a police uniform when he took him to buy a suit in Rome that he could wear in court. During the maxi-trial, Falcone had asked De Gennaro to congratulate Buscetta and Contorno for their composure on the witness stand. It was difficult to see anything improper in any of these episodes.

But Di Pisa ended up involuntarily providing an alternative explanation to his powerful resentment of his colleagues and the government's witnesses. His confrontational manner appeared to have alienated people, causing him to be excluded from the inner circle of magistrates who worked most closely with mafia witnesses. During one deposition, Buscetta had snubbed Di Pisa when the prosecutor had interjected with a question. "Buscetta gave me a dirty look; Falcone smiled and from that moment Buscetta would not even look my way. . . . At a certain point, Buscetta got up and made some coffee (because he had an apartment he was even allowed to make coffee), he offered some to Falcone and Borsellino . . . and didn't ask me whether I wanted any. . . . Afterwards, Falcone told me that my question had been naive."[37]

Di Pisa's strategy backfired disastrously. As he sat grasping for anything that might damage his friends and colleagues, he appeared to many on the judicial Council to be a man consumed by rancor, resentment and jealousy, precisely the kind of person who might vent his frustrations in anonymous letters.

Inadvertently, he seemed to supply his judges with a clear motive for his actions. "Perhaps I have not had the same celebrity in the mass media acquired by some of my colleagues, but I do not consider myself to have operated with any less professionalism or to have obtained lesser results. . . . I practically started the maxi-trial," he said, recalling that General Dalla Chiesa had given the police report on the first 162 defendants to the Procura della Repubblica and not to the investigative office, insinuating that Dalla Chiesa had trusted him and not Falcone and the anti-mafia pool. While technically accurate, Di Pisa's account was grossly distorted. Dalla Chiesa was simply following standard procedure. Italy's old penal code required that all police reports be filed with the Procura, and then, within thirty days, passed on to the investigative office for further inquiry. Moreover this report was not prepared by General Dalla Chiesa, it was the work of police investigator Ninni Cassarà, who had been working in perfect synchrony with Falcone.

Di Pisa criticized Falcone for accepting a request by the American government to help them question an Italian-American mafia witness, who was also a defendant in another trial in Rome. He referred sarcastically to Falcone as a "planetary" prosecutor, "who is busy with everything and everyone, and invades other people's turf."

In his desperate search for new ammunition, Di Pisa resuscitated the criticism of Falcone contained in the private diaries of Rocco Chinnici—criticism that had already been investigated by the CSM and found to have no basis in fact. "I don't want to insinuate anything, but . . ." Di Pisa said. Then, in what was perhaps the lowest blow of all, Di Pisa implied that Falcone had an excessively cozy relationship with Michele Greco, "the Pope," noting that the mafia boss had thrown his arms around Falcone after a deposition. "This isn't an important incident, but I don't know . . . Michele Greco and Falcone's embracing . . . it seemed a little strange . . . to be honest, Falcone didn't initiate this embrace but he didn't push him away either. . . ."

Several members of the CSM were appalled by Di Pisa's performance. "He resembled and behaved like a mortally wounded bull . . . who, in the paroxysms of fury, strikes blindly at anything that moves . . . with the exclusive goal of destroying and killing as much as possible before dying," one anonymous member of the Council was quoted as saying after the session. "A squalid and pathetic spectacle. And to think that Alberto Di Pisa was a respectable and respected magistrate."[38]

Even though Di Pisa's desperate thrusts failed to scratch Falcone, he did succeed in goring another colleague, Giuseppe Ayala, the public prosecutor in the maxi-trial and Falcone's closest friend in the Palace of Justice at the time. "In all of Palermo, not just at the courthouse . . . people are saying that Ayala has a bank debt of 500 million lire [about half a million dollars]," Di Pisa told the CSM. The press began to report rumors that Ayala had accumulated his large bank debt racking up losses at poker and that he had received preferential treatment at the bank because of his position as magistrate. Soon the "Di Pisa case" had become the "Di Pisa–Ayala case," dragging on throughout the fall of 1989.[39]

When Falcone appeared—again—before the CSM in October, he openly expressed his growing anger at being dragged into another pointless controversy. "I am genuinely surprised to hear totally unfounded and flimsy accusations and insinuations . . . coming from someone [Di Pisa] who was the first to congratulate me when I was named deputy chief prosecutor of Palermo. . . . If there were any differences between myself and Di Pisa, he kept them well hidden, I am not aware that he ever expressed these complaints publicly. . . . This desire to attribute messianic powers to me, starting with Di Pisa himself, is beginning to irritate me quite a bit. . . . I would like someone to explain to me what I have to do with this business of Contorno."[40]

Falcone pointed out that even with an army of defense lawyers, no one, during the entire duration of the maxi-trial and its appeal, had shown a single impropriety in the government's use of mafia witnesses. "I challenge anyone in Palermo or elsewhere to tell me when I have done a favor for this or that witness, that I have ever asked for favorable treatment for anyone. . . ."

Even though the charges were easily brushed off, the fact of having to answer charge after charge, in hearing after hearing, was gradually paralyzing the war against the mafia in Palermo. "If we make a 'case' out of every problem, if we spend all our time providing explanations of our conduct, of making comments and being an object of criticism . . . the moment will come when we will arrive to question defendants and they will simply laugh in our face," Falcone said.

And yet there were signs that some people on the judicial Council wanted to create another "case," by trying to make it appear that Falcone had taken the lead in making Di Pisa the prime suspect in the investigation into the anonymous letters. Falcone had clearly explained that High Commissioner Sica had asked him if anyone in the Palermo courthouse had a reputation for sending anonymous letters; when Falcone mentioned Di Pisa's name, Sica replied that other prosecutors in Palermo had said the same thing. Vincenzo Palumbo—one of the Council members who had supported Antonino Meli over Falcone in January 1988—tried to misconstrue Falcone's testimony into its direct opposite: "So do I understand correctly that you were the first to mention Di Pisa's name?"

"No, Sica already had the names," Falcone said. "Sica wanted a confirmation from me that Di Pisa had a reputation as an anonymous letter writer."

At this point, Carlo Smuraglia, one of Falcone's supporters on the Council, saw the potential danger in this apparently innocuous misunderstanding and said: "I want to protest what is happening here this evening, because on tonight's evening news we will hear that Falcone was the first person to suggest Di Pisa and that is not acceptable. Falcone has reconstructed events in an extremely clear manner. Unfortunately, what matters here is not what Falcone says but what we read in tomorrow's newspapers."

The deep divisions on the Council that had formed during the Meli-Falcone battles of 1988 persisted into all of the subsequent controversies. Falcone's supporters were the most adamant that Di Pisa should be transferred from Palermo until his guilt or innocence was proven in his upcoming trial; while most of the other members agreed, they insisted it was only fair, then, that Ayala be transferred at the same time.

While there was no evidence that Ayala had ever done anything improper, it was clear that his family's financial affairs had fallen into serious disarray during an acrimonious divorce. There was no danger, however, of the Ayalas defaulting on the debt: his wife was from an extremely wealthy family and she had used the money to develop some of her considerable real estate holdings. Since the family could (and did) pay off the debt at a moment's notice, the bank would end up making a large profit at Ayala's wife's expense, he insisted. "I am the only magistrate to get into trouble for—not for getting richer on the job—but for getting poorer," Ayala joked.[41]

"This ignoble game had to end in a tie," said Vito D'Ambrosio, who defended Ayala on the Council.[42] "It was a Solomonic decision: one from your group, one from mine," said Carmelo Conti, president of the Palermo Court of Appeals.[43] "But I think some members of the Council wanted to strike at . . . Giovanni Falcone, an undeclared but fairly transparent aim." While there may have been a desire in some to even the score, others were clearly motivated by principle. "Ayala was clearly an honest person, but he was also imprudent," said Stefano Racheli, a strong supporter of Falcone who voted against Ayala. "A magistrate has to live by a higher standard . . . appearances of impropriety count as well as impropriety."[44] It was not a good idea, he felt, for a prosecutor— in a world where bribery and blackmail are everyday occurrences—to run up a huge debt.

And yet Racheli does not exclude the possibility that in the Di Pisa–Ayala case, as in other controversies, the Council may have fallen into an artfully laid trap. "The truly sad feeling I have taken away from my years on the CSM was the sensation that in many instances, I don't even know what side I was playing on because the game was so obscure. . . . The possibility of being used was so great. . . . Did I score a goal for or against the cause of justice?"

On November 7, the Council voted to transfer both Di Pisa and Ayala. The majority decided that Ayala's bank debt was incompatible with the image of an anti-mafia prosecutor and found that even though Di Pisa's authorship of the anonymous letters had not been established in court, the violent and gratuitous criticism he had expressed of his colleagues made it impossible for him to remain in Palermo. In classic Italian style, the two would remain as lame ducks in their old offices in Palermo a few yards down the hall from one another for several more months until the order was executed.

Although many doubts about the mystery of "the Raven" lingered (and Di Pisa would be first convicted and later acquitted), one fact was clear: Palermo was now without two of its best, most experienced mafia prosecutors, Di Pisa and Ayala. The credibility of Domenico Sica, as High Commissioner for mafia affairs, was damaged beyond repair and Giovanni Falcone was further weakened by another bruising battle, not with organized crime but with those who were supposed to be on the same side in the war against the mafia.

"What the mafia was not able to accomplish with dynamite has been accomplished through the weapon of calumny," said Ferdinando Imposimato, a former magistrate who was a member of parliament.[45]

EIGHTEEN

E ven as the mystery of "the Raven" unfolded during the summer of 1989, Giovanni Falcone was forced to grapple with another, equally thorny problem. In the middle of August, he received word that a Sicilian criminal named Giuseppe Pellegriti had sensational revelations to make about mafia and politics. Falcone and Giuseppe Ayala flew to meet Pellegriti in Pisa, where he was in prison. Pellegriti claimed that Christian Democratic leader Salvatore Lima had commissioned the mafia to assassinate his colleague Piersanti Mattarella, the president of the Sicilian Region, in 1980. Although Pellegriti was only a common criminal, he insisted that his information came directly from Nitto Santapaola, the boss of Cosa Nostra in Catania. Falcone and Ayala began to smell a rat. Under close questioning, the inmate began to contradict himself, making obvious factual errors, and it became clear that he could not have gotten his information from Santapaola. "After about ten minutes, Giovanni and I looked at each as if to say: 'Did we come all this way to listen to these fairy tales?' " said Giuseppe Ayala.[1]

From the time that Tommaso Buscetta first began to cooperate in 1984, mafia prosecutors had worried about possible infiltration by phony witnesses planting disinformation. If reliable information got mixed up with artful invention, and credible witnesses became confused with false ones, the entire legal edifice of the maxi-trial could come crashing down. The case was still working its way through the appeals process and a disastrous mistake could be used to discredit the use of mafia witnesses and overturn the sentence in the maxi-trial. Falcone suspected that Pellegriti may have been doing the bidding of another inmate with whom he was on close terms, Angelo Izzo, a right-wing terrorist with a taste for political intrigue. Already sentenced to life in prison, an inmate like Pellegriti risked nothing by lending himself to a disinformation campaign. Falcone was also worried that Pellegriti was being egged on by the people around Leoluca Orlando, the mayor of Palermo, for whom Salvatore Lima was the devil incarnate. Famous for having said that "suspicion is the antechamber of the truth," Orlando seemed convinced that any accusation against his political enemies must, by necessity, be true. The timing of Pellegriti's revelations was also mildly suspicious: Lima's political mentor, Giulio Andreotti, had just become head of the government again, beginning his sixth term as prime minister on July 20, 1989.

Although Falcone was quite certain that Pellegriti was lying, the accusation put him in a tight spot. While prosecutors in the United States are allowed to exercise discretion in deciding whether or not to pursue a given case, under Italian law, magistrates are technically required to investigate any crime that is brought to their attention—regardless of the strength or weakness of the evidence. "He was extremely worried," said Judge Vito D'Ambrosio, whom he stopped off to see on his way back from Pisa to Palermo. " 'They've set a trap for me,' he said. 'This Pellegriti has said things I know not to be true. It's a false trail that will lead nowhere but if I don't follow it, people will immediately say: Why don't you indict Lima?' "[2] When, on October 3, 1989, Pellegriti repeated his accusations against Lima in open court—under pressure from Alfredo Galasso, a lawyer close to Orlando—Falcone immediately charged him with perjury and libel. Pellegriti had been brought in to testify in the appeal of the maxi-trial itself, and the use of a false witness might pollute the whole case, providing a perfect opportunity to those who wanted to find a reason to overturn it. "I had to act right away, I couldn't let any time pass," Falcone told D'Ambrosio. "Naturally, Andreotti tried to use the indictment of Pellegriti as proof of Lima's innocence," D'Ambrosio said. "On the contrary, Falcone was convinced of the falseness of Pellegriti, not of the innocence of Lima."

Not surprisingly, Falcone came under fire, especially from the Orlando camp in Palermo, severely straining their once-close friendship. Soon the rumor began to circulate that Falcone had telephoned Giulio Andreotti to tell him that the accusations against his friend Lima were unfounded and that he intended to indict Pellegriti for libel and perjury. Although there would have been nothing strictly improper had he, in fact, made the call—Andreotti was prime minister—it was not consistent with the image of rigorous independence that Falcone had always enjoyed. Falcone denied having telephoned Andreotti, but in a way that many found ambiguous. When asked about it before the CSM during "the Raven" hearings on October 12, 1989, Falcone said: "And why should I deny every rumor that people spread about me? I have a lot of other things to do. In Palermo we have a saying: 'Don't throw a stone at every dog that barks.' People say everything and the opposite of everything about me: that I'm a Communist or that I'm an anti-Communist, that I am an Andreotti-man or that I have become a Socialist. I don't think I should have to deny it, but if the Council asks me, then I deny it."[3]

"Falcone may have been right to incriminate Pellegriti, but the way he did it was wrong," said Judge Salvatore Barresi, a Palermo magistrate who worked closely with Falcone on the second maxitrial. "Waiting until he pronounced the name of Salvatore Lima in open court and indicting him in this highly public manner and then telephoning Andreotti made it seem—perhaps unintentionally—that he was trying to appear 'trustworthy' in the eyes of the government. I don't think he acted like a magistrate that day."[4]

The growing impression that Falcone was currying support with those in power was supported by the fact that he was, indeed, beginning to cultivate friendships in the Andreotti circle in order to shore up his own dangerously weakened position in Palermo. "This has to be understood in the context of Falcone's life at that time," said Judge Vito D'Ambrosio. "The bomb at Addaura really marked Falcone's life. It was a real turning point . . . Falcone felt completely exposed and unprotected. He became more cautious, more prudent." The lack of political backers had cost him the jobs of chief of the Palermo investigative office and of

High Commissioner for mafia affairs and he had seen eight years of work unravel before his eyes in a matter of months. And, he was convinced, it had almost cost him his life. Now that they were eliminating the investigative office, the only place for him to go was the Procura della Repubblica of Palermo, where the Andreotti faction was said to wield considerable influence.

In his search for political support, Falcone became friendly with Claudio Vitalone, Andreotti's chief legal adviser. In one sense it was natural and perfectly proper: Vitalone was a highly intelligent former magistrate, and had been vice president of the anti-mafia commission. In the new Andreotti government he had been named deputy foreign minister, sponsoring conferences on international drug trafficking and money laundering, at which he invited Falcone to speak. But Vitalone also had the reputation of being an unscrupulous political animal, who, as a magistrate, had placed himself at the service of his powerful friends and been rewarded with a political career. Even the politically cautious Consiglio Superiore della Magistratura had been forced to reject Vitalone for a promotion to Italy's highest court because of his unbecoming conduct as a prosecutor. He had threatened and bullied colleagues who had dared to investigate his friends and relatives, while arranging lavish dinners in order to introduce other prosecutors to his political cronies.[5]

"Falcone was looking for allies in any direction," Judge D'Ambrosio said. "He was severely criticized by the Left for this friendship. He even became brusque with his friends, and reacted badly to any criticism. It was a very bad period for him. His only refuge was work. Because, despite everything, he continued to work."[6]

Aside from any possible desire to cozy up to political power in Rome, Falcone also had another reason for his behavior in the Pellegriti case. He was especially anxious to denounce a false witness in order to protect the credibility of a very real and extremely important new mafia witness, Francesco Marino Mannoia, who, unbeknownst to the public, was about to begin cooperating precisely in those days. By underlining the difference between credible and unreliable criminal witnesses, Falcone wanted to make sure that Marino Mannoia—the first *mafioso* from the winning camp of Cosa Nostra to cooperate with the government—would be taken seriously.

The government's knowledge of the internal workings of the mafia had remained stuck at the great mafia war of the early 1980s. Although Antonino Calderone—the most recent important witness—had begun collaborating in 1987, his knowledge of life in Cosa Nostra ended in 1983 when he fled Sicily for France, and he himself had become an increasingly marginal figure after his brother Pippo's death in 1978. Marino Mannoia's knowledge of Cosa Nostra, instead, was current almost up to the minute. Although he had been in prison since 1985, he knew the composition of the mafia hit squads operating in Palermo right up until the spring of 1989. He knew, because his younger brother, Agostino Marino Mannoia, who visited him each week at Ucciardone prison, was almost invariably a part of those hit squads, having become one of the Corleonesi's favorite killers. Then on April 21, 1989, Francesco Marino Mannoia had heard on the radio in prison that an abandoned automobile belonging to his family had been found with bloodstains in it. As he feared, his brother did not come to visit him in prison that week—or ever again. The Corleonesi had begun devouring their own offspring. When Marino Mannoia's family told him during a prison visit that his brother had disappeared, he did not even flinch, since, he said, "it was considered unseemly for a man of honor to show emotion in situations like that." Not only had he lost a brother, Marino Mannoia understood that, inevitably, he was next. He pretended, publicly, to believe the official explanation that Agostino had been killed by the "losing" families who were trying to make a comeback, but he began to watch his back and, privately, considered his next move.[7] Then in the fall of 1989, Marino Mannoia's mistress appeared at the Rome offices of the Nucleo Anti-Crimine, the police's anti-mafia unit, indicating that the *mafioso* was ready to talk. "We decided, just as precaution, to have her sleep that night in a safe house we had at our disposal," said police investigator Antonio Manganelli. "When our agents went to her hotel to collect her stuff the next day, they learned that the previous evening two men had come looking for her."[8]

After negotiations over security, Marino Mannoia and Falcone finally began their first session on October 8, 1989, just five days after Falcone had charged Giuseppe Pellegriti with libel and perjury. The *mafioso* provided Falcone with a full account of life within Cosa Nostra after the great mafia war.

Marino Mannoia had been a member of the "family" of Stefano Bontate, but was lucky to be in prison during the spring of 1981 when Bontate was assassinated and his closest aides exterminated. Marino Mannoia escaped from prison in 1983, with his brother Agostino's help, and met immediately with Totò Riina to clarify his position within Cosa Nostra. The war had already been won and there was no point in killing all 120 men of honor in Bontate's family, many of whom could be extremely useful. Francesco Marino Mannoia was especially valuable, a "soldier" with ten years' experience, who had shown steady nerves and sound judgment handling all kinds of situations, extortions, murders, drug deals and prison. He had the seriousness, discretion and reserve appreciated in Cosa Nostra: if he resented the men who had killed his boss, he gave no outward sign of it. Moreover, he was intelligent, a talented document forger, who had also learned enough chemistry to become one of the best heroin refiners in Cosa Nostra.

He had prepared much of the heroin for the Spatola-Inzerillo-Gambino ring that Falcone had originally begun investigating. He had met with John Gambino, the boss American police had recently arrested in the "Iron Tower" case. Gambino had personally inspected the quality of the heroin that Marino Mannoia was refining in Palermo—evidence that would help finally induce John and Joe Gambino to plead guilty to drug trafficking in an arrangement with the American government in 1994.

Marino Mannoia was able to identify dozens of recent recruits to Cosa Nostra, the new makeup of the Commission and of the most important mafia hit squads of the last several years.[9]

He knew because his brother, who visited him each week, was usually in the middle of the action. Agostino Marino Mannoia had participated in the assassinations of police investigators Beppe Montana, Ninni Cassarà and Natale Mondo. He confirmed that Salvatore Marino—the man police tortured to death after the killing of Montana—had acted as the mafia's lookout man at the docks where Montana was gunned down. A week later, Agostino Marino Mannoia was again pressed into service during the assassination of Ninni Cassarà and his bodyguard Roberto Antiochia, part of a team of about fifteen men of honor. The assassination was so important that at least four members of the Commission itself, Bernardo Brusca, Francesco Madonia, Giuseppe Gambino and Pino "the Shoe" Greco, were at the scene, with Greco wielding his ubiquitous Kalashnikov, accounting for many of the some 200 bullets sprayed at Cassarà and his men.

Perhaps most important, Marino Mannoia explained the shifting dynamic of power in Cosa Nostra. He described how Totò Riina had gradually eliminated the killers who had "distinguished" themselves in the great mafia war, precisely because their increased prestige had begun to threaten Riina's own power. This, in turn, had led to a nascent rebellion among the mafia's younger ranks, which the Corleonesi had succeeded in crushing. The murder of Agostino Marino Mannoia was one of the final chapters in the story of this failed revolt.

With consummate skill, Riina destroyed his rivals by playing on divisions within the families, personal enmities and ambitions so that he got others to do his dirty work in what appeared like various isolated episodes, but that, in fact, fit into a clear design of Riina's creation.

Perhaps most emblematic of this pattern was the short and bloody career of Pino "the Shoe" Greco, who probably committed at least eighty killings before being eliminated in 1985. Although officially a member of the "family" of Michele Greco, "the Pope," "the Shoe" had become Totò Riina's favorite killer. He had personally eliminated the bosses Stefano Bontate and Salvatore Inzerillo and was said to have cut off the arm with which Inzerillo's teenage son hoped to shoot Totò Riina. He had been part of the audacious hit squad that gunned down General Dalla Chiesa, apparently jumping on the roof of a car in order to aim his Kalashnikov down on the general, his wife and bodyguard. He had participated (as Vincenzo Sinagra testified) in many of the murders in Filippo Marchese's Room of Death.

The cannibalism within the ranks of the Corleonesi began, according to Marino Mannoia, at the end of 1982, with the murder of Filippo Marchese, the boss of Corso dei Mille. Marchese's bloody-minded ferocity had been an asset in a time of war, but in peacetime his recklessness and blind violence were liabilities. With typical shrewdness, Totò Riina had Marchese eliminated by his good friend and business partner, Pino "the Shoe" Greco, by appealing to his greed and ambition. Greco wanted to take full control of the cement company he and Marchese owned jointly and wanted to prevent a possible challenge to his own leadership.

"After the mafia war," said Francesco Marino Mannoia, "Giuseppe Greco, 'the Shoe,' became a kind of charismatic leader, who inspired the admiration and absolute loyalty of many of the younger men of honor." Although Michele Greco, "the Pope," had been his boss and was now nominally head of the Commission, Pino Greco treated "the Pope" like an irrelevant old man, making it clear that he held the real power. "He acted like he was the boss of everything, and ignored the ancient rules of Cosa Nostra," Marino Mannoia told Falcone. For a time, Totò Riina welcomed Pino Greco's rising star because it eclipsed "the Pope." Totò Riina let Pino Greco overplay his hand, knowing that his foolish arrogance would create bad feeling among others, which could be usefully exploited, when needed, in the future. Greco's contempt for the leaders of Cosa Nostra became such that he no longer even bothered showing up for meetings of the Commission, sending his underboss, Vincenzo Puccio, in his stead. (This was the same Vincenzo Puccio who had been among the three killers of Captain Emanuele Basile and who, thanks to the leniency of the Italian justice system, was still on the loose five years later.) The Shoe's own men began to worry about the growing rift between their own family and the Commission and shared their concerns with Totò Riina.

Thus, in late 1985, Pino Greco was shot and killed by his own men, Vincenzo Puccio and Giuseppe Lucchese. Once again, Agostino Marino Mannoia was on the scene, this time, however, not as a member of the hit squad but as an involuntary witness to his own *capo-famiglia*'s murder. He and another "soldier," Filippo La Rosa, were waiting downstairs in Greco's house, while the heads of the family were upstairs talking. When they heard shots, Marino Mannoia and La Rosa ran upstairs to find Puccio and Giuseppe Lucchese standing over Pino Greco's body. "Now you can decide whose side you're on," Lucchese said. Choosing between a dead man and two *mafiosi* holding guns was an easy decision. Because of "the Shoe's" considerable following within

Cosa Nostra, his death was kept secret for some time. The official story was that he had gone to the United States because the Palermo police were hot on his trail. When Vincenzo Puccio was rearrested in late 1986, he gradually became the lightning rod for growing dissent within Cosa Nostra. A lot of the younger members of the organization who, thanks to the Corleonesi's strategy of confrontation, were serving lengthy prison sentences, started grumbling about Totò Riina. Even Riina's brother-in-law, Leoluca Bagarella, complained to Puccio that the boss of bosses was not using his influence to win his release. Riina was also trying to prevent Bagarella from going through with his marriage to Vincenza Marchese, because his fiancée was the niece of Filippo Marchese, whose family's stock was down after Marchese's elimination. Hearing these complaints, Puccio confided his own misgivings to Bagarella and to Antonino and Giuseppe Marchese, the brothers of Bagarella's fiancée, who were also serving time in Ucciardone prison. (Giuseppe Marchese had been the driver of the getaway car in the Christmas Massacre of Bagheria in 1981, whose incriminating fingerprints had led to the murder of Dr. Paolo Giaccone.) Puccio also confided in Francesco Marino Mannoia, assuming, correctly, that Marino Mannoia continued to harbor resentment toward the Corleonesi for the killing of his old boss and good friend, Stefano Bontate. "In the course of my discussions with Vincenzo Puccio I began to realize that he was contemplating a revolt against the suffocating hegemony of Totò Riina, but I told him right away he was burned because, unlike him, I didn't trust either Bagarella or the Marchese brothers, and was afraid they would have informed others of Puccio's plans," Marino Mannoia told Falcone. Going against his own better judgment, however, Marino Mannoia told Puccio that he could count on his support and that of his brother, Agostino. Meanwhile, Bagarella was released and succeeded in marrying Vincenza Marchese, removing his motives for discontent.

Agostino Marino Mannoia's disappearance on April 21, 1989, was a sign that word of the rebels' plans had leaked out. And just three weeks later (May 11, 1989), Vincenzo Puccio himself was murdered in his bunk at Ucciardone prison; he had been killed by his cellmates and confidants, Antonino and Giuseppe Marchese, who smashed in his skull with a barbecue grill while he slept. "This was a killing of unheard-of gravity for Cosa Nostra," Marino Mannoia pointed out. Not only had two men of honor killed their own *capo-mandamento* (district leader), they had done so in prison, which was supposed to be "neutral" territory. Since getting caught was a virtual certainty, there was a strict rule in Cosa Nostra against committing killings in prison. But Totò Riina felt that his would-be rival had to be eliminated immediately, whatever the cost—particularly since the cost would be paid by others. The Marchese brothers evidently decided it was safer to risk longer prison sentences than try to take on the Corleonesi in some foolhardy rebellion. They hoped (as many had before) that by serving up a dangerous rival to Totò Riina, they would be insuring their future. Unfortunately, they made a tragic miscalculation. On the very day of Vincenzo Puccio's murder, another group of assassins outside the prison shot and killed Pietro Puccio (Vincenzo's brother)—short-circuiting any possible retaliation on his part when the news of the killing in Ucciardone became public. While a clever tactical move, it sealed the doom of Antonino and Giuseppe Marchese. They had told authorities that they had been forced to kill Vincenzo Puccio in a sudden argument that had flared out of control. Now that Puccio's brother had been killed on the same day, it became perfectly obvious that the two murders were part of a carefully synchronized plan. Riina, having used them to do his dirty work, had destroyed their alibi and condemned them to life in prison.

The murder of Vincenzo Puccio, in a sense, closed the circle on the gruesome series of killings among the "winners" of the great mafia war. Examined as a whole, the events that Marino Mannoia recounted looked like a "food chain" in the grisly Darwinian struggle of Cosa Nostra, with each fish eating the other until the big fish, Totò Riina, finally swallowed them all. Filippo Marchese had been killed by Pino "the Shoe" Greco, Greco had been killed by Vincenzo Puccio, and now Puccio had been eliminated by Marchese's nephews. Then Riina had killed four birds with one stone, eliminating the Puccios, while making sure that their assassins, the Marchese brothers, were out of the way.

Marino Mannoia's credibility was beyond question: he knew,

quite literally, where the bodies were buried and was able to prove it. Just how much Cosa Nostra feared Marino Mannoia's collaboration became evident in November 1990 when mafia killers murdered his mother, aunt and sister in their Palermo home—making a mockery of the myth that Cosa Nostra does not kill women and children. Nonetheless, Marino Mannoia continued and even returned to Palermo disguised in a policeman's uniform, leading investigators to a garbage dump where they found the remains of numerous murder victims.[10]

Giovanni Falcone and the police investigators who met with and listened to Francesco Marino Mannoia were greatly impressed by his seriousness, his care and precision with details and his sober, unromantic vision of the mafia. "Do you realize how much strength is needed to strangle a man?" he told Falcone. "It can take as long as ten minutes, and sometimes the victim slips out, bites and kicks. Some even manage to break free for a while. But at least it's a professional way of doing the job." Investigators were also greatly impressed with Marino Mannoia's intellect. He was perhaps the most intelligent mafia witness since Buscetta. At one point, in order to break an impasse in the deposition, Marino Mannoia said to Falcone, "When you are skeptical about something I am saying, your eyebrows twitch and I become blocked. Believe me, when I tell you I don't remember something, there's no point in pressing me, it's because I genuinely don't remember."[11]

In their first meeting, Marino Mannoia had pretended to know nothing about relations between the mafia and the government. "I am completely ignorant when it comes to politics," he had said. "Stefano Bontate never told me anything about his political preferences and . . . his political relationships."[12]

But then at a certain point, Marino Mannoia suddenly turned to Falcone and asked him, "Judge, what political color are you?" When Falcone said that he was not a member of any party, Mannoia continued, "I asked because I need to discuss certain very serious things and I don't want there to be any political interference of any kind. Strange things have been happening that never went on before. In the past Cosa Nostra generally voted for the Christian Democrats but . . . in the last parliamentary elections [June 1987], we were given a very specific order in prison to make sure that we voted and got our friends and relatives to vote for the Italian Socialist Party. Somewhat earlier, when the Radical Party needed 10,000 new members to avoid closing down, inside the prison in Palermo, we all signed up on the initiative of Pippo Calò. He himself made a donation of 50 million lire [about $50,000 at the time] . . . I made a contribution of one million lire . . . my cousin Pietro Vernengo contributed five million lire. I mention this because I am very much afraid of the political influence in the magistrature and I believe that this is one of the greatest forces that blocks the struggle against organized crime, in all its forms."

But after about a month of almost daily meetings, Marino Mannoia began to open up. He listed several important Sicilian politicians with whom his former boss Stefano Bontate had close relations. At the top of the list was Salvatore Lima. "He was, I believe, the politician with whom Bontate was on the most intimate terms. I myself saw him with Bontate numerous times . . . both in an apartment, turned into an office . . . as well as in the Baby Luna bar, on the day it was closed for business."

Only a month after taking a beating for his handling of the Pellegriti case, Falcone was once again confronted with the name of Salvatore Lima—Prime Minister Andreotti's man in Sicily. Two years earlier when Antonino Calderone had testified that he had met with Salvatore Lima to arrange for the transfer of a troublesome police officer, Falcone had immediately flown to the United States to try to get Tommaso Buscetta to open up about his relations with Lima. This time Falcone dutifully registered Marino Mannoia's remarks, but he did not follow them up with further investigation. There is an important difference between the two episodes: Calderone had accused Lima of a serious offense (using his influence to help a criminal suspect), while Marino Mannoia had merely stated that he had seen the politician in the company of a mafia boss—not in itself a crime. But when they learned of Marino Mannoia's statement about a year later, many of Falcone's colleagues saw his inaction as part of a general retreat on the mafia-politics front.

"Francesco Marino Mannoia's statement . . . was of genuinely staggering importance," said Judge Salvatore Barresi, "the most important Christian Democratic leader in Sicily met frequently and was on intimate terms with the biggest mafia boss in Palermo at that time. Moreover, he was speaking of events he himself had witnessed, not relating secondhand information. . . . Well, in the face of this explosive statement, which opened up unthinkable scenarios, Giovanni Falcone turned his back and moved on to other topics. . . . At another time, Falcone would have made intensive investigations. But I think that, unconsciously, Giovanni Falcone may have been conditioned by the whole Pellegriti affair. From that point on, Giovanni Falcone concentrated exclusively on the purely criminal dimension of Cosa Nostra, drug trafficking, murders, putting aside, for the moment, the political dimension. Perhaps he understood that the political conditions did not exist to move effectively on this front and therefore decided to ignore the relations of mafia and politics."[13]

Barresi was part of the group of younger, politically minded magistrates that included the two dissidents of the anti-mafia pool, Giacomo Conte and Giuseppe Di Lello, who had begun to challenge Falcone's cautious approach at the time of his compromise with his boss, chief prosecutor Antonino Meli. When Barresi and Di Lello learned of Marino Mannoia's statement, they denounced Falcone's inertia to the Consiglio Superiore della Magistratura. "I broke with Giovanni Falcone over this incident," Barresi said.

Like other friends and colleagues, Barresi is convinced that the bomb at Addaura had a profound effect on Falcone's thinking: "Addaura, I believe, represented a real crossroads for Giovanni Falcone. He understood, for the first time, just how near the threat of death was and that this threat came not only, as he might have imagined, from the mafia itself but some deviant elements within the government itself. He was convinced that people in the secret services had a hand in the bomb." While the bomb made Falcone more cautious, Barresi does not believe that Falcone's changed attitude was a product of concern for his personal safety. "Knowing the personality of Giovanni Falcone, I can rule out that fear of danger was a motivating favor," Barresi said. After all, Falcone had lived with the imminent, daily threat of assassination for nine years, without ever pulling back. Rather, Falcone's attitude was dictated by an increasingly sober evaluation of the balance of power between the magistrature and the government. The events of the past three years—the campaign against the judges, the change in government, his own professional rejections and defeats, the complete legislative inertia on organized crime and, finally, the bomb—had made it painfully clear to Falcone that powerful forces in the government were determined not to sit back and let themselves (or their colleagues) be placed on trial for their links to the mafia. Falcone believed that a head-on battle with the state—at a time when Andreotti was prime minister and Lima his chief representative in Sicily—would have created such a firestorm that it would have ended up backfiring. "Not only would it ruin the possibility of prosecuting those politicians, but it would damage the credibility of the mafia witnesses and compromise the effectiveness of the whole struggle against the mafia," Barresi added. "This was Giovanni Falcone's judicial philosophy. He was not animated by a desire to cover up for these people, or to please anyone—absolutely not. . . . He knew that eventually we would have to pursue the political track, but he was convinced that you had to arrive gradually, step by step, until the political conditions permitted us to do more. The old approach of the frontal attack—which had been adopted, in part, in the first maxi-trial—did not pay. Paolo Borsellino was of the same view."

While many in Palermo challenged Falcone, others believe that, under the extremely difficult circumstances in which he found himself, Falcone made the right decision. "Despite everything, I am convinced that Falcone did well not to try to do more, because he would have been crushed by the reaction of the political class, and by those politicians in particular," said Ignazio De Francisci, one of his protégés from the anti-mafia pool. "Falcone's caution was dictated by the objective difficulties of his work. . . . Also the evidence he had in hand was weak: what would Falcone have obtained by indicting Lima because he was seen ten years earlier meeting with a mafia boss, who was now dead? It's true he was cautious, but in my opinion, he had good reasons to be. . . . In a civilized, democratic country, someone like Lima would have been forced to withdraw from political life on the basis of Marino Mannoia's statement, but, up until the day of his death, Lima was a man who counted in the Christian Democracy, a man who counted a lot . . . One of Falcone's abilities was in weighing the strength of the forces in play and not undertaking battles he knew he was destined to lose," said De Francisci. "He had a clear idea of what and how much he could risk. . . . He had a strategic vision of genuine scope."

But it is precisely this kind of calculation of the balance of power that Barresi and others objected to. "There are two judicial philosophies in Italy, those [like Falcone] who believe the judge has to take outside factors into consideration, and those who believe that the magistrate must do what he has to do and let the chips fall where they may."

"This is the eternal dilemma of the magistrate, you are supposed to pursue every crime, but it is an abstract notion," said Stefano Racheli, a member of the Consiglio Superiore della Magistratura at the time, now a prosecutor in Rome. "I think Falcone had a very Aristotelian idea of ethics: the ethical man tries to understand what his margin of action is and work within that space. . . . Giovanni would never have started a foolhardy battle as an act of protest . . . I think it was part of his being Sicilian. The Sicilians are a profoundly mature and realistic people. Overreaching ambition is the worst thing for a Sicilian, it shows immaturity and lack of dignity."

Falcone's choice was a deeply anguishing and painful one. He fought with and lost some of his closest friends and allies, particularly among the younger generation of magistrates who, inspired by Falcone himself, believed that it was possible to take on mafia power and win. Having grown up in the radical politics of the 1960s and 1970s, they rejected Falcone's traditional caution. "Many of us argued with him over this," said Giuseppe Di Lello. "He reacted by pointing to his past, saying 'How can you doubt me?' . . . And he was right in that. . . . He believed profoundly in the institutions of the state and he was in a sense coherent with that vision." But many, like Di Lello, did not think the institutions of the Italian state—as they were constituted in 1989—were worth believing in.

The repercussions of the new Andreotti government were felt quickly in Palermo. In January 1990, the Christian Democratic Party—under the new leadership party secretary Arnaldo Forlani—forced the resignation of Mayor Leoluca Orlando, putting an end to the five-year experiment in reform. Orlando's alliance with the local Communists and his constant attacks on mafia-tainted politicians within his own party had been a thorn in the side of the Italian Socialists and conservative Christian Democrats and now they had decided to remove the irritation. Although Orlando's administration had created a mood of openness and popular participation in government, its highly vocal anti-mafia stance had remained more rhetorical than real. While it had purged city government of some of its worst elements, mafia interests that had been thrown out the door had crept back in through the window. The hotly debated city maintenance contracts had—with great public fanfare—been reassigned to two apparently clean firms in Rome, which had then turned out to be dummy companies controlled by former mayor Vito Ciancimino, who was awaiting trial for his association with the mafia. Nonetheless, Orlando had made a nuisance of himself by his almost daily tirades against Lima and Andreotti. On January 18, 1990, Prime Minister Andreotti arrived in Palermo and made a not-so-veiled attack on Orlando's supporters within the Jesuit order: "Let the priests take care of our souls, the Lord has given us the grace of the state. What's important is that the DC obtains a good result in the administrative elections." Five days later, Orlando's government fell as many Christian Democratic members of the city council withdrew their support. "It was a bad business from the beginning," Prime Minister Andreotti commented on the death of the Orlando government.[14]

The anti-mafia movement appeared to be in full retreat. In February, two of the principal organized crime prosecutors of Catania handed in their resignations, citing an overwhelming sense of futility and despair. "In this city a prosecutor feels not only isolated but useless," said assistant prosecutor Ugo Rossi.[15]

On May 9, Giovanni Bonsignore, an administrator who had courageously denounced waste and corruption in the Sicilian regional government, was shot and killed outside his home in Palermo. "I know they will kill me sooner or later because doing your duty has become impossible in this city," he had told friends in the weeks before his death.[16]

In the wake of Bonsignore's murder, ex-mayor Orlando made a dramatic attack on the prosecutors of Palermo on national television, accusing them of holding back evidence on the political crimes of Palermo. "I am convinced . . . that inside the file drawers of the Palace of Justice there is more than enough evidence to prosecute these crimes," he said on the prime-time television show *Samarcanda.*[17]

Not surprisingly, prosecutors in Palermo were outraged. "Since the drawers in the Palace of Justice are locked, then how does Orlando know what's in them?" asked Giuseppe Ayala. "The gates to the political world are surrounded by a great stone wall and we have no political witnesses," said Giuseppe Di Lello, an openly left-wing prosecutor, who could hardly be accused of neglecting the political dimension of the mafia. "What does Orlando want us to do? . . . He seems to confuse information that can be used in the political arena and criminal evidence that can be used in a court of law. We don't have criminal evidence."[18]

But in his crude, theatrical way, Orlando had raised a problem whose capital importance was becoming increasingly evident. Throughout local administrative elections being held that spring (May 6–7), a string of political murders took place across southern Italy. Seven local political figures were murdered, while numerous others were shot and wounded or had their cars or houses bombed or set on fire. Moreover, this campaign of terror and intimidation seemed to have worked: many of the candidates elected were themselves under criminal investigation. "We did an investigation and found that 400 candidates either had criminal records or had been charged with crimes such as public corruption, bribery or racketeering," said Judge Pietro Grasso, a Palermo magistrate who had become a consultant to the parliament's anti-Mafia commission.

"The Mafia has always had close ties to the political class," said Francesco Misiani, a magistrate who had worked closely with the High Commissioner for anti-mafia affairs. "But with this last election the Mafia has decided it no longer needs intermediaries between itself and the political world. *Mafiosi* are now being elected directly to political office. Some people talk about the mafia as an anti-state, but in many parts of Italy it is the state."[19]

The situation was clearly being aggravated by the government's continued—and sometimes well-intentioned—efforts to pump money into southern Italy's stagnant economy. A massive government development project in Calabria had set off a feeding frenzy among the local criminal bands, which began killing one another as they competed for hundreds of millions of dollars in government contracts. Literally hundreds of murders had occurred in the valley of Gioia Tauro, a rural area just north of Reggio Calabria, where the government was trying to build a massive new electric plant. The High Commissioner for anti-mafia affairs found that virtually all the work on the plant had been subcontracted out to firms controlled by the 'Ndrangheta, the Calabrian mafia. At one point that summer the entire city council was arrested for collusion with the mafia and plans for the electric plant halted. But not before hundreds of millions of dollars had wound up in the pockets of the local clans. Gioia Tauro had the pollution and ravaged landscape of industrialization, but without the industry. In the meanwhile, the Italian state had involuntarily helped transform a relatively weak, agrarian mafia into a rich, well-organized one that competed and cooperated with Sicily's Cosa Nostra.[20]

In its annual report released in June 1990, the private foundation SVIMEZ announced that the southern Italian economy was being suffocated by the pervasive influence of "mafia-type organizations . . . inside the public administrations of the South." Despite the programs to help the South, the economy gap between North and South was getting wider.[21]

At least in the short term, Falcone's choice brought him only bitter fruits. His promotion to the position of deputy chief prosecutor of the Procura della Repubblica actually gave him less power and autonomy than he had enjoyed in the old, now-defunct investigative office. His new office had about twice as many prosecutors, some of whom had been there ten years or more. While Falcone had paid his dues in the investigative office and was surrounded, for the most part, by colleagues who liked and supported him, he was regarded by some in the Procura as an interloper. Many of them had opposed Falcone's becoming head of the investigative office because they did want him to have more power. "Suddenly he found himself surrounded by colleagues who had historically been his adversaries, who had supported Meli," said Judge Barresi.

"Many colleagues, in perfectly good faith (and it's important to emphasize this), were not prepared to become executors of Giovanni Falcone's orders and give up their own professional autonomy. . . . He began to feel blocked in all his initiatives."

In an attempt to carve out a space for himself, he allied himself with deputy chief prosecutor Pietro Giammanco, who, in early 1990, was the leading candidate to become chief prosecutor. Although Giammanco was considered to be close to members of the Andreotti-Lima faction in Palermo, Falcone agreed to support him, in part because Giammanco had led him to believe that he would give Falcone overall responsibility for the office's mafia investigations. And Falcone's support was important, since many people on the Consiglio Superiore della Magistratura looked to him for guidance on mafia matters. "The nomination of Giammanco was a very difficult decision for the CSM," said panel member Vito D'Ambrosio. "Giammanco had a lot of baggage . . . he was a friend of [Mario] D'Acquisto, a member of the Lima faction, and, therefore, indirectly, a man of Andreotti . . . I asked Giovanni's opinion. He said: 'Probably he's the least bad of the lot. But we're still talking about bad.' "

Falcone's benediction helped guarantee Giammanco's nomination. "Falcone was extremely ingenuous," said Salvatore Barresi. "He was convinced—and he genuinely believed it—that it didn't really matter who you worked with as long as you could achieve certain results. He arrived in the Procura and allied himself with Giammanco . . . because after his disastrous experience with Meli, Giammanco had promised to let him handle the mafia cases. . . . This never happened . . . Giammanco had no intention in giving up his prerogatives as chief, particularly in a city like Palermo. . . . It's obvious that to arrive in a position like that you need a certain kind of political support . . . I won't add any more."

Only a few months after arriving at the Procura della Repubblica, Falcone contemplated leaving Palermo. Some of his friends within the magistrature encouraged him to become a candidate for the Consiglio Superiore della Magistratura, so that he could help shape judicial policy. "We tried to convince him," said Judge D'Ambrosio, a member of the outgoing Council. "He accepted the candidacy in April, but he accepted it unenthusiastically." Falcone was an investigator, not a bureaucrat.[22]

Other friends then tried to talk him out of his decision. "We had a terrible fight," recalled Judge Francesco Lo Voi of the Procura of Palermo. "I tried in every possible way to convince him not to do it, because I knew they wouldn't elect him. . . . And if he were elected, he would be annihilated as just one of thirty members of a panel."

Falcone centered his candidacy around several highly controversial proposals. The Italian judiciary, he argued, needed to be reorganized, particularly the prosecution of organized crime. Rather than having mafia cases splintered off into hundreds of understaffed, small-town prosecutors' offices, each province should have a district office where resources and organized crime investigations would be concentrated. There would be a national anti-mafia prosecutors' office to coordinate the work of the various district offices, so that useful information could be passed between different offices on overlapping cases. The press quickly dubbed this national office as the super-procura. Moreover, Falcone argued, Italy needed a central police force for organized crime, a kind of Italian FBI, with a central data bank, so that local police departments were not constantly bumping into one another in the dark while chasing the same criminals. Because the mafia operated on a national scale, it was necessary for the government to think nationally. "There is no system that allows a prosecutor in one part of the country to learn about other cases that may have a bearing on his own," Falcone said. "I frequently learn about other cases from the newspapers." Falcone offered the proposals knowing that in all likelihood they would be unpopular with the Italian magistrature, always jealous of its autonomy. "Given the degree of collusion between Mafia and government in Italy, a centralized judiciary would be more vulnerable to influence," commented Giacomo Conte, one of the dissidents who had quit the anti-mafia pool in early 1989.[23]

But since Falcone had not been all that eager to join the CSM, he decided to push the proposals he believed in and let the voters decide. He eschewed the more conventional kind of campaigning, asking for support at judicial conferences, calling friends and colleagues, working the corridors of the Palace of Justice and visiting other offices to rally the troops. Falcone felt that since his career and views were well known other magistrates had all the information they needed to decide whether or not they wanted him to represent them. This was seen by some as typical Falcone arrogance. And other candidates who chose the old-fashioned method of "pressing the flesh" were elected over him. "Can you imagine," said Judge Lo Voi. "A prosecutor any country in the world would envy and he can't even get elected to the Consiglio Superiore della Magistratura!"

NINETEEN

While Giovanni Falcone was moving from defeat to humiliating defeat, Paolo Borsellino was enjoying one of the happiest and most productive times of his life. Being out of the limelight in provincial Marsala proved to be a blessing at a time when Palermo was again the center of controversy, power struggles and political maneuvering. Although operating with limited resources, Borsellino was, if nothing else, his own boss. After his first year (1987), in which he had run the entire office with only one other attorney, Borsellino had gradually built up a young but capable staff that by 1990 consisted of seven assistant prosecutors. Although still small, the office began to function effectively, bringing to a successful conclusion the mafia trials Borsellino initiated in his first two years in Marsala, as well as handling the much larger number of ordinary criminal cases. Rather than being a choice of last resort, Marsala began to attract bright young magistrates who were eager to work with Borsellino.[1]

There was an unusually warm and cordial atmosphere in the Marsala prosecutor's office. Visitors were surprised and amused to see Borsellino and his assistants embrace and kiss one another on the cheek when they greeted one another.

Borsellino's hard work and growing reputation also began to attract a very different kind of person to the Procura of Marsala:

mafia witnesses—an entirely new development for a part of Sicily where the code of silence still reigned supreme.

In his first years in Marsala, Borsellino had tried to "turn" certain known *mafiosi* by trying to take advantage of a series of small-scale mafia wars bloodying some of the towns in his territory. When the former boss of Campobello, Natale L'Ala, was nearly murdered in 1989, Borsellino visited him in the hospital. An older man who had lost virtually all his power, had seen his closest friends and family killed, and was himself close to death, L'Ala seemed to have nothing to lose and everything to gain by collaborating. His enemies had first tried to kill him in 1984 but he had escaped unharmed. But this time, he had been shot twice in the face, once in the eye, and lay there with bandages wrapped around his head. Nonetheless, he rebuffed Borsellino's overture. "Let me die a 'man of honor,' " L'Ala told the prosecutor with fatalistic resignation, waiting for a death that would arrive predictably a year later.[2]

Then on September 19, 1989, another *mafioso* from Campobello, Rosario Spatola, telephoned Borsellino's office saying he wanted to talk, but that his life was in danger. (Although they have the same name, this Rosario Spatola was no relation to the Palermo developer that Falcone had prosecuted in the Spatola-Inzerillo and "Iron Tower" cases; although, ironically, he had also been sent to prison by Falcone in a separate drug trafficking case in 1982.) Borsellino's chief investigator, Carmelo Canale, drove four hours across Sicily to fetch Spatola in his hideout in the town of Messina. In order to avoid attracting the attention of *mafiosi* around Marsala, Canale brought Spatola to a police station in Palermo, where Borsellino joined them that same evening and began the deposition immediately.[3]

Spatola was tall, good-looking, a flashy dresser and smooth talker, several cuts above the local mafia thug. Through the drug trade, he had seen a bit of the world—Milan, Switzerland and Spain—and spoke standard Italian as well as Sicilian dialect. "Spatola gives you the impression of being a big con man—although he was very loyal and sincere with us," said Antonio Ingroia, who had joined Borsellino's staff just before Spatola's collaboration. It was more than an impression. Spatola's life was in danger because he had pulled off a few too many cons. He had sold a shipment of phony gold bars for more than $100,000 to someone who turned out to have high-level mafia connections. And he had cheated his mafia bosses in a drug deal, stealing a portion of the delivery in the hope that no one would notice. When they caught on, he had gone into hiding.[4]

"He was a highly extroverted person, like Borsellino, and the two established an immediate rapport," said Ingroia. In that first session, Spatola began talking about a drug deal involving a small Latin American country that Borsellino had never heard of. Skeptical that this might be another tall tale, Borsellino took out a world atlas and was pleased to discover that the witness was correct. "It looks like your geography is better than mine," Borsellino said.[5]

"Paolo was very humble, which helped him both with us assistant prosecutors and with the mafia collaborators," said Ingroia. "He was, above all, a Sicilian. He loved talking in dialect, making jokes and using dialect expressions. . . . He succeeded in creating a kind of feeling, almost of complicity with the witness, whom he succeeded in involving emotionally in the investigation. . . . Borsellino brought the witness over to his side, and the witnesses would struggle to remember further details, make suggestions that could help us corroborate a statement or find a fugitive defendant, by telling us the people and places he was likely to frequent."

But despite his accessibility and warmth, Borsellino could also be tough with his witnesses. Spatola was not entirely candid about his own role in Cosa Nostra, claiming that he was simply a "stray dog" who did business with the mafia without actually being an initiated "man of honor." As he began to describe more and more intimate details of mafia life, this claim became harder and harder to believe. At the same time, Spatola, after having been brought to safety on mainland Italy, began to make extravagant demands, threatening to stop cooperating unless he received more money and a larger apartment. Borsellino then charged him with "mafia association," had him hauled off to prison and held in solitary confinement. Not long afterward, Spatola sent Borsellino a telegram of apology. When Spatola began collaborating again in April 1990, after a three-month hiatus, his testimony took a quantum leap forward. He finally admitted that he had been a member of Cosa Nostra for nearly twenty years and proceeded to draw a complete map of the mafia families of the area.

On the basis of Spatola's testimony, Borsellino was able to arrest dozens of *mafiosi* in and around Marsala.

"Spatola . . . allowed Borsellino to reconstruct the mafia organizations of most of the province of Trapani, the composition of the mafia families of Marsala, Mazara del Vallo, Campobello, and Castelvetrano," Ingroia said. "At the same time, Spatola shed light on an important drug ring involving Spain. . . . Even though Spatola was not a particularly high-level figure, because of his persuasive manner and his ability to form relationships with people, he had succeeded in penetrating various sectors of [mafia life]. . . . He knew a lot about the mafia in Palermo, of relations between the mafia and the Freemasons, of collusion between mafia and judges and politicians."

Spatola revealed the existence of a secret Masonic Lodge in Trapani, where high-level *mafiosi* mingled with local politicians, judges and businessmen. And he provided important testimony about the assassination of Judge Giangiacomo Ciaccio Montalto, the anti-mafia prosecutor of Trapani in 1983. Spatola indicated that Montalto was killed primarily for political reasons. "The motivation of the killing lies in Ciaccio Montalto's intention . . . to go after important people that the mafia has a strong interest in protecting," he said. He confirmed the disturbing role of another Trapani prosecutor, Antonio Costa, who was on the mafia's payroll at the time of Ciaccio Montalto's death. "Ciaccio Montalto had expressed his intentions to his colleague Costa who had, in turn, informed people in the mafia," Spatola told Borsellino. When Costa was arrested, police found a large sum of cash and a supply of arms in his house. Spatola had direct contacts with the *mafiosi* who had corrupted Costa, and had himself been asked to perjure himself in order to give the prosecutor an alibi. "[Rocco] Curatolo [another *mafioso*] . . . proposed that I testify at the Costa trial, claiming to be Costa's wife's lover, and say that I gave her the money that was found in the Costas' house. The money instead came from Girolamo Marino, who was then killed for the carelessness he showed in making this payment to Costa. . . . His killing was both a punishment and a warning to Costa himself to keep silent."[6]

There may also have been a political motivation to the attempted assassination of Ciaccio Montalto's successor, Carlo Palermo, the

Trapani prosecutor who had investigated bribe-taking in the Italian Socialist Party along with arms and drug trafficking. Spatola's boss within Cosa Nostra, the lawyer Antonio Messina, told him that Judge Palermo was much more of a threat to certain politicians than to the mafia. Moreover, Messina had held a series of meetings with Pippo Calò, the member of the Commission who maintained Cosa Nostra's principal political contacts in Rome, in the weeks before the 1985 bombing that nearly killed the prosecutor.

On the heels of Spatola's confession, other important witnesses began to step forward. On May 8, 1990, Natale L'Ala, the old boss of Campobello, who had been shot in the eye a year earlier, was finally killed. Almost immediately afterward, Giacomina Filippello, the woman who had lived with L'Ala for many years, decided to tell Borsellino what her companion had refused to. Unlike some other Italian criminal organizations, women have no role whatsoever within Cosa Nostra. The Sicilians looked on with amusement and contempt at their undisciplined Neapolitan cousins who allowed their women to get mixed up in the Camorra: a woman, Rosetta Cutolo, had even run one of the most important criminal families in Naples, when her brother (Raffaele Cutolo) was in prison. The Sicilian man of honor is not supposed to breathe a word about Cosa Nostra to his family, but like so many other rules, this prohibition had begun to break down in recent years. Sicily was subject to the same social changes as the rest of Italy: women were no longer willing to accept a purely passive role, dressing in black dresses with scarves covering their heads, dividing their time between the kitchen and the parish church. Moreover, the increased violence within Cosa Nostra had strained traditional loyalties. Isolated within the organization, and living like a hunted animal, Natale L'Ala had begun to confide increasingly during his last years with his longtime companion. Giacomina Filippello saw collaboration as her only chance at revenge. Natale L'Ala had told her the names of the killers who had shot at him in the two failed assassination attempts and she had strong suspicions about who might have finally murdered him. She knew about the makeup of local mafia groups and the details of many crimes.[7]

The phenomenon of "mafia women" grew even more important

in 1991 when two other female witnesses stepped forward. Piera Aiello contacted prosecutors after her husband, Nicola Atria, was murdered before her eyes in the pizzeria they ran together.

"My name is Piera Aiello and my life can be told in just a few words: at fourteen I became engaged, at eighteen, a wife, at twenty-one, mother, at twenty-three, a widow," she said. "I was born at eight and a half months, I have been premature in everything from birth, let's hope I won't be in dying."[8]

Her husband was from an important mafia family in the nearby town of Partanna: his father (Vito Atria) had been killed in 1984 and Nicola Atria was a young *mafioso* who dealt in heroin and cocaine. In all likelihood, he was killed because he nourished hopes of avenging his father's death. Coming herself from a very different kind of family, Piera Aiello had relatively little difficulty breaking with the tradition of *omertà* and went to the authorities almost immediately after her husband's death. More difficult and traumatic was the decision of Piera Aiello's sister-in-law, her husband's seventeen-year-old sister, who had grown up in a family permeated with mafia culture. Overcoming powerful resistance, she, too, stepped forward a few months after her brother's death in 1991. Although only a child at the time of her father's death, Rita had heard and seen a great deal in her household. After their father's death, her brother confided a great deal in her and she dated a boy who also moved in criminal circles.

The two women were able to provide a wealth of information on the mafia of Partanna, where a vicious feud had been fought for several years. In a stroke of luck, another woman of Partanna, Rosalba Triolo, tied to the opposite camp of the local mafia, began to collaborate during the same period, and was able to confirm many elements of Aiello's and Atria's testimony from a completely different and independent point of view. Not only were they able to identify killers and drug dealers, they even provided evidence against the mayor of the town, Vincenzino Culicchia, who had gone on to become a Christian Democratic member of parliament. Although Borsellino was naturally skeptical about what a seventeen-year-old girl could know about a powerful politician, police wiretaps and financial investigations confirmed that, indeed, as mayor and president of the local bank, *Onorevole*

Culicchia had extremely close economic and personal ties to the biggest *mafiosi* in the area. It appeared, in fact, that he may have ordered the 1983 murder of a rival candidate for mayor, out of fear that his opponent would discover evidence of wrongdoing when he took control of City Hall.

In a demonstration of how powerful the pull of *omertà* was in the older generation, Rita Atria's mother denounced her daughter and daughter-in-law as *infami* (infamous), the contemptuous term used in Sicily for those who have betrayed the code of silence. Signora Atria claimed that Borsellino had kidnapped her daughter and, despite the murder of her husband and son, insisted that all this nonsense about mafia had been put into her daughter's head by her wicked daughter-in-law, Piera Aiello.

Abandoned by friends and family, Rita Atria and Piera Aiello turned increasingly to Borsellino for emotional support. He pinched Rita on the cheek and kidded her about her tough, street-wise exterior, calling her a *"mafiosa* with a skirt." They telephoned him when they needed to talk and referred to him as "Uncle Paolo." Even after they had finished their depositions, he made a point of seeing them whenever he went to Rome, where they had been moved for their own protection.

At least in one part of the Sicilian provinces, the anti-mafia movement was picking up steam.

In the rest of the country, the problem of organized crime appeared not only to be gaining in ferocity but spreading up the Italian peninsula. In July 1990 the president of the Milan chamber of commerce warned that the great financial capital of northern Italy was becoming the mafia's principal money laundry. "In Milan, there is a river of money flowing," said Piero Bassetti. "In my opinion at least ten of the largest financial companies . . . are accomplices of the mafia or at least know they are working with dirty money."[9]

A dramatic increase in drug seizures, murders, arson and kidnapping was providing increasing evidence that organized crime groups were making substantial inroads in Milan. Prosecutors there had found signs that *mafiosi* were even corrupting local public officials in order to win government contracts and real estate licenses, initiating an investigation known as the "Duomo Connection," after the cathedral that is the symbol of Milan.

Milan had overtaken Palermo among the murder capitals of Italy, with the third highest number of homicides in the country. The top two, significantly, were Reggio Calabria and Naples, symptomatic of the fact that organized crime had become as suffocatingly dominant in the regions of Calabria and Campania as in Sicily.[10]

The public was just waking up to what Falcone had proven in his first cases in the early 1980s: that Milan was a major center of international drug trafficking and that three major southern Italian crime organizations had "colonies" operating in all of the major northern Italian cities. "For many years Milan has acquired a preeminent role . . . as the distribution center for heroin coming from the Middle East and cocaine imported from South American," stated a police report published at the time.

The public impression that violent crime was spinning out of control was borne out by statistics. A police report issued on September 18, 1990, showed a disastrous increase of mafia-related crimes across the board: homicide was up 11.5 percent, extortion up 26.7 percent, dynamite bombings up 22.9 percent, arson up 38.2 percent.[11]

In graphic illustration of the human cost of this reign of impunity, three days later, on September 21, 1990, mafia killers in Sicily gunned down Rosario Livatino, a brave young anti-mafia prosecutor who had worked for years in extreme isolation in the town of Agrigento. Starting while still in his twenties, Livatino had spent a decade working on major mafia investigations out of a tiny office in central Sicily. The details of Livatino's death were particularly chilling. Driving alone without police escort, Livatino was forced off the road by his killers' automobile. Already wounded, he had tried a desperate escape on foot until his predators caught up with him and executed him in cold blood.[12]

In the wake of Livatino's murder and in response to the climate of government indifference, the entire Sicilian magistrature rose up in revolt, threatening to go on strike. They were outraged that a magistrate on the front line of the war against the mafia could be butchered like a pig because he had no protection, while scores of politicians and party hacks in Rome, in no danger whatsoever, had armies of bodyguards and twenty-four-hour limousine service to run errands for their families and take them to and from their favorite restaurants.

"The mafia continues to kill, undisturbed, in Caltanissetta, in Agrigento, everywhere," said Falcone in an interview a few days after Livatino's death. "While on the other hand we have a tired, demoralized magistrature, oppressed by a sense of gloomy resignation. I say: Enough with these phony controversies; enough with these debates that simply use the mafia as a pretext to settle private scores for this or that faction."[13]

On November 1, 1990, two prominent Catanian businessmen were assassinated because they had apparently resisted attempts at extortion. Managers of an important steel mill, one of the largest employers in the city, the two executives were overseeing a 60 billion lire ($50 million at the time) plan for modernizing the Catania plant—money that the Catania mafia evidently wanted to control. In the same period, the Catania branches of Standa, Italy's largest department store chain, had suffered a series of bombs and suspicious fires. The Catania chamber of commerce revealed that 90 percent of all local merchants routinely made extortion payments, some 22,000 people in a city of only 372,000. This, in a place where, according to mafia witness Antonino Calderone, the protection racket had not existed until the 1970s, except against the largest businesses. Describing the tightening grip of the extortion racket, Antonio Mauri, the president of the Association of Catania Industrialists, said in November 1990: "First they ask for money . . . even hundreds of thousands of dollars . . . then they offer you services, they advise you which suppliers to use, they impose their friends, then they want to become your partner and then they take it all. . . . Who, in these conditions, is prepared to invest in the South?"[14]

Later that month, in the small Sicilian city of Gela, eight people were killed and seven others wounded in four different mafia hits in the space of a twenty-five-minute period. War between local clans had claimed more than 100 lives in Gela during the previous three years—an impressive total for a town of only 90,000 inhabitants.[15]

Meanwhile, Giovanni Falcone's working "arrangement" with chief prosecutor Pietro Giammanco was going from bad to worse. Not only did Giammanco not give Falcone control over mafia investigations in Palermo, he frequently kept his chief deputy in the dark about important cases, excluding him from investigations or blocking his path. Falcone learned by accident about important developments in cases he had started, was not free to take initiatives and was denied permission to make trips to gather evidence. When he went to question witnesses, Falcone was invariably shadowed by other prosecutors who were part of Giammanco's inner circle of faithful followers. Things reached the stage where Giammanco would make a point of keeping Falcone waiting outside his office for long periods before receiving him. "This may seem like nothing, but in a highly symbolic place like Palermo, these things have great meaning," said Judge Salvatore Barresi.[16]

"I am like a bear in a cage," Falcone told his old boss Antonino Caponetto. In late 1990, Falcone began recording his frustrations in a diary, recalling Rocco Chinnici's words of warning: "Keep a diary, you never know."[17]

Among the investigations that Giammanco continued to prevent Falcone from investigating was the politically explosive "Gladio" affair. In late 1990, Prime Minister Andreotti announced that, during the Cold War, the Italian government (at the instigation of the United States) had formed a secret civilian militia known as "Gladio," meant to spring into action in the event of a Soviet invasion or Communist takeover. Rather than being dissolved after the Stalin period, the secret military organization continued to exist up into the 1980s. Given Italy's history of secret Masonic lodges, right-wing coups, political killings and suspicious neo-fascist bombings, the idea of a secret anti-Communist army with weapons caches hidden throughout the country raised unpleasant specters. And while there may have been a rationale for having an anti-invasion force in the northern regions of Italy that bordered Communist Yugoslavia, why were there also "Gladio" units in far-off Sicily, where the threats to democracy were of a highly different order? There were rumors that the Sicilian "Gladio" had been activated against the mafia—a highly irregular departure from its original mandate—and something that Giovanni Falcone wanted to investigate.[18]

In diary entries from late 1990 and early 1991, Falcone vented his daily frustrations and humiliations, referring to Giammanco as *il capo,* the boss, or sometimes simply as "he."

—he has asked that certain investigations into the Sicilian regional government be concluded . . . saying that otherwise the Region will lose some of its financing. Obviously some politician told him to do this and it is equally obvious that he intends to close the case . . ." (December 10, 1990)

12.19.1990—He never called [Judge] Giudiceandrea and so we will not have the opportunity to meet with our Roman colleagues that are working on Gladio.

12.19.1990—I learned by chance that several days ago he assigned the investigation of an anonymous letter from Partinico, that regards, among others, the Onorevole [Giuseppe] Avellone [a local Christian Democratic politician], to [Giuseppe] Pignatone, [Vittorio] Teresi and [Francesco] Lo Voi (the last two of whom are not part of the anti-mafia pool) . . .

1.17.1991. I learned today that, during my absence, a colleague [Maurizio] Moscati, assistant prosecutor in Spoleto, had called me about a drug trafficking case, trying to coordinate his investigation with us. Not finding me in the office, [Moscati] spoke with the boss, who naturally, took care of it, assigning it to [assistant prosecutor Teresa] Principato, naturally without telling me anything about it. I learned of it by accident, having called Moscati myself.

. . . 1.26.1991 I learned today, on arriving in the office, from Pignatone, that he, the boss, and [Guido] Lo Forte, that same morning had gone to question Cardinal [Salvatore] Pappalardo, about the Mattarella case [the president of the Sicilian regional government, assassinated in 1980]. . . . I protested with the boss about not being informed in advance, making it very clear that I am perfectly ready to do some other job, but if he wants me to act as the coordinator for anti-mafia investigations, the coordination must be genuine . . .[19]

Falcone kept the diaries to himself, but showed some of it to close friends like Paolo Borsellino. As a precaution, he gave a few pages to a journalist he trusted, Liana Milella, of the economic newspaper *Sole 24 Ore,* asking her not to publish the document for the indefinite future. Falcone may have done this in order that at least one copy of the diary would survive in the event of his death—remembering the documents supposedly kept by General Alberto Dalla Chiesa which allegedly disappeared from his safe the night of his assassination.

"It was perhaps the worst time of his life," said Giuseppe Di Lello, his old colleague from the original anti-mafia pool.[20]

But precisely because things had gotten so bad, the mafia began to become a national issue again. Throughout the postwar period, the war against organized crime had always been fought on "alternating current," with sudden bursts of energy following closely on the heels of some particularly heinous assassination or intolerable crime wave. The outrage following the mafia war of 1981–83 and the killings of Pio Della Torre, General Dalla Chiesa and Rocco Chinnici had provided the political momentum to reach the maxi-trial of Palermo in 1986. And in 1990 and 1991, after a four-year period of inertia, a renewed sense of alarm and anger was growing as people began to realize that the country's mafia problem, rather than having been "solved," was growing demonstrably worse.

The "crime emergency"—declared in huge banner headlines— put the mafia back on the front pages of all of the national newspapers on an almost daily basis, putting the Andreotti government under considerable pressure. In September, Andreotti promised a tough new anti-crime package. But when its centerpiece turned out to be a ban on hunting rifles in southern Italy, Andreotti was greeted with a mixture of derision and contempt.[21] At the same time, he was under growing pressure to replace his much-criticized minister of the interior, Antonio Gava. Not only was Gava rumored to have ties to the Neapolitan Camorra, he had rarely been at work in recent months due to a protracted illness, adding to the overwhelming public impression that the government was quite literally absent from the war on the mafia. In October, Andreotti finally replaced Gava with Vincenzo Scotti, another Christian Democrat from Naples, but much younger and more energetic than his predecessor.

A few months later, after a more extensive cabinet shuffle, Andreotti promised to make the war on organized crime one of his top priorities. In February, Andreotti made Claudio Martelli, the rising star of the Socialist Party, his new minister of justice. Anxious to improve the government's poor anti-mafia credentials, Martelli immediately called Giovanni Falcone in Palermo and asked him to join his staff as "director of penal affairs."

Exhausted and demoralized by his losing battles in Palermo, Falcone decided to accept, leaving behind more than twenty years of work as a magistrate in Sicily. Most of his friends and colleagues tried to talk him out of the move. In Italy, where the "independence" of the magistrature was an almost sacred principle, abandoning the judiciary for the executive branch seemed to some a kind of betrayal. Many magistrates had no idea there was such a thing as "director of penal affairs" let alone what its function was. Falcone's leaving the front line of the war on the mafia in Palermo for an obscure desk job in Rome looked to some like a retreat and admission of failure. Moreover, they were troubled by the identity of Falcone's Roman patron, Claudio Martelli, the dauphin of Socialist leader Bettino Craxi. Martelli, after all, had led the campaign against the judges in 1987, and his party had been promptly rewarded by an avalanche of mafia-inspired votes in Palermo that same year. And it was Martelli who had continued hammering away at Leoluca Orlando's anti-mafia coalition in Palermo, which he called "a shadow government of Jesuits and prosecutors." Now many of Falcone's friends were afraid that Martelli simply wanted to use Italy's most famous prosecutor in a superficial effort to appear tough on crime.[22]

After the disastrous experiences of Falcone's recent past—first with the head of the investigative office, Antonino Meli, and then with chief prosecutor Giammanco—Falcone's move to Rome looked like another dubious compromise with political power. Falcone had a bitter argument with Giuseppe Ayala, one of his best friends left in the Palermo Palace of Justice, resulting in a break in their friendship that lasted several months. Given his naïveté in the political arena, Falcone's friends worried that he would get the worst of any deal with his more cynical and ruthless interlocutors in the Rome power game. "Falcone was a great magistrate but politically naïve, and what made it worse, he was convinced he was politically clever," said Judge Vito D'Ambrosio.[23]

But Falcone, after having experienced the almost total helplessness of the magistrature in Palermo without support from the government in Rome, was convinced that the only way to turn around the war against the mafia was to put his hands on the levers of power. Not only did Falcone understand the problems of organized crime in Italy but, as one of the most widely traveled magistrates in the country, he was familiar with the criminal justice systems, investigative techniques and legislation of virtually all of the other major democracies. He had hundreds of ideas and proposals he was anxious to put into practice.

The main problem with the Italian system, in Falcone's view, was its extreme fragmentation. There were 159 judicial districts, each with its own prosecutors and police forces, who frequently tripped over one another moving in ignorance of the others' work. The mafia, by contrast, moved with ease on an increasingly national and international scale. He was enormously impressed with the United States' system of organized crime "strike forces," located in most major cities, which were independent but had the full force of the federal government behind them. And he could only envy the organization and power of national agencies like the FBI and the Drug Enforcement Agency when he saw the meager staffs and rudimentary resources at the disposal of his Italian police colleagues. Falcone had a whole series of proposals for centralizing and streamlining Italian law enforcement and Martelli supported them.

While many Italian magistrates agreed that a centralized system might work in a country like the United States, with its strong democratic traditions and proven checks and balances, they were afraid that in a small and corrupt country like Italy, it might put the judiciary under government control.

"We were afraid that Martelli would use Falcone in his battle to reshape the magistrature to his own liking," Judge D'Ambrosio said. "We stayed up until two in the morning arguing about it, Giovanni, myself and [Mario] Almerighi [another judge and close friend of Falcone]. Almerighi and I asked him: 'Are you really convinced that Martelli is on your side?' He said: 'No, he's on my side as long as it suits him.' So 'Why,' we said, 'are you on his side, lending him prestige and legitimacy?' To which, Falcone answered: 'Because, as long as he is on my side, I can use him just as he is using me, and then I can accomplish things that I couldn't do

otherwise. . . . Martelli is politically strong and is capable of getting things done. We'll have to see, in the end, who screws whom.'
Those were his words, almost verbatim. This argument didn't
convince us much. . . . 'Martelli is much stronger than you and he
will crush you,' we said. 'You're just a feather in his cap. . . .' This
caused a certain coolness in our friendship. Giovanni felt betrayed
and we felt kind of abandoned by him as well."

But even before he arrived in Rome in March 1991, Falcone
made his presence felt. On Falcone's advice, Martelli issued a decree meant to repair the damage of the latest of the disastrous
court decisions by Corrado Carnevale, the "sentence-killer" on
the Italian Supreme Court. A month earlier, most of the remaining
defendants of the maxi-trial of Palermo were allowed to walk out
scot-free from Ucciardone prison, even though many of them had
been sentenced to life in prison, and their convictions had been
upheld on appeal. Although these defendants had been tried under
Italy's old criminal code, Carnevale, in a highly questionable decision, applied a new feature of the revised penal code according to
which defendants should not be held in prison for more than a
year after their original arrest, if their sentences were not yet definitive. The men were allowed to wait for the second and final appeal (allowed in all Italian criminal cases) in freedom—despite the
fact that many of them were convicted killers who had been fugitives of justice whom police had spent years tracking down. Some
twenty-one thousand criminals had been freed through this mechanism since Italy's new penal code had gone into effect a year and
a half earlier.[24] The "Martelli decree" created an exception for the
most dangerous and led to the immediate rearrest of the bosses of
Palermo. It was an important signal that reversed the atmosphere
of indifference and defeatism in Palermo almost overnight, said
Judge Salvatore Barresi: "If that hadn't been done, you can be certain all these people would be fugitives. It completely disoriented
the bosses. I will never forget for the rest of my life the face of
Michele Greco as he was rearrested. These people who had been
living comfortably at home suddenly, through the will and initiative of Giovanni Falcone, found themselves back in prison."[25]

Falcone began a rigorous review of the whole Italian judiciary,
carefully reading court decisions on organized crime cases across
Italy. Martelli and Falcone began to insist on a more active role in

judicial appointments, taking on Falcone's old nemesis the Consiglio Superiore della Magistratura (CSM). While it continued to leave the final decision to the CSM, the Ministry of Justice started to rank the candidates for major positions within the magistrature based on their professional achievements. By putting the CSM on notice, Falcone was able to weed out some of the highly questionable choices for some of the more sensitive positions in Italian law enforcement. Following the Ministry's recommendation, the CSM kept Pasquale Barecca—a judge whose extremely soft decisions in mafia cases had raised eyebrows in Palermo for years—from becoming general prosecutor of Palermo, in charge of all prosecutions before the Palermo Court of Appeals. In many instances (as in the case of Barecca), Falcone succeeded in identifying magistrates who were later indicted for collusion with the mafia.[26]

Prosecutors across Italy, who had felt largely isolated, now had an ally in Rome. Judge Giacomo Travaglino, a prosecutor in Naples, recalled a pilgrimage he and some of his colleagues took to Falcone's office in Rome. The prosecutors had become increasingly suspicious of a judge on the Naples Court of Appeals, Alfonso Lamberti. "He had made a series of decisions that seemed to us completely senseless," Travaglino said. "He overturned decisions that seemed very solid and granted bail to extremely dangerous criminals in the middle of an incredibly bloody clan war in Naples. To give you an idea of the context: a thirteen-year-old boy was sent by his mother to murder his father's assassin in the courtyard of the Courthouse and Judge Lamberti went ahead and released several other members of this same clan."[27] As they explained their suspicions to Falcone, the Neapolitan prosecutors began to notice a small, ironic smile creep cross Falcone's face. They realized that he already knew about the situation on the Naples Court of Appeals and had reached the same conclusion about Judge Lamberti. Here finally was someone at the Ministry of Justice who understood their problems, had an encyclopedic knowledge of organized crime cases, and had a global vision of the entire field. (These initial suspicions about Lamberti were later borne out by former members of the Neapolitan Camorra who have testified that he was in the pay of local clans.)

Martelli embraced virtually all of Falcone's proposals. They drew up a plan to completely reorganize the prosecution of organized crime by creating a series of "district offices," designed specifically to handle complex mafia cases. Rather than be handled piecemeal by scores of tiny offices, organized crime investigations would be concentrated in twenty-six major cities throughout Italy. Through this legislation, Falcone would regain in a single stroke all of the ground that he had lost in 1988–90 when chief prosecutor Antonino Meli had scattered the anti-mafia pool's cases among the provincial offices of rural Sicily. Three years after being dismantled in Palermo, the model of the anti-mafia pool would be applied in cities across Italy.

Martelli also presented Falcone's plan for an Italian FBI, taking two thousand of the top officers in the various branches of Italian law enforcement and allowing them to work exclusively on the problem of organized crime, with the resources and technology to bring Italy up to a world-class level. They also proposed creating a national office of some twenty magistrates in Rome who would coordinate the investigations into organized crime, something the Italian press dubbed the "super-procura," the super-prosecutor's office.[28]

"In only a few months in Rome, [Falcone] changed the role of the executive branch in the war against the mafia," said Ignazio De Francisci of the old anti-mafia pool.[29]

TWENTY

As 1991 progressed, Falcone's Roman gamble appeared to be paying off. Contrary to most pessimistic predictions, Falcone's new boss, Justice Minister Martelli, kept his word and fought fiercely on behalf of the new crime legislation. One of the most vocal critics of the anti-mafia pool had suddenly become a principal champion of the war on the mafia. "Martelli was converted on the road to Damascus," said Leonardo Guarnotta, Falcone's old colleague in the original anti-mafia pool.

"In my opinion, Giovanni Falcone, with that enormous ability to understand and explain the importance of problems and to identify the instruments needed to combat them, won Martelli over," said Judge Salvatore Barresi.

While a genuine friendship appears to have grown up between Martelli and Falcone, political calculation may also have played a part in the minister's newfound commitment to the anti-mafia cause. "Martelli is an extremely intelligent man . . . and he saw that the war against the mafia could have a great political payoff at that particular moment in history," said Judge Vito D'Ambrosio.[1]

What had happened to make some of the principal adversaries of the anti-mafia movement embrace it suddenly like a long-lost friend? The most obvious answer is that the spread of mafia crime had created a loud public demand for action. But deeper historical forces were pushing the government to go beyond the usual cosmetic changes. In late 1989, the Berlin Wall had collapsed and with it the entire political equation of the Italian postwar system.

The importance of this change for the governing parties was not immediately apparent—after all, they were on the winning side of the Cold War. At first, the consequences seemed to be felt almost exclusively by the Italian Communists themselves. Already by the mid-1980s, during the era of Mikail Gorbachev's perestroika, the Italian Communists had fallen from their historic high of 34 percent (in the mid-1970s) to about 27 percent of the vote. And in May 1990 (after the destruction of the wall), it fell even farther, to a mere 23 percent. That autumn, Communist leader Achille Occhetto announced that his party would change its name to the Partito Democratico della Sinistra (PDS, or Democratic Party of the Left)—a traumatic event that split the Communist vote. While the great majority of members accepted the party's openly social-democratic identity, a full quarter of the PCI's supporters refused to renounce its old name or doctrine, starting a splinter party called Rifondazione Comunista (Communist Refoundation). After the rupture, the Left was weaker and more divided than ever.[2]

After an initial boost, the death of Communism posed serious problems for the principal government parties whose political mainstay had been their staunch opposition to Communism. No longer forced to choose the lesser of two evils, many Italians began to demand more from their governing class, became more intolerant of its rampant corruption and gross inefficiency, and started exploring new options on both sides of the political spectrum. Many who had accepted widespread corruption with a grudging sense of fatalistic resignation now found the level of graft and patronage around them anathema.

New political forces began to fill the growing void. The most significant was the Lombard League—the movement for northern Italian regional autonomy. The Lombard League had existed for several years and had made almost no inroads into mainstream politics. Many of their proposals—instituting street signs in local dialect and removing southern Italians from administrative jobs in the North—seemed hopelessly anachronistic and reactionary. A political movement named after a medieval military alliance whose symbol is a knight in armor brandishing a sword, the Lombard League appeared to offer nostalgic appeal to a vanished past rather than the promise of a bright future. But under the shrewd leadership of its founder Umberto Bossi, the Lombard League began to broaden its appeal, hammering away at political corruption, high taxes, poor government services, the bloated, parasitical government in Rome and the spreading contagion of mafia violence moving from South to North. Suddenly, at the end of the 1980s, a movement that seemed relegated to the lunatic fringe began attracting millions of voters throughout northern Italy.[3]

The appeal of the League lay in the fact that it was the only group to challenge the central premise of the Italian political system, the invasive role of the parties in every sphere of life known as "party-ocracy." The traditional opposition, the Communist Party, rather than reducing the role of government, had helped expand it in the name of egalitarian justice. Instead of rejecting the whole idea of division-of-the-spoils, the Communists had simply demanded their fair share in distributing government jobs and resources. Because Italy remained blocked by the struggle between Communism and anti-Communism, it never experienced an equivalent of the Reagan and Thatcher revolutions. As a result, public resentment over the mounting costs and mixed results of the liberal welfare state continued to grow during the 1980s until its pent-up force began to explode with the end of the Cold War. But in Italy, the revolt against the welfare state had distinct geographical connotations: the followers of the League insisted that the industrious North was being drained to pay for the corrupt patronage state in the South. While its rhetoric was overheated, the League touched on an important truth: the economic gap between North and South had actually become greater during the 1980s—after having narrowed in the previous three decades. By 1990, northern Italy enjoyed a level of prosperity on a par with Switzerland, while the South had a standard of living more similar to Greece or Portugal.[4]

The League's message resonated with the national debate over another great historical change: the economic unification of Europe scheduled for 1992. Many Italian businessmen—based primarily in the center and North—began to worry more about the threat of economic competition than of a Communist takeover.

They, too, began to perceive Italy's enormous expensive, highly centralized bureaucracy as a present danger to their survival. By 1990, the Italian national debt actually exceeded the country's gross national product and drastic measures were needed to bring the country in line with the rest of Europe. Italians were among the most heavily taxed citizens in Europe but, in return, received government services more typical of the Third World. The Christian Democrats and the Socialists fought over which party would control the national phone company but neither seemed to care that it took nearly three months to have a phone installed or that literally half of all phone calls in Italy went dead in the middle of a conversation. In the past, the business community had profited from a cozy relationship with the political system during an era of protectionism; now as markets opened up they viewed the government as a millstone around their neck. "If we don't face our country's problems—the government deficit, inflation but also political reform—we will enter the European market in a position of weakness," said Sergio Pininfarina, the then-president of the Confederation of Italian Industrialists: "Others will have no reason to invest here and our own investors will find better opportunities elsewhere. . . . The de-industrialization of Italy is not a slogan, it's a real danger."[5]

Inevitably, the problem of the mafia became a central issue in the new political discourse. As Europe prepared to open its borders, Italy's problem of rampant organized crime could no longer be regarded as a dirty family secret, about which other nations had no right to comment. In April 1991, German chancellor Helmut Kohl openly stated his fear that after unification Italy might export its mafia problem to the rest of Europe. Sicilian crime families already had active colonies among the Italian guest workers in Germany. What would happen when there were no longer any border checks? Italy's president of the Republic, Francesco Cossiga, after another gruesome series of mafia killings, spoke in even less diplomatic terms: "We cannot bring this disgrace into Europe."[6]

Painting the Christian Democrats as the party of mafia and southern patronage, the Lombard League began eating away at the DC's northern base. The League, which had won less than 1 percent of the vote only a few years earlier, started winning 20 percent of the vote in some northern cities, and polls in early 1991 showed it becoming the first party in the North. In southern Italy, the traditional parties faced a challenge from Leoluca Orlando, the former mayor of Palermo, who had broken with the Christian Democrats and formed his own party called La Rete, "The Network," whose rallying cry was the war against the mafia. According to the government's own statistics some seventeen thousand local administrators throughout Italy were under some form of criminal investigation and the political parties were under new pressure to purge their lists of suspect characters. The new minister of the interior, Vincenzo Scotti, proposed making it illegal for people under indictment or with a criminal record to run for public office and to grant the government power to dissolve local administrations polluted by organized crime.

The Christian Democrats were facing another serious challenge from within their own ranks: Catholic dissidents and members of the opposition were gathering signatures for a series of radical reforms to the electoral system meant to take away power from party leaders and make government more responsive to the popular will. By the time the seventh Andreotti government took office in April 1991, 74 percent of Italians said they favored junking Italy's proportional electoral system in favor of a majoritarian system.[7]

The more astute politicians began to understand that if they did not climb aboard the bandwagon of reform, they might be crushed by it. And one of these was Claudio Martelli. Extremely intelligent and articulate, young, handsome and telegenic, Martelli had the potential to become the Jack Kennedy or Bill Clinton of Italian politics. Unfortunately for Martelli (and perhaps for Italy), he had the misfortune to come of age in the corrupt political machine of Bettino Craxi's Socialist Party during the late 1970s. (In the early 1980s, prosecutors had discovered traces of his involvement in a multimillion-dollar payoff from the Ambrosiano Bank in Milan to a Socialist bank account in Switzerland, brokered by none other than Licio Gelli, the infamous head of the P2 secret Masonic lodge. Naturally, the investigation was squelched and this shadow on Martelli's reputation did not prevent him from becoming minister of justice. When further evidence of the bribe finally came out in 1993, Martelli would be forced to resign.)[8] Perhaps because he knew of the extent of the corruption, Martelli began trying to distance himself from his political mentor and acquire a new political identity. "Martelli understood that scoring points in the war on the mafia paid off very well and he committed himself and used Falcone's great professional capacity to its maximum," said Judge D'Ambrosio. "I think Martelli hoped to become the 'new man' of Italian politics."[9]

Martelli and Falcone's programs met with considerable political resistance, initially; but events in the summer of 1991 suddenly kicked the reluctant parliament into overdrive.

On May 3, Italy was stunned by one of the most bloodcurdling mafia crimes in recent history: in Taurianova, Calabria, killers of the local 'Ndrangheta murdered a butcher in front of his shop in the middle of town, cut off the victim's head with one of his own knives and then used the severed head for target practice in the piazza. This crime riveted national attention not just because of its macabre details but also because Taurianova was a shocking example of just how powerful the grip of organized crime on southern Italian life had become. The severed-head incident had occurred in broad daylight in a central square of the town and had taken some seventeen minutes, and yet no one had seen anything. It was only one of five murders in three days and the thirty-second mafia-style killing in just over two years, an astounding number for a town of just seventeen thousand. Moreover, the execution had a clear political dimension: it came on the heels of (and appeared to be in retaliation for) the murder of Rocco Zagari, a Christian Democratic member of the Taurianova city council, who was also suspected of belonging to the 'Ndrangheta.[10]

As the Italian press rushed to Taurianova, an incredible picture of life there emerged: the town had been run like a private fiefdom by a single family during the entire postwar period. The family patriarch, Giuseppe Macrì, had been mayor and president of the local Christian Democratic Party. His mantle had been inherited by his son, Francesco "Ciccio" Macrì, who expressed his gratitude by having the square where they lived renamed Piazza Macrì and having a statue of his father built (at public expense) in the middle of the square. Thus Don Ciccio made his political speeches from the balcony of Palazzo Macrì, in Piazza Macrì, as the crowd stood next to Giuseppe Macrì's life-size image. The principal source of Don Ciccio's power, however, was his position as president of the local unit of the National Health Service, the great public trough out of which much of the town fed. While few would willingly turn to it for medical help, the health unit had a whopping 1,150 people on its payroll, many of them political cronies occupying no-show jobs. One of them was the murdered city councillor, Rocco Zagari. Macrì had earned the nickname "Ciccio-Mazzetta" (Ciccio "the Bribe") because of his habit of demanding kickbacks from the legion of people he employed, which helped to explain how he was able to drive a Rolls-Royce on his modest civil servant's salary. Don Ciccio's system was so notorious it had attracted the attention of prosecutors. And yet, despite a string of criminal convictions and having been a fugitive of justice, Don Ciccio remained head of the local Christian Democratic Party until 1988. When he was finally forced to step down, his place was taken by his sister, Olga Macrì, who became mayor. Nonetheless, Don Ciccio continued to manipulate the levers of power from his position as the head of the local health unit. Although the Macrìs were not themselves suspected of being *mafiosi,* they ruled with the consent of the local clans, who controlled several seats on the city council and offered their support in exchange for control of lucrative government contracts.[11]

Taurianova's city government had been under the microscope of investigators for some time, but the murder of the city councillor and the episode of the severed head finally forced the government to act. In the wake of the May 1991 killings, Minister of the Interior Scotti announced that he was dissolving the city council of Taurianova and of two other southern Italian towns, because their governments were effectively controlled by the mafia. A government-appointed administrator would run the towns' affairs for a period of up to eighteen months, when new elections would be held.[12]

The next month, on June 9, 1991, Italy voted to eliminate one of the electoral mechanisms that had allowed people like Don Ciccio Macrì to thrive: the system of "preferences." Under Italy's old electoral system, when voters went to the polls, along with voting for a party, they could also express a "preference" for four different candidates of that party. It seemed a democratic measure since it allowed citizens rather than the party leaders to pick their representatives; but it had led to a notorious black market in the selling and trading of "preferences." Politicians or mafia bosses who controlled large packets of votes could quadruple their influence by trading or selling their extra "preferences." If a politician had 1,000 obedient followers, he could promise their "preferences" to three other politicians, who, in return, would get their people to vote for him. Thus, in a kind of multiplication of the loaves, 1,000 "preferences" suddenly became 4,000. This offered unique opportunities for mafia groups, who could steer votes with great precision. Not surprisingly, the "preference" system thrived in southern Italy, where nearly 70 percent of voters used it, twice the number as in many northern regions. (The system was most popular among Christian Democratic voters in Sicily, 86 percent of whom used the "preference" system.) And yet, in a surprising reversal, when the issue was put to the vote on June 9, 1991, the overwhelming majority of voters, in both the South and the North, voted to do away with the system. The vote was a clear warning bell for the government parties and gave new momentum to reformers who vowed another referendum that would completely overhaul the electoral system if the parliament refused to act on its own.[13]

On August 9, 1991, Antonio Scopelliti, a prosecutor at the Italian Supreme Court, was killed in a mafia hit while on holiday visiting his family in Calabria. Scopelliti was preparing to argue the government's case in the final appeal of the original maxi-trial of Palermo, set to be heard by the Supreme Court in the fall. Scopelliti was the second magistrate to be killed during the appeals process: Antonio Saetta, of the Palermo Court of Appeals, had been murdered in 1988.[14]

Later that August, as the government was still debating its crime package, Libero Grassi, a Sicilian businessman who had refused to make extortion payments, was killed outside of his home in Palermo. Although these kinds of murders were an all-too-routine occurrence, the death of Libero Grassi hit a deep nerve. In a world of fear and *omertà,* Grassi had become a symbol of rare courage and proud defiance. Not only had he refused to buckle under to mafia pressure, he had even dared to talk about it. Earlier that year, after receiving a series of threatening phone calls, he published an open letter in *Giornale di Sicilia* (entitled "Dear Extortionist") in which he stated clearly that he had no intention of paying—period. With Grassi's help, police were able to arrest three men on charges of attempted extortion and he continued to discuss the extortion racket with remarkable candor: "Here everybody pays, almost everybody, from $150 a month to $200,000 a year," he said. "Shops, craftsmen, professional firms, small businesses, large industries . . . Palermo is a city of 'conditional freedom.' The free market economy does not exist. And it doesn't exist because the victims won't talk, because the Association of Industrialists remains silent and the Association of Shopkeepers refuses to move a muscle. . . . The silence of death suffocates our economy. . . . Too many pay without even protesting. . . . I am beginning to think that at certain levels there is even a deal. . . . One businessman reached the point of telling a friend of mine, who had also refused to pay, 'If we all pay, we'll pay less.' . . . Extorters and extortionists even have a cup of coffee together and so they move from being victims into accomplices."[15]

Grassi was treated by most other Palermo businessmen as a dangerous lunatic, who was casting aspersion on the good name of the Sicilian entrepreneurial class. But few knowledgeable people doubted the truth of his words. In 1989, police had discovered a hideout of Nino Madonia (son of Commission member Francesco Madonia) that contained an account book of the family's extortion business, with names and numbers clearly laid out. Of the 150 local businessmen listed, only four admitted having paid protection money.[16]

And yet, in other parts of Sicily, others were inspired by Libero Grassi's example. Some 140 shopkeepers in the town of Capo d'Orlando, near Messina, formed an association and decided en masse to rebel against the extortion racket. Their revelations led to the arrest and prosecution of some twenty local *mafiosi*. This represented an intolerable affront and a potentially revolutionary development in Sicily. And after Libero Grassi went on national television to encourage others to stand up against the racket, someone decided to silence him. On August 29, 1991, he was shot and killed.[17]

Only after his death did people seem to grasp the importance of

Libero Grassi's message. The extortion racket in Italy was, according to estimates, a $25 billion business, the equivalent to a massive, illicit tax. Not only a huge drain on the southern Italian economy, it forced hundreds of thousands of people to live in the illegal economy: to keep up with protection payments, shopkeepers underreported their income and underpaid their taxes, reinforcing a culture of corruption as well as shifting money from the treasury of the Italian government into that of Cosa Nostra. "No economic or social problem can be resolved if the state does not address its primary responsibility of defeating crime," the Confederation of Italian Industrialists stated in response to Grassi's death.[18] In the first six months of 1991, the number of organized crime killings in Italy went up by an incredible 73 percent above the already high levels of 1990.[19]

Within ten days of Grassi's death, the Council of Ministers had approved more important anti-crime measures than had been passed in the previous eight years. Virtually the entire package of Falcone's reforms were adopted wholesale: the Italian FBI; the "district" anti-mafia pools; the "super-prosecutor's" office; a plan to hire twenty-three thousand new policemen and *carabinieri*; and a new "anti-racket" law, creating a fund to help businesses that were victims of extortion. The government also voted to put an end to revolving-door justice for mafia bosses: defendants convicted of mafia crimes could be held without bail for up to six years, as their cases worked their way through the lengthy appellate process.[20]

A few weeks after the passage of the crime package, the Council of Ministers agreed to dissolve the town councils of another eighteen local governments polluted by mafia groups.[21]

Then Martelli and Falcone began to address the lax conditions in Palermo that had contributed to Libero Grassi's death. The order to kill Grassi in all likelihood had been issued by Francesco Madonia, the boss who controlled the territory in which Grassi worked, whose family accounting books had been found two years earlier. Although convicted in the maxi-trial of Palermo, Madonia was one of the many bosses who lived in the comfort of the Ospedale Civico in Palermo, where they received visits and made phone calls as if they were in a hotel. When police found the Madonia account books, they noticed an item that said, "Nurses: 11 million lire ($9,000)"—in other words, the orderlies in the public hospital were paid by Madonia to act as his personal servants.[22]

This scandalous situation had been documented years earlier, but had remained substantially unchanged. Martelli and Falcone attempted to address it through a "decree" denying house arrest to convicted *mafiosi* and insisting that they be treated in prison hospitals rather than in outside clinics. In response, prosecutors in Palermo had filed a request asking the Palermo Court of Appeals to send some twenty-two major bosses who were either in the hospital or under house arrest back to prison. The president of the court, Pasquale Barecca, rejected the request, arguing that the law could not be applied retroactively, only in future cases. (It is curious to note that courts had applied the benefits of the new Italian penal code retroactively when it benefited mafia defendants; now they were applying the opposite logic, but with the same end result: the release of convicted bosses.) In light of the murder of Judge Antonio Scopelliti, Barecca's decision appeared particularly grotesque: the defendants could continue to enjoy their freedom as long as the Italian Supreme Court had not considered their appeal but the appeal continued to be delayed by the murder of magistrates connected to the case. Moreover, the court's reasons for granting hospital stays were mind-boggling: one of the defendants, Agostino Badalamenti (a nephew of Gaetano Badalamenti), had been under observation for eighteen months with "suspected hepatitis," which had never been diagnosed. As the government was studying what new measures to take, Pietro Vernengo, one of the twenty-two bosses that Barecca had refused to send to prison, simply walked out of the Ospedale Civico and vanished together with his son and son-in-law, also convicted *mafiosi*.[23]

In response, Martelli demanded the immediate transfer of Barecca, arguing that he had knowingly violated the government's orders. Two days after Vernengo's escape from the hospital, Falcone was in Palermo overseeing a police raid that brought dozens of convicted *mafiosi* back to prison, where, by government decree, they belonged.

The government's decision to crack down on Judge Barecca brought up the larger issue of the Italian Supreme Court and the "sentence-killer" Corrado Carnevale: "Why don't the same measures that have been applied to Doctor Barecca apply to Doctor Carnevale?" asked Luciano Violante, a former magistrate and member of parliament. Violante and others on the parliament's anti-mafia commission had been studying Carnevale's decisions on organized crime and had compiled a long list of judicial and factual errors that raised questions about the Supreme Court judge's competence and good faith.[24]

With the maxi-trial on the Supreme Court's fall calendar, the Carnevale debate acquired special urgency. In 1989, the Palermo Court of Appeals had chipped away significantly at the legal basis of the maxi-trial. While upholding many individual convictions, the court rejected the so-called Buscetta theory, according to which the leaders of Cosa Nostra could be held legally responsible for major assassinations based on testimony that they played an active role on "the Commission" at the time of the killings. This ambiguous decision seemed to offer a perfect opportunity for Carnevale to undo the maxi-trial.

Under growing political pressure, the Italian Supreme Court agreed to change the bizarre system that had given Carnevale, the "sentence-killer," a virtual monopoly on organized crime cases: rather than being funneled automatically to the First Section of the Supreme Court, the cases would now be assigned randomly among the seven sections of the court. Although the judiciary is supposed to be entirely independent, it has always been—for good or ill—highly sensitive to political pressure. For years, the parties in power had defended Carnevale as a judicial "purist"; now he found himself under fire from the same quarters.

Conservative editor Indro Montanelli, whose newspaper, *Il Giornale,* had attacked the anti-mafia pool of Palermo as a nest of Communist agitators, now aimed his guns at the "sentence-killer," calling Carnevale's jurisprudence "nauseating." After a decision in which Carnevale had freed six Neapolitan gangsters who had been sentenced to life in prison, Montanelli wrote: "Is it possible that the law is always, always, on the side of the criminals, and never, in the view of Carnevale, on the side of the courts that convict them?"[25]

Looking into Carnevale's record on the bench, the Ministry of Justice found evidence that he had engaged in a serious breach of judicial ethics, failing to withdraw from a case in which he had a substantial economic interest. Feeling the heat of disciplinary proceedings, Carnevale asked to withdraw from the panel that reviewed the appeal of the maxi-trial.

When the Supreme Court announced its verdict on January 31, 1992, the result was overwhelmingly favorable to the prosecution. Not only did the high court uphold the original convictions but it accepted the so-called Buscetta theory. For the first time in history, the leadership of Cosa Nostra was faced with a nonappealable life sentence. Not only were dozens of major bosses unlikely ever to leave prison, but prosecutors could continue using the same tools to go after the rest of the organization. The decision was a clear signal that the age of impunity that had lasted forty-five years was over.[26]

"It was a result that not even the most optimistic prosecutors in Palermo could have imagined," said Judge Salvatore Barresi. "This, too, was the work of Giovanni Falcone, due in no small measure to his success in sensitizing Martelli to the mafia problem."[27]

To the surprise of many friends and colleagues, Falcone's Roman strategy appeared to be working brilliantly. "I must admit that, in this instance, I was completely wrong," said Judge Barresi, who had criticized Falcone's decision to join Martelli's staff. "Although we were slow to understand it, the mafia understood right away that [Falcone] was much, much more dangerous in Rome than remaining in Palermo." In ten months—starting with the decree of March 1991, ordering the arrest of Michele Greco and the other bosses of Palermo, to the creation of the Italian FBI, the "district offices," the anti-racket law, the abolition of house arrest for mafia defendants and ending with the historic decision of the Supreme Court in the maxi-trial—Falcone had achieved a genuine judicial revolution. "He was conditioning the entire government effort against the mafia, that up until then had been distracted, inconsistent and ineffective, if not worse," said Judge Barresi.

The evening that the Supreme Court handed down the decision in the maxi-trial Falcone and his colleagues held a small, quiet celebration at the Ministry of Justice in Rome. First they telephoned the people who had been most involved in the case, Antonino

Caponetto, Paolo Borsellino, their other colleagues in Palermo; the ministers Oscar Luigi Scalfaro, Mino Martinazzoli and Virginio Rognoni, who had made the trial possible. "Then at about eight-fifteen Falcone sent out for a bottle of champagne and we opened it," said Liliana Ferraro. "But it was not a lighthearted evening. We knew that something big had happened and that, somehow, we would have to pay. There was a sense of great satisfaction but very sober."[28]

D espite its historic importance, the Supreme Court verdict upholding the maxi-trial of Palermo became quickly lost in the flurry of dramatic events that dominated Italian life in the first months of 1992.

Just two weeks after the court decision, on February 17, 1992, police arrested Mario Chiesa, a middle-level Socialist functionary in Milan, as he was in the process of pocketing a $6,000 bribe. When investigators were able to identify some $10 million that Chiesa had socked away in Swiss bank accounts, he began to talk. The larger implications of the scandal were immediately obvious. Milan was the personal fiefdom of Socialist leader Bettino Craxi, who had made his brother-in-law Paolo Pillitteri the mayor and his twenty-eight-year-old son, Bobo Craxi, local party chairman. Bobo Craxi's recent election to the city council had been financed by Mario Chiesa. Rumors began to swirl that prosecutors were moving up the pyramid of power in Milan, and that indictments were imminent for dozens of leading businessmen, city councilmen, party treasurers, members of parliament and the mayor. Clearly, this was not an isolated case of personal dishonesty. An entire system of carefully organized corruption had been uncovered, orchestrated at the highest levels of the leading parties, especially the Socialists and Christian Democrats.[29]

In early March, Prime Minister Giulio Andreotti resigned. Rather than patch together a new coalition, the governing parties—because of the depth of the political crisis—dissolved parliament and called for national elections to be held the next month. As the election campaign got under way, on March 12 a squad of mafia killers gunned down Salvatore Lima near his villa in Mondello, a seaside resort just outside Palermo. At the time of his murder, Lima was busy preparing a rally for his mentor, Andreotti, who was scheduled to start campaigning in Sicily the next day.

E ven for a country all too used to political killings, the Lima assassination was deeply shocking. Dozens of politicians and prosecutors had been murdered by the mafia over the previous fifteen years, but—with the exception perhaps of General Dalla Chiesa—Lima was the most prominent victim. Moreover, the others had been outspoken enemies of the mafia. Lima, instead, was considered to be one of its closest friends in power. While his party colleagues tried to claim that Lima had been a resolute, if silent, adversary of Cosa Nostra, his murder was a profound embarrassment to the Christian Democratic Party. Given Lima's close ties to Andreotti, it was as though the mafia had dumped a dead body on the prime minister's doorstep as a sinister warning.[30]

Although no one understood the exact meaning of the killing, it suggested that something had broken down in the traditional equilibrium between mafia and political power. "The relationship has become inverted: now it's the mafia that wants to give the orders," Giovanni Falcone was quoted as saying. "And if the politicians don't obey, the mafia decides to act on its own."[31]

The parliamentary elections of April 5, 1992, took place under the shadow of the twin scandals of Lima's assassination and the bribery scandal in Milan. Not surprisingly, the election proved a near-total disaster for the governing parties. The Christian Democrats fell to a mere 26 percent of the vote, the lowest total in their history; and the Socialists fell back to only 12 percent. The Lombard League became the largest party in northern Italy, collecting some 10 percent nationally, a small miracle for a party that had won 0.4 percent in the previous parliamentary elections of 1987. But, because the opposition vote was splintered among more than a dozen parties across the ideological spectrum, the government coalition managed to hang on to power by the slimmest of margins. By the admission of the party leaders themselves, the vote was a clarion call for reform. "Either we change or we die," said Interior Minister Vincenzo Scotti.[32]

After the elections, the president of the Republic, Francesco Cossiga, resigned, insisting that the new parliament should pick a new president. (In Italy, the president of the Republic is selected by parliament and serves a seven-year term. Although a largely ceremonial figure, the president does, however, have the power to select the prime minister, who runs the government.) Cossiga's resignation threw the parties into a still-deeper quandary: in a charged atmosphere where everyone was blaming everyone else for the disastrous electoral results they were forced to pick a new president before they could go about forming a new government. While the country was calling for urgent political reform, the parties were busy jockeying for position, negotiating and fighting over the big prize. Before the elections, the Socialists and the Christian Democrats had reportedly worked out a neat political pact: Giulio Andreotti would leave the prime minister's office to Socialist leader Bettino Craxi, and in exchange, the Socialists would help make Andreotti president of the Republic. Christian Democratic leader Ciriaco De Mita would become foreign minister. The elections represented a serious threat to these plans: the recent vote was a clear denunciation of this kind of backroom party politics. Craxi was being hammered by the almost daily indictments coming from the prosecutor's office in Milan, while the figure of Salvatore Lima hovered over Andreotti like Banquo's ghost in *Macbeth*. Through most of May, the new Italian parliament remained completely stalled, trying and failing to elect a new president in secret balloting. In the early rounds, each party put forward dummy candidates with no chance of success, while negotiating furiously about which "real" candidate they would ultimately rally around. When the candidacy of Christian Democratic Party secretary Arnoldo Forlani failed in mid-May, many thought that Giulio Andreotti would now make his move.[33]

During the political crisis, the government's anti-mafia program stalled. The parliament approved its proposal for a "superprosecutor" to coordinate all mafia prosecutions, and Minister of Justice Claudio Martelli proposed Giovanni Falcone for the job. However, Falcone ran afoul once again of his old nemesis the Consiglio Superiore della Magistratura (CSM), which, in a preliminary vote, rejected Falcone for another candidate, Agostino Cordova, chief prosecutor of Palmi, Calabria. Cordova was a dogged investigator with an excellent reputation, but he had worked exclusively in Calabria and did not have Falcone's vast knowledge of the mafia's national and international reach. Cordova had also had the effrontery to investigate links between Socialist politicians in Calabria and local organized crime figures— something that made him anathema to Martelli. The CSM was wary of Falcone's close ties to Martelli, choosing Cordova, in part, as a slap in the face to the Socialist minister. But Martelli did not give up easily and continued to use all of his political muscle to push Falcone's candidacy. The stalemate dragged on throughout April and May.[34]

When a journalist from the Rome daily paper *La Repubblica* went to visit Falcone on Tuesday, May 19, Falcone appeared discouraged by the continued paralysis of the Italian political system. "Cosa Nostra never forgets," he said. "The enemy is always there, ready to strike. . . . This is why we must act quickly to build the super-prosecutor's office. . . . But we are not even able to agree on the election of the president of the Republic."[35]

At the end of the week, on Saturday, May 23, the leaders of the major parties were still meeting to try to unblock the political logjam. After doing a morning's work, Giovanni Falcone left Rome for Palermo, where he returned every weekend. His wife, Francesca, had remained in her job in Sicily, although she was scheduled to be transferred to join Falcone in Rome. That particular week, Francesca had business in Rome and Falcone, rather than leave on Friday evening, postponed his departure until Saturday afternoon so that they could travel together. They left from the Ciampino military airport outside Rome, in a government plane that took off at 4:40 and touched down at Punta Raisi airport in Palermo just over an hour later. A three-car police motorcade with seven bodyguards met them on their arrival. But, since security measures had been cut back in recent years, no helicopter surveyed the route to the city in anticipation of Falcone's arrival. As a result, no one noticed the unusual amount of activity that had taken place earlier in the day next to the highway near the town of Capaci just a few kilometers from the airport. A team of "men of honor," dressed as construction workers, had put the finishing touches on the huge, 500-kilo stash of plastic explosives they had placed in a large metal drain pipe that passed underneath the highway. As evening approached, a group of men clustered around a small shack a hundred yards back from the roadside where a remote-control detonator was hidden, scanning the traffic moving from the airport toward the city.[36]

In a minor breach of standard security procedures, Giovanni Falcone took the wheel of his bulletproof Fiat Croma, a small gesture of freedom in a highly restricted life. Francesca got in beside him in the front seat, while their driver, Giuseppe Costanza, moved to the back seat. As the motorcade drove past Capaci, the entire highway was ripped open by a massive explosion that seemed like the epicenter of an earthquake. All three cars were swallowed up, bent and twisted by the blast that created a huge crater and tore up a quarter mile of road. "All hell seemed to open up before us in a second," said an eyewitness whose car was directly behind the motorcade. "A terrifying explosion . . . a scene from the apocalypse, screams of terror and then an unreal silence. . . . Some people were moaning and others had passed out. I saw Falcone moving, his face, a mask of blood. His head moved back and forth, but he was stuck . . . I don't know if he was conscious. . . . His wife had fainted, her eyes open, looking upward."[37]

The full force of the blast had struck the front of the motorcade, immediately killing the three men in the lead car: Antonio Montinaro, Rocco Di Cillo and Vito Schifani. The three bodyguards in the last car escaped with relatively minor injuries, while Falcone, Francesca and their driver were all badly injured but alive when ambulances arrived. The driver, in the backseat, survived, while Falcone was pronounced dead shortly after arriving at the hospital. If Falcone had not insisted on driving, he might have lived. He was fifty-three years old. Francesca Morvillo seemed to have a chance of survival and briefly regained consciousness. "Where is Giovanni?" she asked when she came to. But after two operations, she died later that evening. She was forty-six years old.[38]

TWENTY-ONE

When news of the bombing of Giovanni Falcone's motorcade was reported, it was as if a head of state had been shot. All the major television networks broke in with a news flash and suspended their regular programming. "When my children, who happened to be watching television at the time, heard the news, they screamed, 'No!' as if there was a sudden death in the family," wrote Claudio Magris, a literary critic living in the northeastern city of Trieste. Millions of Italians remained in front of their television sets as the news bulletins got worse and worse.[1]

At the same time, cheers and applause erupted among the inmates of Palermo's Ucciardone prison. An anonymous caller phoned the Palermo newspaper *Giornale di Sicilia*, taking credit for the bomb: "A wedding present for Nino Madonia." Earlier that day, Nino Madonia, the eldest son of the powerful Madonia clan, was married in the Ucciardone chapel.[2]

The Italian parliament called for a day of mourning and suspended its session until after Falcone's funeral on Monday. In Sicily a general strike was proclaimed, shutting all stores and businesses for a day. The closed coffins of the five victims of the Capaci bombing were laid out the next day in the huge, cavernous marble lobby of the Palermo Palace of Justice, the scene of Falcone's greatest triumphs and bitterest defeats, the place that

Falcone had left in disgust just over a year before. Besides the friends and colleagues of the victims, some were surprised to see thousands of ordinary Palermitans, men and women from the silent majority of a city that, as Falcone had said several years earlier, were "waiting at the window to see who would win the bullfight."

As the parade of government ministers and politicians filed in, the crowd began tossing coins and shouting insults: "Murderers! Clowns! Accomplices. Go home! Go back to your bribes!"[3]

A city that had often shown indifference and sometimes irritation toward the commotion created by Giovanni Falcone and the anti-mafia pool now seemed traumatized by his death. As long as he was alive, it had been good sport to criticize him, complain about the sirens of his police escort and speculate about the behind-the-scenes struggles of the Palace of Justice, but it had been reassuring for the city to know, nonetheless, that he was always there from morning until night, in his bulletproof bunker, pouring through documents, interrogating witnesses, ferreting out money trails and churning out indictments. Now that he was suddenly gone, they felt terribly exposed and vulnerable. "Falcone had always seemed invincible, even though I didn't always agree with him," said a bystander in the crowd that day, quoted in the *Corriere della Sera,* "I never thought they would get him. I somehow expected that he would emerge out of the rubble of the bomb, with his smile, his cigar. . . . Even now, part of me still expects to see him return. Instead, tomorrow we will bury him and he will never come back."[4]

Across the city, a new phenomenon sprang up: people started hanging bedsheets out their windows with slogans of protest or grief written across them: "Palermo demands Justice." "Enough!" "Get the *mafiosi* out of government!" "Falcone, you remain in our hearts." "Falcone lives!"[5]

The funeral of Falcone was a national drama, broadcast live on national television. People wept at the impassioned pleas of Rosaria Schifani, the twenty-three-year-old widow of slain bodyguard Vito Schifani, who cried out "Men of the mafia, I will forgive you, but you must get down on your knees!" Much of the city stood for hours in the street outside the Church of San Domenico, waiting in the rain.[6]

Many commentators saw the assassination of Falcone as symbolic of the death of the Italian state. "Falcone should have been protected better than any other person in our country, because no one more than he embodied the state," wrote Claudio Magris in the *Corriere della Sera.* "The fact that we have been unable or unwilling to protect him means that the state does not exist."[7]

One of Italy's leading philosophers, Norberto Bobbio, declared that the death of Falcone "made me ashamed to be Italian."[8]

Sociologist Pino Arlacchi, a friend of Falcone's, wrote that "the death of Falcone closes a cycle of history that ends in the worst possible way: with the clear and unequivocal defeat of the state. . . . The men of Cosa Nostra are strong because they are allied to other, even more dangerous men, who are inside our institutions, in our midst."[9]

The killing seemed to awake the Italian political world from its sleep. After fifteen unsuccessful ballots, on the day of Falcone's funeral the parliament suddenly made Oscar Luigi Scalfaro Italy's ninth president of the Republic. Although a conservative, seventy-six-year-old Christian Democrat, Scalfaro had a reputation of moral probity, and had kept his distance from the party apparatus. Moreover, he had solid anti-mafia credentials. As minister of the interior in the mid-1980s, he had provided essential logistical support to the prosecutors preparing the maxi-trial of Palermo.

While Italian pundits saw the killing of Falcone as the death of the Italian state, those most familiar with the world of Cosa Nostra saw something quite different going on under the surface. "Such a spectacular public bombing is never in the interest of the mafia . . . it is a sign of weakness," Calderone said in a newspaper interview at the end of May, which received insufficient attention. The killing had become an urgent necessity, Calderone said, because of a series of major defeats. "Giovanni Falcone had been condemned to death a long time ago, but the sentence could no longer be put off for two reasons: the Supreme Court's decision to confirm the life sentences of the bosses of the Commission . . . and the increasing certainty that Falcone would be super-prosecutor. As long as convictions could be overturned in Rome, there was no need to act. But a definitive life sentence unleashed a reaction of rage. The Corleonesi and the winning families lost their heads." The increase in terrorist violence was the result of the fact that the government was now genuinely fighting the mafia. "The Pax

Mafiosa is now a closed chapter," he said. He went on to predict that other killings would soon follow: "I have no doubt: a magistrate, a minister, a police investigator. Cosa Nostra has a little book and for every name there is a time."[10]

When he heard the news that a bomb had struck Giovanni Falcone's car, Paolo Borsellino rushed to the Palermo hospital where his friend had been taken. He was among the few people admitted to the emergency room, just in time to watch Falcone die. When Borsellino emerged, his eldest daughter, Lucia, a university student, was there waiting for him. "Suddenly I saw him . . . his face lost, shaken, he had aged visibly in just a few minutes," she recalled later. When she burst into tears, he told her not to make a scene, but then almost immediately, he broke down, too, and they stood there weeping in one another's arms. But her tears, that day, were not only for Giovanni Falcone. "Now my father's death had grown nearer," she said. " 'Giovanni is my shield against Cosa Nostra,' I had heard my father say a thousand times. 'They will kill him first, then they will kill me.' "[11]

Borsellino participated in all of the funeral rites for Falcone, helping to carry his coffin, and even spoke at the ceremony at the Church of San Domenico. With characteristic consideration for others, he even drenched himself in the rain, looking for a car to take Francesca Morvillo's mother home. But during the first days after the bomb, he was in a powerful state of shock and depression. Uncharacteristically, he sat around the house in almost complete silence, while other colleagues, acquaintances and even adversaries of Falcone scurried to get themselves on television in order to bask in the reflected glory of their "friend" Giovanni.

When the parliament went back into session on the afternoon of the funeral, forty-seven members of parliament, the delegation of the neo-fascist party Movimento Sociale Italiano, voted for Paolo Borsellino to become president of the Republic. When Borsellino learned of the vote, he was furious, phoning to protest with friends in the party whom he had known since their days together at the University of Palermo. No one had asked his permission, he was not a member of any political party, had not been active politically in thirty years and had no intention of becoming a candidate for higher office.

A few days later, he received another unwanted candidacy at a round-table discussion in Rome of the published memoirs of mafia witness Antonino Calderone, which he had agreed to attend weeks earlier. Coming on the heels of the Capaci bombing, the event turned into an emotionally charged commemoration of Falcone, and suddenly Minister of the Interior Vincenzo Scotti, who was also among the speakers, suggested that Borsellino should become the new "super-prosecutor." With Falcone's death, Scotti said, the Consiglio Superiore della Magistratura (CSM) should open up the competition to new candidates; Minister of Justice Martelli seconded the proposal.[12] This spontaneous, unexpected gesture put Borsellino in an extremely uncomfortable position. While he did not want to insult anyone, he disliked the idea of benefiting from his friend's death. Rather than saying anything at the time, he wrote a private letter immediately afterward, declining the candidacy. Borsellino was also bothered by the recklessness with which the politicians in Rome made these kinds of theatrical gestures, which played well in Rome but which could have lethal consequences in a place like Palermo. Many blamed Falcone's death on his stalled candidacy as "super-prosecutor," making him a prominent target of the mafia, without giving him the powers to take the offensive.

As the Italian public began to realize how much they had lost in Falcone, the media shifted the tremendous weight of its attention onto Borsellino. As Falcone was beatified as a martyr, Borsellino was hailed as the new redeemer—a dangerous simplification of the fight against the mafia that drew all eyes to Borsellino. "In order to improve its tarnished image, the government wanted to make my father into the natural 'heir' of Falcone," said Manfredi Borsellino. "Every day, they mentioned his name in conjunction with Falcone's or as the next 'super-prosecutor.' "[13]

Portraying Borsellino as Falcone's "heir" was, in some sense, natural. Not only had they shared the experience of the anti-mafia pool, Borsellino had, at the end of 1991, taken Falcone's old job as deputy chief prosecutor of Palermo. With the creation of the "district offices" in the fall of 1991, Borsellino had asked for a transfer from Marsala, since most major mafia investigations for western Sicily would be concentrated in the capital city. After five years in the provinces, Borsellino had inherited Falcone's mantle as the chief anti-mafia prosecutor in Palermo, working under his friend's former boss and nemesis, Pietro Giammanco. Given the extended jurisdiction of the office under the new legislation, Borsellino would be in charge of all investigations for the south-western provinces of Sicily, from Trapani and Marsala down the coast to Agrigento and Palma di Montechiaro.

While the investigations into the mafia of Palermo remained at something of a standstill, Borsellino was able to build successfully on his work in Marsala. Just before his return to Palermo in December 1991, he succeeded in winning over another important new witness, Vincenzo Calcara, a *mafioso* already imprisoned on the island of Favignana. (Calcara was blamed for a lost drug shipment and preferred the risk of cooperating to certain death.) At one of their first meetings, Calcara revealed that he had been given the job of killing Borsellino himself, but the plan had been dropped when the Commission in Palermo had failed to give its approval. As proof of his claim, Calcara had the names, written in code, of men of honor in Australia, where he was supposed to flee after the assassination. Calcara felt sufficient remorse that every time he found himself face to face with the man he was supposed to have assassinated, he insisted on embracing Borsellino. In early May of 1992, Borsellino ordered a roundup of some forty defendants in Sicily, Rome, northern Italy and Germany based on Calcara's confessions. At the time of Falcone's death—when Borsellino was giving life to the "district office" of Palermo created by Falcone—the old duo of the anti-mafia pool had been working in close synchrony again. In fact, Falcone had hoped that if he became "super-prosecutor," Borsellino would head up the office's operations in Palermo so that the two would be reunited.[14]

When Borsellino's colleagues saw him return to the office at the end of May, he seemed visibly changed. "After the Capaci bombing, he seemed very, very marked by what had happened," said Judge Salvatore Barresi. "There was an air of terrifying sadness about him. Many of us noted that he seemed to have death in his eyes."[15]

As he walked through the lobby of the Palace of Justice to reach his office, people he did not know would come up to him with a greeting, a prayer, a slip of paper containing a tip or suggestion or theory about the Capaci bombing. "They seem to think I'm a saint," Borsellino told his family, feeling the enormous weight of public expectations.[16]

"After that initial moment of disorientation, he rolled up his sleeves and went back to work like a madman," said his son, Manfredi Borsellino. "He dedicated all his energies to shedding light on Falcone's death."[17]

Although he was not assigned to the Capaci bombing case, since all matters involving magistrates in Palermo are handled by the office of Caltanissetta, Borsellino hoped that by pursuing his own mafia investigations he would turn up evidence that might help identify Falcone's killers.

Even before Falcone's death, Borsellino had become the Italian magistrate *mafiosi* asked for when they decided to turn state's witness. When Falcone entered the Ministry of Justice, he ceased, technically, to be a magistrate and lost the authority to question witnesses. So that in early May 1992, when Gaspare Mutolo, a major *mafioso*, decided to talk, he insisted, after learning that Falcone was unavailable, on seeing Paolo Borsellino. Mutolo trusted them because he knew from firsthand experience how hard they had worked in the maxi-trial, at which he was convicted to a heavy sentence. Mutolo had been the chief organizer of the massive heroin ring that Falcone had broken involving Ko Bak Kin in Thailand and the Greek ship that was captured carrying hundreds of kilos of drugs in 1983.

But while Borsellino was eager to meet with Mutolo, he immediately ran into problems with his new boss, Pietro Giammanco, the Procuratore della Repubblica of Palermo. Giammanco raised a bureaucratic obstacle: Borsellino was supposed to work on cases in southwestern Sicily and Mutolo was a Palermo *mafioso*, therefore Giammanco felt that a magistrate working on Palermo cases should have precedence. There was a risk that this administrative snag might jeopardize Mutolo's cooperation; he had refused to talk to other prosecutors and might get cold feet sensing the uncertainty that prevailed in the government camp. The stakes in the Mutolo case were high: Mutolo was perhaps the highest-caliber witness to come along since Francesco Marino Mannoia in 1989. Moreover, he had been the cellmate of Totò Riina when they were in prison during the 1960s—a potentially invaluable source of information about the elusive boss of bosses.

Borsellino's resentment increased when he learned, by pure chance, that the Italian police had reports of a plot to assassinate him of which Giammanco had not thought to inform him. Although Borsellino preferred not to become closely involved in the specific measures to ensure his security, he did want to know when he was in particular danger.[18]

Not surprisingly, Falcone's assassination caused a momentary crisis among the mafia witnesses. Some witnesses stopped talking for a time after the Capaci bombing. Borsellino's own new witness, Vincenzo Calcara, seized with panic, threatened to retract his testimony at trial. Borsellino's chief police investigator, Carmelo Canale, had to travel in the police truck that brought Calcara to Palermo. The witness had descended into a paranoid delirium, convinced that he was about to be killed at any moment. "Do you know who the drivers of this truck are?" he asked Canale, suspecting they might be in on the plot. When they reached Palermo, Borsellino gave him a stern lecture: "Vincenzo, what's happened to your dignity? Didn't I tell you when we first met that it is good to die for something you believe in?" Calcara snapped out of his tailspin and held firm to his testimony.[19]

While still trying to work out a solution to the Mutolo case, Borsellino made another major breakthrough. He won the cooperation of Leonardo Messina, a mafia underboss from Caltanissetta—an area with powerful mafia traditions that had remained almost untouched by the investigations of the preceding ten years. Although still in his late thirties, Messina was from a family of *mafiosi* going back a few generations. "I *am* history," he reminded investigators.

As he had with other witnesses, Borsellino was able—with his warmth and humor—to establish a close rapport with the new witness. At a certain point, as Borsellino listened intently, Messina stopped and asked him: "Why are you staring at me?" "Because I get paid $6,000 a month to stare at you," he replied, breaking the nervous tension with a moment of laughter. Eventually, Messina even asked Borsellino for an autograph to give his children, who admired the legendary prosecutor.[20]

Taking Borsellino into the relatively uncharted waters of the mafia of central Sicily, Messina was a veritable gold mine of new information. His revelations would eventually lead to some two hundred arrest warrants—perhaps the largest single roundup since Buscetta's revelations in the fall of 1984. Not only did he have up-to-the-minute information about the makeup of mafia hit squads and numerous families, he was unusually open about the web of connections between the military arm of Cosa Nostra and the white-collar world of lawyers, doctors, businessmen, bureaucrats and politicians. Government contracts were the biggest source of revenue in the stagnant economy of central Sicily, and virtually nothing got built without the mafia approving it or taking a cut from the winner. As "underboss" of a family with an aging leader, Messina had handled the negotiations for many contracts himself, acting as intermediary between business leaders and important Sicilian politicians.

Messina told Borsellino how a member of the national parliament from Sicily, Gianfranco Occhipinti, had intervened to "fix" a government contract for the mafia. The original aspect of the case was the technique: *Onorevole* Occhipinti removed the "anti-mafia certificate" from the application of the company with the strongest bid, allowing a mafia-run company to win by default. Italian law requires companies to qualify for anti-mafia certificates in order to compete for public contracts, but mafia firms often manage to get around the requirement by hiding the real ownership of their businesses. Messina, however, revealed an ironic new twist on this system of corruption: a mafia company had won a government contract by stealing the anti-mafia certificate of a legitimate company with the help of a member of parliament. Moreover, Messina was able to back up this seemingly incredible story by producing the stolen anti-mafia certificate, which he had kept carefully hidden. As the decision to quit Cosa Nostra matured in him, Messina began quietly preserving evidence of his crimes so that he could establish his credibility when it came time to confess.[21]

Messina also revealed the identity of Totò Riina's "minister of public works" as Angelo Siino, a Sicilian businessman who oversaw Cosa Nostra's government contracts business, collected and received bribes, met entrepreneurs and politicians, made threats and, when necessary, ordered killings. The system of corruption that Messina described was very much like that being uncovered in Milan, with politicians steering contracts to firms willing to make handsome kickbacks—the only difference was that in Sicily there was an extra player at the bargaining table: the mafia. The fact that prosecutors in Milan were moving relentlessly against corruption in northern Italy may have emboldened Messina to tackle the subject of public contracts in Sicily. Messina's testimony about the workings of the government contract racket confirmed Falcone and Borsellino's contention that Cosa Nostra had adopted an increasingly centralized, unitary structure: the local mafia boss was required to pass on a portion of all profits from public contracts to the heads of the organization in Palermo. Totò Riina exerted effective control over the various families by appointing his own personal "ambassadors" to monitor the activities of the local bosses.

Between the drug trade and government contracts, Cosa Nostra had, quite literally, more money than it knew what to do with. To Borsellino's astonishment, Messina described something he called the "House of Money," an apartment that was filled to the brim with cash. Cosa Nostra's profits had become so huge that they simply couldn't launder all of it: so they had to rent a place where they could store it.[22]

While Messina described a criminal world of unprecedented wealth and power, he also revealed Cosa Nostra to be an organization in the midst of profound internal crisis. The reign of terror instituted by the Corleonesi had made life within the organization an intolerable nightmare. "A continuous tragedy," Messina said. While murder had always been part of Cosa Nostra, it had been resorted to more sparingly and rationally in the past—as a means of resolving an obvious conflict or infraction of the rules. Now it was used constantly and in such a capricious fashion to keep everyone off balance and in a state of constant fear. "[The Corleonesi] created tragedy in all the families," Messina said. "They took power by slowly, slowly killing everyone . . . often using us to do the job. . . . We were kind of infatuated with them because we thought that getting rid of the old bosses we would become the new bosses. Some people killed their brother, others their cousin and so on, because they thought they would take their places. Instead, slowly, [the Corleonesi] gained control of the whole system."

Unlike any of his predecessors, Messina did not come from one of the "losing" families in the great mafia war nor was he in immediate danger of being killed because of having stolen drugs or money from the organization. He was a star of the new generation of young bosses, but he saw that his rise would eventually bring him into fatal conflict with his superiors as it had with so many others. "First they used us to get rid of the old bosses, then they got rid of all those who raised their heads, like Giuseppe Greco "the Shoe," Mario Prestifilippo and [Vincenzo] Puccio . . . all that's left are men without character, who are their puppets," Messina said.

Although married, Messina had become involved with an attractive young woman from a well-to-do family, who had taken him outside the closed world of Cosa Nostra. Gradually, he developed a taste for a life in which people didn't have to shoot or strangle or wonder whether their best friends were planning to kill them.

Although his desire to leave Cosa Nostra had grown over a period of years, the final straw, Messina said, was the assassination of Falcone and the heartrending appeal of Rosaria Schifani, the widow of one of the bodyguards killed in the bombing. "My decision is the result of a moral crisis," he told Borsellino in their first meeting. "Even though my grandfather and many of my relatives were 'men of honor,' I no longer identify with the organization. And when I heard the speech of the widow of [Vito] Schifani . . . her words struck me with the weight of boulders and I decided to leave the organization in the only way possible, by collaborating with the justice system."[23]

Along with the crisis within Cosa Nostra, the organization was facing a dangerous challenge from without, as well. Messina was the first witness to explain in great detail a phenomenon that others had alluded to briefly: the growth of a new rival criminal organization in Sicily, known as the *Stidda,* the Sicilian word for "star," because of a star some of the members tattooed on their bodies. Composed originally of former men of honor who had left the organization during the great mafia war of the early 1980s, the new group was particularly strong in the area of southern Sicily around the towns of Agrigento, Caltanissetta and Gela. In fact, many of the original *stiddari* were followers of the old boss of Riesi, Giuseppe Di Cristina, who had warned police of the rise of the Corleonesi shortly before being killed in 1978. And it was the check found in his pocket that helped Giovanni Falcone unravel the financial underpinnings of the Spatola-Inzerillo heroin case. Fourteen years later, another circle closed.

Although the *Stidda* was less organized and less deeply rooted than Cosa Nostra, it was second to no one in violence. As Messina helped Borsellino understand, the terrifying rise in murders in many towns of southern Sicily was due to the vicious war between Cosa Nostra and its new rival.

While the assassination of Falcone had created the appearance of total omnipotence, Messina believed that Cosa Nostra was fighting for its survival. "There are some who believe that Cosa Nostra will disappear within the space of the next decade, destroyed by the intemperance of Salvatore Riina and the war with the *Stidda*," he said.

Messina's revelations about the *Stidda* dovetailed perfectly with another investigation Borsellino was already conducting into a plethora of murders in and around the Sicilian town of Palma di Montechiaro. By tracing the activities and phone calls of a suspicious character from Palma di Montechiaro living in Marsala, Borsellino's investigators had discovered that a whole colony of *stiddari* operated out of Mannheim, Germany. When German police passed on information about a shoot-out in Mannheim involving several Palmesi, Borsellino was able to connect it to the power struggle going on in central Sicily and to issue a series of arrest warrants. One of the men to fall into the net was a young *stiddaro* named Giaocchino Schembri, whom Borsellino flew to meet in his German prison. On July 10—just after Messina had begun talking—Borsellino was able to convince Schembri to cooperate. Already, in their initial informal meeting, Schembri was able to identify the killers of Rosario Livatino—the prosecutor assassinated near Agrigento in September 1991. Contrary to assumptions that the killing was the work of Cosa Nostra, Livatino had been murdered by the *Stidda*, which was evidently anxious to assert its new power by claiming an "excellent cadaver" of its own. As Borsellino was about to leave the Mannheim prison, he gave Schembri a pack of his Dunhill cigarettes, which the inmate jealously conserved as a souvenir. Borsellino promised to return to

Germany later in the month, on July 20, but needed to get back to Italy where urgent business awaited.[24]

By the middle of July 1992, Borsellino was in the extraordinary situation of simultaneously juggling three major new witnesses: Messina, Schembri and Mutolo. After a month a compromise had finally been worked out that would allow the Mutolo case to go forward: Borsellino would be allowed to attend Mutolo's depositions, but the case would remain under the direction of another magistrate, chosen by chief prosecutor Pietro Giammanco. Fortunately, Mutolo accepted the situation in an initial conversation at the beginning of July, while a longer, more detailed deposition was scheduled for July 16.

His family could not recall Borsellino ever working with the frenetic intensity he did in the two months following the death of Falcone—not even during the days of the maxi-trial. In the past, he had always found a few spare hours in the week for his family, now he left for work before they were even up and often came home after they had gone to bed. And—despite his personal phobia of airplane travel—he was constantly on the move, flying to question witnesses and gather evidence.

Even though they rarely saw him, Borsellino became upset when his younger daughter, Fiammetta, announced she was planning a summer trip with friends in rural Africa. "How am I going to let you know if I've been killed?" he said half jokingly.[25] To satisfy her father's concerns, Fiammetta modified her plans, traveling instead to Asia where, at least, she could more easily stay in touch by phone. The family became increasingly unnerved by the drumbeat of new stories on their father. Articles continued appearing proclaiming him the new "super-prosecutor"; photographs and film clips almost invariably showed him together with Falcone—as if they were destined to share the same fate.

"It was as if my father's death had been announced in advance," said Manfredi Borsellino. "During his last days, there was a disinformation campaign, orchestrated by someone, about the mortal danger to [former mayor] Leoluca Orlando. . . . The newspapers on the 17th and 18th of July had long stories about the elaborate security measures taken to protect Orlando. Since Orlando lives near us, there was a general alarm when someone noticed a stolen car parked nearby. 'Failed assassination attempt against Orlando,' people said. But, in fact, that car was closer to our house than to his. . . . All of this created an unbearable atmosphere for us in the family."[26]

"I am convinced that he felt the presence of death very near," said Antonio Ingroia, his assistant prosecutor in Marsala, who followed his boss back to Palermo in 1992. "Marshal [Carmelo] Canale [of the *carabinieri*], who knew him very well, believes the opposite, that it is inconceivable that someone so full of life could imagine his own death. But his behavior in that period was that of a man in a tremendous hurry, of someone who knew that his hours were numbered. If I buzzed the bell to his office, he would say, 'I'm too busy, I don't have time,' something that never happened in the past."

Although they were very close, Borsellino became angry when Ingroia announced that he was taking his family on vacation in the middle of July. "This is no time for vacation," he said. "We have lots of work to do." When Ingroia explained that he had already rented a house and couldn't change his plans, Borsellino fell into an uncharacteristically icy silence. "Before leaving the office, on July 15, I stopped by his office at about 1:30 in the afternoon to say good-bye," Ingroia recalled. "He almost didn't dignify my presence with a glance. He simply said, 'Fine, you've been bothering me about this vacation business for three days. Go on vacation, go on vacation!' He didn't even say good-bye. I was hurt. That afternoon before leaving town, I stopped back at the office, guessing that, even though it was a holiday, the feast day of Santa Rosalia—the patron saint of Palermo—he would still be at work. This time, perhaps realizing that I was hurt by our earlier conversation, he gave me a friendly embrace and I agreed I would come back to work after only ten days off, instead of the month I had planned. . . . I had the impression, that day, that he felt that time was running out on him."[27]

A s Borsellino was making quiet breakthroughs with his new mafia witnesses, the Milan bribery investigation was blowing wide open before the public eye. Literally hundreds of leading politicians and business leaders were under investigation. In June, Carlo Bernini, the Christian Democratic minister of transportation, was indicted for collecting graft from the billions of dollars in public contracts generated by his ministry. On July 14, the turn came for Foreign Minister Gianni De Michelis. Since both men were from Venice, they were known as the two "doges," and were alleged to have split all the bribes being collected in the Veneto region. As foreign minister, De Michelis appears to have had a longer reach: evidence emerged that his party was routinely skimming a percentage from the "humanitarian" aid that Italy was distributing in the Third World. The day of De Michelis's indictment American ambassador Peter Secchia and De Michelis were joint hosts of an enormous going-away party planned weeks earlier. Secchia would be returning to the United States after four years in Rome, while De Michelis was stepping down as foreign minister. The invitation to the party was a cartoon drawing showing De Michelis and Secchia riding together in the same Venetian gondola. Now that it seemed that the doge's gondola might be heading to jail, the joint party was a major embarrassment—symbolic of the United States' warm embrace of some of Italy's most corrupt leaders. Two days after the indictment of De Michelis, police in Milan arrested Salvatore Ligresti, the biggest real estate developer in the city and one of the richest men in Italy, extremely close to Socialist chief Bettino Craxi.

"July 16, the end of a regime" declared the headline of the newsweekly *L'Espresso* reporting on the latest developments in the scandal. "It is the defeat of an entire system," the story ran, "the impeachment of a large part of our governing class."[28] Responding to increasing pressures to resign, Socialist leader Bettino Craxi, after having denied any knowledge of the bribery system, now reversed his position 180 degrees, maintaining that the practice was so widespread that it could not be considered a crime. "Everybody knows that much of the financing of the parties and of the political system is irregular or illegal," he declared before parliament. "And if this material is considered criminal then most of our system would be a criminal system."[29]

The day of Ligresti's arrest, Paolo Borsellino traveled to Rome to resume the deposition of Gaspare Mutolo. Back in the early

1960s, when he was just a common criminal, Mutolo lived for a time in the same prison cell as Totò Riina. From the deference with which his cellmate was treated by other inmates, Mutolo understood that he must be someone important and ingratiated himself with Riina by letting him win at cards. When Mutolo left prison, he acted for a time as Riina's personal driver, a position of great trust. Because Mutolo had more than twenty years of history to recount, he and Borsellino spent their first sessions going over the familiar terrain of the mafia of the 1970s and 1980s. Mutolo saw events from the fascinating angle of a member of a mafia family that had tried to remain neutral in the struggle between the Corleonesi and the established bosses of Palermo. At the end of the session on Friday, July 17, however, Mutolo moved into the explosive and largely unexplored terrain of collusion between Cosa Nostra and high-level government officials. Although he wanted to wait before putting anything on paper, Mutolo told Borsellino about two important figures whom he said had been corrupted by the mafia: Bruno Contrada—a member of the Italian secret services and former police investigator in Palermo—and Domenico Signorino, a prosecutor with the anti-mafia pool at the Procura della Repubblica of Palermo. Suspicions had clouded the reputation of Contrada for years—Buscetta had first mentioned him in 1984 and Falcone had suspected him of involvement in the failed assassination attempt against him in 1989. But hearing Signorino's name was a profound shock for Borsellino. The two had been friends and close colleagues; along with Giuseppe Ayala, Signorino had argued the government's case in the first maxi-trial. When they parted, Borsellino and Mutolo agreed to take up the subject of collusion again when they met the following week. Borsellino was scheduled to fly to Germany to meet with Giaocchino Schembri on Monday, after which he would return to Rome to question Mutolo.[30]

Borsellino returned home that weekend with two important pieces of unfinished business on his mind: Mutolo's confession and Schembri's revelation about the killers of Judge Livatino, neither of which had yet been committed to paper. Agnese Borsellino could tell something was upsetting her husband when he returned home on Saturday, July 18. Finally, after she insisted they go out for a drive, he unburdened himself. Although he did not name names, he said he had heard damning evidence against a police investigator and a prosecutor.[31]

The next morning Borsellino woke at five o'clock when his daughter Fiammetta telephoned from Thailand. An early riser, he remained awake and went into his study to write a reply to a schoolteacher in northern Italy who had invited him to speak to her class. Unable to accept, Borsellino managed to write her a letter of several pages, responding to a long series of questions. At one point, he explained how he had come to dedicate himself to the war against the mafia:

> I became a magistrate because I had a great passion for civil law and . . . up until 1980 I worked mostly on civil cases. . . . On May 4, Captain Emanuele Basile was murdered and chief prosecutor Chinnici asked me to handle the case. Meanwhile my childhood friend Giovanni Falcone had joined my same office and from that time forward I understood that my work had changed. I had decided to remain in Sicily and I needed to give that choice a meaning. Our problems were the very ones that I had begun to deal with, almost by accident, and if I loved this land I had to work on them exclusively. From that day forward I have never left that job. . . . And I am optimistic because I see that young people, Sicilian or otherwise, have a much greater awareness than the culpable indifference in which I lived until I was forty. When these young people are adults they will react with much greater force than I and my generation have.[32]

Borsellino's writing was interrupted at 7:00 A.M. by a phone call from his boss, Pietro Giammanco. Unable to sleep thinking about the trouble he had created in the Mutolo case, Giammanco said he had changed his mind and promised to assign the case to Borsellino when he returned to the office the next day.

Later that morning Borsellino and his wife drove out to their country house in Villagrazia di Carini, a small town by the sea a half-hour's drive from Palermo. Borsellino went out for a spin in the motorboat of a friend and neighbor. And in the early afternoon, the Borsellinos went to lunch at the house of another friend who lived nearby. Afterward, Borsellino returned home for a nap, but clearly did not sleep, leaving five cigarette butts in the ashtray by the bed. When he got up, Borsellino and his six bodyguards drove back into Palermo to see the prosecutor's mother. Maria Pia Lepanto Borsellino lived with her daughter, Rita, who had gone away that weekend. Borsellino was concerned about his mother being alone all day, and he was planning to take her to the doctor to check on her bad heart. Having lost his father when he was twenty-two, Borsellino, as the eldest son, had become the head of the household at an early age and felt a powerful responsibility as well as deep affection for his mother. Although the first rule of good security is to avoid predictable patterns, Borsellino was unwilling to give up his weekend visits to his mother. "Paolo needed to be in regular contact with her, to know how she was and what she was doing," said his sister, Rita. "He couldn't deprive himself of that. This is what made Paolo so human. He always tried to maintain a normal life for everyone. . . . Work was extremely important to Paolo, but his family came first. . . . He was always interested in our lives, he stayed abreast of everything. He lived his family life with great intensity . . . I refuse to regret that."[33]

Cars were parked outside his mother's apartment in Via D'Amelio when Borsellino's three-car escort arrived just after five that afternoon. Several days earlier, his security detail had asked that a "no parking" zone be created in the area to protect against the possibility of car bombs, but the request had not been examined by the committee in charge of government security in Palermo. Borsellino got out of his car, surrounded by five agents—Walter Cusina, Claudio Traina, Vincenzo Li Muli, Agostino Catalano and Emanuela Loi, all of whom held pistols and machine guns. A sixth agent remained at the wheel of the lead car, as he had been trained to do. As Borsellino approached the gate of the apartment building to ring his mother's bell, he and the five bodyguards who surrounded him were blown into the air by an explosion that could be heard miles away across Palermo. Even though there were at least thirty feet between the front gate and the entrance to the building, the blast broke windows all the way up to the eleventh floor. The apartments facing the street on the first four floors were completely gutted. "There were no walls, no furniture," said Rita Borsellino. "The front entrance was just a pile of rubble."

TWENTY-TWO

I t's over, it's all over," said Antonino Caponetto, arriving to survey the carnage wreaked by the bomb of Via D'Amelio on July 19, 1992. The image of the frail-looking, seventy-three-year-old founder of the anti-mafia pool weeping and bowed with grief seemed to sum up the mood of almost total despair created by the death of Paolo Borsellino and his five bodyguards.[1]

Disgusted with the government that was supposed to have protected her husband, Agnese Borsellino rejected the idea of a state funeral, insisting on a private ceremony at their local church with no politicians allowed. There was almost a pitched battle at the Palermo cathedral during the public funeral for Borsellino's bodyguards: when the entourage of government officials arrived from Rome, the crowd went berserk, breaking through the imposing line of 4,000 policemen meant to keep order. Hurling insults and objects, kicking, screaming and punching, they set upon the head of the national police force, Vincenzo Parisi, and jostled president of the Republic Oscar Luigi Scalfaro, who had to be rescued from the mob. Leading the charge were hundreds of infuriated police bodyguards who had come to honor their fallen colleagues and to protest against the government they said used them like cannon fodder.[2]

The next day, most of the leading anti-mafia prosecutors of the

"district office" of Palermo resigned en masse, demanding the re-
moval of their boss, Pietro Giammanco, guilty, in their view, of
obstructing the work of Falcone and Borsellino.[3]

Rita Atria, the seventeen-year-old Sicilian girl who had turned
to Borsellino after her father and brother were murdered by the
mafia, jumped to her death from the balcony of the apartment in
Rome where she lived in hiding. "There is no one left to protect
me," she wrote in a suicide note.[4]

Concluding that the war against the mafia was a lost cause, Gianfranco Miglio, one of the leading spokesmen of the Lombard
League, suggested making Sicily an independent country in order
to protect the rest of Italy from further contagion of the irremedi-
able scourge of Cosa Nostra.[5]

While still reeling from the Borsellino assassination, the newly
formed government of Socialist Giuliano Amato was buffeted on
all fronts. That same week, Italy was forced to withdraw its currency from the European Monetary Union, finally admitting that,
because of the government's massive debt, the Italian lira could no
longer trade as an equal partner with the powerful German mark.
At the same time, the Milan bribery scandal continued to provide
lurid details of how Italy had spent its way out of the Monetary
Union. Rocked by so much bad news, the Italian stock market
plunged.

"These are confused days, punctuated by terrible events," the
lead editorial of the Milanese daily newspaper *Corriere della Sera*
declared on July 26. "We have seen another judge die. We have
seen the state manhandled by an angry crowd. We have seen the
lira and the stock market give way. Above all, in this last week—
seven incredible days—we have palpably felt the growing public
uneasiness. Citizens demand action from a state that so far has appeared impotent in the face of organized crime. But frankly they
doubt that a counteroffensive is possible . . . led by a political class
delegitimized by its own actions . . . by corruption, thievery, by
the immorality brought to light by the magistrates."[6]

With surprising candor, Prime Minister Amato seemed to agree:
"This state is not entirely innocent and we know it," he said, proceeding to raise a series of troubling questions that were on the
minds of millions of Italians. "What portion of the government
has engaged in collusion? has allowed certain things to happen?

has failed to intervene when it might have acted? These are questions about our recent history that need to be answered."[7]

Fighting for its political life, the government took a series of dramatic steps to restore its credibility. Within a few days, it passed Italy's first comprehensive witness protection program, offering sentence reductions and support for *mafiosi* prepared to testify for the government—a measure that prosecutors in Palermo had been demanding for nearly a decade. At the same time, the government decided to transfer the leading bosses of Cosa Nostra to remote island prisons off the Italian coast, where it would be much harder for them to communicate with their organizations. And, in its most dramatic move, Prime Minister Amato decided to send 7,000 Italian army troops to Sicily, acknowledging, in effect, that the government had lost control of the island. Although most were young, ill-trained conscripts, the soldiers did have at least one important function: by performing guard duty at the homes and offices of magistrates and politicians, they freed up hundreds of trained police officers to dedicate themselves to investigative work.[8]

Giving in to overwhelming pressure, Pietro Giammanco stepped down as chief prosecutor of the Procura of Palermo, asking to be transferred to a job in Rome. Replacing him would be Giancarlo Caselli—a highly regarded magistrate of unquestioned courage and integrity. A prosecutor from the northern city of Turin, Caselli had fought in the front lines of the war against terrorism, and was one of the key figures in helping to break the Red Brigades at the height of their power. As a member of the Consiglio Superiore della Magistratura from 1986 to 1990, Caselli had been one of the most passionate and effective defenders of Giovanni Falcone and the anti-mafia pool of Palermo. Although a man of the left, Caselli had repeatedly demonstrated his independent judgment by frequently dissenting from the official positions of his left-wing judicial faction, Magistratura Democratica.

The government remained focused on the mafia in part because of the constant pressure created by public demonstrations in Sicily and the rest of Italy. Palermo remained in a state of constant tumult, with marches, vigils, sit-ins, processions, placards, which continued with unrelenting regularity. The anti-mafia banners that had first appeared scrawled on bedsheets outside the windows of many Palermo homes became a permanent feature. They were brought out between the nineteenth and the twenty-third of each month in memory of the two assassinations. While Palermo has always had a small, politically active minority, these new demonstrations seemed to have a much wider base, with housewives, office clerks and shopkeepers joining with students and religious groups. Rather than being demoralized by the assassinations, Palermo seemed to have become energized by the Capaci and Via D'Amelio bombings. "After the death of General Dalla Chiesa in 1982, someone had a sign that said: 'Here dies the hope of every honest citizen,' " noted Marta Cimino, an organizer of the Committee of the Sheets. "After the death of Falcone someone carried a sign that said: 'Today begins a dawn that will never set.' The two signs are fairly indicative of the change in the last ten years."[9]

In a scene reminiscent of the early Christian martyr cults, the tree that grows on the sidewalk outside of Falcone's Palermo apartment became a kind of public shrine, on which people continued to place flowers and written messages. "Falcone lives!" "Better one day as Borsellino than a hundred as a *mafioso*." "They closed your eyes, but you opened ours."[10]

The same photograph of Falcone and Borsellino—capturing a moment in which the two Sicilian magistrates are talking together and laughing—seemed to dominate every wall and billboard of the city, giving them a strange and happy form of immortality. "Men come and go, ideas remain, they continue to walk on the legs of others," Falcone had said in 1985, a statement that appeared to be borne out by the continual commotion that followed his death.[11] People also made daily pilgrimages with fresh flowers, messages and photographs to a plaque in front of Borsellino's residence in Via Cilea. The plaque was inscribed with a quotation from Borsellino: "I never liked this city, and so I learned to love it. Because real love consists in loving what you don't like in order to change it."

For once, action seemed to accompany government rhetoric. Suddenly, police investigators who had proven themselves against the mafia were moved into positions of responsibility and given the resources to do their jobs effectively. Gianni De Gennaro, who had handled many of the most important mafia witnesses from Tommaso Buscetta forward, was made head of the new Italian FBI, the Direzione Investigativa Anti-mafia (DIA). Antonio Manganelli, who had worked on the confessions of Antonino Calderone, became head of the Servizio Centrale Operativo (SCO). And Colonel Mario Mori, a former aide to General Carlo Alberto Dalla Chiesa who had worked in Palermo from 1988 to 1991, was placed in charge of the anti-mafia unit of the *carabinieri*. All three men had worked hand-in-glove with Falcone, had the same global view of the mafia, and were heading the kind of national police units that Falcone had pushed for. Suddenly, the right people were moving into the right places, like the cylinders of a combination lock lining up.

Results were not long in coming. In the fall of 1992, the Italian police scored an impressive string of successes. In early September, they tracked down Giuseppe Madonia—considered to be the second most powerful man on the Commission after Riina. They also persuaded the Venezuelan government to arrest and extradite Pasquale, Paolo and Gaspare Cuntrera, three Sicilian brothers who were among Cosa Nostra's biggest drug traffickers and money launderers in South America. On September 11, Italian police captured Carmine Alfieri, considered the leading boss of the Neapolitan Camorra, and a fugitive of justice for nine years. A week later, police in Calabria arrested twenty-three men accused of being the leaders of the biggest kidnapping band in southern Italy. At the end of the month, Italian and American police issued 201 arrest warrants on three continents—in what was described as the largest international undercover investigation in history, Operation Green Ice. The "Green Ice" referred to the millions of dollars of drug money that had been frozen in the operation, which broke up a massive money-laundering ring run by Cosa Nostra in Italy and the United States in conjunction with the Medellín drug cartel in Colombia.[12]

In November, they issued some two hundred arrest warrants in central Sicily, building on the evidence Borsellino had gathered from Leonardo Messina.[13]

R ather than shutting the mouths of the mafia witnesses, the assassinations of Falcone and Borsellino seemed to have the opposite effect. With the floodgates finally opened, the police suddenly had more witnesses than they had time in which to question them.

Equally important, existing witnesses became much more cooperative, agreeing to tackle delicate and difficult subjects they had long avoided.

"I was profoundly shaken by the terrible atrocities committed against judges Falcone and Borsellino," Gaspare Mutolo said in October 1992. "These and other recent events . . . have convinced me that Cosa Nostra has undertaken an irreversible strategy of death, that seems to me far from over. . . . I now realize that my decision—choosing the state against Cosa Nostra—cannot have any limits and must be without reserve, whatever the risks and consequences for me."[14]

As a sign of his good faith, Mutolo immediately confessed to two murders of which he had never been suspected even though he was scheduled to be released from prison in a few years. He then proceeded to lift the curtain on the relationship between mafia and politics, the subject Tommaso Buscetta had said was "the crucial knot" of the organized crime problem in Italy. Until recently, Mutolo said, "it was totally understood within Cosa Nostra that we should give our electoral support to the DC [Democrazia Cristiana], which was considered to be the party that could best protect the organization's interests."

This relationship became strained by the maxi-trial of Palermo. As Antonino Calderone had correctly intuited, the Supreme Court's decision upholding the convictions in the case had been the pivotal event that had triggered the recent explosion of political violence. But while Calderone was making logical leaps based on his past experience, Mutolo was privy to the thinking of several members of the Commission with whom he had been in prison until the spring of 1992.

"When the trial began, it was obvious to all 'men of honor' that it was a 'political' trial, whose outcome would be decided by the government in Rome," Mutolo explained. "We all unanimously believed that the trial verdict would invariably be a conviction, because the government had to demonstrate to public opinion—within Italy and abroad . . . that it could strike a hard blow to Cosa Nostra." But after the initial guilty verdicts in 1987 the organization assured its men that, with the help of its political friends, the sentence would be quietly modified on appeal, when public attention was distracted. To make sure this happened, Cosa Nostra sent a precise warning to the Christian Democrats by abandoning them for the Socialists in the elections of 1987. Cosa Nostra was greatly reassured by the events between 1988 and 1991.

Especially encouraging was the Court of Appeals decision in the maxi-trial, which overturned some of the convictions and questioned the Buscetta theorem, which would allow the court to hold the Commission of Cosa Nostra for its most important crimes. The scene appeared to have been set for Judge Corrado Carnevale, who Mutolo described as "the greatest guarantee for Cosa Nostra," to overturn the case. "There was the mathematical certainty within Cosa Nostra, based on assurances from our lawyers, that the Supreme Court would overturn the original court decision engineered by Falcone," he explained. "This would have produced a double result: of . . . freeing the defendants and, finally, demolishing the professional reputation of Giovanni Falcone, who would have appeared to have been a 'persecutor' of innocent victims. This would have represented the ultimate triumph of Cosa Nostra over him."

Falcone's death, Mutolo said, had already been decided back in the early 1980s, but his defeat in the courts might have delayed an execution of the sentence indefinitely. "The climate surrounding Falcone alternated, the danger relaxing or increasing, depending on the course of the maxi-trial in its various phases," he explained. "The climate relaxed with the end of the anti-mafia pool in the investigative office and the introduction of the new Italian penal code, considered more favorable to Cosa Nostra and, finally, with the transfer of Falcone to Rome."

The organization had underestimated the importance of Falcone's presence at the Ministry of Justice. "He was now considered less dangerous for the organization," Mutolo said. "I remember, in fact, that we used to joke that he would end up as the ambassador to some South American country. . . . Gradually, we began to understand that Doctor Falcone was becoming even more dangerous in Rome than he had been in Palermo. We understood that the position of Director General of [Penal Affairs] of the [Justice] Ministry—which no one had even heard of before— had been transformed in Falcone's hands into a powerful instrument against Cosa Nostra. It was obvious that the various government decrees of Ministers Martelli and Scotti were inspired by Falcone." In prison at Spoleto, Mutolo had a chance to speak with Giuseppe Giacomo Gambino, his *capo-mandamento* (district leader) and a member of the Commission, who had suddenly become pessimistic. "He told me that everything was going to go badly, contrary to what we had all believed until recently. . . . In fact, Gambino said that President Carnevale, who constituted our greatest guarantee, was forced to step down from the maxi-trial . . . above all because of the pressures of Doctor Falcone who, with the support of Minister Martelli, wanted to save 'his' case."

When this prediction came true, its effects on Cosa Nostra were devastating. "The sentence in the maxi-trial was a real blow, not simply because it made so many convictions definitive, but above all because it represented an historic defeat of Cosa Nostra, whose existence and internal structure were—for the first time—identified, recognized and punished. . . . This unexpected reversal of the Supreme Court was attributed with total certainty by Cosa Nostra to the intervention of Giovanni Falcone . . . the 'time of guarantees' had ended."

The court's sentence in the maxi-trial was as much a disaster for the leadership outside prison as for the bosses in it. The verdict represented the ultimate failure of the military-minded strategy of Totò Riina and the Corleonesi. Riina had gambled everything on the belief that in a head-to-head confrontation with the state he could intimidate the government into annulling the verdict at the last moment. Hundreds of *mafiosi,* including many of Cosa Nostra's most powerful figures, had sat patiently in prison waiting for the decision to be reversed. Now that all hope was lost, and many *mafiosi* were unlikely ever to see the outside of a prison again, they realized that Riina's strategy had backfired disastrously. Cosa Nostra's relentless violence had alienated public opinion to such a point that the government had no choice but to adopt extraordinary measures—including the transfer of Carnevale—to ensure a conviction in the maxi-trial. The angry reaction to the sentence created serious internal problems for Riina, who had to do something dramatic to stem a possible rebellion in his ranks. Rather than back down, Riina had no choice but to step up the violence severalfold, showing that he was prepared to risk all-out war with the state in order to avenge the life sentences of his friends in prison.

"It was time for a new strategy, a strategy of frontal conflict," Mutolo said. "The phrase you heard was: 'Ora ci rumpemu i corna a tutti' (Now we are going to break all their heads)."

Although Mutolo was not informed about which specific targets Cosa Nostra was going to strike, he knew something very big was in preparation in early 1992. "At this point, something very strange happened for someone who knows the mentality of the members of Cosa Nostra," Mutolo said. "Various men of honor, fugitives, some of them facing rather heavy sentences, spontaneously and, of their own free will, turned themselves in to police. This was strange because, as is well known, a member of Cosa Nostra never turns himself in voluntarily, even if he only has to serve a month in jail." While this signal had escaped outside observers it had a precise meaning to those who knew how to read the writing on the wall. "Within Cosa Nostra something very serious had occurred and all men of honor were placed in the position of deciding freely to turn themselves in or to stay out—with the clear risk that they might be implicated in what was about to happen."

The murder of Salvatore Lima was the first response to the Supreme Court decision. "*Onorevole* Lima was killed because he was the greatest symbol of that part of the political world which, after having adopted a policy of peaceful coexistence with the mafia, doing favors for Cosa Nostra in exchange for its votes, was no longer able to protect the interests of the organization at the time of its most important trial, and, in fact, had tried to change direction," Mutolo testified. Although men of honor in prison spoke as little as possible for fear their conversations might be bugged, several bosses of the Commission (Giuseppe Calò, Salvatore Montalto and Giuseppe Giacomo Gambino) managed to communicate their clear satisfaction that the mafia had begun to pay back the politicians who had turned against them, Mutolo testified. "More explicitly, on one occasion when I met Montalto in the corridor, he exclaimed, with obvious satisfaction, 'Accuminciaru finalmente!' (Finally, they've started!)"

At the same time, Leonardo Messina, the other major new witness, confirmed Mutolo's testimony about Lima and the maxi-trial while adding new details about Supreme Court Judge Corrado Carnevale, the "sentence-killer." "Everyone assured us that the trial would be assigned to the First Section and its president, Carnevale, who was a guarantee for us, and certainly not only because of his ideas of jurisprudence: the word was that he was 'malleable.' . . . As for the killings of Falcone and Borsellino, without doubt the result of the maxi-trial played a determining role. . . . A reaction was absolutely necessary to improve morale and to reassert the power of Cosa Nostra. That reaction had to be against the magistrates who had handled the case and against the politicians who had failed to guarantee the positive outcome of the trial and had allowed Carnevale to be removed from the case and had even passed a series of laws that affected the defendants in the maxi-trial. There was widespread resentment toward the Andreotti faction of the Christian Democracy and the Craxi group with the Socialist Party, who had allowed themselves to be influenced by younger, emerging figures within their parties, like Minister of Justice Martelli."[15]

In early September, a member of Totò Riina's inner circle, Giuseppe Marchese, decided to cooperate with the government. One of a new generation of recruits whose membership was kept secret within Cosa Nostra, Marchese had been a personal protégé of Riina's. Marchese became a member of Riina's family when his sister married Leoluca Bagarella, Riina's brother-in-law. Riina liked to repeat that the young Marchese, nephew of boss Filippo Marchese, was "in his heart." While still a teenager, Giuseppe Marchese had participated in the notorious Christmas Massacre of Bagheria in December of 1981. By the time of Borsellino's death, Marchese had already spent ten of his twenty-eight years in prison and, thanks to Riina, he was likely to remain there forever. In 1989, Marchese had dutifully obeyed Riina's orders by bashing in the brains of his cellmate, Vincenzo Puccio, the mafia boss who wanted to rebel against the Corleonesi; but Riina had made a mockery of Marchese's claim of self-defense by having Puccio's brother murdered on the same day. Cosa Nostra had even prevented Marchese from marrying his fiancée. Because the girl's father had left his wife and was living with another woman, the marriage would be "dishonorable." The only way Marchese could marry the girl would be to kill her father first, the young *mafioso* was told by both his brother and his brother-in-law, Leoluca Bagarella. At a certain point, they indicated that if he didn't kill

the man, they would do the job themselves. "As a result," Marchese testified, "the only way for me to avoid [his] being killed was
for me to break off the engagement with the girl I loved, pretending that I no longer cared for her. This decision, naturally, was
very painful and my relationship with my brother and with
Bagarella were no longer the same." Now, even if Giuseppe
Marchese should ever be released, he no longer had anyone waiting for him on the outside. He decided to collaborate because he
realized that Riina had simply used him and thrown him away.
"To Riina we are just dead meat," he said.[16]

With his close ties to the Corleonesi, Marchese knew quite a bit
about the mafia's ties to numerous public officials. He also added
an important detail to the investigation of the murder of Salvatore
Lima; Giuseppe Madonia, the son of Commission member
Francesco Madonia (and one of the killers of Captain Emanuele
Basile), told him that Lima had been given very strict orders to fix
the maxi-trial—or else. "Madonia told me that they had told him:
'stick to your promise or we'll kill you and your family.' "

Together with past testimony, the prosecutors were now in a
strong position to demonstrate that Salvatore Lima was indeed the
mafia's "ambassador" in Rome. After questioning Marchese in
early September, prosecutors in Palermo flew to the United States
to meet with Tommaso Buscetta. Moved by the deaths of Falcone
and Borsellino, and acknowledging the new climate in Italy,
Buscetta decided to break his long silence on the politics of Cosa
Nostra. With his knowledge of the mafia stretching back to the
1940s, Buscetta revealed that Salvatore Lima's father had himself
been a man of honor and that Buscetta himself had had extensive
contacts with Salvatore Lima since the early 1960s when Lima
was mayor of Palermo. "Salvo Lima was in fact the politician to
whom Cosa Nostra turned most often to resolve problems for the
organization whose solution lay in Rome," he testified. As Falcone had suspected, Lima was indeed the member of parliament
Buscetta had met in a Rome hotel in 1980. "Lima himself asked
for the meeting through Nino Salvo," Buscetta said. "In the course
of the meeting, [Lima] spoke to me about politics in Palermo. . . .
In that period, Lima was especially close to Stefano Bontate and
was politically at odds with Vito Ciancimino, who was tied to
Totò Riina and the Corleonesi." Thus the divisions within Cosa

Nostra corresponded to divisions in the political world. Lima and the Salvo cousins, in fact, wanted to convince Buscetta to remain in Palermo in order to reinforce Stefano Bontate and the moderate faction within the mafia.[17]

As with everything else in Cosa Nostra, the balance of power between mafia and politics had changed during the past fifteen years. Under the reign of the "moderate" bosses of Cosa Nostra, the relationship was one of compromise and negotiation. But as the mafia got richer and more powerful through the drug trade, the new leaders became more demanding and confrontational. At the same time, the increased public awareness of the mafia problem had made it more difficult for politicians to maintain relations with and perform favors for mafia members. After the killing of Bontate, Lima and the Salvo cousins had no choice but to adapt themselves to the new hegemony of the Corleonesi. "Lima became the prisoner of a system," said Leonardo Messina. "Before this latest generation, being a friend of *mafiosi* was easy for everybody. . . . It was a great honor for a *mafioso* to have a member of parliament at a wedding or a baptism. . . . When a *mafioso* saw a parliamentarian he would take off his hat and offer him his seat. . . . Now, it has become an imposition: do this or else."[18]

The escalation of the drug trade and the constant killings sponsored by the Corleonesi put more and more pressure on the government to get tough on the mafia and boxed men like Lima more and more into a corner. The ultimate test was the Supreme Court's verdict of the maxi-trial, and when Lima was unable to deliver, he had to be killed—effectively putting an end to the unholy alliance between part of the Christian Democratic Party in Sicily and the mafia that had started at the time of the elections of 1948.

The new round of witnesses allowed prosecutors to solve another crime that had perplexed investigators. On September 8, 1992, mafia killers had assassinated Ignazio Salvo, the wealthy Sicilian businessman convicted at the maxi-trial of belonging to the mafia. Salvo was said to be the go-between Cosa Nostra used for contacting Salvatore Lima and other politicians. The Salvo and Lima killings—together with the assassinations of Falcone and Borsellino—were part of the same strategy. Cosa Nostra had killed those it blamed for the verdict of the maxi-trial: the two enemies who brought the case, the two political friends who were supposed to have it overturned on appeal.

When the Procura della Repubblica of Palermo indicted twenty-four people in October 1992 for the murder of Salvatore Lima, it made a deep impression on public opinion for various reasons. Although none of the defendants was a politician, never before had a criminal indictment treated the problem of political collusion with such frankness. By revealing the cooperation of so many important new witnesses, the indictment showed that the war against the mafia, rather than being stopped by the murders of Falcone and Borsellino, was moving ahead at full speed. After the resignation of Giammanco, the prosecutors of Palermo had recovered a sense of unity and were working together to great effect. It was clear that the mafia was in trouble, hemorrhaging badly. By late 1992, the government had more than two hundred mafia witnesses—a veritable exodus from the principal criminal organizations.[19]

N ot surprisingly, the Lima indictment was a massive blow to the prestige of former prime minister Giulio Andreotti and the Christian Democratic Party. Andreotti retreated into semiretirement as a "senator for life"—in Italy a certain number of elder statesmen are given permanent seats in the parliament's upper house. Rumors began to circulate that he might be implicated in the mafia collusion scandal. Moreover, the Christian Democrats were becoming almost as battered as the Socialists by the ever-expanding bribery investigation, Operation Clean Hands.

The treasurer of the DC, Senator Severino Citaristi, was well on his way to becoming the record holder for most indictments in the scandal—as analogous cases sprang up in every corner of Italy. On September 31, 1992, virtually the entire government of the Abruzzi—the region of Italy east of Rome—was arrested on charges of misappropriating some 436 billion lire ($350 million at the time) in European Community funds.[20] On October 1, the mayor and six city council members of the northern town of Vercelli were dragged off to jail through a cheering crowd yelling "Thieves! Thieves!"[21] Throughout Italy, Antonio Di Pietro, the leading magistrate of the Milan bribery case, had become a national hero. "Di Pietro" T-shirts were selling like hotcakes and anticorruption graffiti proliferated on walls across the country: FORZA DI PIETRO! (Go, Di Pietro!) GRAZIE, DI PIETRO! (Thank you, Di Pietro!). The investigation had entered an incandescent phase that many compared to the early stages of the French Revolution.

In late November, Salvatore Ligresti—a wealthy businessman close to Craxi—admitted having made payments amounting to 16 billion lire (about $13 million) to the Socialists and the Christian Democrats. A growing chorus of important leaders within the Socialist Party—including Justice Minister Claudio Martelli—called on Bettino Craxi to step down as party leader. Soon afterward, the long-awaited indictment of Craxi arrived: the magistrates in Milan accused him of forty episodes of corruption or illegal campaign financing for a total of 36 billion lire (about $30 million). Although he continued attacking his enemies with the fury of a cornered animal, it was clear that Craxi's fifteen-year reign was coming to an end.[22]

The bribery cases in northern Italy and the mafia investigations in the South moved forward relentlessly like the pincer movement of an army surrounding and attacking the same enemy from two directions. On December 1, news leaked out that Judge Domenico Signorino and four other Palermo magistrates were under investigation for collusion.[23] Two days later, an even more stunning development: the most powerful political leaders of Reggio Calabria—including two former mayors and a member of parliament—were accused of ordering the mafia killing of another leading Calabrian politician. According to the indictment, the murdered man was killed not because he opposed city corruption, but because he wanted a cut of the bribes being pocketed on over $1 billion in public contracts. In Calabria, political corruption and organized crime appeared to have come together in a new lethal apotheosis: political bosses killing other politicians, acting like chiefs of mafia clans.[24]

On Christmas Eve 1992, Italian police arrested Bruno Contrada, the former Palermo police investigator and secret service agent, whom Buscetta had warned Falcone about in 1984.[25] Gaspare Mutolo had told Borsellino about Contrada just three days before the bomb of Via D'Amelio. Now Giuseppe Marchese revealed three specific incidents in which Contrada had allegedly tipped off mafia bosses about imminent police raids. In one case, Marchese said that Contrada had prevented the arrest of Totò Riina himself. "The first time I heard Contrada's name was in 1981. . . . My uncle Filippo [Marchese] told me to go immediately to see Salvatore Riina, because Doctor Contrada had informed us that the police had figured out where Riina lived and were planning on conducting a raid the following morning. . . . I went right away to Riina . . . who immediately grabbed a few clothes and got into a white Mercedes with his family."[26]

Then, on January 15, 1993, came the ultimate breakthrough: *carabinieri* in Palermo arrested Totò Riina, as he was riding unarmed in a plain Citroën sedan through downtown Palermo—exactly where he had been for most of the last twenty-three years during his life as a fugitive. Only six months after the devastating bombs of Capaci and Via D'Amelio the war against the mafia seemed to crystallize in a new and very different image: the short, paunchy, sixty-three-year-old Riina, his head lowered and his hands cuffed together, posing for a police photographer. Visible on the back wall was a photograph of General Carlo Alberto Dalla Chiesa, who had been assassinated with Riina's blessing ten years earlier. Finally, the tables had turned.[27]

There was a sense of shock, disbelief, even disappointment when the photographs of Riina under arrest were released to the public. With his inexpensive, ill-fitting clothes, crudely cut short hair and thick, stubby fingers, Riina looked like what his false identity card said he was: a Sicilian farmhand on a visit to the big city. The man known as *la belva* (the Beast) was a model of soft-spoken, old-world courtesy; insisting he was simply "a poor, sick old man" who knew nothing about Cosa Nostra, he addressed police deferentially and stood up whenever they entered the room. Could this be, people began to wonder aloud, the man who had pulled the strings of the world's dominant criminal organization? But, despite his respectful air, Riina showed an acute interest in the thing he understood best: power. "He was clearly trying to figure what everyone's rank was," said Colonel Mario Mori, the officer overseeing the operation. "He wanted to know whether I was really in command or whether there was someone over me."[28]

Riina seemed an anomalous, almost impossible figure in the Europe of Maastricht, bullet trains and the GATT treaty, like the

Japanese soldiers who supposedly emerged from the Philippine jungles of Asia in the 1960s believing that World War II was still on. Riina's capture was a sign that Italy, slowly and painfully, was changing. "With the arrest of Riina, Italy enters Europe," one commentator wrote.[29]

Gradually, the details of Riina's capture began to emerge.

On January 8, 1993, a Sicilian criminal named Baldassare Di Maggio was arrested in the northern city of Novara. Although he faced only minor charges, Di Maggio immediately admitted that he was a man of honor and told police that he could help them find Riina. Di Maggio was typical of the new generation of *mafiosi* who had become disillusioned with the domination of the Corleonesi. He had risen within the organization by committing countless murders for Riina and for the mafia of San Giuseppe Jato, a town between Palermo and Corleone, whose bosses were among Totò Riina's closest allies. When the *capo-famiglia,* Bernardo Brusca, a member of the Commission, and his son, Giovanni, went to prison, Di Maggio became acting head of the family. But after Giovanni Brusca was released, Di Maggio became an uncomfortable presence that needed to be eliminated. Riina held a meeting whose apparent purpose was to make peace between Di Maggio and the Brusca family, but Di Maggio saw through this theatrical production. While siding with the Bruscas, Riina had gone overboard to reassure Di Maggio: "Balduccio non e' un'arancia buttata via!" (Balduccio is not some used orange to be thrown away!) the boss had said in his folksy Sicilian idiom. But Di Maggio had seen him order enough killings to know that Riina was the most dangerous when he was soft-spoken and honey-tongued. Di Maggio fled Sicily for his life and when police caught up with him in Novara, he was ready to talk.[30]

Di Maggio was brought to Palermo, where a special team of *carabinieri* had been formed whose exclusive purpose was to capture Riina. They had shot thousands of hours of videotape of people they believed to make up the boss of bosses' inner circle. "That's Riina's driver!" Di Maggio exclaimed, viewing the film. Along with helping to locate Riina, Di Maggio helped police dismantle the whole protective structure the boss had created around himself in Palermo, identifying a highly secret group of apparently respectable citizens most of whom had eluded the attention of the police in the past.[31]

The incredible string of successes that culminated in Riina's capture raised an uncomfortable question: why couldn't this have been done years ago? "They arrested Riina because they *decided* to," said Giuseppe Di Lello, Falcone and Borsellino's old colleague from the original anti-mafia pool. After all, Riina was captured in the center of Palermo, where he had evidently been living for years.[32]

TWENTY-THREE

A fter the arrest of Totò Riina, the tangle of collusion between mafia and politics began to unravel with even greater
rapidity. Heartened by the sense that the government was finally
serious about the war against the mafia, witnesses cast off any
residual reticence about discussing Cosa Nostra's political ties. In
the fall of 1992, Gaspare Mutolo and Tommaso Buscetta, while
implicating Salvatore Lima, preferred not to answer when asked if
they knew who in the government Lima contacted when he
needed favors done for his friends in Cosa Nostra. Only Leonardo
Messina had said openly, "*Onorevole* Lima . . . acted as the liaison with *Onorevole* Andreotti for the needs of the Sicilian
mafia."[1]

In March 1993, after Totò Riina had made his first rather menacing appearance in court—broadcast on national television—
Mutolo changed his mind. "I am convinced that we are going
through a very dangerous period and that . . . politicians tied to
Cosa Nostra will try to do everything possible to block the effective actions that the magistrature, with the help of witnesses, has
undertaken in these last months," he said. "I have realized, therefore, that I must put aside once and for all any fears that . . . have
kept me from revealing everything I know on this subject, starting
with the most important problem . . . Cosa Nostra's most power-

ful political ally: Senator Giulio Andreotti." Mutolo recounted a meeting in 1981 at which Rosario Riccobono, the boss of his family, asked Ignazio Salvo to use his influence to fix a trial. "Ignazio Salvo said he would talk to *Onorevole* Salvo Lima, who would discuss it personally with Senator Andreotti. . . . After the killing of Stefano Bontate . . . the 'normal circuit' for all problems that needed attention in Rome was: Ignazio Salvo, *Onorevole* Salvo Lima and Senator Giulio Andreotti."[2]

In order to investigate these charges, prosecutors in Palermo had to draft a detailed request asking the Italian parliament to waive Andreotti's immunity. The lengthy document—laying out all the preliminary evidence against Andreotti and the members of his political faction in Sicily—became a political bombshell the moment it was filed. Although Andreotti's alleged ties to Cosa Nostra had been the subject of gossip, speculation and even public political protest for nearly two decades, no government document had ever leveled such serious charges.

Only a few days later, even more shocking revelations surfaced after prosecutors traveled to the United States to question Francesco Marino Mannoia, who was in the American witness protection program. Marino Mannoia provided the first eyewitness testimony tying Andreotti directly to bosses of the mafia. He described a high-level summit in 1980 with the bosses Salvatore Inzerillo and Stefano Bontate at which Andreotti allegedly arrived with Lima in a bulletproof Alfa Romeo belonging to the Salvo cousins. Although Marino Mannoia did not participate in the private discussions, his boss, Stefano Bontate, later described the contents of the meeting to him. Andreotti had supposedly come to protest the recent killing of the Sicilian president of the Democrazia Christiana (DC), Piersanti Mattarella, murdered on January 6, 1980, to which Bontate responded: "We're in charge here in Sicily and if you don't want to destroy the DC you will do what we say. Otherwise we will take away our votes not just here but . . . in the whole of southern Italy. Then you will be left with only the vote in the North, where everyone votes Communist."[3]

On the same trip to the United States, the team of prosecutors also met with Tommaso Buscetta, who made perhaps the most devastating accusation of all: that Andreotti had commissioned a mafia murder. The victim was Carmine "Mino" Pecorelli, a blackmailing journalist who had been shot to death in Rome in March of 1979. "The Pecorelli murder was a political crime commissioned by the Salvo cousins, at the request of *Onorevole* Andreotti," Buscetta told Giancarlo Caselli, the chief prosecutor of Palermo in April 1993. Buscetta's sources were Stefano Bontate and Gaetano Badalamenti, who indicated that they had helped plan the killing themselves. Badalamenti had also told Buscetta that he had met personally with Andreotti in the former prime minister's private office in Rome in order to ask him to help his brother-in-law, Filippo Rimi—whose conviction on mafia charges was later overturned.[4]

When Caselli and his assistant prosecutors returned to Italy, still another bombshell awaited them. Baldassare Di Maggio, the *mafioso* who had helped capture Totò Riina, claimed to have been present at a second mafia summit with Andreotti in 1987 during the maxi-trial of Palermo. "Salvatore Riina asked me to go see [Ignazio] Salvo—in order to get him to contact Salvatore Lima to arrange a meeting about the maxi-trial with our 'mutual friend.' The name of the 'mutual friend' was *Onorevole* Giulio Andreotti." Told to dress in his best clothes, Di Maggio was part of the entourage that drove with Riina to the meeting at the apartment of Ignazio Salvo. "On our arrival I recognized among the people present, without a shadow of doubt, Giulio Andreotti and Salvo Lima, who stood up and greeted us. . . . I shook the hands of the two parliamentarians and I kissed Ignazio Salvo. . . . Riina greeted all three men, Andreotti, Lima and Salvo, with a kiss. . . ."[5]

Andreotti dismissed the charges against him as "lies and slanders . . . the kiss of Riina, mafia summits . . . scenes out of a comic horror film." He insisted that the attacks against him were a vendetta for his government's tough stance against Cosa Nostra. "There is something monstrous and paradoxical that I, the prime minister whose government dealt the most decisive blows against organized crime, should be portrayed as a friend of the mafia. . . . I am embittered but not surprised."[6]

This latest revelation went beyond the wildest imaginings of all but the most conspiratorially minded Italians. For those who saw Andreotti as the occult hand behind all the unsolved crimes of recent Italian history this was the smoking gun they had been waiting for. To others—even some of Andreotti's harshest critics—it seemed inconceivable that a man of his unquestionable intelligence would expose himself by becoming personally involved with bosses of the mafia. It was difficult to imagine a man who had moved among the great historical figures of the late twentieth century—from De Gaulle, Eisenhower and Adenauer to Reagan, Thatcher and Gorbachev—meeting secretly with gangsters and killers. It was equally hard to envision a man of Andreotti's stiff and glacial reserve exchanging kisses with Totò Riina, "the Beast."

The charges against Andreotti cannot, however, be dismissed out of hand.

Even the most incredible accusation of all—that Andreotti commissioned the murder of journalist Mino Pecorelli—is not quite as implausible as it might seem. At the very least, the Pecorelli case paints an extremely disturbing portrait of the rampant illegality of life within the Andreotti faction.

Editor of a scandal sheet called *OP,* Pecorelli made money through the art of political blackmail, threatening to print damaging revelations about Italy's corrupt ruling elite. His articles hinted tantalizingly at explosive information to come in future issues, sending veiled messages to the interested parties. In some cases he would actually print a dummy copy of a journalistic scoop that he would then withdraw for a price. Although he was a phony journalist, Pecorelli's information was real enough. A member of Licio Gelli's mysterious P2 Masonic Lodge, Pecorelli had numerous sources in the Italian secret services and many people used his magazine to leak classified documents, plant damaging stories and settle scores with their political opponents. When he was killed in March 1979, it was clear that Pecorelli had finally gone too far and that someone—almost certainly in the political world—had decided to silence him once and for all. But, not surprisingly, the Pecorelli murder investigation went nowhere. It was being handled by the Procura of Rome, that black hole that so many political inquiries entered and from which so little light emerged.

The investigation began to open up in November 1992, when Tommaso Buscetta told prosecutors that Stefano Bontate had told him in 1980, "We did the Pecorelli killing because the Salvo cousins asked us to." In a later conversation with Buscetta, Gaetano Badalamenti allegedly confirmed Bontate's claim. In April 1993, Buscetta added a new detail to his account: Badalamenti had told him that "Andreotti was worried because the journalist was pulling out a lot of dirt on him; that the journalist had let Andreotti know about it and Andreotti was afraid that if they were made public they would damage him politically."[7]

In late 1992 and early 1993, prosecutors gathered evidence that is consistent with the scenario Buscetta outlined. Shortly before his death in March 1979, Pecorelli had prepared a cover story entitled "All the President's Checks" on Andreotti's involvement in a major bribery scandal. In early 1979, Pecorelli met with Andreotti's "legal adviser," Claudio Vitalone, at a Rome restaurant and the cover story on Andreotti was withdrawn. (It should be pointed out that at the time Vitalone was a prosecutor in the Procura of Rome—the office that was supposed to investigate political corruption in Rome and would later be assigned the Pecorelli killing itself.) Although Vitalone admits to meeting Pecorelli he denies negotiating any blackmail payment. He is contradicted flatly by Andreotti's right-hand man at the time, Franco Evangelisti, who testified under oath that he paid 30 million lire (about $42,000 at the time) to get Pecorelli to suppress the cover story on Andreotti. "*Onorevole* Evangelisti personally brought the 30 million lire in cash to the typographer's office where *OP* was printed," prosecutors in Rome wrote in June 1993. "Evangelisti says he got the money from Gaetano Caltagirone, who told him that he himself had already paid Pecorelli another 15 million lire."

Evangelisti and Caltagirone were already notorious for having performed much of the dirty work for the Andreotti faction over the years. Evangelisti, a member of parliament, was discovered to have met with Michele Sindona in 1978, when the Sicilian banker was a fugitive from Italian justice. Gaetano Caltagirone made large illegal campaign contributions to the Andreotti faction, while, in turn, receiving massive loans from Italcasse, a government-owned bank.[8]

At the time of Pecorelli's death, police found the following note among the journalist's personal papers: "It's a bombshell! The Italcasse scandal is not over. It's just begun. At the beginning of the year it will come out who took the checks." Pecorelli's information proved extremely reliable. In early 1980, Caltagirone's financial empire went bankrupt, leaving Italcasse (and the Italian taxpayer) with more than $200 million in bad loans.[9] Then, in a famous interview in 1980, Evangelisti openly admitted having repeatedly taken large under-the-table campaign contributions from Caltagirone. "We've known one another twenty years and every time we saw one another he would ask me: 'Franco, how much do you need?' " Evangelisti told the journalist Paolo Guzzanti with characteristically disarming candor. "Who imagined any scandal? Who ever thought there was any harm?" When asked what the money was for, Evangelisti replied: "To finance our 'faction.' To finance my election campaign, to finance the party."[10]

Even though the Italian parliament had passed a stringent campaign finance law in 1977, Caltagirone's illegal campaign contributions were never prosecuted. Evangelisti was minister of the merchant marine at the time, and while he was forced to resign his cabinet post, he kept his seat in parliament and remained Andreotti's chief of staff.

Pecorelli's story "All the President's Checks" was the natural parallel to the Caltagirone affair. Once again, hundreds of millions of dollars were pumped out of Italcasse in bad loans to a shadowy company called SIR—a portion of which found their way back to the coffers of Andreotti's political machine. SIR issued a series of bank checks to various nonexistent people, which were in fact cashed by some of Andreotti's closest aides (Evangelisti, Giuseppe Ciarrapico). As with Caltagirone, SIR went belly-up, leaving Italian public banks to swallow a debt of 218 billion lire (about $310 million in 1979 dollars). "It has been shown that some 1.4 billion lire (about $2 million) in bank checks issued by SIR were placed at Senator Andreotti's disposal," prosecutors in Rome wrote in their indictment of June 1993.[11]

Another of Andreotti's political operatives, Ezio Radaelli, has admitted having received 170,000,000 lire (about $240,000) in the illegal bank checks from SIR directly from Andreotti in order to organize campaign rallies. Moreover, Radaelli has testified that, on two different occasions, he was pressured not to mention Andreotti's name to prosecutors investigating the scandal. Even the man doing the pressuring has admitted the charge. "In effect, I did ask Radaelli—on President Andreotti's request—not to mention his name in relation to the business of the checks," Carlo Zaccaria, an aide-de-camp of Andreotti, told prosecutors recently.

In typical fashion, Andreotti has tried to brush off his relations with Pecorelli with a humorous anecdote, which revealed, none-theless, that he was fully aware of Pecorelli's threats. *"Onorevole* Evangelisti told me that Pecorelli intended to publish an article against me about certain checks. . . . I gave no weight to the matter, also because of the reputation of the magazine *OP*. Evangelisti told me that he had found Pecorelli devastated by terrible headaches from which he suffered periodically and which—perhaps jokingly—he attributed to the toughness of some of his journalistic attacks. Because I, too, have suffered from migraine for many years, I sent him a medicine I have found to be very helpful, with a note wishing him every relief." While Andreotti has insisted he was much too busy to be bothered with the financing of his faction, his anecdote shows him intimately involved with its most minute aspects. His concern for Pecorelli's migraine also demonstrates his legendary attention to detail and his exquisite sense of irony: sending headache medicine to a political enemy who was creating a political migraine for Andreotti.

Despite Andreotti's repeated denials, preliminary evidence makes it quite clear that he was a knowing player in a scheme of illegal campaign financing, suborning perjury and the paying of hush money to a blackmailer. But this does not, of course, prove that he commissioned the murder of Pecorelli. There is, however, another side to the SIR check scandal, which leads back to the world of organized crime. "Some of these checks, for a total of 55 million lire ($70,000), were cashed by a company controlled by the financier Ley Ravello and Domenico Balducci; the latter—murdered in 1982—was a member of the so-called Magliana Gang," prosecutors in Rome wrote in the Andreotti indictment of June 1993. The Magliana Gang was one of Rome's principal criminal organizations during the 1970s and 1980s, and Domenico Balducci was one of its leaders. He was also a business partner and close friend of Giuseppe "Pippo" Calò, the boss of Buscetta's mafia family, who lived (in wealth and style) as a fugitive in Rome until his arrest in 1985. (Indeed, Balducci was one of the people Buscetta met when he skipped parole in 1980 and spent several weeks living with Calò in his Rome hideout.) Police investigators believe that the Magliana Gang was a satellite of Cosa Nostra, distributing drugs, laundering money and even performing murders for the mafia on mainland Italy. Members of the Roman gang (along with right-wing terrorists) helped carry out the terrorist bombing of train 904 in December 1984—a crime Pippo Calò has been convicted of organizing as a diversionary tactic in response to the revelations of Buscetta earlier that fall. The proven financial and criminal links between Calò and Balducci, and between Balducci and the SIR-Italcasse scandal—create the distinct possibility that Calò—known as "the treasurer" of the mafia—may have been using SIR and Italcasse to launder Cosa Nostra's drug profits. This is much more than a fanciful hypothesis: one of the many bank checks issued by SIR had been found in the pocket of Giuseppe Di Cristina, the mafia boss of Riesi, when he was killed in the streets of Palermo in 1978. It was one of the checks that Giovanni Falcone used in his first big mafia case to reconstruct the Spatola-Inzerillo heroin and money-laundering ring. A year after his death, it was more clear than ever how true Falcone's aim and how sound his intuitions had been.

If SIR was being used both to launder money for the mafia and to make under-the-table political contributions, many powerful interests were in danger when Pecorelli began threatening to blow the lid off the scandal. The bosses of the mafia and of the political class would both have had reasons for wanting to get rid of Pecorelli—the kind of convergence of interests that seems to result in excellent cadavers.

Buscetta dismissed the possibility that the mafia would have acted alone in a delicate case of this kind. "The Salvo cousins would never have commissioned a political crime with such unpredictable consequences without first consulting the interested party," he said in a deposition of June 2, 1993.

While this scenario provided Andreotti with a strong motive for eliminating Pecorelli, ultimately the case against the former prime minister depends on proving a solid link between Andreotti and the bosses of Cosa Nostra.

Andreotti and many of his chief supporters insist that he is the victim of a carefully orchestrated conspiracy. They find it suspicious that new accusations against the former prime minister seem to emerge with each round of depositions, that witnesses who never mentioned his name before have suddenly stepped forward with devastating charges. They see the Andreotti case as part of the strategy to destroy the Christian Democratic Party by its many political opponents in its time of greatest crisis. Although Andreotti was careful not to be too specific about who was behind the conspiracy, the remaining lieutenants of his now tattered army have offered several theories.

The most popular one is that Cosa Nostra has planted false witnesses in order to punish Andreotti for his stalwart efforts against the mafia. But this notion does not bear up under close scrutiny. While Andreotti's seventh government (1991–92) made a major contribution to the war against the mafia, he had never distinguished himself in this vein during the previous forty-five years of his career—something that is consistent with the mafia witnesses' testimony that the Lima killing was a retaliation for Andreotti's sudden reversal in crime policy. Furthermore, a mafia conspiracy to get Andreotti would be a near practical impossibility. The various mafia witnesses accusing Andreotti were held in different secret locations—some in different countries—and have little or no opportunity to contact one another. Recent witnesses like Messina, Marchese and Di Maggio were from a different generation and did not know older *mafiosi* like Buscetta, Contorno, Calderone, Marino Mannoia and Mutolo. Most importantly, why would men who broke with the mafia ten years ago, whose families have been hunted down and killed and who had, in return, dealt devastating blows to Cosa Nostra, suddenly lend themselves to a mafia plot to destroy Andreotti?

The other leading theory is that the witnesses are being manipulated into attacking Andreotti by Giancarlo Caselli, the new chief prosecutor of Palermo, in order to fulfill a left-wing political agenda. Quite aside from the fact that Caselli has a long record of unblemished professional integrity, this theory has many problems. Caselli does not work alone. The case against Andreotti was developed together with several other magistrates who can hardly be accused of being left-wing zealots: many worked in the Procura of Palermo when the office was accused of being soft on the Andreotti faction of the Christian Democracy in Sicily. In fact, the outlines of the Andreotti case were already present in the indictment in the murder of Salvatore Lima that was drawn up in October 1992, three months before Caselli arrived in Palermo. Moreover, the prosecutors hardly have exclusive control over the mafia witnesses, who are in the primary custody of police agents who are responsible for their protection and are present at all depositions. A conspiracy against Andreotti would require the participation of at least three different Italian branches of the Italian police—not to mention agents of the U.S. Marshals Service, the FBI and the Drug Enforcement Agency who watch over Buscetta and Marino Mannoia in the United States.

The gradual escalation of accusations against Andreotti can be explained by the witnesses' well-articulated fear of tackling the problem of mafia and politics. As Buscetta repeated often to Giovanni Falcone: "It would be foolish for us to touch this subject, which is the crucial knot of the mafia, when many of the people of whom I would have to speak have not left the active political scene." Privately, Buscetta had mentioned Andreotti to U.S. prosecutor Richard Martin back in 1985.[12]

If there is no organized conspiracy against Andreotti, then the testimony of the witnesses must be examined carefully, one by one.

While witnesses like Leonardo Messina, Gaspare Mutolo and Tommaso Buscetta have an excellent track record for reliability, they are repeating things told to them by others. They insist that "men of honor" never lie when discussing mafia business, but one would not want to convict a former prime minister on blind faith in the inviolability of the mafia's code of honor. It is impossible to exclude the possibility that their sources of information—bosses like Stefano Bontate, Gaetano Badalamenti and Rosario Riccobono—might have wanted to exaggerate their political influence in order to increase their prestige within Cosa Nostra. Moreover, only Badalamenti told Buscetta that he had met Andreotti personally. Bontate and Riccobono may have simply assumed that Andreotti would have been involved given Lima's extensive contacts with the mafia.

Because of these potential difficulties, the case against Andreotti is likely to hinge on the testimony of the only two eyewitnesses directly tying him to the bosses of the mafia—Baldassare Di Maggio and Francesco Marino Mannoia. While Di Maggio has told the seemingly incredible story of the kiss between Andreotti and Riina, he was also the man who had Riina captured, proving in the most eloquent manner possible that he was a member of the boss's inner circle. Moreover, Marino Mannoia is a witness who has also greatly impressed investigators with his seriousness and reliability. "It may seem inconceivable that Andreotti might have met with Stefano Bontate, but it is no less inconceivable to me that Francesco Marino Mannoia would make something like that up," said Antonio Manganelli, the director of the Servizio Centrale Operativo, one of the Italian police's main anti-mafia units. Unlike witnesses (Buscetta and Calderone) who have given interviews and coauthored books about their experiences, Marino Mannoia has always avoided the spotlight, anxious to bury his old identity in the anonymity of the U.S. witness protection program. "Mannoia has absolutely no interest in stirring up controversy," Manganelli added. "If he never heard of Italy again in his life, he would only be too happy."[13]

Andreotti's own credibility under oath, on the other hand, is open to question. He was forced to retract previous testimony, admitting that he had in fact given 170,000,000 *lire* in bank checks from SIR to his aide, Ezio Radaelli, and that he had asked Radaelli not to implicate him in the scandal. Moreover, it appears he was not telling the truth when he vehemently denied ever having met the Salvo cousins of Palermo. In 1994, the Palermo photographer Letizia Battaglia discovered an old news photo she had shot years earlier of Andreotti at a Christian Democrat rally held at the Salvos' Zagarella Hotel complex. The picture shows Andreotti being greeted personally by Nino Salvo. It is highly unlikely that a man who remembered sending migraine medicine to Mino Pecorelli—someone he had never met—fourteen years after the fact, would forget having been the personal guest of one of the richest men in Sicily and one of the Christian Democratic Party's largest donors.

Since then, magistrates have turned up five other photographs showing Nino Salvo at public events with Andreotti. According to Vito Ciancimino, the former mayor of Palermo: "There is no question that Andreotti and the Salvos knew one another, it was a well-known fact." Andreotti has tried, with increasing difficulty, to maintain his original position: "I insist that I never saw that person . . . or rather, if I saw him, I did not know it was Nino Salvo."

Moreover, recent investigations have produced damning evidence against Carnevale, the "sentence-killer," who was given the responsibility of presiding over all organized crime cases in Italy for several years. He was wiretapped fixing a case with a mafia defense attorney in 1994. Carnevale had been suspended from his job but continued going to the courthouse every day and remained in contact with his colleagues. An important new mafia witness (Salvatore Cancemi) has testified that he gave 100 million lire (about $80,000) to his lawyer to bribe Carnevale—a claim that appears to have been confirmed by still another wiretapped conversation. Carnevale mentions the 100 million lire to his son-in-law, who is heard saying: "Let's hope this thing about Cancemi doesn't come out." While not bearing directly on Andreotti, the evidence against Carnevale confirms the mafia witnesses' claims of collusion at the highest levels of government.

Despite this mounting evidence, the court may not want to convict a former prime minister on the testimony of a group of convicted killers. But the question of Andreotti's legal and criminal responsibilities has obscured what is perhaps the larger and more important matter: Andreotti's political and moral responsibility for the well-documented collusion with the mafia of the leaders of his faction in Sicily. Andreotti was an important player—perhaps the most important player—in a political class that accepted a culture of illegality and knowingly used the mafia's strength in southern Italy for its own political advantage.

Several facts about Andreotti are uncontrovertible. When Salvatore Lima joined the Andreotti faction in 1968, he was already the subject of persistent rumors and investigations. Andreotti has always hidden behind the fact that Lima was never convicted of any crime and deserved the presumption of innocence. But the threshold of proof for the political arena should be somewhat higher than that of criminal court. Lima was mayor of Palermo during the years when the bosses of the mafia obtained almost every building license in the city. And during a trial in the 1960s, Lima was forced to acknowledge knowing Angelo La Barbera, one of the biggest bosses of the period. Lima was close friends with Nino and Ignazio Salvo—both of whom were arrested by Falcone in 1984 and ultimately convicted in the maxi-trial of Palermo as members of Cosa Nostra. None of this, or the growing number of witnesses who tied Lima directly to the mafia during the 1980s, caused Andreotti to reconsider whether someone with Lima's reputation should belong to the prime minister's inner circle. The

parliament's anti-mafia commission (including its Christian Democrat members) concluded unanimously in 1993 that Lima had
been in league with Cosa Nostra.

For several years, Andreotti also accepted the support provided
by Vito Ciancimino, whose ties to the mafia were even more notorious than Lima's. Already by the early 1970s, Ciancimino had
been publicly branded as one of the pillars of the mafia's power in
Palermo. This did not prevent the Andreotti faction from concluding a strategic alliance in which Ciancimino agreed to support Andreotti at the Christian Democrats' party congresses. To accept
support from someone like Ciancimino is to knowingly acquiesce
in a system based on corruption and violence.

Andreotti has treated all criticism with cynicism and contempt.
"You Sicilian Christian Democrats are strong, that's why everyone speaks ill of you," he said in a rally in Palermo, meant to reassure his troops in the wake of public protest over the murder of
General Dalla Chiesa in late 1982. "We reject the false moralism
of these critics who foam at the mouth while you get stronger and
stronger with each election," he added, to the obvious delight of a
crowd that included both Lima and Ciancimino.[15]

Andreotti is the sum of all the contradictions of modern Italian
life, the friend of popes and criminals, a bizarre mixture of holy
water and Realpolitik. A deeply religious Catholic who attends
Mass each morning at six o'clock, Andreotti is also legendary for
his corrosive cynicism. "[Andreotti] seemed to have a positive
aversion to principle, even a conviction that a man of principle
was doomed to be a figure of fun," former British prime minister
Margaret Thatcher wrote in her memoirs. "Andreotti belongs to a
certain Jesuitical, clerical tradition in which you accept that in a
fallen world you have to work with the material at hand," said
Gerardo Bianco, a longtime colleague in the Christian Democratic
Party. "He is a genuinely religious and even charitable man, but
he has a pessimistic view of human nature and of original sin that
allows him to tolerate the presence of people of dubious reputation."[16]

Giulio Andreotti is simply the most prominent figure in a much
larger pattern from the immediate postwar period to the present.
There are hundreds of politicians—large and small—who have relationships with the mafia that range from active collusion to pas-

sive coexistence. The case against Andreotti's former minister of interior and fellow Christian Democrat, Antonio Gava, is in some ways even more disturbing and much more fully documented. Rather than simply relying on the testimony of mafia witnesses, prosecutors in Naples have dozens of wiretapped phone conversations between organized crime figures and members of Gava's political machine. One of the central figures is Francesco Alfieri, the owner of a large construction company and first cousin of Carmine Alfieri, the most powerful boss of the Camorra, the Neapolitan version of the mafia. As they watched Francesco Alfieri's house, police observed a continuous parade of candidates coming to ask for Alfieri's electoral support. As they tapped his phone, they heard the mayor of a local town telling Alfieri: "Voi siete il mio padrone" (You are my boss). Explaining his relations with so many elected representatives, Alfieri told prosecutors: "I don't invite the politicians, they invite themselves at election time. It's they who need me." Asked why they needed him, Alfieri replied: "I am well liked in the area because of my goodness of soul. So I recommend people, including politicians, to people who like me. Once in a while I ask a little favor of the politicians, but not for myself." The prosecutors went on to list all "the little favors" Alfieri received from the politicians in the form of lucrative public contracts.[17]

After Carmine Alfieri was captured in the fall of 1992, he and his former underboss, Pasquale Galasso, both became government witnesses. Both men have implicated Gava and dozens of the other politicians. They claim not only to have met Gava but insist that the minister of the interior used his influence to win the release of several convicted *camorristi*.

Although the case against Gava has not yet been proven, it is extremely striking that so many previous "untouchable" fugitive bosses like Alfieri and Riina were suddenly arrested after their alleged political protectors were forced from public life.

A long with the crackdown on collusion, another sign that the government has turned an important corner against the mafia is the impressive progress prosecutors have made in the investigations into the murders of Falcone and Borsellino. While almost all of the political killings in Palermo of the last fifteen years have remained unpunished, prosecutors in Caltanissetta believe they have identified nearly everyone involved in the two bombings, from the men detonating the explosives to the bosses who planned it. Police have charged one man with stealing the car used in the bombing of Via D'Amelio and have arrested a phone technician accused of tapping Borsellino's mother's phone so that Cosa Nostra knew exactly when he would be arriving on the afternoon of July 19, 1992.

The success is the result of new witnesses and superb police work. The initial investigative thread into the killing of Falcone was Antonino Gioè, a mafia killer the police kept under careful observation for months. Placing bugging devices in his apartment and tapping his phone, investigators overheard Gioè talking about the Falcone bombing and indiscreetly criticizing some of Cosa Nostra's top bosses. When they heard him discussing plans for a new assassination, they were forced to move in and arrest him.

Overcome with guilt and terror at having unwittingly betrayed his co-conspirators, Gioè committed suicide by hanging himself with his shoelaces from the bars of the window of his Rome prison cell. But his involuntary confessions provided police with the first sketchy account of the murder. Prosecutors were able to flesh out the details when three *mafiosi* who participated in the bombing decided to confess. One of them, Salvatore Cancemi, a member of the Commission, actually walked into a police station in downtown Palermo of his own free will and gave himself up— another sign of the organization's deep internal crisis. He claimed that he was sick of the endless violence of the Corleonesi whose terrorist strategy had been the ruin of Cosa Nostra. Cancemi was involved in the planning of the assassination, helping pick the best spot to plant the bomb and a safe place on a nearby hill where they could store the explosives on land owned by a friend of Cosa Nostra. Another of the new witnesses, Santino Di Matteo, was one of the crew of five men who placed the explosives underneath the highway and drove at high velocity along the airport highway so that the killers could test the remote-control detonator device against the speed of an oncoming car. The third, Gioacchino La Barbera, was the lookout man who alerted the killers when Falcone's plane touched down at the Punta Raisi airport.[18]

The three witnesses have enabled prosecutors to reconstruct the attack in its every phase, minute by minute. The decision to kill Falcone was taken, they said, by Totò Riina, who assigned the planning of the job to Salvatore Biondino, the man with Riina when he was arrested in January of 1993. All in all, some eighteen men participated in the preparation and execution of the bombing. A man of honor with a butcher shop near Giovanni Falcone's house was assigned the job of alerting the others when the prosecutor's bodyguards arrived to pick up his bulletproof car—something they always did before he arrived at the airport. Another was stationed in Rome to follow Falcone around the capital, calling Palermo when he left the Ministry of Justice and headed for the airport. A third stood by at the airport of Punta Raisi, watching for the plane to land. Two other lookout men were placed between the airport and the point of attack, ready to warn the group on the hill of the motorcade's approach. Pressing the detonator was Giovanni Brusca, whose father is the boss of San Giuseppe Jato. Presiding over the scene was Leoluca Bagarella—Riina's brother-in-law. Cancemi and Di Matteo described the victory celebration that followed the Capaci bombing, with Totò Riina ordering French champagne for the occasion. As the others toasted, the two future witnesses looked at one another and, under their breath, exchanged a gloomy assessment of Totò Riina and their future: "Stu cornutu ni consumo' a tutti!" (This cuckold will be the ruin of us all!).[19]

Their reconstruction confirmed what police had learned through brilliant investigative work. By identifying the cellular telephone numbers of the various participants, police were able to document the crisscrossing of calls that led up to the attack. They can show that the *mafioso* in Rome did indeed call the man at the Palermo airport as Falcone's plane took off and can document the sudden volley of calls between the lookout men and the group with the detonator, which increased in intensity in the final minutes and then ended with the explosion at 5:56.

These records—combined with Gioè's uncensored, recorded comments—prove that the testimony of the new witnesses is anything but the work of malicious fantasy.

The one point that still remains unclear is whether the mafia acted alone in killing Falcone and Borsellino or whether it was coordinated with someone in the government or the secret services.

"It is not *only* the mafia," insists Falcone's friend Judge Vito D'Ambrosio.[20] But, so far, no concrete evidence has emerged to support this claim. While investigating the murder of Giovanni Falcone, prosecutors in Caltanissetta found that Rudi Maira, a member of parliament in Rome, was speaking on his cellular phone with an organized crime figure back in Sicily when the bomb exploded, killing Falcone, his wife and bodyguards. The conversation was interrupted by the bomb blast, suggesting that the *mafioso* was in the vicinity of the assassination. Prosecutors do not believe that Maira bears any responsibility in the murder of Falcone, but the coincidence of the two events provides for an eloquent snapshot of the state of the Italian Republic at 5:56 on the evening of May 23, 1992: five loyal government servants are blown up by one band of *mafiosi,* while a member of parliament is chatting amiably with one of their associates.[21]

That Italian police are now able to reconstruct important crimes within months of their occurrence and even anticipate and prevent other crimes is an indication of how far they have come from the late 1970s when Cosa Nostra was an obscure and impenetrable world whose existence some had come to doubt.

"At an earlier time, all this would have been unthinkable," Alfredo Morvillo, anti-mafia prosecutor in Palermo and Falcone's brother-in-law, said in an interview after the arrest warrants were issued for the Capaci bombing. "Times have changed: a mechanism is in place that now moves on its own. . . . We owe this working method above all to Rocco Chinnici, Giovanni Falcone and Paolo Borsellino."[22]

Anti-mafia prosecutors in Italy describe the period from Borsellino's death in July of 1992 to the spring of 1994 as a "magic moment." Italian police dismantled entire criminal organizations, arrested mafia figures who had eluded capture for decades, broke up money-laundering rings, foiled assassination attempts, seized billions of dollars in illegal assets and indicted scores of businessmen, politicians, magistrates and police officials accused of protecting known *mafiosi.* Prosecutors enjoyed the full support of both public opinion and the power of the central government in Rome. For the first time, investigators had the resources, the tools and the organizational structures they needed to attack the mafia in a coordinated, global manner. The prosecutor's office in Palermo was now headed by a man of unquestioned commitment and ability and, after years of conflict and controversy, the assistant prosecutors worked in close harmony. The best police investigators to emerge in the 1980s moved to positions of power in the 1990s. More than six hundred people became government witnesses—an almost biblical exodus from the ranks of organized crime. *Omertà* among ordinary citizens also appeared to be breaking down.

From a statistical point of view, the results were genuinely astounding: in two years, arrests in southern Italy went up by 46 percent and the murder rate in *all of Italy* went down by 42 percent. That the murder rate of an entire nation can be so dramatically influenced by a police crackdown demonstrates clearly that violence in Italy is largely a problem of organized crime rather than a general sociological phenomenon.

But anti-mafia prosecutors who came of age during the 1980s are acutely aware of how fragile this kind of success is. If there is a single theme that runs through the careers of Giovanni Falcone and Paolo Borsellino it is the fundamental importance of the changing political winds in the war against the mafia in Italy. The war has been fought in a schizophrenic fashion, with long periods of inertia interrupted by sudden bursts of energy in response to public protest over some particularly heinous crime. When prosecutors have enjoyed the support of the government, they have achieved success. After the first mafia war of the early 1960s, Cosa Nostra was forced to disband for several years but came back stronger than ever when the government lost interest in the problem during the 1970s. The second mafia war and the assassination of General Alberto Dalla Chiesa led to the maxi-trial of Palermo. But the anti-mafia pool was dismantled by political forces who wanted a more docile, toothless judiciary. The political support for this most recent crackdown was determined by the assassinations of Falcone and Borsellino. The importance of politics in law enforcement can be proven mathematically. When the government has acted, the number of arrests and trials have jumped and the number of murders and deaths by overdose have gone down. When the government has relaxed its grip, the figures have reversed themselves.

The experience of the last forty years has made clear what should have been obvious from the start: a governing class that lives enmeshed in a pattern of illegality is in no position to conduct a serious, sustained campaign against organized crime. The stunning successes of law enforcement since 1992 have gone hand in hand with a much larger attempt to clean up the system of government corruption. The political support for this most recent crackdown was determined, in part, by the anomalous atmosphere created by the massive government bribery investigation, Operation Clean Hands. With a third of the Italian parliament under indictment, the Italian judiciary temporarily became the dominant arm of government. The parliament was forced to commit a kind of collective suicide: it passed long-awaited electoral reform, adopted a new majoritarian voting system and dissolved itself, bringing about new national elections on March 27, 1994.

The electoral triumph of Prime Minister Silvio Berlusconi in March put an end to this period of judicial interregnum. With a new parliament, the executive and legislative branches have vowed to take back the power lost to the magistrature. Although the new government insists it will continue both the corruption investigations and the war on the mafia, there is considerable anxiety in Italian law enforcement. Even before Berlusconi entered political life, many of the top executives of his financial empire, Fininvest, were under investigation in the Milan bribery scandal, including his brother, Paolo Berlusconi. Furthermore, Prime Minister Berlusconi has extremely close ties to many members of the old political parties who have been hit hardest by the investigation. Bettino Craxi, the former head of the Italian Socialist Party, who is a fugitive of Italian justice in Tunisia, was the best man at Berlusconi's wedding. Berlusconi's chief representative in Sicily, Marcello Dell'Utri—although not charged with any wrongdoing—has documented ties to organized crime figures. During the election campaign, rumors surfaced that Dell'Utri might be indicted—creating the perception that anti-mafia prosecutors were hostile to the future prime minister.[23]

At another point during last spring's election campaign, one of the chief bosses of the Calabrian mafia, Giuseppe Piromalli, declared in open court, "We will vote for Berlusconi." After the elections, there were a series of bombings and arson fires against opposition political figures in Sicily—a sign that the mafia believes it can take advantage of the new situation.

"We know from several witnesses that the mafia has high expectations from this government," said Vincenzo Macrì, a prosecutor with the Direzione Nazionale Anti-mafia in Rome, which coordinates mafia prosecutors in Italy. "We don't know whether this reflects actual promises made or hopes on the mafia's part."[24]

These hopes may not necessarily spring from direct contacts between Berlusconi's Forza Italia Party and the mafia, but rather from his party's often-stated desire to limit the power of the magistrature. But it is nonetheless disturbing that several members of the new parliament have called for drastic changes in Italy's witness protection program and the elimination of the island-prisons for the most dangerous mafia bosses, two of the most effective weapons against organized crime.

In 1993 and 1994 unemployment reached 10 percent nationally, so economic growth replaced clean government as the country's top priority. The corruption investigations had frozen many public works projects, creating the impression for some that the cleanup is bad for business. Berlusconi was elected in part because he promised to create a million new jobs, but he has also vowed to dismantle the state-owned industries that are the principal instrument of political patronage, corruption and mafia penetration of government.

The year of the Berlusconi government has been anything but encouraging. The battle between the prime minister and the magistrates of Milan has intensified. In the summer of 1994—as prosecutors were about to arrest several executives of Berlusconi's Fininvest—the Berlusconi cabinet hastily issued a decree making it illegal for magistrates to arrest defendants for a series of white-collar crimes. Although mafia crimes were excluded from the government's decree, it contained a little-noticed clause that would have been a potential bonanza for organized crime. The decree required magistrates to notify potential suspects within three months that they were objects of investigation, which would have made any complex organized crime investigations impossible. Suspected *mafiosi* under investigation would have to be informed that their phones were being tapped. Fortunately, the decree was withdrawn when Berlusconi's own government allies—the Lombard League and the neo-Fascists of Alleanza Nazionale (National Alliance) refused to support it.[25]

With the filing of bribery charges against Prime Minister Berlusconi himself in November of 1994, the conflict between the government and the magistrature reached the breaking point. Berlusconi's Minister of Justice immediately called for an inspection of the Milan prosecutor's office and filed charges against the chief prosecutor with the Consiglio Superiore della Magistratura. The Italian Supreme Court intervened, removing the investigation from Milan and sending it to a much smaller office in the city of Brescia. In the midst of this ugly battle, Judge Antonio Di Pietro, the magistrate who had started the Operation Clean Hands investigation, resigned, saying he was exhausted by having been turned into a political football. His resignation throws the future of the corruption investigation into doubt. The big question is whether, as in the past, the government's war against the magistrature will sabotage the war against the mafia.[26]

The future of the mafia, however, also depends on economic factors. The desire to stimulate the economy has created great temptations for the government. The quickest and easiest solution is to reopen the faucet of government spending and not pay too close attention to who controls the contracts. But the experience of the last forty-five years has shown this formula to be an unmitigated disaster. The government must keep in mind that mafia dominance and economic health are irreconcilable.

Southern Italy finds itself in a predicament not unlike that of the Eastern European countries after the fall of the Berlin Wall. Like Bulgaria or Czechoslovakia, Sicily has lived for decades under a corrupt and inefficient system that is now suddenly exposed to the rigors of the marketplace. In all of Sicily, with a population of 5 million people, there are only 110,000 jobs in industry and a good number of them are in state-owned industries kept open for political reasons. Many of these will disappear, in the short term, as government industries are sold off. The police and the magistrature can only address the problem of law enforcement, the government must devise a comprehensive plan for developing southern Italy—a strategy that weans the economy from dependence on the government and creates a private sector without greatly increasing the already high levels of unemployment.[27]

The government's actions in the near future will determine whether the great cleanup of the last few years will simply become another parenthesis in Cosa Nostra's long reign in Sicily or whether it represents the beginning of the end of the mafia.

While Cosa Nostra has absorbed punishing blows, the organization has not been defeated. Despite the arrest of Totò Riina, the leadership of the Corleonese faction seems still to be solidly in place. Riina's principal associates, Bernardo Provenzano and his brother-in-law Leoluca Bagarella, are still at large and are believed to be calling the shots. And the relatively low number of mafia killings indicates that the level of internal strife is under control.

Although there are many people who are trying to restore the old status quo, there are reasons to believe that something important has changed in Sicily in the last ten to fifteen years. The social consensus the mafia once enjoyed has been seriously eroded. "The mafia is not disappearing, but the people who used to revere us and used to identify with the mafia, now tolerate us because they are afraid," Leonardo Messina testified before the Italian parliament. "People in Sicily are beginning to believe in the state because now even the son of a street sweeper or a shoemaker may go to university and no longer wants to be subject to the mafia," he said.[28]

Falcone and Borsellino had a lot to do with this social change. Past crusaders against the mafia, from Mussolini's "Iron Prefect" Cesare Mori to General Dalla Chiesa were, like Garibaldi's conquering troops, northern Italians on a mission to civilize the island and link it to the rest of Italy. Falcone and Borsellino offered a new image of the state: serious, uncompromisingly honest and profoundly Sicilian. By bringing the mafia to trial, they proved that the mafia is not invincible. And they did so through the scrupulous use of the legal code. "The most revolutionary thing you could do in Sicily," Falcone once said, "is simply to apply the law and punish the guilty."[29]

Clearly, crime will continue to exist in Sicily and the rest of Italy, as it does in almost all modern democracies. But Cosa Nostra's extraordinary power over daily life has derived in good part from its ability to infiltrate the political system. If the bond of collusion can be broken, the mafia can be isolated much more easily and its power reduced to that of other organized crime groups that operate at the periphery rather than the center of society.

Berlusconi may be sincere in his stated desire to fight the mafia, but there are indications that—at least on a local level—organized crime has made a concerted attempt to infiltrate his party. On March 29, 1994, two days after the government coalition won fifty-four out of the sixty-one seats in parliament representing Sicily, Giuseppe Mandalari, Totò Riina's accountant, was wiretapped by police as he made the following comment about the election results: "Beautiful, all the candidates are my friends, all of them got elected."[30]

Berlusconi resigned in December 1994. His place has been taken by his former Treasury Minister, Lamberto Dini, heading a new "nonpolitical" government. This may help bring a truce to the war between the government and the magistrature. But Berlusconi is already planning his return to power and is pressing for elections in June of 1995. The problem, however, is not one of personalities. The question is whether the new political parties that have grown up from the ruins of the old will have the strength to reject the "help" offered by organized crime figures.

"There is no question that the mafia is looking for new allies in government," said Giuseppe Tricoli, a close personal friend of slain prosecutor Paolo Borsellino and a member of the right-wing National Alliance, which is part of the government coalition. "And it is logical that they should try to infiltrate Forza Italia, which has recycled many figures from the old political parties. But it is our role in the government to keep a new alliance between mafia and politics from developing. The outcome of that struggle will determine the whole game."[31]

1838. Courts in Sicily make first mention of criminal "unions, brotherhoods and sects."

1860. Giuseppe Garibaldi lands with northern Italian troops in Marsala, unifying Sicily with the newly created Italian state.

1863. I Mafiusi di la Vicaria opens. The play, about a group of criminals in the Palermo jail, is the first recorded use of the term *mafioso* (or *mafiuso*) to refer to members of a criminal organization.

1876. The parliamentary inquest by Leopoldo Franchetti and Sidney Sonnino into the origins of violence in Sicily.

1890. The police chief of New Orleans is killed in a feud between two Sicilian criminal groups, leading to a lynching of Italian-Americans.

1893. The former mayor of Palermo, Emanuele Notarbartolo, is murdered. Raffaele Palizzolo, a member of parliament from Sicily, is accused of ordering his killing.

1916. Salvatore Lucania, a.k.a. Lucky Luciano, immigrates to the United States.

1924. Benito Mussolini appoints Cesare Mori "Prefect of Palermo" and gives him extraordinary powers to fight the mafia.

1943. July 9. Allied troops invade Sicily, defeating fascism. Known *mafiosi* join the new movement of Sicilian separatism and obtain positions of prominence during the Allied occupation.

1946. The first Italian postwar government grants Sicily special autonomy, including its own parliament, effectively putting an end to the separatist movement. The United States deports Lucky Luciano and numerous other Italian-American gangsters to Italy.

1947. May 1. The bandit Salvatore Giuliano and his men fire on the May Day rally of Sicilian Communists and peasants held at Portella della Ginestra to celebrate their strong showing at recent local elections. In the decade after the end of World War II, forty-three Socialists, Communists or union organizers are murdered in Sicily.

1955. October 1. Italian-American and Sicilian members of Cosa Nostra hold a mafia summit at Palermo's Hotel delle Palme. Six weeks later police in the United States break up a follow-up summit of American gangsters in Apalachin, New York. The Sicilian Cosa Nostra, following the American model, forms a "Commission," whose head is Salvatore Greco.

1963. June 30. A car full of dynamite explodes and kills seven Italian *carabinieri,* the culmination of an escalating mafia war in Palermo. The killings provoke a manhunt in which 1,903 suspected *mafiosi* are arrested and the Italian parliament convenes its first anti-mafia commission. Salvatore Greco and other important *mafiosi* (including Tommaso Buscetta) move to North and South America. Cosa Nostra temporarily dissolves the Commission.

1969. The major trials against the mafia end in the mass acquitals of defendants. Salvatore Riina and Bernardo Provenzano break their parole and become fugitives.

December 10. A mafia hit squad, directed by Riina and Provenzano, kills Michele Cavataio, the man blamed for starting the first mafia war. Calogero Bagarella, the brother of Riina's future wife, dies in the shoot-out.

A triumvirate is formed to govern the Sicilian mafia during a period of reorganization. The triumvirate is composed of Gaetano Badalamenti (the boss of Cinisi), Stefano Bontate (the boss of Santa Maria di Gesù in Palermo) and Salvatore Riina (of Corleone).

1973. Leonardo Vitale, a *mafioso* of Palermo, confesses, indicating Salvatore Riina as one of the new bosses of the mafia. Vitale is sent to an asylum for the criminally insane and charges are dropped against those he accused.

1974. The full Commission of Cosa Nostra is reestablished with Gaetano Badalamenti as head. Only eight deaths by drug overdose are recorded in Italy.

1975. An "inter-provincial" Commission is established, uniting all the clans of Sicily in order to reduce conflict between Palermo and the other provinces. The chief sponsor of the idea is Giuseppe Calderone, the boss of Catania.

1977. Colonel Giuseppe Russo, a mafia investigator of the *carabineri,* and a friend are murdered in Ficuzza, near Corleone. The killing was carried out without the authorization of the Commission and without the knowledge of its head, Badalamenti.

1978. May 30. Giuseppe Di Cristina, the boss of Riesi and a member of the Commission, is shot dead in Palermo. A few days earlier, Di Cristina had warned police of the rise of the Corleonese mafia and the imminent assassination of several public officials.

September 30. Giuseppe Calderone, boss of Catania, and a close friend of Di Cristina, is killed. The new boss of Catania is Nitto Santapaola.

Gaetano Badalamenti is removed from the Commission and expelled from Cosa Nostra. Michele Greco, the boss of Ciaculli (Palermo), known as "the Pope," becomes the new head of the Commission.

1979. March 9. Michele Reina, the head of the Christian Democratic Party for the province of Palermo, is assassinated.

July 11. Giorgio Ambrosoli, the attorney investigating the bankruptcy of the financial empire of Sicilian banker Michele Sindona, is murdered in Milan.

July 21. Boris Giuliano, deputy police chief of Palermo, who had begun the first major investigations of heroin trafficking between Sicily and the United States, is killed near his home in Palermo.

August 2. Michele Sindona disappears from New York, where he is under indictment, staging a fake terrorist kidnapping with the aid of John Gambino and other members of the U.S. mafia. After spending several weeks in Sicily in the care of Sicilian *mafiosi* Rosario Spatola and Salvatore Inzerillo, Sindona reappears in New York on October 16.

September 25. Cesare Terranova is murdered in Palermo. A former magistrate and Communist member of parliament, he was preparing to return to the magistrature as head of the Ufficio Istruzione (investigative office) of Palermo.

1980. January 6. Piersanti Mattarella, the president of the region of Sicily, and an important Christian Democrat reformer, is murdered in Palermo.

May 5. Captain Emanuele Basile of the *carabineri* is killed in front of his wife and child in Monreale. Together with Paolo Borsellino, Basile had been conducting an important investigation (initiated by Boris Giuliano) into heroin trafficking and murder involving the Corleonese mafia. Paolo Borsellino is assigned to investigate the murder.

Procuratore della Repubblica chief prosecutor Gaetano Costa signs fifty-five arrest warrants against the heroin ring of the Spatola-Inzerillo-Gambino clans. The case passes to the investigative office and is assigned to Giovanni Falcone. Costa is killed later that summer on August 6.

1981. April 23. Stefano Bontate, boss of Santa Maria di Gesù, a member of the Commission, is murdered on the evening of his forty-third birthday.

May 11. Salvatore Inzerillo, one of Bontate's allies on the Commission, is killed with the same Kalashnikov rifle. The second mafia war of Palermo goes into full swing with more than a hundred people being murdered or disappearing in the course of the year.

June. Police intercept a phone call from Tommaso Buscetta in Brazil to Ignazio Lo Presti, a Palermo businessman, inquiring about the death of Salvatore Inzerillo and the ongoing mafia war. Lo Presti disappears later that summer.

December 25. The Christmas Massacre of Bagheria, in which three *mafiosi* and a passerby are killed in the center of town. Police find the getaway car with the fingerprints of Giuseppe Marchese, nephew of boss Filippo Marchese.

1982. April 30. Pio La Torre, head of the Italian Communist Party in Sicily, and a member of the parliament's anti-mafia commission, is killed with his driver, Rosario Di Salvo, in Palermo.

May 1. Carlo Alberto Dalla Chiesa becomes the new prefect of Palermo.

July 12. Major police roundup in Palermo led by Ninni Cassarà, based on his report implicating Michele Greco and 161 others.

September 3. General Carlo Alberto Dalla Chiesa, his wife and driver are killed.

September 13. The Italian parliament creates the office of High Commissioner of Anti-mafia Affairs with powers of investigation denied Dalla Chiesa. It also passes the Rognoni–La Torre law, conceived by slain Communist leader Pio La Torre, giving prosecutors the power to confiscate mafia-controlled assets.

November–December. Rosario Riccobono, the boss of Partanna-Mondello, and Filippo Marchese, the boss of Corso dei Mille, disappear. The brother, nephew and son-in-law of Tommaso Buscetta are all murdered in Palermo.

1983. May 24. Police capture a ship in the Suez Canal carrying 233 kilos of heroin to Palermo.

July 9. Giovanni Falcone and chief prosecutor Rocco Chinnici issue fourteen arrest warrants for the assassination of General Dalla Chiesa. Chief defendant is Michele Greco.

July 12. Ko Bak Kin, one of Cosa Nostra's principal heroin suppliers, is arrested in Bangkok and agrees to cooperate with police.

July 31. Rocco Chinnici, head of the investigative office of Palermo, together with two bodyguards and the concierge of his building, are blown up by a car bomb.

August. Bettino Craxi becomes Italy's first Socialist prime minister. Mino Martinazzoli and Virginio Rognoni become ministers of justice and interior, providing critical support to the war against the mafia.

November. Antonino Caponetto replaces Rocco Chinnici as head of the investigative office of Palermo and forms the anti-mafia pool, composed of Giovanni Falcone, Paolo Borsellino, Giuseppe Di Lello and Leonardo Guarnotta.

1984. June. Giovanni Falcone and Vincenzo Geraci travel to Brazil to meet Tommaso Buscetta who is extradited to Italy and becomes a government witness.

September 29. On the basis of Buscetta's testimony, 366 arrest warrants are issued.

October 1. Salvatore Contorno, soldier of Stefano Bontate, begins cooperating, leading to 127 more arrest warrants.

October 3. Two ex-mayors of Palermo, Giuseppe Insalaco and Elda Pucci, and current mayor, Nello Martellucci, appear before the anti-mafia commission and discuss the influence of organized crime on city government. Two weeks later, Insalaco's car is burned outside his home in Palermo.

October 4. The Italian parliament votes against forcing the resignation of Foreign Minister Giulio Andreotti because of his ties to financier Michele Sindona, who has just been extradited to Italy for commissioning a mafia murder.

November 3. Vito Ciancimino, former mayor of Palermo, is arrested on charges of association with the mafia.

November 12. Nino and Ignazio Salvo, the heads of one of Sicily's largest business empires, are indicted for association with the mafia.

December 2. Leonardo Vitale, the first modern mafia witness, is murdered.

December 23. The Naples-Milan train 904 is blown up by a terrorist bomb, killing 16 and wounding 262. Giuseppe Calò, a member of the Commission, is later charged with organizing the bombing.

1985. May. Leoluca Orlando becomes mayor of Palermo.

July 25. Giuseppe Montana, the head of the "fugitive squad" of the Palermo police, captures eight high-level mafia fugitives, as preparations for the special "bunker-hall" courthouse needed to hold the maxi-trial of Palermo are in full swing. Three days later Montana is killed.

August 6. Ninni Cassarà, deputy chief of the Investigative Squad of the Palermo police, and his bodyguard are assassinated. Giovanni Falcone and Paolo Borsellino are evacuated to the island of Asinara as protection against possible assassination.

October 24. The Pizza Connection case, with Tommaso Buscetta and Salvatore Contorno as witnesses, begins in New York.

November 8. Falcone, Borsellino and the anti-mafia pool file the 8,607-page *ordinanza-sentenza* for the maxi-trial of Palermo.

1986. February 10. The maxi-trial of Palermo opens with 475 defendants, 117 of whom are still fugitives.

February 20. Michele Greco, "the Pope," is captured and joins the defendants of the maxi-trial.

March 19. Michele Sindona is convicted of murder. The following day he dies in his prison cell after drinking a cup of poisoned coffee.

April 2. Tommaso Buscetta and Salvatore Contorno arrive from the United States to testify in the maxi-trial of Palermo.

May 22. Paolo Borsellino prepares to leave Palermo after being selected to become chief prosecutor of Marsala.

1987. January 10. The novelist Leonardo Sciascia publishes a prominent article attacking the anti-mafia prosecutors.

June. National elections are held for a new parliament. Championing the cause of defendants' rights, the Radical Party runs a successful subscription drive in Italian prisons, to which numerous mafia bosses contribute heavily. The Socialist Party, attacking the power of the judiciary, nearly doubles its vote in Palermo. The new minister of justice, Giuliano Vassalli, is an outspoken opponent of any plea bargaining or any witness protection for mafia witnesses.

November. The referendum to limit the power of the judiciary, sponsored by the Socialist and Radical parties, prevails.

December 16. After a year and a half, the first maxi-trial of Palermo ends with 344 convictions and 114 not guilty verdicts. Antonino Caponetto, chief prosecutor of the Palermo investigative office, prepares to return to Florence.

1988. January 12. Giuseppe Insalaco, former mayor of Palermo, is killed.

January 14. Palermo anti-mafia investigator Natale Mondo is killed.

January 19. The Consiglio Superiore della Magistratura chooses Antonino Meli over Giovanni Falcone as new head of the investigative office of Palermo.

March 9. Falcone issues 160 arrest warrants on the basis of the testimony of Antonino Calderone, brother of former boss of Catania, Giuseppe Calderone.

April 13. Antonio Gava, a Christian Democrat rumored to have ties to organized crime in Naples, becomes minister of the interior.

July 21. Paolo Borsellino publicly denounces the dismantling of the anti-mafia pool of Palermo.

July 30. The Consiglio Superiore della Magistratura opens hearings to investigate Borsellino's charges.

August 5. The government in Rome chooses Domenico Sica over Giovanni Falcone as new High Commissioner for Anti-mafia Affairs.

September 25. Judge Antonio Saetta, who was scheduled to hear the appeal of the maxi-trial of Palermo, is assassinated together with his son.

November 23. Italy's Supreme Court decides against Falcone and in favor of Meli, dividing up the Calderone cases among twelve different offices.

1989. May 26. Witness Salvatore Contorno is arrested with other criminals in Palermo.

June 6. Anonymous letters begin to circulate accusing Giovanni Falcone and others of sending Contorno to Sicily to kill mafia defendants.

June 20. A powerful bomb is discovered outside Falcone's summer house in Addaura as Falcone confers with Swiss magistrates about money laundering in Italian-speaking Switzerland.

July 20. High Commissioner Domenico Sica accuses Alberto Di Pisa, a mafia prosecutor of Palermo, of orchestrating the anonymous letters campaign against Falcone and others.

July 23. Giulio Andreotti becomes prime minister for the sixth time.

October 3. Giuseppe Pellegriti accuses Salvatore Lima, a former mayor of Palermo, of ordering the assassination of General Carlo Alberto Dalla Chiesa. Giovanni Falcone charges Pellegriti with libel.

October 8. Francesco Marino Mannoia begins collaborating with Falcone.

1990. January 24. Leoluca Orlando resigns as mayor of Palermo.

May 6. Administration elections are held, during which numerous political candidates are murdered, shot at or threatened in southern Italy.

May 9. Giovanni Buonsignore, a Palermo bureaucrat who denounced mafia influence in local government contracts, is killed.

May 19. Leoluca Orlando accuses the prosecutors of Palermo of covering up evidence against the mafia's political protectors.

September 21. Judge Rosario Livatino, anti-mafia prosecutor of Agrigento, is murdered.

October 16. Antonio Gava steps down as minister of the interior, and is replaced by Vincenzo Scotti.

1991. February 1. Claudio Martelli becomes minister of justice, asking Giovanni Falcone to be one of his chief aides.

February 26. Michele Greco, "the Pope," and forty-one convicted defendants of the maxi-trial of Palmero are released by Italy's Supreme Court—only to be rearrested by a special decree made by Martelli in consultation with Falcone.

May 3. Massacre in Taurianova, Calabria. Organized crime killings in Italy up by 73 percent in the first half of the year.

August 3. Minister of Interior Scotti dissolves the city council of Taurianova, polluted by organized crime—the first of more than seventy city councils to be dissolved during the next two years.

August–November. Paolo Borsellino wins the cooperation of three new witnesses in Marsala: Piera Aiello, Rita Atria and Vincenzo Calcara.

August 9. Antonio Scopelliti, a prosecutor scheduled to argue the government's case in the final appeal of the maxi-trial of Palermo before the Italian Supreme Court in Rome, is assassinated while on vacation in Calabria.

August 29. Libero Grassi, a Palermo businessman who publicly defied the mafia's extortion racket, is murdered in Palermo.

September. The government in Rome adopts Falcone's plans to reorganize the war against the mafia in centralized police and prosecutors' offices.

December 11. Paolo Borsellino returns to Palermo as deputy chief prosecutor, playing a leading role in new mafia investigations.

1992. January 31. The first department of the Italian Supreme Court, minus its president, Corrado Carnevale, upholds the convictions in the maxi-trial of Palermo.

February 17. Mario Chiesa, a Socialist administrator in Milan, is arrested for bribery, opening the massive political corruption investigation known as Operation Clean Hands.

March 12. Salvatore Lima, Prime Minister Giulio Andreotti's top aide in Sicily, is shot and killed near his villa in Mondello, outside Palermo.

April 5. Governing parties suffer major loss in national elections, almost losing their majority in parliament.

May 23. Giovanni Falcone, his wife, Francesca Morvillo, and three bodyguards are killed by a massive bomb at Capaci near the Palermo airport. On the day of Falcone's funeral, the Italian parliament elects Oscar Luigi Scalfaro president of the Republic.

June 30. Leonardo Messina begins collaborating with Paolo Borsellino.

July 10. Giaocchino Schembri, a *mafioso* in prison in Germany, begins cooperating with Paolo Borsellino.

July 14. Socialist foreign minister Gianni De Michaelis is indicted on bribery charges.

July 16. Gaspare Mutolo begins collaborating with Paolo Borsellino.

July 19. Paolo Borsellino and five bodyguards are killed by a car bomb placed outside his mother's home in Palermo.

July 23. Prime Minister Giuliano Amato sends 7,000 troops to Sicily and adopts tough new crime package containing the witness protection program pushed by Falcone and Borsellino.

October 11. Prosecutors in Palermo indict twenty-four people for the murder of Salvatore Lima, described as Cosa Nostra's ambassador in Rome.

1993. January 15. Salvatore Riina is arrested in Palermo, ending twenty-three years as fugitive.

February 11. Former prime minister Bettino Craxi resigns as head of the Socialist Party after numerous indictments for bribery.

March 27. Former prime minister Giulio Andreotti is accused of collusion with the mafia by prosecutors in Palermo.

April 18–19. By an overwhelming margin, Italian voters pass a national referendum rejecting the country's proportional electoral system in favor of a new majoritarian system.

July 23–26. The Christian Democratic Party, the party that has led all Italian governments since 1946, formally dissolves, giving birth to *Il partito popolare.*

1994. March 27–28. Businessman Silvio Berlusconi wins in new national elections, leading a coalition formed of his new Forza Italia party, the separatist Northern League and the neo-Fascist National Alliance.

December 6. Antonio Di Pietro, the magistrate who began the Operation Clean Hands investigation into political corruption, resigns after having initiated proceedings against Prime Minister Berlusconi on charges of bribery.

NOTES

PROLOGUE

1. Leopoldo Franchetti, *Condizioni politiche e amministrative della Sicilia*, pp. 5–6.
2. The initial story on the charges against Signorino appeared in *Giornale di Sicilia*, December 1, 1992. The stories on his suicide appeared in *Giornale di Sicilia*, *Corriere della Sera* and *La Stampa*, December 4, 1992.
3. The *mafioso* who accused Signorino is Gaspare Mutolo. See interrogation of Mutolo.
4. The police chief *(questore)* of Palermo was Matteo Cinque. The accusations against him were reported in *Corriere della Sera*, May 29, 1993.
5. Description of Palermo is based on author's reporting in Palermo during November and December, 1992. The Comitato delle Lenzuola published a documentation of its activities during the year after the assassinations of Falcone and Borsellino: *Un lenzuolo contro la mafia* by Robert Alajmo (Palermo, 1993).
6. On the "excellent cadavers" of Palermo, see Saverio Lodato, *Quindici anni di mafia* (Milan [1990], 1994; and Lucio Galluzzo, Franco Nicastro, and Vincenzo Vasile, *Obiettivo Falcone* (Naples [1989], 1992).
7. Giovanni Falcone (with Marcelle Padovani), *Cose di Cosa Nostra*, p. 49.
8. Buscetta's statement is contained in a television interview reprinted in *Panorama*, August 2, 1992.
9. On the decision to send troops to Sicily, see *Corriere della Sera* and *La Stampa*, July 20–25, 1992.
10. The statistics on the number of mafia witnesses and fugitives arrested in 1992 and 1993 are from the Italian Ministry of the Interior.
11. The most important source of information on the Lima assassination is the *Atto di accusa* of the Procura of Palermo, filed October 11, 1992. It was published in pamphlet form under the title *Delitto Lima* (Agrigento, 1992).
12. Author interview with Vittorio Foa.
13. Author interview with Pietro Scopolla.

14. Paul Ginsborg, *A History of Contemporary Italy* (New York, 1990), p. 375.
15. *The New Yorker,* March 1, 1993.
16. Figures on Italian and southern economy: Centro Studi Confindustria report, *Squilibri di bilancio, distorsioni economiche dell'economia italiana,* October 1991, by Stefano Micossi and Giuseppe Tullio; and Centro Studi Confindustria report, *L'industria in Sicilia,* September 1992.
17. Leonardo Messina's testimony before anti-mafia commission, December 4, 1992.
18. On the illegal building in Agrigento and elsewhere in Sicily, see the report of the Legambiente, *L'ambiente illegale* (Rome, 1993), p. 31.
19. See Dacia Maraini's *Bagheria* (Milan, 1993).
20. The figures on the number of city councils dissolved came from the Italian Ministry of the Interior. On the town of Platì, see *La Repubblica,* September 22, 1992.
21. Enrico Deaglio, *Raccolto Rosso* (Milan, 1993), p. 9.
22. Leonardo Sciascia, *La Sicilia come metafora: Intervista di Marcelle Padovani* (Milan, 1979).

CHAPTER ONE

1. For the early history of the mafia, see Salvatore Lupo, *Storia della mafia* (Rome, 1993); Francesco Renda, *Storia della Sicilia,* vol. 1 (Palermo, 1984); Christopher Duggan, *Fascism and the Mafia* (New Haven, 1989); and Gaetano Falzone, *Storia della mafia* (Palermo, Falzone, Gaetano, (Palermo [1973], 1987); and Henner Hess, *Mafia* (Rome-Bari, 1984).
2. Francesco Petruzzella, *Sulla pelle dello stato,* p. 163.
3. Franchetti, *Condizioni politiche e amministrative della Sicilia,* pp. 19–21.
4. Cesare Mori, *Con la mafia ai ferri corti* (Palermo [1932], 1993), p. 228.
5. Duggan, pp. 195–99.
6. For the colorful account of Luciano's alleged involvement in the invasion of Sicily, see Michele Pantaleone, *Mafia e politica* (Turin, 1960), pp. 48–63. For a more sober and careful reconstruction, see Lupo, p. 159.
7. On the deportation of Italian-American gangsters, see the anti-mafia commission's report on mafia and politics, *Relazione sui rapporti tra mafia e politica,* approved April 6, 1993.
8. On Vito Genovese and Charles Poletti, see Claire Sterling, *Octopus* (New York, 1990), pp. 56–57.
9. On the killing of Socialists and Communists, see Renda, *Storia della Sicilia,* vol. 3, pp. 276–82.
10. Renda, vol. 3, p. 278.
11. Renda, pp. 285–86.
12. Author interview with Renda.
13. On the killing of Giuliano and the trial of Gaspare Pisciotta, see anti-mafia commission report on mafia and politics, April 6, 1993.
14. Lo Schiavo is quoted in Pino Arlacchi, *La mafia imprenditrice* (Bologna, 1983), p. 59.
15. Letter of Palazzolo, quoted in Giorio Chinnici and Umberto Santino, *La Violenza Programmata* (Milan, 1989), p. 272.
16. Antonio Maria Di Fresco, *Sicilia: 30 anni di regione* (Palermo, 1976), p. 15.
17. On the "Sack of Palermo" and the roles of Lima and Ciancimino, see Orazio

Cancilla, *Palermo* (Rome-Bari, 1988), pp. 525–42, and the anti-mafia commission's *Relazione conclusiva, 4 febbraio, 1976, VI Legislatura, doc. XXIII, n.2,* pp. 214–37, reprinted in Nicola Tranfaglia, *Mafia, politica e affari* (Rome-Bari, 1992), pp. 72–108. The quotation on suspicious building licenses is from Tranfaglia, p. 94.

18. On the abandonment of the center of Palermo, see Cancilla, p. 532.

19. Johann Wolfgang von Goethe, *Italian Journey,* 1816–1817, trans. W. H. Auden and Elizabeth Mayer (New York, 1962), pp. 225–52.

20. On the family backgrounds of Falcone and Borsellino, author interviews with Maria Falcone and Rita Borsellino Fiore and Maria Pia Lepanto Borsellino. See also, Umberto Lucentini, *Paolo Borsellino: Il valore di una vita* (Milan, 1994); and Francesco La Licata, *Storia di Giovanni Falcone* (Milan, 1993).

21. Falcone, *Cose di Cosa Nostra,* p. 14.

22. Falcone, p. 39.

23. Author interview with Giuseppe Tricoli.

24. Examples of this anthropological approach are to be found in the work of Hess, Duggan, and in Arlacchi's early book, *La mafia imprenditrice.* For a discussion of the anthropological interpretation of the mafia, see Lupo, and Sterling, p. 41.

25. For the state of Italian politics in 1978, the rise of the Communists and the Moro kidnapping, see Ginsborg, *A History of Contemporary Italy,* pp. 374–87.

26. From an account of the funeral of Di Cristina, *L'Unità,* June 3, 1978.

27. A full account of the confession of Di Cristina is contained in the report of the Legione Carabinieri di Palermo, of August 25, 1978. It is also quoted extensively in the massive indictment of the maxi-trial of Palermo, *Ordinanza Sentenza contro Abbate + 706,* filed in Palermo on November 8, 1985. A generous selection of the 8,607-page document is reprinted in the book *Mafia: L'atto di accusa dei giudici di Palermo,* edited by Corrado Stajano (Rome, 1986). The confessions of Di Cristina are on pp. 18–37.

28. A full account of the murder of Boris Giuliano was filed by the Questura di Palermo on December 16, 1979. Accounts of deaths of Giuliano and Terranova are given in Lodato, *Quindici anni di mafia,* pp. 13–20, while that of Mattarella is treated on p. 35. On the death of Terranova, see Galluzzo, p. 125.

29. For an account of the death of Basile and the arrest warrants against Inzerillo, see *La Repubblica,* May 6, 1980, and Lodato, pp. 40–42. On the debate in the Procura della Repubblica, see Galluzzo, pp. 132–43. Also, author interview with Vincenzo Geraci.

CHAPTER TWO

1. Lucio Galluzzo, Francesco La Licata and Saverio Lodato, eds. *Falcone vive* (Palermo [1986], 1992), p. 37.

2. On the release of defendants and the complete details of the investigation, see *Requisitoria, Rosario Spatola + 84,* filed by Giusto Sciacchitano, of the Procura della Repubblica of Palermo, December 7, 1981; and the *Sentenza istruttoria del processo contro Rosario Spatola + 119,* filed by Giovanni Falcone, Palermo, 1982. A partial reconstruction is given in Lodato, pp. 44–50. Also, author interviews with Sciacchitano and Francesco Lo Voi.

3. On the career and death of Costa, see Galluzzo, *Obiettivo Falcone,* pp. 126–43, and Lodato, *Quindici anni di mafia,* p. 54. Also, author interview with Rita Bartoli Costa.

4. Author interview with Maria Falcone.

5. Author interview with Giusto Sciacchitano.

6. On the discovery of the heroin laboratory, the arrest of Alberti and the killing of Jannì, see the *Requisitoria, Rosario Spatola + 84;* Lodato, pp. 44–50; and *La Repubblica,* August 28, 1980.

7. *Falcone vive,* p. 47.

8. Sterling, *Octopus,* p. 199; Cancilla, p. 541.

9. On the loan from Sindona to Fanfani and his relations with other Christian Democrat leaders, see *Commissione parlamentare d'inchiesta sul caso Sindona; Relazione conclusiva, VIII Legislatura, doc. XXIII, n.2-sexies,* Roma, *1982,* pp. 161–78, reprinted in Tranfaglia, *Mafia, politica e affari,* pp. 203–20. See also, *L'Espresso,* October 25, 1981, and November 1, 1981.

10. On death of Ambrosoli, see *Sindona: gli atti d'accusa dei giudici di Milano* (Rome, 1986), pp. 47–52; Stajano, *Un eroe borghese* (Turin, 1991); Sterling, pp. 192–94.

11. *Falcone vive,* 44–45.

12. Author interview with Giuliano Turone.

13. Author interview with Elio Pizzuti.

14. Tranfaglia, pp. 203–20.

15. *Relazione della commissione parlamentare d'inchiesta sulla loggia massonica P2, IX Legislatura, doc. XXIII, n.2,* July 12, 1984. On Berlusconi's membership in the P2, see Giovanni Ruggeri and Mario Guarino's *Berlusconi: Inchiesta sul Signor TV* (Milan, 1994).

16. Author interview with Turone.

17. See *Sindona* and Stajano.

18. *Corriere della Sera,* May 20, 1984.

19. The Andreotti aide who met with Sindona was Franco Evangelisti. The meeting and the relations between Sindona and Andreotti are described in the parliamentary report on the Sindona affair, reprinted in Tranfaglia, pp. 260–67.

20. *L'Unità,* May 26, 1981.

21. *L'Unità,* May 29, 1981.

22. *Falcone vive,* p. 55.

23. Author interview with Leonardo Guarnotta.

24. Author interview with Turone.

25. Lodato, p. 39.

26. Author interview with Pizzuti.

27. Author interviews with Guarnotta, Ignazio De Francisci, Giovanni Paparcuri, Barbara Sanzo and Vincenzo Geraci.

28. Author interview with Pizzuti.

29. The number of convictions was reported in *L'Espresso,* April 22, 1984.

CHAPTER THREE

1. *La Repubblica,* May 6, 1980, and Lodato, *Quindici anni di mafia,* pp. 40–42.

2. Author interviews with Maria Pia Lepanto Borsellino, Rita Borsellino Fiore, Agnese Borsellino and Manfredi Borsellino.

3. *Ordinanza Sentenza contro Abbate + 706,* vol. 17, filed in Palermo, November 8, 1985.

4. *La Repubblica,* May 6, 1980, and Lodato, pp. 40–42.

5. This quote and the entire reconstruction of Borsellino's investigation into the death of Basile is from vol. 17 of the *Ordinanza Sentenza contro Abbate + 706,* which Borsellino wrote.

6. The murder of Fra Giacinto (Stefano Castronovo) was reported in *La Repubblica,* September 9, 1980; *L'Espresso,* September 21, 1980; and in Lodato, pp. 63–66.

7. The relations of Paolo Bontate with Raytheon are described in *La Repubblica,* April 25, 1981, and in Lupo, *Storia della mafia,* p. 189.

8. The death of Stefano Bontate was reported in *La Repubblica,* April 25, 1981, and described in Lodato, pp. 66–68. Falcone's reconstruction of the killing is contained in vol. 13 of the *Ordinanza Sentenza* of the maxi-trial, pp. 2516–41.

9. *L'Espresso,* May 4, 1981.

10. The death of Inzerillo was reported in *La Repubblica,* May 12, 1981, and is discussed in Lodato, p. 68. Falcone's reconstruction of the crime is contained in vol. 13 of the *Ordinanza Sentenza* of the maxi-trial, pp. 2542–67.

11. Pino Arlacchi, *La mafia imprenditrice* (Bologna, 1983), p. 153.

12. A full discussion of the Salvos' economic empire and criminal associations is outlined by Falcone in the maxi-trial indictment and is reprinted in Stajano, ed., *Mafia: L'atto di accusa dei giudici di Palermo,* pp. 313–58.

13. Author interview with Elio Pizzuti.

14. The wiretapped conversation between Lo Presti and Buscetta is in *Mafia: L'atto di accusa dei giudici di Palermo,* pp. 320–25.

15. Galluzzo, La Licata and Lodato, eds., *Falcone vive,* p. 59.

16. The interview with Nino Salvo appeared in *L'Espresso,* July 4, 1982.

17. Author interview with Pizzuti.

CHAPTER FOUR

1. There were an estimated thirty mafia killings in the first three months of 1982, Nando Dalla Chiesa, *Delitto imperfetto* (Milan, 1984), p. 61.

2. A full description of the attack on Contorno as well as the principal crimes of the mafia war of Palermo, 1981–82, is contained in the *Rapporto giudiziario di denuncia a carico di Greco, Michele + 161 persone,* written by Antonino Cassarà, filed jointly by the police and *carabineri* of Palermo, July 13, 1982. A second, fuller account (based on Contorno's own testimony) is contained in the maxi-trial indictment (vol. 13, pp. 2603–31), written by Falcone. A description of the crime is also in Lodato, *Quindici anni di mafia,* pp. 74–76.

3. Cassarà report, *Michele Greco + 161.*

4. A long indictment on the misappropriation of water in Palermo, *Sentenza contro Ciacciofera, Michele + 88,* was filed by Giacomo Conte of the Ufficio Istruzione di Palermo on March 1, 1988. The indictment quotes extensively from a series of earlier studies of the wells of the city. Michele Greco was one of the defendants and his wells are discussed at length.

5. *L'Espresso,* May 29, 1983.

6. Perhaps the definitive and most up-to-date account is contained in the report on the principal mafia killings in Palmero over the previous decade: *Richiesta di custodia cautelare nei confronti di Agate, Mariano + 57,* filed by the Procura della Repubblica di Palermo, February 20, 1993.

7. Borsellino's reconstruction of the Giaccone killing is contained in the maxi-trial indictment, vol. 17, pp. 3428–51.

8. The statistics on heroin use in Italy come from the annual reports of the Direzione Centrale per i Servizi Antidroga of the Ministero dell'Interno.

9. On the appointment of Dalla Chiesa, see Stajano, ed., *Mafia: L'atto di accusa dei giudici di Palermo,* pp. 221–27.

10. On the career and death of La Torre, see Lodato, pp. 81–91.

11. Author interview with Giuseppe Ayala.

12. On the press campaign against Dalla Chiesa, see Falcone's reconstruction in Stajano, ed., *Mafia,* pp. 227–40.

13. Dalla Chiesa's interview with Bocca appeared in *La Repubblica,* August 10, 1982. It is reprinted in full in *Delitto imperfetto,* pp. 247–52.
14. Falcone's reconstruction is reprinted in its entirety in *Mafia,* pp. 221–311. These diary entries are from pp. 225–40.
15. Dalla Chiesa, p. 52.
16. Dalla Chiesa's letter to Spadolini is reprinted in *Mafia,* p. 232.
17. *L'Espresso,* May 9, 1982.
18. *Mafia,* p. 230.
19. *Mafia,* pp. 291–92.
20. *Wall Street Journal,* February 12, 1985. Partially reprinted in *Mafia,* p. 240.
21. Falcone's reconstruction of the investigation into Graci and the Knights of Labor of Catania is in *Mafia,* pp. 254–66. Also, author interview with Elio Pizzuti.
22. *Mafia,* pp. 255–57.
23. *Mafia,* pp. 240–88.
24. *Mafia,* p. 293.
25. *Mafia,* p. 298.

CHAPTER FIVE

1. Lodato, *Quindici anni di mafia,* p. 122.
2. *L'Espresso,* April 14, 1985.
3. *L'Espresso,* February 6, 1983.
4. Report of the Cutolo wedding appeared in *L'Espresso,* May 1, 1983.
5. *L'Espresso,* May 15, 1983.
6. The history of the Basile case is given by Borsellino in vol. 17 of the maxi-trial indictment, pp. 3361–78.
7. Author interview with Manfredi Borsellino.
8. Author interviews with Agnese Borsellino, Rita Borsellino Fiore and Maria Pia Lepanto Borsellino. Borsellino's comment in an interview on Swiss television is on videocassette: *Intervista a Paolo Borsellino,* © 1992, RTSI.
9. The history of Gasparini's cooperation is explained by Falcone in the maxi-trial indictment, reprinted in Stajano, ed., *Mafia,* pp. 105–13.
10. *Mafia,* pp. 122–29.
11. *Mafia,* p. 296.
12. *Mafia,* pp. 139–47
13. Author interview with Gianni De Gennaro.
14. Author interview with Elio Pizzuti.
15. Author interview with Domenico Signorino.
16. Lodato, pp. 130–32. Author interview with Giovanni Paparcuri.
17. *Mafia,* pp. 293–96.
18. The first excerpts of the Chinnici diaries appeared in *L'Espresso,* September 18, 1983. For discussion of the Chinnici diaries, see Lodato, pp. 137–42, and Galluzzo, *Obiettivo Falcone,* pp. 151–63.
19. A more complete sampling of the Chinnici diaries, including this quotation, is reprinted in *Antimafia,* vol. 1 (1991), a publication of the Coordinmento Antimafia of Palermo.
20. *L'Espresso,* October 23, 1983.
21. *Antimafia,* vol. 1 (1991).
22. Galluzzo, La Licato and Lodato, eds. *Falcone vive,* p. 37.
23. *Antimafia,* vol. 1 (1991).
24. *Falcone vive,* p. 37.

25. The Consiglio Superiore della Magistratura discussed the case of the Chinnici diaries in its meeting of September 28, 1983.

CHAPTER SIX

1. Antonino Caponetto, *I miei giorni a Palermo* (Milan, 1992), p. 31.
2. Caponetto, p. 37.
3. Caponetto, p. 31.
4. Caponetto, p. 40.
5. Author interview with Antonino Caponetto.
6. Caponetto, p. 37.
7. Author interview with Barbara Sanzo.
8. Caponetto, p. 38.
9. Author interview with Leonardo Guarnotta.
10. Author interview with Liliana Ferraro.
11. Stajano, ed., *Mafia,* p. 15.
12. The contributions of these witnesses are discussed in *Mafia:* Gasparini (pp. 105–23); Totta (p. 289); Calzetta (p. 180); Sinagra (p. 47); and Marsala (pp. 63–69). See also the interrogations of Sinagra and Marsala deposited in the Tribunale di Palermo.
13. Interrogation of Salvatore Contorno.
14. Sterling, *Octopus,* p. 75.
15. Fabrizio Calvi, *Vita quotidiana della mafia* (Milan, 1986), p. 98.
16. Sterling, pp. 114–15.
17. *Mafia,* p. 115.
18. Sterling, p. 267.
19. Sterling, p. 266.
20. *L'Espresso,* January 16, 1983.
21. *L'Espresso,* January 30, 1983.
22. Sterling, pp. 272–73.
23. Author interview with Vincenzo Geraci; Lodato, pp. 145–46.

CHAPTER SEVEN

1. Falcone, *Cose di Cosa Nostra*, pp. 49–50.
2. Falcone, p. 44.
3. Interrogation of Tommaso Buscetta.
4. Interrogation of Tommaso Buscetta.
5. Author interview with Antonino Caponetto.
6. Interrogation of Tommaso Buscetta.
7. The organization of Cosa Nostra, as explained by Buscetta, is outlined by Falcone in the maxi-trial indictment and reprinted in Stajano, ed., *Mafia: L'atto di accusa dei giudici di Palermo,* pp. 38–55.
8. Interrogation of Tommaso Buscetta.
9. Author interview with Richard Martin.
10. Author interview with Antonio Manganelli.
11. For an extended discussion of the summits of Palermo and Apalachin, see Sterling, *Octopus,* pp. 82–92.
12. Sterling, p. 103.
13. Sterling, p. 111.
14. Interrogation of Tommaso Buscetta.
15. Interrogation of Tommaso Buscetta.
16. The confessions of Di Cristina appear in the report filed by the Legione Cara-

binieri di Palermo on August 25, 1978, and are partially reprinted in *Mafia,* pp. 18–37.

17. This quote and those that follow are from the interrogation of Tommaso Buscetta.

18. This description of the death of Rosario Riccobono is contained in the *Richiesta di custodia cautelare nei confronti di Agate, Mariano + 57,* filed by the Procura della Repubblica di Palermo, February 20, 1993.

19. This quote and those that follow are from the interrogation of Tommaso Buscetta.

20. Galluzzo, La Licata and Lodato, eds. *Falcone vive,* p. 61.

21. This quote and those that follow are from the interrogation of Tommaso Buscetta.

22. *La Stampa,* November 22, 1992.

23. Falcone, p. 51.

24. Falcone, p. 52.

25. *La Stampa,* November 22, 1992.

26. Author interview with Antonino Caponetto.

27. On the dozing of Geraci, see the testimony of Alberto Di Pisa before the Consiglio Superiore della Magistratura, September 21, 1989. On the private remarks of Buscetta to Falcone, I have relied on an interview with Antonino Caponetto, who was present at the December 18, 1984, deposition of Buscetta at which Geraci was not present.

28. Falcone, p. 87.

29. Interrogation of Tommaso Buscetta.

30. Falcone, p. 82.

31. Author interview with Leonardo Guarnotta.

32. Falcone, p. 72.

33. Falcone, p. 70.

CHAPTER EIGHT

1. Falcone, *Cose di Cosa Nostra,* p. 41.

2. Interrogation of Tommaso Buscetta.

3. The confessions of Marsala are quoted extensively in Stajano, ed., *Mafia: L'atto di accusa dei giudici di Palermo,* pp. 63–72.

4. The wiretapped conversations between Violi and Cuffaro are reprinted in *Mafia,* pp. 55–63.

5. Author interview with Richard Martin.

6. The division of labor of the anti-mafia pool was explained to me in interviews with Antonino Caponetto, Giuseppe Di Lello and Leonardo Guarnotta.

7. Author interview with Giuseppe Ayala. See also, Giuseppe Ayala, *La Guerra dei giusti* (Milan, 1993), pp. 83–85.

8. *Corriere della Sera,* September 31, 1984; *La Stampa,* October 1, 1984.

9. Author interview with Richard Martin.

10. Interrogation of Tommaso Buscetta.

11. For a fuller discussion of the Pizza Connection case, see Sterling, *Octopus,* pp. 180–89 and pp. 249–64. Also, Alexander, Shana, *The Pizza Connection,* (New York, 1988) and Ralph Blumenthal, *The Last Days of the Sicilians,* (New York, 1988). The figure on John Gambino's ownership of pizza parlors is from *L'Espresso,* April 22, 1984.

12. Sterling, p. 242.

13. Sterling, p. 244.

14. Interrogation of Tommaso Buscetta.

15. *Ordinanza Sentenza* of the maxi-trial, vol. 11, pp. 2139–71.
16. Sterling, p. 54. See also, *L'Espresso,* April 22, 1984, and November 18, 1984.
17. Author interview with Richard Martin.
18. *La Repubblica,* October 4, 1984.
19. Lodato, *Quindici anni di mafia,* p. 154.
20. Interrogation of Salvatore Contorno.
21. Author interview with Antonio Manganelli.
22. Interrogation of Salvatore Contorno. Falcone also reconstructs the assassination attempt against Contorno in the indictments of the maxi-trial *Ordinanza Sentenza,* vol. 13, pp. 2603–31).
23. Lodato, p. 154.
24. Interrogation of Salvatore Contorno.
25. Author interview with Richard Martin.

CHAPTER NINE

1. The cable is quoted in *Europeo,* July 2, 1993.
2. Ciancimino's career was outlined by the final report of the Italian parliament's anti-mafia commission, *Relazione conclusiva, 4 febbraio, 1976, VI Legislatura, doc. XXIII, n.2,* pp. 214–37, reprinted in Tranfaglia, *Mafia, politica e affari,* pp. 72–108. See also, the indictment of Ciancimino, Tribunal of Palermo, *Procedimento penale contro Vito Ciancimino + 4, n.411/90* and the sentence of the court: *Sentenza contro Vito Ciancimino,* Tribunale di Palermo, January 17, 1992. On Ciancimino's role in the water system of Palermo, see: *Sentenza contro Ciacciofera, Michele + 88* filed by the Ufficio Istruzione di Palermo on March 1, 1988.
3. See the essay on Lima written by Vincenzo Vasile in Tranfaglia, Nicola, ed., *Cirillo, Ligato e Lima* (Rome-Bari, 1994); and the *Atto di accusa* of the Procura of Palermo, filed October 11, 1992, and the anti-mafia commission's *Relazione conclusiva, 4 febbraio, 1976, VI Legislatura, doc. XXIII, n.2,* pp. 214–37, reprinted in Tranfaglia, pp. 72–108.
4. Giorgio Galli, *Storia della Democrazia Cristiana* (Milan, 1993) and *Storia dei partiti politici italiani* (Milan, 1991). Also author interview with Galli.
5. *La Repubblica,* October 23, 1992.
6. *La Repubblica,* October 23, 1992.
7. Sterling, *Octopus,* p. 229.
8. Author interview with Galli.
9. Galuzzo, *Obiettivo Falcone,* p. 172.
10. Interview with Elda Pucci in *L'Espresso,* July 29, 1984.
11. Nino Rocca and Umberto Santino, eds., *Le tasche di Palermo* (Palermo, 1992), p. 22.
12. Leoluca Orlando, *Palermo* (Milan, 1990), pp. 42–43.
13. Interview with Elda Pucci in *L'Espresso,* July 29, 1984.
14. Orlando, pp. 50–51.
15. Interrogation of Tommaso Buscetta. *Sentenza contro Vito Ciancimino,* Tribunale di Palermo, January 17, 1992.
16. *La Repubblica,* October 4, 1984.
17. Alfredo Galasso, *Mafia e Politica* (Milan, 1993), p. 33.
18. Interview with Elda Pucci in *L'Espresso,* July 29, 1984.
19. *La Repubblica,* October 3, 1984.
20. *La Repubblica,* October 5, 1984.
21. Giuseppe di Lampedusa, *Il Gattopardo* (Milan, 1958) and *The Leopard,*

trans. by Archibald Colquhoun (New York, 1960). This quote is from p. 42 of the Italian edition, my translation.

22. Ginsborg, *History of Contemporary Italy*, p. 375.

23. Centro Studi Confindustria report on *Squilibri di bilancio, distorsioni economiche dell'economia italiana,* October 1991, by Stefano Micossi and Giuseppe Tullio.

24. On the period of the "historic compromise," see Ginsborg, pp. 375–402.

25. Giulio Andreotti, *Il Potere Logora* (Milan, 1990), p. 34.

26. Enzo Biagi, *Il Boss è solo* (Milan, 1986), p. 181; cited in Sterling, p. 74.

27. Buscetta interrogation.

28. Sterling, pp. 272–74.

29. Author interview with Gianni De Gennaro.

30. Interrogations of Tommaso Buscetta and Francesco Marino Mannoia.

31. Lodato, *Quindici anni di mafia,* p. 154.

32. Interrogation of Tommaso Buscetta. Also, Stajano, ed., *Mafia: L'atto di accusa dei giudici di Palermo,* pp. 326–29; Caponetto, *I miei giorni a Palermo,* pp. 54–56.

33. *La Repubblica,* October 19, 1984.

34. Lodato, p. 158.

35. Interrogation of Vincenzo Marsala.

36. Author interview with Antonino Caponetto.

37. Interrogation of Tommaso Buscetta.

38. Caponetto, pp. 54–56.

39. Alessandro Silj, *Il Malpaese* (Rome, 1994), pp. 257–58.

CHAPTER TEN

1. *Processo alla mafia,* a film produced by the Italian state television, RAI, 1986. Lodato, *Quindici anni di mafia,* 189–192. Sterling, pp. 277–281. Author interview with Liliana Ferraro.

2. Lodato, p. 155.

3. Galluzzo, *Obiettivo Falcone,* p. 175.

4. Lodato, pp. 209–12, and Orlando, *Palermo.*

5. Caponetto, *I miei giorni a Palermo,* p. 50.

6. The estimate on the number of Sicilian families dependant on the illegal economy came from an interview with Francesco Misiani, formerly a staff member of the High Commission for anti-mafia affairs. The statistics on income and consumption are from the Italian government statistics office, *ISTAT,* and are quoted in the *Relazione di Minoranza* filed by the parliament's anti-mafia commission, on January 24, 1990, *X Legislatura, doc. XXIII, n.12-bis/1.*

7. *Giornale di Sicilia,* April 14, 1985, quoted in Galluzzo, p. 190.

8. Author interview with Antonino Caponetto.

9. Author interview with Domenico Signorino.

10. Author interview with Gianni De Gennaro.

11. Author interview with Antonino Caponetto.

12. Author interview with Ignazio De Francisci.

13. Author interview with Leonardo Guarnotta.

14. Author interview with Giuseppe Ayala.

15. Falcone, *Cose di Cosa Nostra,* p. 15.

16. Author interview with Stefano Racheli.

17. Author interview with John Costanzo.

18. Luca Rossi, *I disarmati* (Milan, 1992), p. 267.

19. Author interview with Diego Cavalliero.
20. Interrogation of Vincenzo Sinagra.
21. Chinnici and Santino, *La Violenza Programmata,* p. 213.
22. Interrogation of Vincenzo Sinagra.
23. Author interview with Vincenzo Sinagra.
24. Interrogation of Vincenzo Sinagra.
25. Borsellino's reconstruction of the Giaccone killing is contained in the maxi-trial indictment, vol. 17, pp. 3428–51.
26. The number of mafia fugitives is from *L'Espresso,* August 25, 1985.
27. On the career of Montana, see Lodato, pp. 159–61.
28. Petruzzella, ed., *Sulla pelle dello stato,* p. 111.
29. Lodato, p. 162.
30. *Sulla pelle dello stato,* p. 112.
31. Lodato, pp. 168–69.
32. Testimony of Vincenzo Pajno, Procuratore della Repubblica, before the Consiglio Superiore della Magistratura, on July 30, 1988.
33. Lodato, p. 169; *L'Espresso,* October 20, 1985.
34. Galluzzo, *Obiettivo Falcone,* pp. 191–92; Lodato, 170–72.
35. Lodato, p. 174.
36. *Sulla pelle dello stato,* p. 113.
37. Caponetto, pp. 68–69.

CHAPTER ELEVEN

1. Author interview with Rita Borsellino Fiore.
2. Stajano, ed., *Mafia: L'atto di accusa dei giudici di Palermo,* p. viii.
3. *Mafia,* p. 5.
4. *Mafia,* pp. 84–88.
5. *Mafia,* p. 14.
6. *Ordinanza Sentenza contro Abbate + 706,* vol. 17.
7. *Mafia,* p. 2.
8. *Mafia,* pp. 244–45.
9. *Mafia,* p. vii.
10. Author interviews with Maria Pia Lepanto Borsellino and Rita Borsellino Fiore.
11. Caponetto, *I miei giorni a Palermo,* p. 70.
12. Aurelio Angelini et al. *Uno Sguardo dal bunker: cronache del maxi-processo di Palermo* (Siracusa, 1987), pp. 17–31.
13. Lodato, *Quindici anni di mafia,* p. 182.
14. Orlando, *Palermo,* p. 102; Lodato, p. 179.
15. Lodato, pp. 178–79.
16. Angelini, p. 18.
17. Angelini, p. 21.
18. Angelini, pp. 18–20.
19. Sterling, *Octopus,* p. 280.
20. *Processo alla mafia* (1986 film).
21. Author interview with Giuseppe Ayala.
22. Leonardo Sciascia, *A futura memoria* (Milan, 1989), p. 116.
23. The full transcript of the maxi-trial was reprinted in the *Giornale di Sicilia,* between February 1986 and December 1987. Substantial excerpts appear in a volume edited by Lino Jannuzzi, *Così parlò Buscetta* (Milan, 1986). This quote is from p. 115.

24. Jannuzzi, p. 135.
25. Jannuzzi, p. 140.
26. Jannuzzi, pp. 144–45.
27. Jannuzzi, p. 137.
28. Jannuzzi, p. 148.
29. Jannuzzi, pp. 194–95.
30. Jannuzzi, p. 203.
31. Jannuzzi, pp. 197–201.
32. Caponetto, p. 55.
33. Jannuzzi, pp. 207–8.
34. Jannuzzi, pp. 220–25.
35. Jannuzzi, pp. 91–92.
36. Jannuzzi, p. 169.
37. Sterling, p. 284.
38. Jannuzzi, p. 158.
39. Sterling, p. 285.
40. Angelini, p. 117.
41. *Mafia*, p. 328.

CHAPTER TWELVE

1. Lodato, *Quindici anni di mafia*, pp. 186–87.
2. Interrogation of Vincenzo Marsala.
3. On the marriage of Falcone I have relied on author interviews with Barbara Sanzo, Rita Fiore Borsellino, Pasqua Seminara and Francesco Lo Voi.
4. Author interview with Giuseppe Ayala.
5. *Corriere della Sera*, January 10, 1987, reprinted in Sciascia, *A futura memoria*, pp. 128–30.
6. *A futura memoria*, p. 130.
7. Author interview with Rita Borsellino Fiore.
8. Orlando, *Palermo*, p. 71.
9. Lodato, p. 208.
10. *Giornale di Sicilia*, January 14, 1987, quoted in Lodato, p. 207.
11. Rossi, *I disarmati*, p. 211.
12. Galluzzo, *Obettivo Falcone*, p. 189.
13. Vitalone's conduct as a magistrate and his rejection for the Corte di Cassazione are the subject of debate at the hearings of the Consiglio Superiore della Magistratura on May 6, 1982, and November 28, 1985. See also: *L'Espresso*, May 18, 1986.
14. Chinnici and Santino, *La Violenza Programmata*, p. 126.
15. Lodato, p. 214; *Richiesta di custodia cautelare nei confronti di Agate, Mariano + 57*, filed by the Procura della Repubblica di Palermo, February 20, 1993.
16. Interrogation of Tommaso Buscetta.
17. Arlacchi, *Gli Uomini del disonore*, p. 28.
18. On Craxi's rise to power in the Socialist Party, see Ginsborg, *A History of Contemporary Italy*, pp. 377–78.
19. From Bitetto's confessions to the Procura della Repubblica di Milano, excerpted in the book *Tangentopoli* (published by *Panorama*, Milan 1993), pp. 50–62.
20. Carlo Palermo's vicissitudes are chronicled in *L'Espresso*, April 14, 1985; May 19, 1985; July 29, 1984, and in his book *Attentato* (Trento, 1992).
21. On the IRI slush fund see: *L'Espresso*, January 13, 1984; *Panorama*, February 10, 1985; *L'Espresso*, February 17, 1987; *L'Espresso*, May 3, 1987; *L'E-*

spresso, August 16, 1987. On the protest of the assistant prosecutors in Rome, see *L'Espresso,* June 16, 1985.

22. *Panorama,* September 27, 1987.
23. On the election results of 1987, see Massimo Morisi et al., *Far Politica in Sicilia* (Milan, 1993), p. 156.
24. Orlando, *Palermo,* pp. 74–79.
25. Morisi, p. 144. Interview with Claudio Martelli, *Panorama,* September 6, 1987.
26. Author interview with Antonino Caponetto.
27. Author interview with Ignazio De Francisci.
28. Rossi, *I disarmati,* p. 269.
29. Lodato, pp. 220–23.

CHAPTER THIRTEEN

1. Caponetto, *I miei giorni a Palermo,* p. 90.
2. *Corriere della Sera,* January 13, 1988; Lodato, *Quindici anni di mafia,* pp. 230–32.
3. Lodato, p. 235.
4. Lodato, pp. 234–35; Galasso, *Mafia e Politica,* pp. 32–40. The most complete text of the "testament" of Insalaco was printed in *Antimafia,* vol. 2 (1990).
5. Caponetto, p. 89.
6. Caponetto, p. 88.
7. Caponetto, p. 87.
8. *Corriere della Sera,* January 20, 1988.
9. Caponetto, p. 89.
10. Author interview with Giuseppe Di Lello.
11. Rossi, *I disarmati,* p. 268.
12. Author interview with Vito D'Ambrosio.
13. Author interview with Ignazio De Francisci.
14. Author interview with Stefano Racheli.
15. Author interview with Giuseppe Di Lello.
16. The quotes from the debate on the nomination are all contained in the minutes of the hearings of the Consiglio Superiore della Magistratura from January 18, 1988.
17. Caponetto, p. 82.
18. This and the quotes that follow come from author interviews with Vincenzo Geraci, Leonardo Guarnotta, Giuseppe Ayala and Ignazio De Francisci.

CHAPTER FOURTEEN

1. The discussion of Calderone is derived principally from the depositions he made to Falcone. Those confessions were reworked by Pino Arlacchi into the book that became *Men of Dishonor.* Although the page references given here correspond to the English-language edition of the book, the translations are my own based on the original Italian edition.
2. Arlacchi, *Men of Dishonor,* p. 75.
3. Arlacchi, p. 22.
4. Arlacchi, p. 172.
5. Arlacchi, p. 172 [pp. 198–99, Italian ed.].
6. Arlacchi, p. 93.
7. Arlacchi, p. 183 [p. 212, Italian ed.].

8. Election figures are provided by the Italian Ministry of the Interior and published after each election by the Italian parliament.
9. Arlacchi, pp. 184–85 [pp. 213–14, Italian ed.].
10. Arlacchi, p. 184 [p. 214 Italian ed.].
11. Arlacchi, p. 177 [p. 205, Italian ed.].
12. Author interview with Antonio Manganelli.
13. Interrogation of Tommaso Buscetta; also quoted in the indictments into the death of Salvatore Lima, *Il delitto Lima.*
14. From the minutes of the hearings of the Consiglio Superiore della Magistratura (CSM), July 31, 1988, Falcone testimony.
15. CSM, July 30, 1988, Palmieri testimony.
16. Caponetto, *I miei giorni a Palermo,* p. 91.
17. CSM, July 30, 1988, Meli testimony.
18. Lodato, *Quindici anni di mafia,* and CSM, July 30, 1988, Meli testimony.
19. CSM, July 31, 1988, Borsellino and Falcone testimony.
20. CSM, July 30, 1988, Palmieri testimony.
21. CSM, July 30, 1988, Meli testimony.
22. CSM, Falcone testimony, July 31, 1988.
23. Author interview with Giuseppe Di Lello.
24. CSM, July 31, 1988, Borsellino.
25. CSM, July 30, 1988, Palmieri and Meli testimony.
26. CSM, July 31, 1988, testimony of Giaocchino Natoli.

CHAPTER FIFTEEN

1. Author interview with Diego Cavalliero.
2. Author interview with Calogero Germanà.
3. Author interview with Diego Cavalliero.
4. Author interview with Calogero Germanà.
5. Minutes of the hearings of the Consiglio Superiore della Magistratura (CSM), July 31, 1988, testimony of Paolo Borsellino.
6. *Domanda di autorizzazione a procedere contro il Senatore Antonio Gava, XI Legislatura, doc. IV, n.113,* filed April 7, 1993.
7. Sterling, *Octopus,* pp. 292–96.
8. Sterling p. 293.
9. Sterling, p. 292. On Carnevale, see Sterling, p. 294 and the anti-mafia commission's *Relazione di minoranza, X Legislatura, Doc. XXIII n. 12/bis/1,* January 24, 1990.
10. Caponetto, *I miei giorni a Palermo,* p. 85.
11. Caponetto, pp. 84–85.
12. CSM, July 30, 1988, Meli testimony.
13. Author interview with Liliana Ferraro.
14. Falcone's letter appeared in the *Corriere della Sera* and other Italian papers on July 31, 1988. It has been reprinted in numerous books, including Galuzzo, *Obiettivo Falcone,* and Rossi, *I disarmati.*
15. CSM, July 30, 1988, testimony of Carmelo Conti and Antonio Palmieri.
16. CSM, July 30, 1988, Meli testimony.
17. CSM, July 31, 1988, Falcone testimony.
18. CSM, July 31, 1988, Borsellino testimony.
19. Author interview with Vito D'Ambrosio.
20. *Giornale,* July 31, 1988, and August 1, 1988.
21. Author interview with Vito D'Ambrosio.

22. Author interview with Vincenzo Geraci.
23. Author interview with Vito D'Ambrosio.

CHAPTER SIXTEEN

1. *Giornale,* September 10, 1988.
2. *L'Espresso,* December 11, 1988.
3. Galluzzo, *Obiettivo Falcone,* pp. 280–81.
4. *L'Espresso,* April 16, 1989.
5. Letter of September 5, 1988, reprinted in Galluzzo, pp. 282–83.
6. Lodato, *Quindici anni di mafia,* pp. 261–63.
7. The report of these killings and the quotes that follow are from *Corriere della Sera,* September 29, 1988.
8. *Europeo,* November 18, 1988.
9. *Corriere,* November 16, 1988.
10. Galluzzo, p. 284.
11. *Corriere,* November 14, 1988.
12. *Corriere,* November 18, 1988. The member calling for Falcone and Meli's transfer was Erminio Pennachini, a Christian Democrat appointee.
13. Author interview with Ignazio De Francisci.
14. *Europeo,* November 25, 1988.
15. Author interview with Vito D'Ambrosio.
16. Sterling, *Octopus,* p. 294; Galluzzo, p. 283.
17. Author interview with Giuseppe Ayala.
18. *L'Espresso,* April 16, 1989.
19. Galluzzo, p. 283; Sterling, p. 295.
20. Author interview with Giuseppe Ayala.
21. Author interview with John Costanzo.
22. Galluzzo, p. 285.
23. *L'Espresso,* December 18, 1988.
24. Sterling, p. 307.
25. *Corriere,* December 2, 1988.
26. This reconstruction of Operation Iron Tower is based on conversations with Gianni De Gennaro, Antonio Manganelli as well as accounts in Sterling, pp. 305–307; *Corriere,* December 2, 1988; *L'Espresso,* December 11 and December 18, 1988.

CHAPTER SEVENTEEN

1. Author interview with Giuseppe Di Lello.
2. Author interview with Vito D'Ambrosio.
3. Sterling, *Octopus,* p. 296.
4. Author interviews with Vito D'Ambrosio, Giuseppe Di Lello and Ignazio De Francisci.
5. *Relazione di Minoranza* filed by the parliament's anti-mafia commission, on January 24, 1990, X *Legislatura,* doc. XXIII, *n.12-bis/1,* chapter III.
6. Sterling, p. 291.
7. *L'Espresso,* February 19, 1989.
8. For a treatment of the state of health care in Palermo and particularly at the Ospedale Civico, see a recent book, *Sanità alla sbarra* by Riccardo Arena (Palermo, 1994), p. 60 and pp. 205–18.
9. *L'Espresso,* April 16, 1989.
10. *L'Espresso,* April 16, 1989.
11. *Corriere della Sera,* January 25, 1989.

12. *L'Espresso,* June 25, 1989.
13. *L'Espresso,* June 11, 1989.
14. Salvatore Parlagreco, *Il mistero del corvo* (Milan, 1990), p. 66.
15. *Il Sabato,* February 11, 1989.
16. *L'Espresso,* May 28, 1989.
17. *L'Espresso,* July 2, 1989.
18. Falcone, *Cose di Cosa Nostra,* pp. 55–56.
19. Falcone, CSM, July 13, 1989.
20. Author interview with Vito D'Ambrosio.
21. Galluzzo, *Obiettivo Falcone,* p. 304.
22. Lodato, *Quindici anni di mafia,* p. 276.
23. Galluzzo, pp. 311–13.
24. Author interview with Antonio Manganelli.
25. Galluzzo, p. 299.
26. Author interview with Ignazio De Francisci.
27. *Corriere,* June 28, 1994.
28. Parlagreco, pp. 67–68.
29. Parlagreco, p. 61.
30. Parlagreco, p. 66. For various interpretations of the *corvo* case, see Parlagreco's *Il mistero del corvo* (written in defense of Di Pisa), and *L'intrigo,* written by Parlagreco and Di Pisa together. For a different perspective, see *Per fatti di mafia* (Rome, 1991), pp. 55–112 by Francesco Misiani, a close aide to High Commissioner for anti-mafia affairs at the time. For the factual reconstruction of events, I have relied on the testimony before the Consiglio Superiore della Magistratura (CSM) and its final report of November 6, 1989, as well as the sentence of the court of Caltanisetta, *Sentenza contro Di Pisa, Alberto,* February 22, 1990.
31. Galluzzo, p. 316.
32. Author interview with Vito D'Ambrosio.
33. Testimony of Vincenzo Pajno, CSM, July 22, 1989.
34. Falcone testimony before CSM, October 12, 1989.
35. *Sentenza contro Di Pisa, Alberto,* February 22, 1990, Tribunale di Caltanisetta, February 22, 1992.
36. Di Pisa testimony, CSM, July 24, 1989.
37. Di Pisa testimony, CSM, July 24, 1989.
38. *La Repubblica,* October 6, 1989.
39. Di Pisa testimony, CSM, September 21, 1989.
40. Falcone testimony before CSM, October 12, 1989.
41. Ayala testimony before CSM, September 28, 1989.
42. Author interview with Vito D'Ambrosio.
43. *L'Espresso,* March 4, 1990.
44. Author interview with Stefano Racheli.
45. *La Repubblica,* July 28, 1988, quoted in Parlagreco, *Il mistero del corvo,* p. 71.

CHAPTER EIGHTEEN

1. Accounts of the testimony of Pellegriti appeared in the *Corierre della Sera,* October 11, 1989, and October 13, 1989. The quote is from an author interview with Giuseppe Ayala.
2. Author interview with Vito D'Ambrosio.
3. Falcone testimony before Consiglio Superiore della Magistratura (CSM), October 12, 1989.
4. Author interviews with Salvatore Barresi and Vito D'Ambrosio.

5. CSM hearings on Vitalone.
6. Author interview with Vito D'Ambrosio.
7. Interrogation of Francesco Marino Mannoia.
8. Author interview with Antonio Manganelli.
9. The reconstruction of Marino Mannoia's career is based on his own interrogation and is contained in the *Richiesta di custodia cautelare nei confronti di Agate, Mariano + 57*, filed by the Procura della Repubblica di Palermo, February 20, 1993.
10. *Corriere della Sera*, November 25, 1989, December 5, 1989, December 6, 1989.
11. Falcone, *Cose di Cosa Nostra*, pp. 27 and 59.
12. Interrogation of Francesco Marino Mannoia.
13. Author interviews with Salvatore Barresi, Vito D'Ambrosio, Ignazio De Francisci, Stefano Racheli and Giuseppe Di Lello.
14. *Corriere della Sera*, January 24, 1990.
15. *Corriere*, February 11, 1990.
16. *Corriere*, May 10, 1990.
17. *Corriere*, May 19, 1990.
18. *Corriere*, May 19, 1990.
19. Author interviews with Pietro Grasso and Francesco Misiani. The results of the investigation into the elections are contained in the anti-mafia commission's report entitled: *Relazione sulle risultanze dell'attivita' del gruppo di lavoro della Commissione incaricato di indagare sulla recrudescenza di episodi criminali durante il periodo elettorale. X Legislatura, doc. XXIII, n.20*, July 25, 1990.
20. On the situation in Gioia Tauro, see Misiani, *Per fatti di mafia*, pp. 113–52.
21. *Corriere*, June 29, 1990.
22. Author interviews with Salvatore Barresi, Vito D'Ambrosio and Francesco Lo Voi.
23. Author interviews with Giacomo Conte and Giovanni Falcone.

CHAPTER NINETEEN

1. The reconstruction of this period of Borsellino's career is based on author interviews with Diego Cavalliero and Antonio Ingroia. See also, Lucentini, *Paolo Borsellino: Il valore di una vita*.
2. Interrogation of Giacomina Filipello, deposited in the Tribunal of Marsala. Filipello's collaboration is also discussed in Liliana Madeo, *Donne di mafia* (Milan, 1994), pp. 49–59, and Lucentini, pp. 177–80.
3. Lucentini, pp. 165–67.
4. Interrogation of Rosario Spatola.
5. Author interview with Antonio Ingroia.
6. Interrogation of Rosario Spatola.
7. Lucentini, p. 176.
8. This quote is from a brief biography of Rita Atria by Sandra Rizza, *Una ragazza contro la mafia* (Palermo, 1993), p. 61. Rita Atria's collaboration is also discussed in Madeo, pp. 185–211 and Lucentini, pp. 181–201.
9. *Corriere della Sera*, July 7, 1990.
10. *Relazione di Minoranza* filed by the parliament's anti-mafia commission, on January 24, 1990, X Legislatura, doc. XXIII, n.12-bis/1.
11. *L'Espresso*, September 30, 1990.
12. On the career and death of Livantino, see Nando Dalla Chiesa, *Il giudice ragazzino* (Turin, 1992), and Lucentini, pp. 184–86.

13. *La Repubblica,* September 26, 1990.
14. *La Repubblica* and *Corriere della Sera,* November 2, 1990.
15. *La Repubblica, Corriere* and *L'Unità,* November 29, 1990.
16. Author interview with Salvatore Barresi.
17. Author interview with Antonino Caponetto.
18. *L'Espresso,* November 11, 18, 1990. Silj, *Il Malpaese,* pp. 42–49.
19. Falcone's diary notes are from the archive of the Italian parliament's anti-mafia commission (*Il Sole 24 Ore,* June 24, 1992).
20. Author interview with Giuseppe Di Lello.
21. *La Repubblica,* September 26, 1990.
22. Morisi, *Far Politica in Sicilia,* p. 144.
23. Author interview with Vito D'Ambrosio.
24. *La Repubblica,* May 23, 1991.
25. Author interview with Salvatore Barresi. On the freeing and rearrest of Michele Greco, see *Corriere,* February 26, 1991, and *L'Unità,* February 27, 1991.
26. *Il Messaggero,* October 4, 1991; *Corriere,* November 13, 1991. Author interviews with Liliana Ferraro and Ignazio De Francisci.
27. Author interview with Giacomo Travaglino.
28. *Corriere,* October 25, 1991; *La Repubblica,* October 27, 1991.
29. Author interview with Ignazio De Francisci.

CHAPTER TWENTY

1. Author interviews with Leonardo Guarnotta, Salvatore Barresi and Vito D'Ambrosio.
2. On the crisis of the Italian Communist Party, see *L'Unità* from the fall of 1989—when party secretary Achille Ochetto first announced the proposal to change the name—to the following year when the new name was finally announced, on October 10, 1990, and reported the following day. See also, *Oltre il PCI* by Paolo Flores D'Arcais (Milan, 1990).
3. For a good analysis of the rise of the political tensions that led to the Lombard League, see Giorgio Bocca's *La Disunità d'Italia* (Milan, 1990).
4. *The International Economy,* September/October 1991. *Corriere della Sera,* May 9, 1991.
5. *Corriere,* April 10 and September 1, 1991.
6. *La Repubblica,* November 8, 25 and 27, 1990; *Corriere,* November 20, 1990.
7. *La Repubblica,* April 21, 1991.
8. The accusations against Martelli for his role in the *conto protezione* payment were made public on February 10, 1993, prompting his immediate resignation. *Corriere della Sera,* February 11, 1993; *L'Espresso,* February 21, 1993. The accusations are outlined in the Milan prosecutors' request to investigate, made to the committee on parliamentary immunity, *Domanda di autorizzazione a procedere nei confronti dei deputati Craxi e Martelli, XI Legislatura, doc. IV, n.225,* March 11, 1993.
9. Author interview with Vito D'Ambrosio.
10. *L'Unità,* May 10, 1991; *Europeo,* May 17, 1991; *Panorama,* June 9, 1991; *La Repubblica,* June 5, 1991.
11. Misiani, *Per fatti di mafia,* pp. 155–95.
12. *Europeo,* May 17, 1991; *Panorama,* June 9, 1991.
13. Morisi, *Far Politica in Sicilia,* pp. 275–78.
14. *La Stampa,* August 10, 1991.
15. *Corriere,* August 30, 1991. For a general discussion of Grassi's life and death, see Saverio Lodato, *I Potenti* (Milan, 1992), pp. 37–54.

16. *Corriere,* October 2, 1991.
17. The conviction of the extortionists of Capo d'Orlando is reported in *La Stampa,* November 27, 1991. For a general treatment, see *Contro il racket* (Rome-Bari, 1992), by Tano Grasso, the head of the shopkeeper's anti-mafia group.
18. *Corriere,* August 30, 1991.
19. *Corriere,* September 10, 1991.
20. *Corriere,* September 1, 1991.
21. *La Repubblica,* October 1, 1991.
22. *Corriere,* October 2, 1991.
23. *Corriere,* October 17, 1991; *La Repubblica,* October 17, 1991.
24. *L'Unità,* October 18, 1991.
25. *Giornale,* October 31, 1991.
26. *Il delitto Lima.*
27. Author interview with Salvatore Barresi.
28. Author interview with Liliana Ferraro.
29. On the early phase of the corruption investigation, see *Le mani pulite,* by Enrico Nascimbeni and Andrea Pamparana (Milan, 1992); *I Saccheggiatori,* by Giuseppe Turani and Cinzia Sasso (Milan, 1992); and Antonio Carlucci's *Tangentomani* (Milan, 1992).
30. *Corriere,* March 13, 14, 15; *Il delitto Lima.*
31. *La Stampa,* May 24, 1992.
32. *L'Espresso,* March 22, 1992; *Panorama,* March 22, 1992; *The New Yorker,* March 1, 1993.
33. *Corriere,* May 24, 1992.
34. *L'Espresso,* April 5, 1992.
35. *La Repubblica,* May 24, 1992.
36. The most complete and detailed reconstruction of the assassination is contained in the various documents filed by the Procura distrettuale anti-mafia of Caltanisetta, which has handled the investigation: the *Richiesta per l'applicazione di misure cautelari,* filed November 1, 1993; the *Richiesta per l'applicazione di misure cautelari,* filed November 10, 1993; the *Ordinanza di custodia cautelare in carcere,* filed November 11, 1993; the *Richiesta di rinvio a giudizio contro Aglieri, Pietro + 36,* filed April 30, 1994.
37. *La Repubblica,* May 25, 1992.
38. *Corriere,* May 24, 1992.

CHAPTER TWENTY-ONE

1. *Corriere della Sera,* May 25, 1992.
2. *Corriere,* May 29, 1992. *Giornale di Sicilia,* May 24, 1992.
3. *La Repubblica,* May 25, 1992.
4. *Corriere,* May 25, 1992.
5. *Corriere,* May 27, 1992.
6. *La Repubblica,* May 26, 1992.
7. *Corriere,* May 25, 1992.
8. *La Repubblica,* May 25, 1992.
9. *La Repubblica,* May 25, 1992.
10. *La Repubblica,* May 30, 1992.
11. Lucentini, *Paolo Borsellino,* p. 238.
12. *Corriere,* May 29, 1992.
13. Author interview with Manfredi Borsellino.
14. Interrogation of Vincenzo Calcara and Lucentini, pp. 231–34.

15. Author interview with Salvatore Barresi.
16. Lucentini, p. 250.
17. Author interview with Manfredi Borsellino.
18. Lucentini, p. 254.
19. Lucentini, p. 252.
20. These two quotes are from an author interview with Antonio Manganelli.
21. Interrogation of Leonardo Messina. The portions of his confessions regarding Occhipinti are contained in the *Domanda di autorizzazione a procedere in giudizio contro il deputato Occhipinti,* presented to the Italian parliament, *XI Legislatura, doc. IV, n.149,* December 28, 1992.
22. This and the two quotes that follow are from Leonardo Messina's testimony before the Italian parliament's anti-mafia commission, XI Legislature, December 4, 1993.
23. This quote and the growing role of the *Stidda* are from the interrogation of Leonardo Messina.
24. Lucentini, pp. 275–78.
25. Lucentini, p. 296.
26. Author interview with Manfredi Borsellino.
27. Author interview with Antonio Ingroia.
28. *L'Espresso,* July 26, 1992.
29. *Corriere,* July 4, 1992.
30. Mutolo first made these revelations in his session with Borsellino on July 17, 1992, but they were not recorded until the session with Giaocchino Natoli, on October 23, 1992.
31. Lucentini, p. 287.
32. Lucentini, p. 289.
33. Author interview with Rita Borsellino Fiore.

CHAPTER TWENTY-TWO

1. Caponetto, *I miei giorni a Palermo,* p. 18.
2. *La Repubblica,* July 22, 1992.
3. A copy of the letter, signed on July 23, was provided to the author by Giuseppe Di Lello. Di Lello explained the reasons behind the letter in an article that appeared in *Il Manifesto,* July 28, 1992.
4. *Corriere della Sera,* July 28, 1992.
5. *La Stampa,* July 27, 1992.
6. *Corriere,* July 26, 1992.
7. *Corriere,* July 29, 1992.
8. *L'Unità,* July 25, 1992.
9. Author interview with Marta Cimino; see also Alajmo, *Un lenzuolo contro la mafia* (Palermo, 1993).
10. *The New Yorker,* March 1, 1993.
11. Galluzzo, La Licata, and Lodato, eds., *Falcone vive,* p. 81.
12. For the arrest of Carmine Alfieri, see the *Corriere della Sera,* September 12; on the extradition of the Cuntrera brothers, see *Panorama,* September 27 and October 4, 1992; on Operation Green Ice, see *La Repubblica,* September 28, 29 and 30, 1992 and *Panorama,* October 11, 1992. On the arrest of Giuseppe Madonia, see *Panorama,* January 24, 1993.
13. The blitz based on the confessions of Leonardo Messina occurred on November 17, 1992, and was reported in all the major Italian papers the following day.
14. Interrogation of Gaspare Mutolo.

15. Interrogation of Leonardo Messina.
16. Interrogation of Giuseppe Marchese.
17. Interrogation of Tommaso Buscetta, quoted also in the *Domanda di autoriz-zazione a procedere contro il Senatore Giulio Andreotti,* filed with the Italian parliament, March 27, 1992.
18. Leonardo Messina's testimony before the Italian parliament's anti-mafia commission, XI Legislature, December 4, 1993.
19. Giammanco's decision to seek a transfer from Palermo was reported in *La Stampa,* July 29, 1992. The statistics on the number of witnesses is from the *Direzione investigativa anti-mafia.*
20. *La Stampa,* October 1, 1992.
21. *Corriere,* October 2, 1992.
22. *Panorama,* December 6, 1992.
23. The initial story on Signorino appeared in *Giornale di Sicilia,* December 1, 1992; his death was reported in all the major Italian papers, December 4, 1992.
24. *La Stampa,* December 3, 1992.
25. The accusations against Contrada are collected in the *Ordinanza di custo-dia cautelare in carcere,* filed by the Tribunal of Palermo, December 23, 1992.
26. Interrogation of Giuseppe Marchese.
27. *Corriere,* January 16, 1993.
28. Author interview with Mario Mori.
29. *La Stampa,* January 16, 1993.
30. The reconstruction of Baldassare Di Maggio's role is based primarily on an interview with chief judge Giovanni Tinebra. His role is discussed in *La Stampa* and *La Repubblica,* on January 16 and 17, 1992. See also, *Totò Riina: La sua storia,* by Pino Buongiorno (Milan 1993), pp. 3–20.
31. Author interview with Giovanni Tinebra.
32. *La Stampa,* January 16, 1992.

CHAPTER TWENTY-THREE

1. Interrogation of Leonardo Messina. This and the principal accusations of mafia ties are also contained in the lengthy request filed by the Procura della Repubblica of Palermo for a waiver of Andreotti's parliamentary immunity on charges of collusion with the mafia, *Domanda di autorizzazione a procedere contro il Senatore Giulio Andreotti, XI Legislatura, doc. IV, n.102,* March 27, 1993. The results of further interrogations were added to this initial request but are filed under the same case number.
2. Interrogation of Gaspare Mutolo.
3. Interrogation of Francesco Marino Mannoia. Mutolo's statement is contained in an addendum to the *Domanda di autorizzazione,* filed with the parliament on April 14, 1993.
4. Interrogation of Tommaso Buscetta, also in the addendum to the *Domanda di autorizzazione,* filed with the parliament on April 14, 1993, reported in *L'U-nità,* April 15, 1993. Buscetta's latest confessions are also contained in the au-tobiographical book he has published together with Pino Arlacchi, *Addio Cosa Nostra* (Milan, 1994).
5. *Corriere della Sera,* April 21, 1993.
6. *La Stampa,* April 28, 1993.
7. This quote and the description of the Pecorelli case is based on the extensive brief filed by the Procura della Repubblica of Rome requesting a waiver of An-

dreotti's parliamentary immunity, on charges of his role in the death of Pecorelli, *Domanda di autorizzazione a procedere contro il Senatore Giulio Andreotti, XI Legislatura, doc. IV, n.169,* June 9, 1993.

8. The meeting between Evangelisti and Sindona is discussed in the parliamentary report on the Sindona affair, reprinted in Tranfaglia, *Mafia, politica e affari,* pp. 260–67.

9. The *Domanda di autorizzazione a procedere* against Andreotti of June 9, 1993.

10. *La Repubblica,* February 28, 1980.

11. This and the next several paragraphs are based closely on the *Domanda di autorizzazione a procedere* against Andreotti of June 9, 1993.

12. This quote is from the interrogation of Tommaso Buscetta. It is also contained in the lengthly request filed by the Procura della Repubblica of Palermo for a waiver of Andreotti's parliamentary immunity on charges of collusion with the mafia, *Domanda di autorizzazione a procedere contro il Senatore Giulio Andreotti, XI Legislatura, doc. IV, n.102,* March 27, 1993.

13. Author interview with Antonio Manganelli.

14. *La Stampa,* and *La Repubblica,* September 22, 1993.

15. *L'Espresso,* November 18, 1984.

16. Author interview with Gerardo Bianco.

17. *Domanda di autorizzazione a procedere contro il Senatore Antonio Gava, XI Legislatura, doc. IV, n.113,* filed April 7, 1993.

18. The most complete and detailed reconstruction of the Falcone assassination is contained in the various documents filed by the Procura distrettuale antimafia of Caltanisetta, which has handled the investigation: the *Richiesta per l'applicazione di misure cautelari,* filed November 1, 1993; the *Richiesta per l'applicazione di misure cautelari,* filed November 10, 1993; the *Ordinanza di custodia cautelare in carcere,* filed November 11, 1993; the *Richiesta di rinvio a giudizio contro Aglieri, Pietro + 36,* filed April 30, 1994. On the Borsellino killing, see *La Stampa,* October 10, 1993, and *Corriere,* January 4, 1994. On the suicide of Gioè, see *Corriere,* August 1, 1993.

19. *Corriere,* November 13, 1993.

20. Author interview with Vito D'Ambrosio.

21. *Domanda di autorizzazione a procedere contro il deputato Rudi Maira, XI Legislatura, doc. IV, n.153* filed December 28, 1992.

22. *Corriere,* November 13, 1993.

23. The number of organized crime witnesses comes from the Italian Ministry of the Interior.

24. The crime figures from 1992 and 1993 comes from the annual report of the parliament's anti-mafia commission, *Relazione conclusiva, XI Legislatura, Doc. XXIII N. 14,* February 18, 1994.

25. The headquarters of Berlusconi's company, *Fininvest* were searched on March 9, 1994, and Dell'Utri was questioned by prosecutors that same day, *Corriere,* March 10, 1994. Dell'Utri was wiretapped talking with Vittorio Mangano, a major heroin dealer convicted in the maxi-trial of Palermo, the conversation is recorded in a police report reprinted in Ruggeri and Guarino's *Berlusconi: Inchiesta sul Signor TV,* pp. 129–30. On the leaks about possible indictment of Dell'Utri, see *Corriere,* March 23, 1994.

26. Author interview with Vincenzo Macrì.

27. On the government decree, see *La Stampa, La Repubblica* and *Corriere,* July, 14–20, 1994.

28. On the resignation of Di Pietro, see *La Stampa* and the *Corriere,* December 7, 1994.

29. *Sole 24 Ore,* December 2, 1992. Interview with Salvatore Butera, of the *Banco di Sicilia.*

30. Leonardo Messina's testimony before the Italian parliament's anti-mafia commission, XI Legislature, December 4, 1993.

31. *L'Espresso,* May 28, 1989.

32. On the arrest of Mandalari and his wiretapped statements, see *Corriere,* December 14, 1994 and January 6, 1995.

33. Author interview with Giuseppe Tricoli.

SELECT BIBLIOGRAPHY

For general background on Sicily and the mafia:

Arlacchi, Pino. *La mafia imprenditrice*. Bologna, 1983.
Cancilla, Orazio. *Palermo*. Rome-Bari, 1988.
Catanzaro, Raimondo. *Il delitto come impresa*. Milan, 1988.
Colajanni, Napoleone. *Nel regno della mafia* [1900]. Catanzaro, 1984.
Dalla Chiesa, Carlo Alberto. *Michele Navarra e la mafia del corleonese*. Palermo, 1990.
Di Fresco, Antonio Maria. *Sicilia: 30 anni di regione*. Palermo, 1976.
Duggan, Christopher. Fascism and the Mafia. New Haven, 1989.
Falzone, Gaetano. *Storia della mafia*. Palermo [1973], 1987.
Fentress, James, and Chris Wickham. *Social Memory*. Oxford, 1992.
Franchetti, Leopoldo. *Condizioni politiche e amministrative della Sicilia* [1877]. Rome, 1992.
Gambetta, Diego. *La mafia siciliana*. Turin, 1992. In English, *The Sicilian Mafia*. Cambridge, 1993.
Gatto, Simone. *Lo stato brigante*. Palermo, 1978.
Genah, Raffaele, and Valter Vecellio. *Storie di ordinaria ingiustizia*. Milan, 1987.
Hess, Henner. *Mafia*. Rome-Bari, 1984.
Lupo, Salvatore. *Storia della mafia siciliana*. Rome, 1993.
Maraini, Dacia. *Bagheria*. Milan, 1993.
Mori, Cesare. *Con la mafia ai ferri corti* [1932]. Palermo, 1993.
Morisi, Massimo, et al. *Far politica in Sicilia*. Milan, 1993.
Nicolosi, Salvatore. *Il bandito Giuliano*. Milan, 1977.
Pantaleone, Michele. *Mafia e politica*. Turin, 1960.
———. *Anti-mafia occasione peduta*. Turin, 1969.
———. *A cavallo della tigre*. Palermo, 1984.
Paternostro, Dino. *A pugni nudi: Placido Rizzotto e le lotte popolari a Corleone nel secondo dopoguerra*. Palermo, 1992.
Poma, Rosario. *Onorevole Alzatevi*. Florence, 1976.

Renda, Francesco. *Storia della Sicilia.* Palermo: vol. 1, 1984; vol. 2, 1985; vol. 3, 1987.
———. *I beati Paoli.* Palermo, 1988.
Riolo, Claudio. *L'identità debole: il PCI in Sicilia tra gli anni '70 e '80.* Palermo, 1989.
Sciascia, Leonardo. *Il giorno della civetta.* Turin, 1961.
———. *A ciascuno il suo.* Turin, 1966.
———. *A futura memoria.* Milan, 1989.
———. *Una storia semplice.* Milan, 1989.
———, with Marcelle Padovani. *La Sicilia come metafora,* Milan, 1979.
Smith, Dennis Mack. *Storia della Sicilia medievale e moderna.* Rome-Bari, 1983.
Tajani, Diego. *Mafia e potere: Requisitoria, 1871.* Pisa, 1993.

Books that touch directly on the recent history of the Sicilian mafia:

Alajmo, Roberto. *Un lenzuolo contro la mafia.* Palermo, 1994.
Alexander, Shana. *The Pizza Connection.* New York, 1988.
Arena, Riccardo. *Sanità alla sbarra.* Palermo, 1994.
Ayala, Giuseppe. *La guerra dei giusti.* Milan, 1993.
Blumenthal, Ralph. *The Last Days of the Sicilians.* New York, 1988.
Buongiorno, Pino. *Totò Riina.* Milan, 1993.
Calvi, Fabrizio. *La vita quotidiana della mafia.* Milan, 1986.
———. *Figure di una battaglia,* Bari, 1992.
———. *L'Europe dei parrains,* Paris, 1993.
Caponetto, Antonio, with Saverio Lodato. *I miei giorni a Palermo.* Milan, 1992.
Dalla Chiesa, Nando. *Delitto imperfetto.* Milan, 1984.
———. *Storie.* Turin, 1990.
———. *Il giudice ragazzino.* Turin, 1992.
Deaglio, Enrico. *Raccolto Rosso.* Milan, 1993.
Di Lello, Giuseppe. *Giudici.* Palermo, 1994.
Di Pisa, Alberto, and Salvatore Parlagreco. *Il grande intrigo.* Rome, 1993.
Fava, Claudio. *La mafia comanda a Catania: 1960–1991* Rome-Bari, 1991.
———. *Cinque delitti imperfetti.* Milan, 1994.
Galasso, Alfredo. *La mafia politica.* Milan, 1993.
Galluzzo, Lucio, Franco Nicastro, and Vincenzo Vasile. *Obiettivo Falcone.* Naples [1989], 1992.
Grasso, Tano. *Contro il racket.* Rome-Bari, 1992.
Lodato, Saverio. *Dieci anni di mafia.* Milan, 1990. Recently rereleased in an updated form under the title *Quindici anni di mafia.* Milan, 1994.
———. *I potenti.* Milan, 1992.
Misiani, Francesco. *Per fatti di mafia.* Rome, 1991.
Orlando, Leoluca. *Palermo.* Milan, 1990.
Palermo, Carlo. *Attentato.* Trento, 1992.
Parlagreco, Salvatore. *Il mistero del corvo,* Milan, 1990.
Provisionato, Sandro. *Segreti di mafia.* Rome-Bari, 1994.
Rossi, Luca. *I disarmati.* Milan, 1992.
Sterling, Claire. *Octopus.* New York, 1990.
Tranfaglia, Nicola, ed. *Cirillo, Ligato e Lima.* Rome-Bari, 1994.

Books directly concerning or written by Giovanni Falcone and Paolo Borsellino:

Falcone provided a lengthy interview in late 1985, which has been reprinted together with a collection of photographs in the volume *Falcone vive* (Palermo [1986], 1992).

Falcone's autobiographical reflections on the mafia appeared in a book prepared with Marcelle Padovani, *Cose di Cosa Nostra* (Milan, 1991).

Storia di Giovanni Falcone, by Francesco La Licata (Milan, 1993), written in conjunction with his sisters.

Paolo Borsellino: Il valore di una vita by Umberto Lucentini (Milan, 1994).

The volume *Sulla Pelle dello Stato* (Palermo, 1991), contains speeches of Borsellino, Falcone and other magistrates. *Magistrati in Sicilia* (Palermo, 1992), contains the last public debates in which Falcone and Borsellino participated.

A collection of Falcone's speeches is contained in *Discorsi di Giovanni Falcone* (Palermo, 1994).

Perhaps the most important expression of the work of Giovanni Falcone and Paolo Borsellino is contained in the 8,607 pages of the indictment of the maxi-trial of Palermo, officially *Ordinanza Sentenza contro Abbate + 706,* filed in Palermo on November 8, 1985. The principal sections of the *ordinanza* have been reprinted in the volume *Mafia: L'atto di accusa dei giudici di Palermo,* edited by Corrado Stajano (Rome, 1986).

Also of fundamental importance is Falcone's *Sentenza istruttoria del processo contro Rosario Spatola + 119, Tribunale di Palermo,* 1982. The *Requisitoria, Rosario Spatola + 84,* filed by Giusto Sciacchitano, of the Procura della Repubblica di Palermo, December 7, 1981, provides a record of the investigation. An important parallel investigation to the Spatola case was that conducted by prosecutors in Milan into the criminal career of Michele Sindona, which has been reprinted in partial form in the volume, *Sindona: gli atti d'accusa dei giudici di Milano* (Rome, 1986). An excellent account of Sindona's murder of Giorgio Ambrosoli is *Un eroe borghese* by Corrado Stajano (Turin, 1991). See also: *Il Crack: Sindona, La DC. Il Vaticano e gli altri amici* by Paolo Panerai and Maurizio De Luca (Milan, 1977); *Il Caso Marcinkus* by Leonardo Coen and Leo Sisti (Milan, 1991); *L'Italia della P2* by Andrea Barberi et al. (Milan, 1982); *St. Peter's Banker: Michele Sindona* by Luigi Di Fonzo (New York, 1983).

Another fundamental record of their work is contained in the depositions of various mafia witnesses they questioned over the course of their career. These interrogations are filed in the court of Palermo by name of the defendant/witness:

The interrogation of Tommaso Buscetta.
The interrogation of Salvatore Contorno.
The interrogation of Vincenzo Marsala.
The interrogation of Vincenzo Sinagra.
The interrogation of Antonino Calderone.
The interrogation of Francesco Marino Mannoia.
The interrogation of Rosario Spatola.
The interrogation of Giacomina Filipello.
The interrogation of Rita Atria.
The interrogation of Piera Aiello.
The interrogation of Vincenzo Calcara.
The interrogation of Leonardo Messina.
The interrogation of Gaspare Mutolo
The interrogation of Giaocchino Schembri.
The interrogation of Giuseppe Marchese.

The full transcript of the maxi-trial of Palermo was reprinted in the *Giornale di Sicilia,* between February 1986 and December 1987. Substantial excerpts appear in a volume edited by Lino Jannuzzi, *Così Parlò Buscetta* (Milan, 1986). Another book that discusses the maxi-trial is Aurelio Angelini et al., *Uno*

Sguardo dal bunker: cronache del maxi-processo di Palermo (Siracusa, 1987). Variations on Buscetta's confessions have appeared in the volumes *Il boss è solo* by Enzo Biagi (Milan, 1986). An updated memoir has appeared more recently, *Addio Cosa Nostra* by Pino Arlacchi (Milan, 1994).

The confessions of Antonino Calderone have been reproduced in the book *Uomini del disonore*, by Pino Arlacchi (Milan, 1992), which has been translated into English as *Men of Dishonor* (New York, 1993).

The careers of the female mafia witnesses Filipello, Atria and Aiello appear in the book *Donne di mafia* by Liliana Madeo (Milan, 1994).

The best single-volume discussion of postwar Italian history is Paul Ginzborg's *A History of Contemporary Italy* (New York, 1990). A good overall history of political corruption and organized crime in Italy is Alessandro. Silj's *Il Malpaese* (Rome, 1994). See also, Sergio Turone's *Corrotti e corruttori dall'Unità d'Italia alla P2* (Rome-Bari, 1984). On the corruption investigation that started in Milan, see: Barbacetto Veltri's *Milano degli scandali* (Rome-Bari), 1991; Enrico Nascimbeni and Andrea Pamparana's *Le mani pulite* (Milan, 1992); Giuseppe Turani and Cinzia Sasso's *I saccheggiatori* (Milan, 1992); Antonio Carlucci's *Tangentomani* (Milan, 1992). Good general books on very recent political events in Italy are Giorgio Bocca's *La disunità d'Italia* (Milan, 1990) and *L'inferno* (1992); Corrado Stajano's *Il disordine* (Turin, 1993).

The Centro siciliano di documentazione Giuseppe Impastato has published an important series of statistical studies of the mafia and of Palermo: *La violenza programmata* by Giorgio Chinnici and Umberto Santino (Milan, 1989); *L'impresa mafiosa* by Umberto Santino and Giovanni La Fiura (Milan, 1990); *La città spugna* by Amelia Cristantino (Palermo, 1990); *Le tasche di Palermo*, ed. Nino Rocca and Umberto Santino (Palermo, 1992); *Gabbie vuote: processi per omicidio a Palermo dal 1983 al maxiprocesso* by Giorgio Chinnici et al. (Milan, 1992).

I have also relied heavily on the minutes of the Consiglio Superiore della Magistratura, the governing body of the Italian judiciary, which has disciplinary powers over all judges and magistrates.

Extremely important were dozens of reports of the anti-mafia commission of the Italian parliament, published over the course of the last decade. An excellent selection of some of the commission's most important reports from the 1960s to the present can be found in the volume *Mafia, politica e affari*, edited by Nicola Tranfaglia (Rome-Bari, 1992). Particularly important were the public hearings of Tommaso Buscetta, Leonardo Messina and Gaspare Mutolo and the *Relazione sui rapporti tra mafia e politica*, released on April 6, 1993; and the *Relazione di Minoranza, X Legislatura, Doc. XXIII, n.12-bis/1*, January 24, 1990; *Relazione sulle risultanze dell'attivita' del gruppo di lavoro della Commissione incaricato di indagare sulla recrudescenza di episodi criminali durante il periodo elettorale, X Legislatura, Doc. XXIII, n.20, July 25, 1990*.

Among the most important documents for understanding the problem of mafia and politics are the many requests filed with the Italian parliament requesting waivers of parliamentary immunity. In particular:

Domanda di autorizzazione a procedere contro il deputato Gunnella, VII Legislatura, Doc. IV, n.120, November 22, 1978.

Domanda di autorizzazione a procedere contro il senatore Antonio Natali, X Legislatura, Doc. IV, n.82, January 18, 1990.

Domanda di autorizzazione a procedere contro il deputato Gunnella, X Legislatura, Doc. IV, n.225-A and *A-bis*, October 23, 1991.

Domanda di autorizzazione a procedere contro il senatore Sisinio Zito, X Legislatura, Doc. IV, n.105, January 13, 1992.

Domanda di autorizzazione a procedere contro il deputato Principe, X Legislatura, Doc. IV, *n.*244, January 23, 1992.

Domanda di autorizzazione a procedere contro il deputato Culicchia, XI Legislatura, Doc. IV, *n.*1, May 11, 1992.

Domanda di autorizzazione a procedere contro il deputato Principe, XI Legislatura, Doc. IV, *n.*49, July 3, 1992.

Domanda di autorizzazione a procedere contro il senatore Sisinio Zito, XI Legislatura, Doc. IV, *n.*30, September 2, 1992.

Domanda di autorizzazione a procedere nei confronti dei deputati Craxi e Martelli, XI Legislatura, Doc. IV, *n.*225, March 11, 1993.

Domanda di autorizzazione a procedere in giudizio contro il deputato Occhipinti, presented to the Italian parliament, XI Legislatura, Doc. IV, *n.*149, December 28, 1992.

Domanda di autorizzazione a procedere contro il senatore Giulio Andreotti, XI Legislatura, Doc. IV, *n.*102, March 27, 1993.

Domanda di autorizzazione a procedere contro il senatore Guilio Andreotti, XI Legislatura, Doc. IV, *n.*161, May 31, 1993.

Domanda di autorizzazione a procedere contro il senatore Giulio Andreotti, XI Legislatura, Doc. IV, *n.*169, June 9, 1993.

Domanda di autorizzazione a procedere contro il senatore Giulio Andreotti, XI Legislatura, Doc. IV, *n.*196, July 21, 1993.

Domanda di autorizzazione a procedere contro il senatore Antonio Gava, XI Legislatura, Doc. IV, *n.*113, filed April 7, 1993.

Domanda di autorizzazione a procedere contro il deputato Cirino Pomicino, XI Legislatura, Doc. IV, *n.*258, April 8, 1993.

Domanda di autorizzazione a procedere contro il deputato Mastrantuono, XI Legislatura, Doc. IV, *n.*259, April 8, 1993.

Domanda di autorizzazione a procedere contro il deputato Rudi Maira, XI Legislatura, Doc. IV, *n.*143, December 28, 1993.

ACKNOWLEDGMENTS

My greatest thanks go to the scores of people who consented to be interviewed for this book. Many of them are quoted in the text, but many others, who were not quoted, were no less helpful. I feel special gratitude to Maria Falcone, Agnese Borsellino, Manfredi Borsellino, Rita Fiore Borsellino and Maria Pia Lepanto Borsellino, whose participation cannot have been without pain.

In helping me to amass a mountain of documentation, I am deeply indebted to the staff of the Italian parliament's anti-mafia commission, especially Enzo Montecchiarini and Piera Amendola and the commission's president during the period of my research, Luciano Violante. Equally valuable was the ample documentation kindly provided by the Consiglio Superiore della Magistratura with the help of Judge Vincenzo Maccarone. The staffs of the "Giunte per Autorizzazione per Procedere" of the Italian Senate and House of deputies were also extremely helpful and unstinting with their time. The same is true for the public information offices of various government ministries, in particular, Interior, Justice and Defense. The personnel of the Palermo "bunker-hall" courthouse were a model of efficiency and courtesy in locating and copying enormous quantities of depositions and trial testimony.

I want to thank the many friends I met in Palermo who were unfailingly generous and hospitable as well as full of insight and understanding, in particular, Marta Cimino, Giuliana Saladino, Paolo Viola, Beatrice Monroi and Marco Anzaldi.

I also owe a great debt to many friends in Rome, especially Vittorio Foa and Sesa Tatò for their warm encouragement and intelligent observations; and the many people at the American Academy in Rome with whom I lived for three years, its director Joseph Connors, its deputy director Pina Pasquantonio and its president Adele Chatfield Taylor. My wife, Sarah McPhee, was perhaps the greatest force in encouraging me to pursue this subject as a book and also performed the thankless, but critically important, task of reading the first and roughest drafts of the manuscript. Jenny, Martha and Laura McPhee, were also extremely kind to take the time to give me assiduous and sharp-eyed readings of various drafts. My agent, Sallie Gouverneur, helped from proposal to finished book. Dan Frank at Pantheon has been everything I could have hoped for in an editor. He was involved, interested and enthusiastic, available whenever needed, but respectful of an author's autonomy. His assistant, Claudine O'Hearn, has been of great help in shepherding the book through the editorial process.

INDEX